PHILOSOPHIA TOGATA

# PHILOSOPHIA TOGATA I

## *Essays on Philosophy and Roman Society*

EDITED BY

MIRIAM GRIFFIN

AND

JONATHAN BARNES

CLARENDON PRESS · OXFORD

*Oxford University Press, Great Clarendon Street, Oxford* OX2 6DP
*Oxford New York*
*Athens Auckland Bangkok Bogota Bombay*
*Buenos Aires Calcutta Cape Town Dar es Salaam*
*Delhi Florence Hong Kong Istanbul Karachi*
*Kuala Lumpur Madras Madrid Melbourne*
*Mexico City Nairobi Paris Singapore*
*Taipei Tokyo Toronto*
*and associated companies in*
*Berlin Ibadan*

*Oxford is a trade mark of Oxford University Press*

*Published in the United States*
*by Oxford University Press Inc., New York*


*First published, with corrections, in paperback 1997*



*British Library Cataloguing in Publication Data*
*Data available*

*Library of Congress Cataloging in Publication Data*
*Data available*

*ISBN 0-19-815085-7*

*1 3 5 7 9 10 8 6 4 2*

*Printed in Great Britain on acid-free paper by*
*Biddles Ltd., Guildford and King's Lynn*

# Preface

THE papers assembled in this volume were all originally delivered at the seminar on Philosophy and Roman Society which we have held in Oxford over the last three years. The aim of the seminar was interdisciplinary, in the proper sense of that much abused word. We thought that if historians, philosophers, and classical scholars met and discussed a subject of common interest in a common forum, the ideas and methods and approaches proprietary to each group might prove mutually informative and inspiring. The meetings—in our no doubt partial judgement—met with some success. We are sanguine enough to hope that the present book may convey to its readers something of the excitement which the seminar generated.

Interest in our subject has grown enormously, and in various quarters, over the past decade or so. Historians have become ever more involved with social and intellectual issues. Classical scholars are showing an increasing interest in the philosophical background and presuppositions of literary texts. Ancient philosophers are once again willing to recognize that there was philosophy after Aristotle and that Roman authors are of the first importance for the history of their subject.

It is, moreover, a topic which invites—indeed, which demands—the combined attention of scholars from all three disciplines. Philosophical exegesis of Cicero's works is jejune when it ignores the historical and literary dimensions of his texts. A historical investigation of the political importance of Stoicism is empty and unreal unless the philosophical tenets of the Stoic system are analysed and understood. The literary study of Lucretius would be insubstantial if it did not consider the philosophical complexities and the historical circumstances of Epicureanism. Such reflections are perhaps platitudinous. But it is one thing to profess a platitude, another to act on it.

The subject is broad and its history long. In publishing a selection of the papers given at the seminar we have chosen to concentrate on a relatively brief chronological period. Indeed, although three of our contributors trace themes into the early

Empire, most of them are concerned with intellectual life in the first century BC. There is something to be said about earlier generations, although the sources here are meagre and reconstruction is largely conjectural. There is, evidently, very much to be said about later ages, when the texts are numerous and rich. But the first century BC was formative. It is well documented. It must constitute the starting point for any inquiry into the mutual interaction of philosophy and Roman life.

Our volume is not and does not pretend to be a comprehensive history of the place of philosophy in Roman life; nor do its component parts add up to a full account of our subject in the first century BC. We do not mention the renascence of Aristotelian studies in our period; nor do we discuss, save incidentally, the most significant philosophical development of the epoch: the revival of Platonism. Again, since only writers of philosophy are discussed, the book contains no account of the less explicit influence of philosophical ideas on Latin literature. Readers will doubtless lament other omissions.

But we make these confessions without any profound sense of sin. The book assembles a collection of soundings, of preparatory studies. We suppose that many more such soundings must be made, and that much further work of a fundamental nature must be undertaken, before a complete and serious history of the subject can be written. And we contemplate this supposition not with disappointment but rather with anticipatory pleasure.

Many people have helped us. We thank our contributors for their patience and punctuality. We thank the members of the seminar for their lively and valuable participation. We are grateful to Philippa Smith for compiling the Bibliography and to Julia Griffin for her help with the Index. We thank the Oxford University Press for its generosity, and in particular John Cordy, Hilary Feldman, and Jane Stuart-Smith for their help at different stages of publication.

M. T. G.
J. B.

*Oxford*
*December 1987*

# Contents

# Editors' Note

## *on the Paperback Edition*

*Philosophia Togata* was first published in 1989. This new edition incorporates corrections and modifications made by the contributors to their chapters, as well as substantial additions to the bibliography. The book has been renamed *Philosophia Togata I* to mark the simultaneous appearance of a companion volume *Philosophia Togata II: Plato and Aristotle at Rome.*

M. T. G.
J. B.

*(Oxford and Geneva, March 1996)*

I

# Philosophy, Politics, and Politicians at Rome

MIRIAM GRIFFIN*

A DISCUSSION of the relation between philosophy and politics may appropriately begin with the famous dictum of Plato in the *Republic*:

Unless either philosophers become kings in our states or those whom we now call kings and rulers take to the pursuit of philosophy seriously and adequately, and there is a conjunction of these two things, political power and philosophical intelligence, there can be no end of troubles for our states or, I think, for the human race. (473 D)

No profession has ever devised a piece of self-advertisement more blatant or more successful. The link that Plato saw between *δύναμις πολιτική* and *φιλοσοφία* was to have a long history and an enduring fascination.

Though the Romans may not have agreed with Plato that the philosopher-king was essential to the health of individual states, they knew the doctrine. Cicero described his own consulship and his brother's proconsulship in Asia as realizations of Plato's dream (*QFr.* I. 1. 29), and Marcus Aurelius, who could justly claim the title of 'philosopher-king', is plausibly said to have had Plato's prescription ever on his lips (SHA *M. Ant.* 27. 7).[1]

In a more sober vein, Cicero wrote that the only case of a man pre-eminent 'et doctrinae studiis et regenda civitate' was Demetrius of Phalerum, the Peripatetic philosopher who ruled Athens for a decade in the late fourth century BC. That was to discount various philosophers brought in for short spells as petty dynasts in various Greek cities, like the Peripatetic philosopher Athenion who, in Cicero's own lifetime, had ruled

* I am indebted to Jonathan Barnes for providing some vital references and for trying to clarify my arguments.

[1] Marcus had, however, a modest conception of what a philosophical ruler could and should aim to achieve (*Med.* IX. 29), see Rawson, below, p. 252.

Athens under the auspices of Mithridates.[2] Though Athenion was not an encouraging example, the Romans were to continue this tradition themselves: Augustus sent first a Stoic, Athenodorus, the son of Sandon, and then a follower of Plato's own school, the Academy, to govern their native city of Tarsus (Strabo XIV. 675).

The philosopher-ruler was, however, the exception among the numerous examples of the philosopher-cum-politician type. It was a type common enough in the Hellenistic world to merit a treatise by Hermippus in the third century BC entitled *On Those Who Have Passed from Philosophy to Tyranny and Despotic Rule* (*Περὶ τῶν ἀπὸ φιλοσοφίας εἰς τυραννίδας καὶ δυναστείας μεθεστηκότων*, *Acad. index Herc.* col. XI. 1 ff.; cf. Plut. *Mor.* 1126 A ff.). Many of them were political advisers to kings and despots, as Plato himself and some of his pupils had been for a time. Hermippus collected such titbits as the story of the Stoic Persaeus who insisted that the *sapiens*, the Stoic wise man, would prove a good general, but who, when put in charge of the Acrocorinth by his patron Antigonus Gonatas, suffered defeat through being drunk on duty (in the year 244, Athenaeus IV. 162 d). Sphaerus, another third century Stoic, advised King Cleomenes of Sparta, particularly on the restoration of the communal institutions attributed to Lycurgus (Plut. *Cleom.* 11). Even Epicureans, who advocated abstention from public life as the norm, were found hanging around the Seleucid court (Ath. V. 211 b–d).[3]

## I. ROMAN EXPOSURE TO PHILOSOPHY

Perhaps the most familiar type of politicized philosopher the Romans encountered, at least initially, was the philosopher

[2] Cic. *Leg.* III. 14; Ath. V. 211 d ff. (from Posidonius), on whom see Badian [188] and Kidd, below, pp. 41–6. Aristion the Epicurean who probably succeeded Athenion as tyrant at Athens did little to improve the reputation of philosopher-rulers (App. *Mith.* 28–9).

[3] Demetrius of Phalerum and the philosophers at the Hellenistic courts are briefly discussed in F. L. Vatai, *Intellectuals in Politics in the Greek World* (London, 1984) 116 ff.; on the subsequent history of Plato's notion see Rawson, below, pp. 233 ff. On the Epicureans see M. L. Clarke, *Higher Education in the Ancient World* (London, 1971), 71. In Epicurean doctrine participation was permissible for special reasons (below, pp. 13; 30; 33) and is specifically allowed for in this form in D.L. X. 121 b: [*τὸν σοφὸν*] *μόναρχον ἐν καιρῷ θεραπεύειν*, on which see Fowler, below, pp. 129–33 .

serving as ambassador. Strabo's lists of native sons that accompany his accounts of the Greek cities include a number of these, but the most famous instance of such intervention in Rome's diplomatic relations with the East was the visit in 155 BC of an Athenian embassy composed of three leading philosophers, the Stoic Diogenes, the Peripatetic Critolaus, and Carneades, the brilliant sceptic who headed the Academy. They were sent to Rome to beg for the remission of a fine imposed on Athens for the sack of Oropus. They succeeded in having the fine reduced, for, as the Elder Cato remarked, 'These men argue so well that they could gain anything they ask for'. Plutarch also recounts what large audiences they drew when they used their spare time in Rome to deliver lectures. Carneades chose to debate the role of justice in international affairs: he argued on the first day that there is such a thing as natural justice which should be followed as a guide, and on the next day that natural justice does not exist. It was this performance in particular that led Cato to urge the Senate to settle the matter of the fine quickly, 'so that these men may return to their schools and lecture to the sons of Greece, while the youth of Rome give ear to their laws and magistrates, as in the past'.[4]

It was precisely in this period, the middle of the second century BC, that Greek school philosophy really began to establish its hold on educated Romans. For the eastern wars that culminated in the conquest of Macedonia and Greece resulted in an influx of Greek hostages, ambassadors, and teachers. In 161 BC the Senate, typically and ineffectively, had instructed the urban praetor not to allow rhetoricians or philosophers to live in Rome (Suet. *Rhet.* I. I; Gellius, *NA* XV. II). The most that the official attitude may have achieved was the inhibition of teaching in public, which could help to explain why the typical situation in which we meet Greek philosophers in Rome in the Republic is living in the houses of great men or accompanying them on their travels. Such philosophical companions can be attested for many of the familiar figures of the late Republic: L. Licinius Lucullus took the Academic Antiochus of Ascalon with him on his eastern campaigns (Cic. *Luc.* 4–7); Brutus 'lived with' Antiochus' brother Aristus, also a philosopher

[4] Plut. *Cat. Mai.* 22; cf. Cic. *Luc.* 137; Gell. *NA* VI. 14, 8–10; Pliny, *NH* VII. 112.

(Plut. *Brut.* 2. 2); the Stoic Athenodorus Cordylion lived in the house of the younger Cato (Plut. *Cat. Min.* 16), and the Stoic Diodotus lived and died in that of Cicero (Cic. *Brut.* 309).[5] The degree of dependence on their noble patrons varied considerably. Panaetius and Posidonius, who had held high positions in their native Rhodes (Strabo XIV. 655), were closer to being social equals than Philodemus, who requests in a poem financial support from L. Calpurnius Piso (*Anth. Pal.* XI. 144). Even if the house to which he invited Piso for an Epicurean celebration[6] was a present from his patron,[7] his was still a more dignified position than that of the Peripatetic philosopher Alexander who travelled everywhere with Crassus, receiving a cloak for the journey which he had to give back on his return (Plut. *Crass.* 3).

In the Republic the Romans also went east to find their philosophy, which became for many the final stage in their education.[8] The practice is attested for the second century BC, at least as a diversion from official duties. Metellus Numidicus, the consul of 109, had listened to Carneades in Athens in his youth (Cic. *De Or.* III. 68), and it was in 119 that Q. Mucius Scaevola Augur, on his way out to govern Asia, stopped at Athens and insulted T. Albucius who had gone to Athens to study and had 'gone Greek', emerging a complete Epicurean and Graecophone (Lucilius II. 88 ff. Marx; Cic. *Brut.* 131; *Fin.* I. 8). That was too much for Scaevola, though he himself had studied Greek philosophy with Panaetius (Cic. *De Or.* I. 75). But the heyday of the Greek tour came in the first century. It is in 79/8 BC that we find Cicero, as depicted in his own *De Finibus* V, studying in Athens, along with his brother Quintus, their cousin Lucius, and their friends Atticus and M. Pupius Piso. Varro studied there in the 80s with Antiochus, and in 44 and 43 BC it was at the lectures of Cratippus, the eloquent Peripatetic

[5] Rawson [94] 81–3; for a convenient list of Greek and Greek-speaking scholars (including philosophers) attached to prominent Romans in the late Republic see Balsdon [80] 54–8.

[6] *Anth. Pal.* XI. 144 = Gow–Page, *Garland of Philip.* no. 23. Note that the problem concerning Philodemus' celebration of Epicurus' birthday on the 20 Gamelion, a date that D.L. X. 18 appeared to contradict, was solved by D. M. Lewis's emendation of the text of Diogenes Laertius in *CR* 19 (1969) 272.

[7] The possibility is discussed in R. G. M. Nisbet's edition of *In Pisonem*, Appendices 3 and 4.

[8] Daly [90]; Rawson [94] 6–12.

philosopher, that Marcus Cicero junior and Horace were recruited for the Republican cause. Brutus was in Athens, listening to the professors and drafting their audiences (Cic. *Off.* I. 1; *Fam.* XVI. 21).

Philosophical knowledge was even more widespread and fashionable under the Principate. In the *Dialogus de Oratoribus* of Tacitus the apologist for modern oratorical techniques points out that in the Republic an orator could create a sensation with a few philosophical commonplaces: 'they were novel and unknown, and only a small minority of the orators themselves knew the principles of rhetoric and the tenets of philosophy; but now it is all common knowledge, and there is scarcely anyone in the crowd who is not familiar with, if not actually instructed in, the rudiments of both' (19). We recall the rich freedman Trimalchio in Petronius' *Satyricon* who claims as a notable distinction, worth including in his epitaph, 'He left 30 million sesterces and never listened to a philosopher' (*Sat.* 71. 12). And indeed, however much he may boast of having devoted his *otium* not to culture but to profit, he has not escaped exposure to philosophy entirely, as is shown by the clichés he spouts about the equality of all men including slaves, a favourite Stoic doctrine (*Sat.* 71. 1; cf. 56. 7).[9]

## 2. POPULARITY OF DIFFERENT SCHOOLS

All of the four major schools, Stoics, Epicureans, Academics, and Peripatetics, claimed adherents in the Principate as in the Republic, while the Cynics seem to have acquired new vigour.[10] The standard view of the popularity enjoyed by different sects at different times as a guide to conduct for the Roman governing class posits variety in the late Republic, followed by the triumph of Stoicism in the Principate, succeeded

[9] On Trimalchio's epitaph see now the thorough discussion by J. H. D'Arms, *Commerce and Social Standing in Ancient Rome* (Cambridge, Mass., 1981), 108 ff., who points out that the mention of these alternative ways of spending *otium* from public office respectably is part of Trimalchio's pretensions to equestrian behaviour. It is too simple, however, to say that 'active engagement in this class of pursuits (philosophy and literature) held no fascination for Trimalchio' (p. 113). Rather, Trimalchio's verses, literary lectures, and philosophical clichés are meant to suggest that he thinks he has acquired these attainments but without effort.

[10] On the history of Cynicism in Rome see now Billerbeck [79] ch. 1.

eventually by Neo-Platonism in the third century AD. It is a scheme easier to qualify than to explain.

It is clear that, after the great impact made by Panaetius and his pupil Posidonius in the second and early first century BC, the Stoa experienced very strong competition from the three other major schools. The take-over of Athens by a Mithridatic faction encouraged the Greek equivalents of *optimus quisque* to flee to Rome along with the head of the Academy, Philo of Larissa (Cic. *Brut.* 306). Cicero was permanently converted by Philo, and Atticus by the Epicurean Phaedrus whom they both heard, probably for the first time, in Athens (Cic. *Fin.* I. 16; V. 3).[11] Several inscribed bases at Athens show that his converted hearers, Lucius and Appius Saufeius, erected statues of Phaedrus as their καθηγητής, a technical term for private tutor. Atticus seems to have taken up the position of benefactor to Phaedrus' whole family: his daughter put up a statue recording their gratitude to Phaedrus' ἀκουστής.[12] We also hear of active politicians who subscribed to the sect, not only L. Calpurnius Piso, consul in 58 BC, but L. Manlius Torquatus, praetor in 49 (Cic. *Fin.* II. 74), Vibius Pansa, consul in 43, and others whom we shall note later among Caesar's assassins.

Plato's Academy, having passed, under the leadership of Carneades (214–129 BC) and Clitomachus (187–110 BC), through a period of scepticism and demolition work on other schools, started with Cicero's teacher, Philo of Larissa, to place more emphasis on the notion that at least probability, if not

[11] See Badian [188] for the situation in Athens. At p. 46 n. 44 he discounts Cic. *Fam.* XIII. I. 2 as evidence that Phaedrus visited Rome.

[12] Raubitschek [200]. Cornelius Nepos (*Att.* 3. 2) says that the Athenians erected statues to Atticus and (on one emendation of the text) to Pilia, though this was done in Atticus' absence as he had resisted the move. Bailey [199] noted that this reluctance was in keeping with the Epicurean doctrine that the desire for statues in one's honour was one of the unnecessary desires (schol. on *Kuriai Doxai* 29; cf. Lucr. III. 78). Nepos also says that the statues were set up in sacred places, and the statue of Atticus set up by Chrysothemis, like the one of Phaedrus set up by Appius Saufeius, was dedicated to the Eleusinian deities. Perhaps this would make them more acceptable, for the Epicureans believed in maintaining traditional worship (Plut. *Mor.* 1095 C; D.L. X. 10; Lucr. VI. 75), including honouring the gods with statues (D.L. X. 121b 1–2, cf. Lucr. VI. 75), and Epicurus himself had been initiated into the Eleusinian mysteries (see Brunt, below, pp. 186–7). In any case the wise man, if honoured in this way, should accept it with unconcern (D.L. ibid.). On the exceptional importance attached by Epicureans to statues of their teachers and their disciples see Frischer [37]. For the meaning of the term καθηγητής see Glucker [71] 132.

certainty, was attainable. Philo's pupil Antiochus abandoned scepticism and Philo and called his sect the 'Old Academy', claiming to return to the teaching of Plato and his pupil Aristotle. Stoic doctrines, particularly in epistemology, he absorbed on the grounds that their founder Zeno had really only changed the terminology of the ancestral doctrines. The teaching of Antiochus was very popular: it combined the advantage of moral respectability to an all but Stoic level with the snob appeal of spiritual descent from the greatest ancient philosophers (Cic. *Fin.* v. 7; *Acad.* 15–18; *Luc.* 13–15; *Tusc.* I. 55). On a more practical level, Antiochus valued eloquence and was thought to provide useful techniques for orators. His brochures laid claim, through his philosophical ancestors, to more orators, generals, and statesmen than any other sect (Cic. *Fin.* v. 7).

Scarcely to be distinguished from this 'Old Academy' were the Peripatetics of the period. The philosopher Staseas of Naples is found in the Tusculan villa of M. Pupius Piso even before Piso went to Athens to study, there to become a convert to Antiochus (Cic. *De Orat.* I. 104; *Fin.* v. 8), while M. Licinius Crassus had a Peripatetic philosopher resident in his house (Plut. *Crass.* 3). But the leading Peripatetic philosopher to emerge in the Republic was Cratippus, who had once been a pupil of Antiochus and Aristus (*Acad. index Herc.* xxxv. 10–16). Caesar's implacable enemy M. Claudius Marcellus studied with him when in exile at Mitylene (Cic. *Brut.* 250), Pompey is said by Plutarch to have discussed philosophy with him (*Pomp.* 75), and Cicero eventually obtained the Roman citizenship for him from Caesar (Plut. *Caes.* 24). In the period of the dictatorship Cicero regarded Cratippus as the *princeps philosophorum* (*Off.* I. 2).

All of these sects continued to claim adherents at least up to the time of the foundation of chairs in Athens for each of them by Marcus Aurelius (Philostr. *VS* II. 566; Lucian *Eun.* 3). Under the Principate philosophers graced the palace itself. The two most influential cultivated by Augustus himself were Stoics. Athenodorus continued to carry out his pastoral duties from Tarsus, sending Octavia a philosophical consolation on the death of her son Marcellus (Plut. *Poplic.* 17); when Livia's son Drusus died, it was the turn of Areus to administer solace (Sen.

*Marc.* 4). But the dominance of Stoicism must not be overrated. Augustus' nephew Marcellus was tutored by the Academic Nestor of Tarsus who, like Athenodorus, ended his life governing his native city (Strabo XIV. 675), and the Peripatetic philosopher Xenarchus was honoured with the Emperor's friendship (Strabo XIV. 670). Plutarch and Favorinus bear witness to the continuing attractions of the Academy. Even the Epicureans, discreet by creed, can be detected in considerable numbers. The Julio-Claudian period yields, for example, the historian Aufidius Bassus (Sen. *Ep.* 30) and Seneca's correspondent Lucilius (*Epp.* 23. 9; 20. 9). Later several of Statius' addressees seem to be cultivating an Epicurean *quies*, and a number of Pliny's correspondents can be suspected.[13] And then there is Trajan's widow Plotina who obtained a notable concession for the Garden from the Emperor Hadrian: an inscription records her success in gaining for the head of the school the right to appoint a successor who was not a Roman citizen (*IG* II$^2$ 1099). Still later the efforts of Galen to refute the Epicureans show their vitality in the second century AD, perhaps even more than the pious devotions of Diogenes in Oenoanda.

There is considerable evidence that, to many Romans, Stoicism as a moral philosophy seemed like a rationalization of (or a poor substitute for) Rome's own traditional ideals (Cic. *Tusc.* I. 2; *Fin.* II. 67). Perhaps nothing demonstrates more clearly the basic attraction this doctrine held for the Romans than the fact that Q. Sextius, founder of the one native sect Rome ever produced, is described by Seneca as 'magnus vir, et, licet neget, Stoicus' (*Ep.* 64. 2). Therefore it might be said that what needs explaining is not the dominance of Stoic moral philosophy for nearly two centuries after Augustus had endorsed traditional Roman morality, but its failure to dominate the scene in the late Republic when a return to traditional values was constantly being urged as a remedy for political anarchy.

Cicero himself suggests (*Cael.* 40–1) that the loosening of

[13] Statius' *Silvae* exhibit: Pollius Felix (III proem. and II. 2. 113 ff. with Epicurean motifs noted by Nisbet, *JRS* 68 (1978) 1 ff.); Manilius Vopiscus (I. 3, 94 ff.); perhaps Atedius Melior (II. 3, 64 ff.). In Pliny's *Letters* we meet the *corrector* Maximus (VIII. 24; cf. Epict. III. 7) and perhaps Bruttius Praesens (VII. 3, with R. Syme, 'Legates of Cilicia under Trajan', *Hist.* 18 (1962) 352 = *Roman Papers* ii (Oxford, 1979), 774).

*mores* in Rome and the change of political circumstances in Greece had given the sect which pronounced pleasure to be the end for man the edge over the austerity of Stoicism. Scholars have often favoured a similar type of explanation, tracing to the political strife and turbulence of the Late Republic the attractions of a doctrine promising security and tranquillity.[14] This type of explanation, however, does little to explain the vitality of the other sects popular in this period, and it may be more helpful to suggest some less nebulous factors. One is the fact that the Epicureans were the first school to present their doctrines in Latin in works which, according to Cicero, were read all over Italy despite their inaccuracy and crudeness.[15] Another Epicurean asset was Philodemus, the gifted pupil of Zeno of Sidon, who came to Rome some time in the 70s and attached himself to Calpurnius Piso. Philodemus was not, like Epicurus himself, an avowed enemy of culture. Not only did he follow his teacher Zeno of Sidon in his interest in rhetoric and poetry, but he composed verses too elegant for Cicero to be rude about them while attacking him and his patron (*Pis.* 70). Until his death in the 30s BC Philodemus and the Epicurean teacher Siro provided a focus for Epicurean study and discussion in Campania, sessions in which Virgil and his friends Quintilius, L. Varius Rufus and Plotius Tucca took part. Horace frequented the same haunts.[16]

Nonetheless, it was the Academy and the Lyceum that fostered the oratorical skills so necessary for political success under the Republic. Cicero insists that for the budding orator—and hence for the budding statesman—the Academics and Peripatetics provide the best training (Cic. *De Orat.* III. 57 f.; *Brut.* 119 ff.; *Tusc.* II. 9). There were two reasons for that: Peripatetics were best at rhetorical theory, and each of these schools taught a form of argument useful to the orator. The Peripatetics gave

[14] C. W. Chilton, *Diogenes of Oenoanda* (Oxford, 1971) favours this view in his Introduction (p. xxii), but it is hard not to doubt the helpfulness of such an explanation when he himself (pp. xxiv–xxv) alleges a surge of interest in the Garden in the period of the Antonine peace, adducing its resistance to superstition as the attraction.

[15] *Fin.* II. 44; *Tusc.* IV. 6–7; *Fam.* XV. 16. 1; 19. 3 (Cassius on Catius and Amafinius). Cicero is also rude about L. Saufeius (*Att.* I. 3. 1; II. 8. 1; IV. 6. 1; VII. 1. 1), Epicurean writer and friend of Atticus. See now on these writers Rawson [94] 9, 284.

[16] Hor. *Serm.* I. 5. 40 ff.; 10. 81; *Cat.* 5; cf. Gell. *NA* VI. 20; Hor. *Serm.* I. 2. 119 ff.; *Epist.* I. 15. 11–12. On Philodemus and Siro see Rawson [94] 23–4, and on the importance of Philodemus as a teacher, Sedley, below, p. 103.

practice in debating both sides of the question; the Academics in rebutting any argument (Cic. *Fin.* v. 10). Cicero, urging on Brutus his duty to press on with the study of oratory, asks, 'Why else where you trained by the Old Academy and the philosopher Aristus?' (*Brut.* 332). The Stoics, by contrast, laboured under the disadvantage of an austere theory of style. In practice, too, they were thought to be good at drawing fine distinctions and at puncturing arguments, but their discourse was regarded as arid and graceless. Those like P. Rutilius Rufus, who put into practice their belief that eloquence was simply a matter of speaking the truth and that only the wise man was fit to be an orator, did not succeed in the Roman courts (Cic. *De Orat.* I. 227).

It could then be argued that Stoic morality achieved its natural triumph in Roman upper-class circles when the other schools lost their particular advantages and when the coming of the Principate meant that oratory was of less importance in politics. Tacitus, whatever his own convictions, could make a persuasive case for thinking that effective oratory was not as essential under the Principate (*Dial.* 37 ff.). In any case, as we saw above, the development Cicero already deplored had reached completion, and the teaching of rhetoric belonged to the schools of declamation which imparted, in a pre-digested form, the fruits of philosophical theory and wisdom.[17] Finally, the vitality of the example of the younger Cato both illustrates and helps to explain the ascendancy of Stoicism as a guide to conduct. The Romans were moved more by the example of their *maiores* than by precept, and Cato gave them an example of freedom and victory in the face of defeat and despotism. His suicide demonstrated that the independence of the individual from external circumstances, which Epicureanism also aimed to achieve, was combined in Stoicism with enhanced dignity and prestige. Cato managed to appeal simultaneously to Stoic paradox and Plato's *Phaedo*, thus outflanking the 'Old Academy', so that Brutus, who initially condemned his suicide

[17] Cic. *Inv.* I. 1; *De Or.* I. 22; III. 131, cf. *QFr.* III. 3. 4. With Aper's view at Tac. *Dial.* 19, however, compare Quintilian XII. 1–2 who, following Cicero, still advises a broad education for the orator, including first hand acquaintance with philosophy. He disapproved of the current slick oratory of the *delatores* (on which see Winterbottom [206] without, however, differing from Domitian's own low opinion of philosophers (see below, p. 22).

on good Platonic grounds, ultimately changed his mind and followed his example (Plut. *Brut.* 40. 4).[18]

### 3. PHILOSOPHY AND CONDUCT

We come now to an even more puzzling question: what effect did philosophy have on the conduct of Roman statesmen who were exposed to philosophical lectures in Rome and abroad, and who, for whatever motives, frequently had a philosophical companion in their entourage?[19] In *De Natura Deorum* Cicero claims, 'In my public and private life alike I have practised the precepts taught by reason and by theory' (I. 7). Five years before, when he had governed Cilicia and conquered his mountain tribe in hopes of gaining a triumph, he wrote to Cato that the two of them had brought philosophy into the forum and almost on to the battlefield itself (*Fam.* XV. 4. 16). Similarly Varro, to whom Cicero would have been nervous of ascribing totally alien sentiments about philosophy (*Att.* XIII. 12. 3; 16. 1; 19. 5; *Fam.* IX. 8. 1), is made to remark in the *Academica*, 'I adopt for myself the pursuit of philosophy in its entirety, both as a standard for living, so far as I am able, and as recreation for the mind' (*Acad.* 7).

Yet in recent scholarship there has been a strong strain of scepticism about the relevance of philosophical doctrines to the behaviour of Roman politicians. Some have supposed that there was a 'dichotomy between Greek theories and Roman practice', as Earl says in connection with Terence. Stanton uses similar language when discussing the policies of Marcus Aurelius.[20] Others suppose that the Romans had a light-

[18] On Cato's suicide see Griffin [192] 194–6. Plutarch represents Brutus' criticism of Cato as based on *φιλοσοφία*, and the charge of running away and the expression *οὐχ ὅσιον* are reminiscent of *Phaedo* 61 B–62 D. For Brutus as an adherent of the 'Old Academy' of Antiochus: Cic. *Brut.* 120; 149; 332; *Tusc.* V. 21; *Att.* XIII. 25. 3. Moles [196] argues for the authenticity of Plutarch's story and thinks the eventual justification of suicide there attributed to Brutus is Stoic (779 n. 52), but it is possible to read it as an attempt to square his decision with the Platonic view: he had given his life to the Republic, thereby fulfilling his duty; what was left of it was useless to her and therefore he was entitled to dispose of it. See also Pelling, below, pp. 225–6.

[19] For different conceptions of the role of such philosophical companions—political advisers, domestic chaplains, intellectual companions see Glucker [71] 21–7; Rawson [94] 81–3, and below, pp. 237 ff.; Barnes, below, pp. 56–7; 58–9; 62.

[20] D. C. Earl, 'Terence and Roman Politics', *Hist.* 11 (1962) 469 ff.; Stanton [175].

hearted attitude to philosophy. Thus Shackleton Bailey writes of Atticus' Epicureanism, 'He may be supposed to have professed it partly to be in fashion and partly because as a devotee of things Hellenic he had to have a philosophy and Epicureanism suited him better than any other.'[21] Brunt has given us a picture of Arrian even more complex and puzzling: a man sufficiently impressed by the Stoic teaching of Epictetus to publish a version of his discourses years later, yet not enough to judge Alexander by Stoic standards in his *Anabasis*.[22]

## 4. THE NEGATIVE EVIDENCE

The ancient sources provide some support for both the dichotomy and the frivolity theory. For the dichotomy idea, one can start by pointing to many places in Cicero's philosophical works where he shows that, in matters such as the best constitution and the tenets of the state religion, no doctrine could be held to have more authority than the tradition and experience of Rome. In *De Re Publica*, for example, Scipio is made to show deference towards the political theories of Plato and then justifies his disagreement with them on the basis of his traditional Roman training. You must listen to me, he says, as a Roman given a liberal education, yet better trained by experience and *domestica praecepta* than by books (I. 36). In *De Natura Deorum* the Stoic spokesman, Lucilius Balbus, after presenting his proof of the existence of a providential divine nature, appeals to C. Aurelius Cotta as 'a leading citizen and a pontiff' to support him (II. 168). Cotta, an adherent of the sceptical Academy founded by Carneades, demurs. He replies that, as a Cotta and a pontiff, he does accept, without proof, the traditional lore, but, he adds, that does not prevent him from demanding of a philosopher that his proofs be cogent (III. 6–7, see Brunt, below, pp. 190–1).

When this dichotomy between conduct and philosophical belief was found in Epicureans, Cicero found it less attractive. He ridicules senators like L. Manlius Torquatus for avoiding

[21] D. R. Shackleton Bailey, *Cicero's Letters to Atticus* i (Cambridge, 1965) 8. That the impact of philosophy on the Roman governing class throughout the Republican period was superficial is maintained by Jocelyn [195].

[22] Brunt [158].

Epicurean arguments in the senate and the law courts, talking instead of *officium*, *dignitas*, *recta*, *honesta*, and taking risks for one's country—concepts more suited to Peripatetics and Stoics (*Fin.* II. 76). What is most striking about the Epicureans, however, is the number who entered public life, for Epicurus advocated abstention from politics as the norm (D.L. X. 119). Cicero notes that T. Albucius, convicted for extortion as governor of Sardinia, bore his exile like a true Epicurean, happy wherever pleasure was to be found, but points out that he could have saved himself the trouble by following his sect's advice to abstain from public life (*Tusc.* V. 108). Josephus remarks of the Tiberian senator Pomponius that he 'held almost all the magistracies, but otherwise was an Epicurean pursuing an ἀπράγμων βίος' (*AJ* XIX. 32). And Epictetus scolded an imperial official with Epicurean beliefs for perversely laying down base doctrines while doing noble deeds (III. 7; cf. Pliny *Ep.* VIII. 24).

There is also ample evidence for Romans maintaining that philosophical problems and controversies should not be taken too seriously. At the beginning of *De Finibus* Cicero attempts to answer objections to his decision to write philosophy. Some, he says, disapprove of the study altogether; others think that it is all right if done in a casual way without too much interest or effort; others think it beneath the *dignitas* of a *princeps civitatis*, though they find it appropriate enough for leading statesmen to debate the minutiae of civil law. That offers a significant clue to the Roman attitude, for *ius civile* was a Roman product. In fact, the Roman attitude to philosophy was inseparable from their complex attitude to all things Greek. They were not to be ruled by something which they had learned from their subjects. Yet the intellectual superiority of the Greeks had to be admitted, albeit grudgingly: Cicero hoped to show that Latin could match, or even surpass, Greek in the vocabulary necessary for literature, including philosophical writing (*Fin.* I. 10; *Nat. D.* I. 8). But what he was particularly concerned to show was that Greek theories had proved inferior to the military, political, and moral practices of the Romans. This point, made forcibly in *De Re Publica* (e.g. II. I. 2) and the *Tusculan Disputations* (I. 1–3), is echoed in Quintilian's dictum, 'Greek superiority in moral precept is matched by Roman pre-eminence in examples of conduct—which is the greater thing' (XII. 2. 30).

In *De Oratore* Cicero's hero, L. Licinius Crassus, explains that systematic expositions of abstract subjects do not befit Roman statesmen. He compares this attitude favourable with that of *eruditissima illa Graecorum natio*, men who, regardless of place and company, are always ready to embark on the finer points of useless subjects. Nor is it appropriate, he says, for Roman statesmen to spend their *otium* on such debates, and Crassus gives as a model the childish diversions that Laelius and the younger Scipio enjoyed when free of public business (II. 22). This passage is virtually an admission that the discussions reported in *De Oratore*, supposedly on the authority of a participant (C. Aurelius Cotta), are fictional. It not only reminds us of the *mos dialogorum* (*Fam*. IX. 8. 1), but also warns us against thinking that Scipio and Laelius, or most of Cicero's other well-born interlocutors, were really in the habit of holding formal philosophical discussions of this type with each other.

Cicero was, in fact, criticized for putting such discussions in the mouths of Lucullus, Catulus, and Hortensius in the first edition of the *Academici Libri*: some thought it a slur on the reputations of these statesmen to suggest that they had such expert knowledge or would waste so much time on it. Cicero replied (*Luc*. 4–7) that men like Lucullus, who took the philosopher Antiochus around with him on campaign, did have expert knowledge. Unfortunately for him, we have his letters to Atticus admitting that in that work he had attributed to his original interlocutors an expertise they were known to lack (*Att*. XIII. 12. 3; 16. 1; 19. 5).[23]

One Roman who could see the humour in this contrast of national attitudes was L. Gellius Poplicola, newly appointed governor of Asia, who arrived in Athens in 93 BC on the way to his province. He called together all the philosophers then in the city and urged them to settle their differences if they were not to waste their lives in argument; a settlement of their controversies was possible, he said, and he offered himself as arbitrator (Cic. *Leg*. I. 53). I cling to Cicero's interpretation of this

[23] See Barnes, below, pp. 60–1. One should avoid drawing general conclusions from this episode: the *Academici* contained more technical material than most of Cicero's philosophical works; he nonetheless believed that not only Varro, but Cato and Brutus, would be truly suitable speakers (*Att*. XIII. 16. 1), and despite his *apologia* in *Luc*. 4–7 he did actually change the speakers. For other examples of Romans with technical philosophical knowledge see my forthcoming ch. 18 in *CAH*[2] ix.

incident as a deliberate joke, rejecting the rather owlish notion that it has to do with the political friction between the philosophical schools in Athens that led up to the tyranny of Athenion.[24]

In the Republic the use of Academic and Peripatetic philosophy as a form of rhetorical training probably contributed to this attitude of detachment towards philosophical controversy. Philosophy provided the θέσεις, or abstract questions, used in rhetorical practice already before Cicero's time and continuously into the Empire. The budding orator learned to debate on both sides of such questions as: Is the world governed by Providence? Did law originate naturally or by contract between men? Should the wise man engage in politics? What is the difference between a king and a tyrant? Quintilian, agreeing with Cicero that the Academics and Peripatetics offer the best training in debate and rhetorical theory, explicitly draws the conclusion that the Roman orator is not bound to be faithful to one doctrine as the philosophers themselves are. He can copy all of the most eloquent methods of argument and take over the most noble precepts, which he should then embellish with Roman examples (xii. 2. 23–30). The important point here for our purposes is not the mixing of doctrines in itself, but the basis of choice, here rhetorical expediency, and the lack of interest in the disputes between the schools.[25]

[24] Badian [188] 126 n. 46; but cf. Rawson [94] 7 n. 17.

[25] On these general questions or θέσεις see S. F. Bonner, *Roman Declamation* (Liverpool, 1949), 2–5. Although, as Winterbottom [206] remarks, Quintilian goes beyond Cicero's *De Oratore*, his inspiration here, in insisting that the perfect orator must be a virtuous man and show the effect of the moral philosophy he learns in his *mores* as well as his *eloquentia*, his question at xii. 2. 23, 'quae secta conferre plurimum eloquentiae possit', and his comments on the various schools there, are in line with Cicero's practical concerns in that work. As for the mixing of doctrines, eclecticism itself, even when not a system in itself (D.L. i. 21) or a selection of doctrines based on a philosophical rationale, such as Cicero and Antiochus exemplify in their very different ways (see Barnes, below, pp. 79–81 and *CAH*² ix ch. 18), need not mean a lack of commitment to live by the precepts chosen (as is argued for Horace by Mayer [204]). Indeed, under the Empire we find serious philosophers not given a specific school label, e.g. Augustus' Areus, probably included among the Stoics by D.L., according to the index to Bk. VII in codex P, but not labelled by Strabo, Plutarch, Dio, later Greek writers, Seneca, Suetonius, or Marcus Aurelius (references in Rawson, below, nn. 59–64); Dio Chrysostom; Flavius Archippus (Pliny, *Ep.* x. 58). Lucian explicitly says of his Demonax, the best of philosophers (2), that he combined many types of philosophy (5). Galen believed that uncritical adherence to a sect showed one was not a true doctor or philosopher (*Nat. Fac.* ii. 52–3 K) and proclaimed his own independence of any sect and his willingness to select what was true and reject what was false in the doctrines of different sects (*Libr. Propr.* xix. 13 K). Cf. Sedley, below, n. 48.

The seriousness of Seneca and Marcus Aurelius in dealing even with abstract philosophical problems and arguments, without showing any of the self-conscious urbanity of Cicero, may suggest a change of attitude as Greek philosophy became more integrated into Roman life.[26] But we cannot assume that was true of even upper-class society as a whole. In Lucian indeed we meet the extreme of frivolity in his portrayal of the woman who listens to the house-philosopher at the same time as she is having her hair done or eating dinner: 'While the philosopher is delivering a discourse, the maid comes and hands her a note from her lover, so that the lecture on chastity is kept waiting until she has written a reply to her lover. Then she hurries back to hear it' (*Merc. Cond.* 36).

The Romans had a word for the serious-minded Greek wrapped up in his logical puzzles, namely *baro* = block-head or simpleton. It is used particularly, but not exclusively, of Epicurean philosophers, the most dogmatic of all:[27] their founder's maxims formed a sort of catechism, and Epicurus' picture was put on their rings and cups (Cic. *Fin.* v. 3). This word *baro* occurs in an important Ciceronian letter of 51 (*Att.* v. 11) applied to Patro, the current head of the Epicurean school at Athens, and his disciples. It is an episode that sheds much light on the complex Roman attitude to Greek philosophy.

Patro had appealed to Atticus to have rescinded a decree of the Athenian Areopagus allowing C. Memmius (the patron of Lucretius), now in exile in Greece, to use the ruins of the house of Epicurus as a site for some building project. Though the gardens were probably still the seat of the school (*Fin.* v. 3), the house, perhaps ruined in Sulla's sack, had left its hands. The head of the school wanted Memmius to cede it to him. Atticus asked Cicero, then governor of Cilicia, to intervene, and Cicero, as he informs Atticus in this letter, wrote to Memmius. Now we also have Cicero's letter to Memmius (*Fam.* XIII. 1) in

[26] Fuller discussion in 'Philosophy for Statesmen: Cicero and Seneca', in H. W. Schmidt and P. Wülfing (eds.), *Antikes Denken–Moderne Schule*, *Gymnasium* Beiheft 9 (Zurich, 1988).

[27] *Baro* of Epicureans: e.g. Cic. *Fam.* IX. 26. 3; *Att.* v. 11. 6 (on which see Shackleton Bailey's commentary, iii. 209: in *Fin.* II. 76, however, it is not applied to Epicureans). For Epicurean orthodoxy see Sedley, below, pp. 97 ff. The Stoics, according to Seneca, differed from the Epicureans in this respect (*Ep.* 33. 3–4) and were allowed the freedom to disagree even with Zeno (*Ep.* 33. 4; 8–11; cf. 82. 9; 83. 9; *Otio* 3. 1).

which Cicero is not respectful about Patro. Knowing that the scholarch's importunity has annoyed Memmius, Cicero rests his plea on his own friendship with Memmius while making fun of Patro's *contentio* and *ineptiae* (the same word as Cicero had made Crassus use of the hair-splitting Greeks in *De Oratore*). He mentions that Patro had adduced, in appealing to Memmius and himself, the respect due to wills and the authority of Epicurus, adding that if we want to criticize his insistence, we can ridicule his whole life and *rationem quam sequitur in philosophia*.

On the basis of Cicero's references to Patro in these letters some scholars have even argued that neither Atticus nor Memmius was an Epicurean. Moreover, Cicero says in his letter to Memmius, speaking of Atticus' support of Patro, 'not that he is one of them; for he is highly cultured.' But in fact Patro could hardly have appealed to *Epicuri auctoritas* had Memmius not been sympathetic to philosophy, while Atticus' adherence to the sect is amply attested by Cicero (*Leg.* I. 21; 54; III. 1; *Att.* IV. 6. 1). The *ratio* which Patro follows is his method of argument, not his school (cf. *Nat. D.* I. 12), and his lack of culture was common to many Epicurean philosophers. Cicero's point is that neither Memmius nor Atticus were simple-minded dogmatic Epicureans who argued earnestly and without any taste or style. As Cicero makes the Stoic spokesman say to the Epicurean Velleius in *De Natura Deorum:*

> If your school would take my advice, you would give up all attempts at wit. It sits ill upon you, for it is not your *forte*. . . . This does not, of course, apply to you personally—you have the polished manners of your family and the urbanity of a Roman; but it does apply to all the rest of you and especially to the founder of the system, a man without taste or literary culture, who attacked everyone and was entirely devoid of sharpness, authority or grace. (II. 74)

The Memmius episode then provides no argument against the natural assumption that both Atticus' abstention from public life and his energetic cultivation of personal friendships were connected with his Epicurean convictions.[28] Indeed, it is interesting

[28] I am closer here to the view of Rawson [94] 100–101 than to that of Shackleton Bailey (above, p. 12), though I do not think we have grounds for saying that Atticus was not a 'serious Epicurean', only that he was less serious in manner than many members of the sect. That Cicero does not make him the major speaker in any dialogue may be ascribed to Atticus' dislike of being in the limelight or solemnly expounding principles of any kind. For Memmius' attitude, see Fowler, below, p. 121.

that his biographer Cornelius Nepos, a younger contemporary, describes Atticus' motivation on several occasions in Epicurean terms, though he nowhere states his adherence to that sect (or indeed that of other well-attested Epicureans whom he mentions).[29] On the other hand, he also attributes motives and attitudes with Stoic and Platonic overtones, thus illustrating his own characterization of Atticus as using the precepts of the leading philosophers 'ad vitam agendam non ad ostentationem' (17. 3). As Nepos was himself contemptuous of philosophy (Cic. *Att.* XVI. 5. 5) and despised most of its adherents as hypocrites (Lact. *Inst.* III. 15. 10), it is therefore all the more notable that, in a eulogistic Life, he felt that he had to mention Atticus' knowledge of philosophy (if not his actual questionable creed) and ascribe philosophical sounding reasons to him. Presumably this side of Atticus was too well known or too important to Atticus himself to be ignored. Thus Nepos furnishes Atticus (6. 1–2) with a Stoic-sounding rationale for abstention from public life, namely, the corrupt state of contemporary politics and government, but combines it with the kind of nautical imagery about political involvement familiar from Lucretius. The alternative explanations for this would seem to be that Nepos is either echoing Atticus' Epicurean sentiments and diluting them himself, or echoing Atticus' use of arguments of varied philosophical provenance.[30] In the first case, Nepos emerges as one of those who failed to avoid picking up philosophical notions; in the second, Atticus is revealed, not as having no serious belief in Epicureanism, but as finding it natural to draw from his broad knowledge of philosophy additional arguments to justify his decisions in the eyes of others.

## 5. THE POSITIVE EVIDENCE

Despite all this testimony to detachment and casualness, there

[29] The language was noted by Bailey [199]: *tranquillitas* at 6. 5; *quies* at 7.3, and see further n. 30. Other known Epicureans he mentions are L. Saufeius (12. 3, cf. Cic. *Att.* IV. 6. 1; VII. 1. 1; XV. 4. 2 and 3) and Lucretius (12. 4).

[30] Stoic rationale: Sen. *Otio* 3. 2 (citing Zeno); D.L. VII. 121. Nautical imagery (also at 10. 5–6): Lucr. II. 1–2, cf. Cic. on Epicurean abstention in *Rep.* I. 1; IV. 9 (but *Off.* III. 2 for non-Epicurean context) and Statius' echoes of Epicurus' γαληνισμός in *Silv.* II. 2 (above, n. 13). The first explanation was suggested to me by Nicholas Horsfall; for the second, Cic. *Leg.* III. 1 might suggest that Atticus might have alluded to Plato at least. For the philosophic terms used by Nepos of Atticus' suicide, see Griffin [192] 67 and 76 nn. 6, 7.

is, in fact, abundant evidence that the Romans did expect their fellows to be affected in their conduct by their constant exposure to philosophy. When general consistency between moral tenets and conduct is cited among the merits of Atticus, or Cato, or Flavius Archippus,[31] when charges of hypocrisy are levelled against Cicero, or Cato, or Seneca,[32] general acceptance of an ideal is presupposed (though it is also recognized that consistency, like most other ideals, is not often realized). On the other hand, hypocrisy is a convenient charge to hurl at an enemy in any age, and we may hesitate to take such expressions of outrage as evidence that the Romans actually expected to find, or even seriously demanded, consistency between conviction and conduct. As long as people profess moral principles, with whatever degree of seriousness, their enemies will quote their words against their deeds.

More revealing is praise and advice of a more specific kind. Thus when Marcus Aurelius and his son Commodus proposed to the senate in 177 AD a measure imposing price controls on the sale of gladiators and renounced for the imperial treasury the taxes it had received on these sales, one senator noted in his speech of praise that these emperors did not think it consistent with their *secta* (Stoicism, of course) to preserve bad regulations. This remark, preserved on a remarkable inscription (*ILS* 5163. 24–6), clearly alludes to the Stoic idea that there is a natural law which provides an absolute standard by which to correct human laws (Cic. *Leg.* II. 9 ff.).

By far the most significant testimony to a widespread belief that philosophy had consequences for conduct, however, is the copious evidence for suspicion and fear of those consequences. The first well-attested expulsion of philosophers from Rome in 161 BC seems simply to have reflected the kind of suspicion of something new threatening the traditional modes of education that we have seen in the Elder Cato's reaction to Carneades (above, p. 3). As Seneca put it later, 'Philosophers are expelled from Rome as *corruptores iuventutis*' (*Helv.* 10. 8). And even after

[31] Atticus (Nepos, *Att.* 17. 3); Cato (Cic. *Mur.* 62); Flavius Archippus (see below, p. 22); cf. also Scipio Nasica (below, p. 23).

[32] Cicero: letter from Brutus to Atticus, *ad Brut.* I. 17. 5, on whose authenticity I agree with Moles [196] 765 that the negative verdict of Shackleton Bailey does not seem justified. Cato: Plut. *Cat. Min.* 11. 4; 36; 52; Sen. *Tranq.* 17. 9. Seneca: Tac. *Ann.* XIII. 42; Dio LXI. 10. 4.

philosophy had become a familiar part of cultural life, there remained a feeling that excessive enthusiasm for doctrine went beyond what was suitable to a Roman of senatorial standing. Tacitus puts this most clearly in the *Agricola*, where he explains the efforts made by his hero's mother to curb his passion for the Greek philosophy that he picked up in Massilia (4. 4).

Behind this attitude of suspicion lay the belief that philosophy could actually diminish a man's usefulness to the state in one of several ways.

(1) It might seduce him away from public life. This was of course a stock charge against Epicureans with their doctrine of *λάθε βιώσας*. The feeling that Epicureans were unsuited to any social activity is strikingly attested in Suetonius' story of the grammarian M. Pompilius Andronicus in the late Republic: because he was an Epicurean he was thought unsuitable for keeping a school and had to give up, retire, and write a history (*Gram.* 8). Under the Empire, when political apathy became a practical problem for emperors, Stoicism too became associated with the temptation to the contemplative life. For the Stoa, though fundamentally in favour of men entering politics to discharge their obligations to fellow men, held that there were a good many circumstances in which abstention or retirement was legitimate, and there were Stoics prepared to exploit this doctrine to avoid a life that was tedious when it was not dangerous. Thus Tacitus could write of the Stoic Helvidius Priscus, 'He devoted himself to philosophy, not, as so many, to make the high-sounding name of philosophy a pretext for *segne otium*, but to take up public life, protected against the blows of fortune' (*Hist.* IV. 5).

(2) It might inculcate doctrines that were impractical and inappropriate to the realities of public life. The key text for the Republic is, of course, Cicero's *Pro Murena*, where Cato is held up to ridicule for applying the austere doctrines of the Stoa to public life. Cato, says Cicero, refused a request of the *publicani* for a revision of their tax contract—because it is wrong to give in to *gratia*; he pressed an accusation of the consul designate for electoral corruption—because pity is ruled out by his sect. Cato, as we shall see, was not always as rigid as that, but what Cicero alleged against his sect was clearly still felt in Seneca's day. For he writes in *De Clementia*, 'I know that among the

ignorant the Stoic sect has a reputation for being too harsh and hence unable to offer good advice to *principes* or *reges*' (II. 5. 2). Then again, Tacitus paints a ludicrous picture of the Stoic Musonius Rufus tagging on to a senatorial legation to parley with the advancing Flavian armies and preaching the virtues of peace (and no doubt the natural obligation of all men to each other) to the soldiers.[33]

(3) It might make him recalcitrant to authority and subversive of government. In fact, the idea that philosophy was responsible for political opposition does not seem to have taken hold in Rome except for a period of about forty years under Nero and his Flavian successors. That is when Seneca felt moved to write, 'It is a mistake to believe that those who have loyally dedicated themselves to philosophy are stubborn and rebellious and defiant towards magistrates or kings or those who administer affairs' (*Ep.* 73).

This low estimate of philosophy as a preparation for public life is reflected in the policy of the Roman government towards philosophers in the matter of privileges and immunities. Following Hellenistic precedents, Caesar and Augustus had granted certain limited privileges to doctors and teachers, the last category including *grammatici* and *rhetores*. Much later these same groups received from Vespasian additional immunities and privileges (Suet. *Iul.* 42; Dio LIII. 30; Suet. *Aug.* 42; 59; Riccobono, *FIRA* I., nos. 73, 77). But from the beginning philosophers had been omitted from these privileged ranks, and Vespasian does not seem to have made any change. The omission is significant, for there were Hellenistic precedents for giving similar rights to philosophers. One reason for hesitation about them may have been the cynical Roman feeling that real philosophers were hard to identify. As Quintilian wrote, 'philosophia enim simulari potest, eloquentia non potest' (XII. 2. 12). Again, even after the omission was corrected, Antoninus Pius, when confirming Hadrian's privileges, pointed out that no restriction of the number of immunities allowed each city need be laid down in the case of philosophers (as it was for the other privileged categories) because philosophers are few; he went on to explain that the numbers who profess philosophy are not few

[33] Tac. *Hist.* I. 81.

but that those who argue about contributing to their cities are clearly too concerned about money to count as real philosophers (*Dig*. XXVII. 1. 6. 7). But the principal reason for the omission must have been a feeling that philosophers were not among those educators 'qui publice iuvenibus prosunt', as the jurist Paulus points out, for these privileges were meant as rewards for service to the state (*Dig*. XXVII. 1. 6. 5).

The date when the omission was corrected is revealing. Pliny's letters from Bithynia show that a philosopher called Flavius Archippus had received special honours *ad hominem* from Domitian whose description of him as 'bonum virum et professioni suae moribus respondentem' illustrates that emperor's low estimate of the profession in general. In the reign of Trajan, Archippus could claim exemption from jury duty *ut philosophus* (*Ep*. x. 58)—that is, as a member of a privileged category. The reign of Nerva or Trajan seems indicated for the change, exactly the time when the expulsions of philosophers as subversive, started by Nero and continued by Vespasian and Domitian, came to an end.[34] Clearly there had been a deep-seated feeling that philosophy was useless as education for public life, a feeling intensified for a time by the troubled relations between emperors and philosophers into a belief that it was an actual liability.

## 6. PROBLEMATIC EXAMPLES

If these fears we have mentioned provide a *prima facie* case for the influence of philosophy on the conduct of Romans in public life, it is harder to draw convincing connections between philosophy and politics in particular cases. If we were to set down the minimal requirements for demonstrating that a Roman statesman, in supporting a particular policy or taking a particular decision, was governed by the specific doctrines of a philosophical school to which he adhered, they would surely be:

(1) to show that the man adhered to the sect in general or that there is reason to think he was under its influence at this time.

[34] For the problem of dating the change, see Bowersock [98] 30 ff. and my review in *JRS* 61 (1971) 279–80.

(2) to show that the policy or decision in question would be the one clearly indicated by the creed of that sect for these circumstances. This would usually be done by adducing texts giving the sect's views or, more questionably, inferring from a strict consistency of action or viewpoint among those known to hold to that creed, that some doctrine of the sect was involved.

Such a proof would hardly be conclusive, for the man might still in fact be differently motivated on that occasion. Thus it has recently been argued that when Demetrius the Cynic defended a Stoic philosopher who had been bribed to testify falsely against his friend and pupil in the last years of Nero (Tac. *Ann.* XVI. 32. 3), he was acting out of adherence to a Cynic tradition of humanity (φιλανθρωπία). Yet we cannot exclude the possibility that his contemporaries were right to believe, as Tacitus claims they did, that Demetrius, despite his profession of Cynicism, had defended Celer more to advance himself or show off than out of any honourable purpose ('ambitiosius quam honestius': *Hist.* IV. 40; cf. IV. 10).[35]

For a Roman in public life, it can be even harder to show that he has chosen a course of action because it was prescribed by his philosophy, for he may have been following Roman tradtion. Thus Posidonius remarks of Scipio Nasica, the consul of 111 BC, after noting that his grandfather had fought to maintain high standards of justice in the treatment of Rome's subjects, 'in practising his philosophy in his life, and not just in words, he maintained the tradition of his family and his heritage of virtue' (*FGrH* 87 F 112).

Another impediment to ascertaining Roman motivation is the nature of our sources, and in particular of Plutarch, who is the most informative on philosophical interests. A Greek and a philosopher himself, he seems to have sought out incidents that could demonstrate the importance of Greek philosophy to the best of the Romans. He was concerned to show that, far from eroding Roman greatness (as the Elder Cato had prophesied), Greek learning had become an established part of Roman

[35] Moles [208], in an interesting discussion of Cynicism, shows that Demetrius *could* have been motivated by a strain of Cynic thinking rather different from the harsh critical attitude more often associated with that school. His paper, in any case, shows that even Cynicism, whose tenets were comparatively crude and simple, could have generated very different ideas of what to do on particular occasions.

culture at the height of the city's power (*Cato Mai.* 23. 3). Thus he believed, and even exaggerated, Cicero's account of Lucullus' philosophical expertise in the first edition of the *Academici Libri* (Plut. *Luc* 1. 4; 42. 2–4).[36] Can we then trust him when, even before mentioning that Crassus was attached to Aristotelian doctrine, he gives as Crassus' own reason for personally training and educating his slaves that he thought it the duty of a master to care for his slaves as living tools of domestic science (ὄργανα ἔμψυχα τῆς οἰκονομικῆς, Plut. *Crass.* 2. 6)? Perhaps Crassus was really acting as a hard-headed businessman, ensuring that his slaves were profitable. We naturally feel less sceptical when reading about the philosophical motives of Brutus, whose expertise is well attested.[37]

Again, Plutarch retails from the biography of the younger Cato by his Stoic admirer Thrasea Paetus a philosophical explanation of Cato's divorce and remarriage of his wife Marcia (*Cat. Min.* 25. 4; 52. 4). Shortly after 56 BC Cato gave up his wife Marcia, by whom he had had three children, to the rich and elderly Hortensius, on whose death in 50 he took her back to his house, now an heiress. According to Plutarch Hortensius originally asked for Cato's daughter in marriage in order to realize the community of wise men. The allusion to the community of women and children advocated by Zeno in his πολιτεία and then by Chrysippus is clear (D.L. VII. 131) Cato refused his daughter but agreed to hand over his wife. Now the ascription of such an argument to Hortensius is absurd, for as Cicero tells us (*Att.* XIII. 12. 3), Hortensius knew little about philosophy and thought it a waste of time. Nor would the argument have had much appeal for Cato, as Stoicism had moved

[36] Glucker [71] esp. 380 ff., argues conclusively that Plutarch's account of Lucullus' role in the *Sosus* affair (*Luc.* 42. 3–4) derives ultimately from Cicero, whose first edition of the *Academica* Plutarch mentions here: he suggests Nepos' biography of Cicero as the immediate source. See also Barnes, below, pp. 60; 92–3.

[37] Moles [196] argues for the authenticity, not only of the views Plutarch ascribes to Brutus on suicide, but also of the philosophically resonant utterance at *Brut.* 51. 2–4. For Cicero, however, Plutarch's view that Antiochus of Ascalon (and unnamed friends at Rome) urged him successfully to return to Rome when he had made contingency plans for staying in Athens, deserting public life and devoting his life to studying philosophy (*Cic.* 4. 3), has no support in Cicero's autobiographical account at *Brut.* 314–17, which makes it clear that he always planned to return to be an orator at Rome. Even if (implausibly) Cicero is here concealing a political motive for his absence, he had no reason to conceal the role of philosophy and philosophers in his plans. For Plutarch's emphasis, see also Pelling, below, pp. 199 ff., and Rawson, below, pp. 236–7.

on from its Cynic phase and was no longer attacking existing institutions,[38] while nothing suggests that Cato saw himself in that earlier tradition. In view of the emphasis in Plutarch and in our other sources for this incident (Appian, *B. Civ.* II. 99; Lucan II. 344) on Hortensius' desire for an heir, the most likely explanation is that Hortensius, who had a grown son of whom he disapproved (Val. Max. v. 9. 2; Cic. *Att.* VI. 3. 9) and whom he threatened to disown, wished to produce another heir to his great wealth before he died. He may also have wished his wealth to be used on the right side in the political conflict that seemed imminent to some even in 56. In the end, Hortensius did make this son his heir (Cic. *Att.* VII. 3. 9), but Marcia also benefited handsomely in the will.

It was the will, of course, that gave rise to Caesar's allegation in his *Anticato* (Plut. *Cat. Min.* 52. 5; cf. 11. 4) that Cato agreed to the arrangement in order to acquire Hortensius' fortune through Marcia. That charge had to be answered, and what Plutarch records is one attempt at a philosophical explanation. Unfortunately, it satisfies neither of our minimal requirements, failing on the first count for Hortensius and on the second for Cato. The Stoic philosopher Seneca had a simpler explanation: Marcia, he said, was fickle (Haase fr. 74, from *De Matrimonio*). It is hard to feel that the philosophers did better here than the Greek geographer Strabo who invoked anthropology:

> It is reported of the Tapyri (who lived near Parthia) that it was a custom of theirs to give their wives in marriage to other husbands as soon as they had had two or three children by them; just as in our times, Cato gave Marcia in marriage to Hortensius at his request, in accordance with an ancient custom of the Romans (XI. 515)

Modern efforts to provide philosophical motives for the political activities of Romans in public life have been less amusing than this venture, but hardly more successful. For example, it has been suggested at various times that Tiberius Gracchus was inspired in his tribunate by Stoic ideas.[39]

[38] See Annas, below, pp. 167 ff. On Plutarch's attitude here see Babut [333] 173–4.

[39] Dudley [185] discusses previous attempts, notably that of F. Taeger, *Tiberius Gracchus* (Stuttgart, 1928) 16 ff. More recently Smuts [187] has tried to align Gracchus with a strain of Stoicism that he claims was championing equity against the strict justice required by another strain (but see below, n. 44). Becker [184] suggests that Panaetian Stoicism generated a sympathy for social justice and practical morality that encour-

It is certainly true that Tiberius Gracchus was close to the philosopher Blossius of Cumae, a pupil of the Stoic Antipater of Tarsus and a φιλόσοφος himself, according to Plutarch (*Ti. Gracch.* 8. 5; 20. 3). Blossius was interrogated after Tiberius' death as one of his supporters—Cicero (*Amic.* 37) makes Laelius describe him as the *dux* of Gracchus; in Valerius Maximus (IV. 7. 1) he is his faithful *comes*. In all the accounts Blossius' first line of defence is that he obeyed Tiberius.

Now there is evidence that Blossius at least shared the view of Tiberius that the tribune had an unqualified duty to serve the good of the people (Plut. *Ti. Gracch.* 17. 4; 20. 4), a view Tiberius manifested by deposing his fellow tribune Octavius for opposing the people's interests (Appian, *B. Civ.* I. 12; Plut. *Ti. Gracch.* 15. 2; 5). There is also reason to think that Blossius would have sympathized with Tiberius' programme of redistributing land in the interests of social justice, for he subsequently joined the revolt of Aristonicus in Asia, which drew its support largely from the poor, notably slaves and peasants (Plut. *Ti. Gracch.* 20. 4).

Where does this evidence take us? Even if we pass over the difficulties about the relation of Blossius to Tiberius and assume that Tiberius accepted from him Stoic doctrines, it is not possible to show that the Stoa inculcated democratic views at all with regard to the constitution, or unequivocally with regard to agrarian reform.

Polybius in his highly theoretical account of the Roman constitution, written not long before the tribunate of Tiberius, says that the tribunes are bound to follow the will of the people (VI. 16. 5). But that only helps to identify the notion as Greek, not specifically Stoic, and traditionally the Stoa did not discuss political institutions in any detail (Cic. *Leg.* III. 14). As for the land bill, Tiberius is said to have had help in drafting from P. Mucius Scaevola (Plut. *Ti. Gracch.* 9. 1; Cic. *Luc.* 13) who was a Stoic sympathizer (Cic. *Off.* II. 47, cf. *Brut.* 114) and had some patronal relationship to Blossius (Cic. *Amic.* 37). Then one can

aged land reform, but also rejected 'unethical tactics' in politics and favoured the mixed constitution as a means to political harmony; that when the two aims came into conflict in his tribunate Tiberius Gracchus maintained the priority of the first, Scipio and his friends that of the second. Hadot [185b] and now, more elaborately, Erskine [185a] attempt to analyse the views of Tiberius and of his opponents according to a supposed split in the second century BC Stoa over the interpretation of the school's view of justice as applied to political issues.

appeal to Tiberius' argument, as reported by Plutarch, that it was shocking to see beasts having caves to dwell in while Italian soldiers were homeless, for the Stoa held that men and gods were higher beings than animals who were intended for their use (e.g. Cic. *Fin.* III. 63; 67). This is a pretty thin argument, especially when one remembers that the Stoa was not prone to stress the importance of material goods, holding that only virtue mattered to happiness. Blossius' teacher Antipater, however, is credited by Seneca (*Ep.* 92. 5) with a more liberal attitude to externals, and by Cicero with the view that business transactions should be governed by the Stoic conception of man's obligations to human society, interpreted in the most generous sense (*Off.* III. 52–3).[40]

At this point, however, we encounter real difficulty, because Stoic influence can be ascribed with at least equal plausibility to those who disagreed with Tiberius Gracchus on both the issues under discussion. Tiberius' activity lost him the support of his Stoic friend Q. Aelius Tubero (Cic. *Amic.* 37; *Brut.* 117) and his kinsman Scipio Aemilianus. Now in Cicero's *De Re Publica* (I. 34), Laelius remarks that Scipio often discussed politics with Polybius and the Stoic philosopher Panaetius. If we do not simply write this off as part of Cicero's romantic and exaggerated account of the 'Scipionic circle',[41] what can we deduce about the views that Scipio and Panaetius might have shared?

Little is preserved of the discussion of the tribunate in *De Re Publica* (I. 69; II. 57–8), but the general distrust of popular power there attributed to Scipio and his friends might suggest that the view given would have been close to what Cicero says in *De Legibus* (III. 23–5), where he disapproves of the Gracchi and justifies the tribunate as an instrument of control over the power of the people, which would otherwise be too violent.

[40] See Annas, below, pp. 151 ff. In order to show that democratic reform could be Stoic-inspired, a parallel is often drawn with the influence of Sphaerus on the land reforms of King Cleomenes of Sparta in the second century BC. But even Plutarch, not one to underrate such influence, says not a word about Sphaerus' influence on these reforms, but notes only that he fired the king's ambition and determination and was interested in the revival of the Spartan ἀγωγή (*Cleom.* 2. 2; 11. 2), while Diogenes Laertius VII. 178 lists a work by Sphaerus on the Spartan constitution. Vatai (above, n. 3) 126–9 is unimpressed by the alleged political influence of Sphaerus and Blossius.

[41] See on the 'Scipionic Circle' Astin [183] Appendix 6; Rawson, below, pp. 37–8.

Though it is hard to see what is particularly Stoic about this, Cicero does tell us, also in *De Legibus* (III. 14) and while discussing the different offices of state, that Panaetius wrote more practically than older Stoics about political institutions.[42] As for the proposal for land reform, Laelius in *De Re Publica* specifically condemns the agrarian scheme of Tiberius Gracchus (III. 41), and this view is also that of Cicero in *De Officiis* (II. 72; 78–80) where Panaetius is the main source (e.g. II. 60).

Should we then take the opposite view and argue, as Dudley has done, that the Stoa was identifying with the position of Gracchus' conservative opponents?[43] The Stoic principles behind the attack on such *largitiones* in *De Officiis* are, first, their view of justice (derived from Aristotle) as distribution according to desert (II. 78), and second, their view of man's obligation to the larger community of gods and men and to those smaller communities of which it is made up, i.e. the interests of society as a whole are not to be sacrificed to those of some part of it (II. 72). We are back to the principle invoked by Antipater which, as we said, could have been used to support Gracchus' agrarian reform.[44] Indeed it is not hard to see that principles of this kind could be applied in opposite senses to the issue at hand and that, while there could be Stoic arguments for and against, there was no Stoic dogma unequivocally covering the case. More rewarding is the subtle approach of Nicolet who suggests that philosophical language was used by the Gracchi and their opponents, all of whom belonged to a milieu open to Greek influences and used to political and philosophical discussion.[45] We do not know of course that the particular Stoic arguments considered above were used by either Gracchus and his supporters or his opponents.

Similar difficulties confront us in dealing with a much more

[42] Cicero also mentions Diogenes in this context, on whose interest in the maintenance of private property transactions as opposed to the imposition of an unlimited obligation to forward the interests of others, see Annas, below, pp. 151 ff.

[43] Dudley [185] 96–7.

[44] Dudley [185] argued that the sympathy of Blossius with Tiberius' scheme is explained, not by his Stoicism, but by the democratic and anti-Roman tradition of his family.

[45] Nicolet [186] shows convincingly that appeals to an equity beyond strict justice were used by both sides in this political struggle.

sophisticated attempt to connect philosophy and politics, this time concerning the Epicureans. In a celebrated book review, published in 1941, Arnaldo Momigliano wrote:

There is a conspicuous date in the history of Epicureanism: the date (46 BC) at which Cassius turned Epicurean (Cic. *Fam.* xv. 16; 19), not to enjoy the *hortulus*, but to reach quickly the conclusion that the tyrant had to be eliminated. . . . Surely, the last struggle for Roman aristocratic government [Caesar's murder and the subsequent opposition to Antony] cannot be reduced to ideological formulae. . . . Yet it was also a philosophical *affaire*.[46]

Momigliano rested his theory of an Epicurean struggle for republican government (1) on the conversion of Cassius and (2) on a sudden enthusiasm for the cause of the tyrannicides and a corresponding hostility to Antony that he thought he detected in Epicureans after the assassination of Caesar.

It is important to be clear about what this theory does *not* claim. It does not claim that the assassination was principally the work of believing Epicureans: indeed, it could not, as the spiritual leader, M. Junius Brutus, was an adherent of the Old Academy (above, p. 7), and no certifiable Epicurean besides Cassius is to be found among the sixteen conspirators we can identify by name.[47] Nor does the theory claim that Epicureanism gave clear directives for dealing with tyrants by assassination, or even for preferring Republican government to rule by one man. Again, it could not have made these claims for Epicureanism, because, although the abuse of tyrants was a favourite pastime of all the philosophical schools, there were plenty of texts suggesting that the cruelty of tyrants should be met by the ἀταραξία of the practised Epicurean (Cic. *Tusc.* II. 17–18; D.L. x. 118). Thus when Statilius the Epicurean, in discussion with Brutus, said that it was not fitting for the wise man to forfeit his imperturbability because of stupid and senseless men, he was giving a perfectly sound Epicurean reply (Plut. *Brut.* 12). As for preferring Republican government, Momigliano correctly saw that the Epicurean view that society arose out of a natural agreement between men (a sort of social

[46] Momigliano [47]: the citations are from pp. 151 and 155.

[47] There were more than sixty conspirators in all (Suet. *Iul.* 80. 4): the sixteen names are collected by Groebe, *RE* x (1919), 254–5.

contract) for mutual protection and security did not lead to any great interest in the virtues of particular types of constitution. Similarly, the doctrine that active political life was not normally worth the trouble for the individual was not likely to induce Epicureans to leap into the fray when a government failed to do its job of providing security.

What Momigliano did claim was that action against tyrants could be justified in Epicurean terms, and was in fact justified in this way at this time. As regards the first, he was clearly right: Lucretius had constructed a schematic history of human society in Book v 988 ff. which departed from its Epicurean model Hermarchus in distinguishing between a monarchical stage of society and a later stage when magistrates and laws provided a social structure. The latter, Lucretius held, was more effective at ensuring order and security. (See Fowler, below, pp. 141–5.) That Lucretius was uttering a rallying cry is unlikely, given that he was writing in the 50s, some years before Caesar's dictatorship. He simply shared the usual Roman admiration for their ancestral constitution, and Epicureanism did not rule out his expressing his preference in an Epicurean framework. Similarly, breakdown of true justice could form one of the exceptional cases when the wise man could enter politics (Cic. *Rep.* I. 6; Sen. *Otio* 3. 2). Lucretius may be alluding to this latter doctrine when he says of Memmius, his addressee, 'neque Memmi clara propago | talibus in rebus communi desse saluti' (I. 43: see Fowler, below, p. 128).

What the theory fails to prove, however, is the second point, that Cassius and other Epicureans did in fact square their actions on this occasion with their philosophy. First, Cassius. His conversion came, not in 46, but in 48 when, after fighting for Pompey at Pharsalus, he decided not to join the diehards in Africa but to come home 'spe pacis et odio civilis sanguinis' (Cic. *Fam.* xv. 15. 1).[48] In a letter to Cicero of early 45, Cassius lays stress on the need for peace and clemency: he prefers to bear with Caesar as an old and clement master rather than have a new and cruel one such as Pompey's son might prove to

[48] The date of Cassius' conversion is pointed out by Shackleton Bailey, *Cicero Epistulae ad Familiares* ii (Cambridge, 1977) 378, commenting on the *nuper* of *Fam.* xv. 17. 3 and adducing 'si iam biennium aut triennium est cum virtuti nuntium remisisti' in *Fam.* xv. 16. 3 (both letters written early in 45).

be (*Fam.* xv. 19. 4).[49] At that time many known Epicureans were on Caesar's side, and Caesar's camp had for some time been known as a hot-bed of Epicureanism (*Fam.* vii. 12, written in 53). In fact, Cicero suggests, in writing to Cassius in January 45, that his conversion from Stoicism to Epicureanism was a reflection of the victory of Caesar in the civil war (*Fam.* xv. 16. 3).[50] Given our evidence, we have no reason to think that Cassius put his decision to kill Caesar, even to himself, in philosophical terms. Despite the problems in using Plutarch (above, pp. 23–5), it is worth noting his observation about the assassination, running, as it does, counter to his usual tendency to adduce philosophical motives:

> Cassius, turning his eyes toward the statue of Pompey before the attack began, invoked it silently, although he was much addicted to the doctrines of Epicurus [which did not credit survival after death or intervention by the supernatural]. But the crisis apparently, when the dread deed was imminent, replaced his former rational calculations with divine inspiration. (*Caes.* 66. 2)

No more convincing is the attempt to establish a role for Epicurean precept in the thinking of such Epicureans as became exasperated with Antony. Philodemus, the philosophical mentor of L. Calpurnius Piso, may have made a remark hostile to Antony when discussing the evil ambitions of politicians which justify aloofness from public life (see Fowler, below, pp. 125–6). Yet such a remark could be an incidental reflection of the political attitude of Piso rather than a call for action justified by philosophy. For Philodemus elsewhere, when noting the tendency of the good man to be condemned in free states and in tyrannies, ends with the expected Epicurean exhortation to *ἀταραξία*: 'I am amazed by people who think that such a condemnation, pronounced not by good men but evil ones, or

[49] The emphasis here is compatible with Epicureanism (cf. the *ἡμερότης* and *ἐπιείκεια* attributed to Epicurus himself (D.L. x. 10) and advocated by Philodemus in *Ir.* 44. 25; 45. 5), though not exclusive to it.

[50] Cicero's expression 'ex qua *αἱρέσει* "vi hominibus armatis" deiectus' (*Fam.* xv. 16. 3) is illuminated by his letters of 53 to the lawyer Trebatius, who had converted to Epicureanism in Caesar's camp, on which Cicero remarks (in the context of the conversion) 'o castra praeclara' (*Fam.* vii. 12. 3), adding that everything there is ruled by force (vii. 13. 2). It is surely Caesar's victory that Cicero is blaming for his conversion. I do not understand why Shackleton Bailey (above, n. 48) 379 thinks that the context of the remark in xv. 16. 3 suggests that Cassius was formerly an Academic, not e.g. a Stoic.

rather by beasts, makes life no longer worthwhile' (*Mort.* xxxv, col. vi. 11 ff.). In fact Piso, a loyal Caesarian to the end (Suet. *Iul.* 83. 1) did lose patience with Antony (Cic. *Fam.* xii. 2. 1), but was still noted for taking a more moderate line towards him, when real strife started, than passionate Republicans like Cicero (Cic. *Phil.* i. 6; 10; xii. 14; App. *B. Civ.* iii. 50–60). He had earlier in fact resisted pressure from supporters of the Liberators to ignore Caesar's will and, in doing so, referred to the followers of the Liberators as tyrants (App. *B. Civ.* ii. 135–6). Piso simply had a reasonable dislike of coercion from any quarter.

## 7. SOME CONCLUSIONS

These attempts to establish connections between philosophical doctrines and particular policies and decisions fail, but, in failing, they are instructive. They teach us that establishing such connections is difficult, and they point to some of the reasons why it should be.

Even if we leave out of account the problem common to all aspects of ancient history, that our evidence is usually insufficient to decide between possible motives; even if we ignore the various sorts of eclecticism the period exhibits,[51] still the ethical doctrines of the dogmatic schools themselves were usually too general to give unambiguous directives in particular situations. In fact, the most popular schools in the period of the late Republic and early Empire only made reference to politics in the most general terms. It is not even possible to show that they had a clear preference for a particular type of constitution.[52]

Their ethical doctrines were flexible, both in their generality and often in their subtlety. It is well to remember that all these schools developed and valued to a high degree the art of casuistry, that is, skill in deciding what particular action here and now actually followed from a general philosophical

[51] See above, n. 25.

[52] Stoics for the mixed constitution: D.L. vii. 131; for monarchy: Sen. *Ben.* ii. 20, with the discussion in Griffin [146] 202 ff. For the Epicureans the purpose of society was to ensure the security of individuals. That did not lead to a preference for any constitutional form, though one could argue for the effectiveness of one, as Lucretius did (see above, p. 30). Epicureans despised public office of all kinds (Plut. *Mor.* 1127 A), but could advise monarchs on occasion (see above, n. 3).

dogma, what remedies for the soul were appropriate on each occasion.[53] Thus, on the fundamental question, whether or not to participate in politics, the Stoics had to decide if any of the recognized obstacles obtained at any one time; the Epicureans, if an emergency existed great enough to justify participation (Sen. *Otio* 3. 2–3; 7. 1–4).

Given this flexibility, it is not surprising that the adherents of these schools found no incompatibility between traditional Roman ideas and their broad ethical doctrines. For example, the Epicureans admitted that virtue was an excellent means to the aim of life, which was pleasure (Cic. *Fin.* I. 34–6; II. 69 ff.; Sen. *Vit. Beat.* 7. 1), and Cassius alludes to the doctrine in praising the clemency of his fellow Epicurean Vibius Pansa (Cic. *Fam.* XV. 19. 2). But the virtue recommended could also be good old Roman courage in battle or traditional Roman discipline in putting patriotism above loved ones and children (see below, p. 36). Similarly, as Brunt has shown, the Stoics insisted on a man's fulfilling the duties attached to his various social roles; but it was his knowledge of Roman standards that told Marcus Aurelius what made a good emperor and Helvidius Priscus what made a good senator.[54] When men such as Thrasea Paetus acted on the Stoic doctrine that withdrawal from political life was appropriate when the state was corrupt, they had already judged Nero's government corrupt by traditional senatorial standards.[55]

Finally, if the long history of these schools provided a stock of *exempla* showing the application of the doctrines to specific situations, it also illustrated the variety of conclusions one could draw. These creeds would never have survived so long if they had not proved adaptable.

What kind of connection between philosophy and politics can we reasonably expect? Perhaps we should look more to the language in which choices are analysed and justifications framed when we are seeking to understand the role that philosophy played in the life of Roman statesmen.

[53] Seneca (e.g. *Epp.* 70. 11; 71. 1; 81. 10; 95. 5; *Ben.* II. 16. 1; *Ep.* 64. 8–9) and Epictetus (e.g. I. 22. 1–8; II. 11. 8–9; 17. 7–9; IV. 1. 41–2) are quite explicit about this.

[54] Brunt [201].

[55] See Wirszubski [85] 138 ff., though not enough is made there of the language of justification used by these Romans 'who held Stoic views'; Griffin [146] 365–6.

It was not just for intellectual exercise that Cicero in March of 49, when he was trying to decide whether or not to join Pompey in the East, was debating in Greek and in Latin a series of philosophical *θέσεις* on tyranny: 'ought a man to remain in his country when it is ruled by a tyrant?', 'should he use any means to upset tyranny, even if the safety of the state is thereby endangered?' (*Att.* IX. 4). At the same period he was writing to S. Sulpicius Rufus and his former questor Mescinius Rufus about his uncertainty whether or not to join Pompey (*Fam.* IV. 2; V. 19). He divides the question into the *honestum* and the *utile*: 'what is right [to leave Rome] is clear, but not what is expedient; but we should be the sort of men who allow no such distinction [an allusion to the Stoic doctrine that nothing could be truly *utile* that was not *honestum*, *Off.* II. 9–10; III. 13–19]. Therefore we must go, but where?' As with the tyrant *θέσεις*, philosophy does not tell Cicero what to do, even, as here, when he accepts particular doctrines. It provides him with the terms in which to cast the problem, but only he can decide what is *honestum* in this case.

Again, in Cicero's deliberations after the murder of Caesar, Atticus at one point gives him the advice '*μὴ πολιτεύεσθαι*' and then withdraws it as inappropriate (*Att.* XIV. 20. 5). For the notion of staying in Rome, Atticus is fortifying himself with the Stoic arguments rehearsed in *Tusculan Disputations* I about death being a refuge, not an evil (*Att.* XV. 4). For the idea of leaving, Cicero is strengthening himself with the idea of finding a better death abroad, freer and less horrible, having in mind Cato's suicide and its Stoic justification as a release from a dishonourable life and unpleasant death (*Att.* XVI. 7. 4, cf. XV. 20. 2).[56] The philosophical language is not just veneer, though no doctrine decides the issue. Philosophy supplies the language for thinking men trying to make moral and political choices, pitting Epicurean views against Stoic and, in the second case, one Stoic doctrine against another. Similarly, Seneca's *De Tranquillitate Animi*, *De Otio*, and the *Letters to Lucilius* show us how Stoics could invoke the school's complex doctrine about political participation to justify courses of action.

[56] For Cicero's deliberations about his *officium* in his letters, using the terminology of *De Officiis*, see Brunt [190]; cf. Pelling on Plutarch's treatment, below, pp. 219–22. On Stoic justifications for suicide, see Griffin [192] 72–5.

The subtlety or generality of school doctrines made them ideal for use in justification, including the insincere variety. What one could do and did do with Stoicism is immediately clear to anyone reading the interchange of letters between Cicero and Cato (*Fam.* xv. 4 and 5) about the value of a triumph (and the subordinate honour of a *supplicatio*). Cicero is asking for Cato's support in the senate for the *supplicatio* he desires. His request is grounded on past mutual benefits, but the letter is written in full deference to Cato's philosophical standards and ends with an appeal to their joint efforts to bring philosophy into public life. In this exchange it is common ground between Cato and Cicero that the pursuit of glory and good repute is a reasonable aim. *Eudoxia* = true glory was, according to some Stoics, one of the *commoda* or desirable indifferents, not a good but worthy of pursuit (Cic. *Fin.* III. 56–7; *Off.* I. 83; II. 88). What they debate is the sort of glory involved, for the same Stoics distinguished *vera gloria*, that based on virtuous action and accorded by good men, from *ficta gloria*, that accorded by the ignorant and based on popular, but bad, actions (*Fin.* III. 57; *Off.* II. 43, cf. I. 65).

Cicero's job is to persuade Cato that the honours he hopes for fall in the first category, though he knows that Cato can say that they would be empty tributes from the *vulgus* based on *res bellicae*, which Cato regards as a trivial type of achievement. Cato respects the moral qualities a governor shows in managing his province, so Cicero points out that his military successes were only made possible by his *aequitas* and *continentia* towards the provincials, who were therefore willing to support him. Cato's support for his *supplicatio* would in itself fulfil the second condition for true glory. Cato refuses in a masterpiece of rebuke and admonition—all the way to the final apology for writing *at such length* a letter which is brief and laconic by comparison with Cicero's. He applauds Cicero's virtues, his *innocentia* and *diligentia*, but argues that a *supplicatio*, which gave honour to the gods, was inappropriate as these achievements were Cicero's own. Cato, however, managed to switch off his Stoicism (or chose to accept arguments closer to Cicero's) when it came to his own family: just after this he supported the vote of a *supplicatio* of unusual length to his son-in-law Bibulus for a victory over the Parthians that he had not even won (Cic. *Att.* VII. 2. 6–7; 3. 5).

Four years earlier, we find Epicurean doctrine being used on both sides on the same issue. Cicero's speech *In Pisonem* suggests that L. Calpurnius Piso used his Epicureanism to explain why he had not asked the senate to grant him a triumph when he returned home from his governorship of Macedonia. According to Cicero, Piso had not dared to make the request because of the stories of his greed and general unpopularity that preceded him home, and said that he had never desired a triumph (56), calling men who did *idiotae*, that is, philosophically ignorant (60). Cicero makes fun of this claim by inventing two philosophical lectures for Piso to recite to his ambitious son-in-law Caesar (59–60): (1) Why do you want a thanksgiving, for the gods are never propitious or angry towards men (cf. Cic. *Nat. D*. I. 45; D.L. X. 139)? (2) Why do you want a triumph, for neither the booty, nor the procession, nor the applause contribute at all to *voluptas corporis*? The latter is, of course, only Cicero's crude version of Epicurean doctrine, but it is not implausible that Piso himself would have said that he placed a higher value on *quies* than *gloria* (Lucr. II. 37 ff.) or political power (Lucr. V. 1127). Cicero points out that on this occasion Piso was rebuked for his conduct in his province (47, 92) by L. Manlius Torquatus, the consul of 65 BC, who is adduced as an example of a normal governor of Macedonia who did not disdain being hailed as imperator (44). Torquatus is the father of the Epicurean spokesman in *De Finibus*, and there is some suggestion in that work (I. 39) that he was an Epicurean too. In any case, his son propounds there good Epicurean arguments in favour of the pursuit of hardship and fame (I. 34–6), based on the idea of forgoing pleasure and incurring pain for the sake of gaining greater pleasures (praise and love, which guarantee a life without fear) and avoiding greater pains (danger and contempt).[57]

The doctrines of the dogmatic sects were too complex to provide definite directives on particular occasions. But they provided the moral vocabulary for weighing alternatives and justifying decisions. To write or speak in philosophical terms, even insincerely, is to think in those terms. Philosophy thus

[57] The seventh of the *Kuriai Doxai* (D.L. X. 141) laid down that if, and only if, becoming ἔνδοξοι made men secure, then to seek good repute was to pursue a natural good, cf. also D.L. X. 120a and Plut. *Mor.* 1100 A, D.

played an important role in a society where religion had little metaphysics and less ethics.

If providing a moral background seems a modest role, there is a comparison to be made with Christianity. It too has served to provide terms and concepts. It notoriously can be employed both for and against on various political issues such as apartheid. Indeed, with a little ingenuity, it can be made relevant to issues such as human rights and the position of women, questions formulated in terms never dreamed of by its founder or his early followers.

The comparison with Christianity is apt in another sense also. We often find in the ancient writers traces of philosophical vocabulary and argument, mixed up with more ordinary political ones. Sometimes such expressions are mouthed by people not known to be adherents of a sect or by speakers apparently unconscious that they are philosophizing. Philosophy supplied ethical preconceptions on which moral choices were often based even by those who neither knew nor cared much about the philosophical sects.

2

# Posidonius as Philosopher-Historian

I. G. KIDD

POSIDONIUS, the Stoic philosopher and polymath of Apamea and Rhodes, one of the most dominant intellectual figures in the first half of the first century BC, had in general an astonishingly encyclopaedic range of interests and writings. In particular, he was the only major professional philosopher of the ancient world who also wrote a large and important historical work. This fairly obvious but interesting statement has been made before, of course, most recently by Jürgen Malitz in his useful book, *Die Historien des Poseidonios*.[1] But strangely little has been done to pursue it, and I suspect for two main reasons: first a δύσερως ἔρως for *Quellenforschung* preoccupied with the possible influence of Posidonius on other writers, instead of with the character of the *History* itself; and second, not unconnected with the first, the paucity and in most cases unrewarding historical content and context of the surviving fragments. As for the first reason, source detection seems to me of little help for the particular problem which concerns me here, and indeed dangerous, because derivatory material is largely dependent on the attested evidence for its validation, but more importantly because its character, whether through reshaping by the author for his own purposes or more simply by his principles of selection out of context, makes it of little use for questions of this sort. For example, it is certain that Diodorus Siculus used Posidonius for parts of his Books V and XXXIII–XXXVII, but the extent and form of this use remains quite problematical, and it can certainly be shown in places that it is not all-pervading; and in any case, Diodorus' kind of redeployment of material in the very few instances where we have a control is quite unfruitful for the historical character and nature of Posidonius' work. But the second reason points to an unavoidable difficulty. The evidence is dreadful. I am tempted to say that, despite the relative

[1] Malitz [222] 409.

quantity, the quality of evidence for Posidonius' *History* is worse than for any other department of his writing. The main reporters. Athenaeus and Strabo, refer to Posidonius as the philosopher, never the historian, and do not cite him for historical reasons, nor indeed in historical contexts. Plutarch too refers to Posidonius as the philosopher, and although one of the great quoters of the ancient world, refers explicitly to Posidonius remarkably seldom.

The *History* was a massive work in its own right: it ran to fifty-two books covering from the end of Polybius (146/145 BC)[2] to, in my opinion, the middle or late 80s,[3] and was possibly, like Thucydides' *History*, unfinished. So the first question to ask is whether it was simply another aspect of Posidonius' πολυμαθία, or whether it was organically related to his philosophy. The first of these alternatives is by no means excluded without consideration or argument. After all, we have the case of Hume, a major philosopher, who yet wrote a famous large history, which seems to owe little or nothing to his philosophical ideas. Hume himself claimed that he wrote it for literary fame.

In a well-known passage (T 80 EK), Athenaeus (IV. 151 e) expressly characterizes the *History* as being composed by Posidonius in a manner consonant with his philosophy (ἐν ταῖς Ἱστορίαις αἷς συνέθηκεν οὐκ ἀλλοτρίως ἧς προήρητο φιλοσοφίας[4]) particularizing that general statement with 'reporting many habits and customs of many people', i.e. ethnography. But Athenaeus nowhere gives any indication that he understands this, and what follows these lines is part of the description of eating and drinking habits from Posidonius' Celtic ethnography (F 67 EK), which shows no connection with or relation to any philosophy, Stoic or otherwise. This suggests to me that Athenaeus, who knew the *History*, and cites it by book numbers, might have picked up the characterization from an original profession elsewhere in Posidonius himself.

Fortunately we can do much better than this. In *Ep*. 88. 21–8 (F 90 EK), Seneca details a quadripartite Posidonian

[2] T 1a (fragments and testimonia are referred to by their Edelstein–Kidd numbers).

[3] Kidd [5] vol. II (i), F 51.

[4] The phrase οὐκ ἀλλοτρίως ἧς προήρητο φιλοσοφίας must be taken with the main verb συνέθηκεν, not with the following participial clause πολλὰ παρὰ πολλοῖς ἔθιμα καὶ νόμιμα ἀναγράφων, as Gulick takes it in the Loeb translation of Athenaeus.

classification of arts and sciences with their relationship. I have argued elsewhere[5] that the passage shows that Posidonius regarded the top class of 'arts' as philosophy, that is to say, natural philosophy, ethics, and logic, calling them ἐλεύθεραι τέχναι, which led some modern scholars to confuse them with the Liberal Arts. But it is the second class of 'arts' that contained what we call the arts and sciences, and the Romans the *liberales artes*. These are not philosophy, but are related to philosophy (the top class) as necessary tools for philosophy.[6] And what is meant by that is clarified for the sciences in a fragment from Geminus' Epitome of Posidonius' *Meteorologica* reported by Simplicius through Alexander (F 18 EK), which shows that for Posidonius the sciences helped to fill out and establish the descriptive framework of the natural world and to present theories of its organization from hypotheses, which is like aetiology, but not proper explanation.[7] Now what interested Posidonius was aetiology (τὸ αἰτιολογικόν), explanation, causation. But ultimate explanation and principal causes were the province of philosophy only, not of the sciences or arts, although the sciences could illustrate them and fill out possible or alternative intermediate or proximate causes in the complete chain of explanation.[8] All this demands an organic rather than an episodic view of Posidonius' variety of interests and writing. And therefore it seems to me inescapable that by analogy the *History* performed the same function for ethics as the sciences did for natural philosophy, and if it comes to that, probably mathematics for logic.[9] Incidentally, this is one of the major reasons why it seems to me inconceivable that the notorious introduction at the opening of Diodorus I on the character and function of historiography can be from Posidonius as is so persistently claimed, most recently by Theiler and Malitz, who then build whole theories on this basis.[10] But Diodorus' presumptuous claim that history is 'the prophetess of truth and as it were the metropolis or mother city

[5] Kidd [215]; [5] vol. II (i), F 90.

[6] 'Aliquod nobis praestat geometria ministerium: sic philosophiae necessaria est quomodo ipsi faber, sed nec hic geometriae pars est nec illa philosophiae', F 90. 23–6; cf. F 134. 55 ff.; Kidd [215] 10; [5] vol. II (i), F 90.

[7] Kidd [215] 10 f.; [5] vol. II (i), F 18. 24–8.

[8] Kidd [5] vol. II (i), T 85, F 18; Kidd [215] 10 f.

[9] Cf. Kidd [216].

[10] Theiler [6] F 80; Malitz [222] 413 f.

of the whole of philosophy'[11] is in stark and ludicrous opposition to Posidonius' carefully defined relative positions of the arts and philosophy.

But we then must ask what signs there are of this in our miserable collection of historical fragments. Let me begin with the largest, most complete, and indeed most notorious of them all, Posidonius' account of the brief tyranny of the Peripatetic Athenion in Athens in 88 BC, given in Athenaeus v. 211 d–215 b, F 253 EK. Moreover, this looks to me like straight Posidonius, a quotation: the language is Posidonian and certainly not Athenaean. The fragment is, however, extremely complex, raising a succession of historical problems which have been the subject of much debate. For the details of this, the reader should consult my *Commentary* on *The Fragments of Posidonius*.[12] For my present purpose I must confine myself to our particular issue.

The background is this. By the beginning of 88 BC the political situation in Athens was in some confusion. After three consecutive years when Medeios of Peiraeus secured election as eponymous archon, there followed a year (88/87 BC) of *ἀναρχία*, in the technical sense of the omission of an eponymous archon in the archon list (IG II$^2$ 1713, 1714).[13] Meanwhile Mithridates was in full control in Asia and beginning to loom over the West, while Rome was embarrassed by the Social War and political unrest, and so the situation in Athens was dangerously volatile. An appeal to the Roman senate to sort things out brought no response,[14] and Medeios vanished from the scene. Meanwhile, this Athenion, an erstwhile Peripatetic professional teacher, got himself elected as ambassador to Mithridates, became an official Friend of the King, returned full of promises from Mithridates, fanned the passions of the mob in his favour, had himself voted Hoplite General in an *ad hoc* ecclesia engineered by himself, and intensified a brief reign of terror, culminating in a disastrous attempt to take Delos and its treasure.[15] He then

[11] Diod. I. 2. 2, *πόσῳ μᾶλλον ὑποληπτέον τὴν προφῆτιν τῆς ἀληθείας ἱστορίαν, τῆς ὅλης φιλοσοφίας οἱονεὶ μητρόπολιν οὖσαν* ... This is more in line with Cicero's apotheosis of history in *De Or.* II. 36 as *lux veritatis* and *magistra vitae*.

[12] Kidd [5] vol. II (ii), F 253.

[13] Kidd [5] vol. II (ii), F 253. 23–32, 103–11.

[14] F 253. 95–7.

[15] F 253. 23–179.

apparently disappears, and we hear of another tyrant Aristion, who ruled Athens for the King until Sulla took it 86 BC.[16] This is a situation obviously full of interest for the historian. But what happens?

First Athenaeus' context: the Athenion story is followed in Athenaeus by that of the Epicurean Lysias who became tyrant of Tarsus (*FGrH* 166 F1), and this is topped by a long and sarcastic tirade against Plato's account of Socrates, with an appendix on the minor Socratics. Athenaeus selected this particular extract from the *History* not for its historical value, nor yet for its historical context, but solely for its satirical attack on a philosopher's pretence to power.

Now look at Posidonius. This is his introduction to Athenion (F 253. 12–23 EK):

Athenion, an assiduous attender at the school of the Peripatetic Erymneus, bought an Egyptian slave girl with whom he had sex. Her child, whether by Athenion or another, also named Athenion, was brought up in the master's house. The boy [our Athenion] was taught to read, would help his mother prop the old man up when he went out, became his heir on his death, and was slipped illegally into the citizen roll to become an Athenian citizen. He married a shapely wench with whose help he set off on the hunt for young pupils in the life of a professional teacher. Having made his pile as a sophist in Messene and Larissa in Thessaly he returned to Athens.

This is scandalous stuff both in language and innuendo. It is the style of Attic oratorical invective. It is clearly not meant to be historical objectivity. Posidonius is manipulating rumour to heighten the contrast of Athenion's beginnings with his political pretensions, and to use this anarchic interlude in Athens as a historical demonstration of the dangers of such a character in command of a city.

After a sneer about Athenion insinuating himself (ὑποδραμών, F 253. 25 EK) into the King's good graces on his embassy, Posidonius turns to Athenion's reception at Athens in a vivid portrait of a frenzied hybristic emotional welcome home of a supposed saviour, where the excessive emotions (πάθη) of the crowd of Kekropids grotesquely outrun all reason and

[16] App. *Mith.* 28–9; Strabo IX. 398; Plut. *Sulla* 12, 13, 23; *Luc.* 19; *Num.* 9; *Mor.* 558 C, 809 E; Pausanias I. 20. 5.

control; as if a later historian were to highlight an umbrella-waving Chamberlain declaring peace in our time. It is the function of a statesman and leader in Stoic philosophy to control such outbursts of *πάθη*, as in an individual the *ἡγεμονικόν* of reason must discipline the emotions. But Athenion, a supposed philosopher, sought power by fanning them with disastrous results. The studied sarcasm of the language is searing. Here is an example (F 253. 36–47 EK):

> Aye but there he was now coming into the city, and practically the greatest part of the city had poured out for his reception; and running with them to join them were many other spectators wondering at the paradox of fortune, when the illegally enrolled Athenion to Athens is conveyed on a silver-footed couch with scarlet coverings, a man who had never seen scarlet before on his scholar's gown, when not even any single Roman had insulted Attica with such a presentation of effeminate luxury. So they were running all together to this spectacle, men, women, children, expecting the best from Mithridates, when Athenion, the pauper who had held subscription lectures, because of the King now farts his way arrogantly through town and country in escort.

This is a deliberately high-coloured passage employing vivid detail, rhetorical devices such as chiasmus, punning, asyndeton, and a final carefully engineered, indignant explosion of sarcasm in *σιληπορδῶν* (F 253. 46 EK). It is very much in Posidonius' most powerful style. And he continues with the description of the extravagant reception of Athenion by the Dionysiac artists, and of his housing in the mansion of the wealthy Dies (F 253. 47–58 EK).

Now come the crucial elections; but what we get are a vivid thirty-nine lines of Athenion's rabble-rousing speech (F 253. 64–103 EK), followed by only eight and a half lines of the action, infuriatingly brief and lacking in detail for the historian, where Athenion is elected Hoplite General, and appoints the rest of the archons himself.[17] Posidonius seems more interested in causes than in details of procedure. There follow thirty-two lines (F 253. 112–144 EK) of the subsequent reign of terror in Athens and Attica with graphic embroidery, explicitly illustrating the philosopher turned tyrant (F 253. 112 EK). They

[17] See Kidd [5] vol. II (ii), F 253; 64–103; 103–11.

have frequently been suspected of contamination,[18] wrongly in my opinion; we have not a confusion of doublets but a rhetorical *variatio* heightening the colour. Finally (F 253. 145–179 EK) comes a corrosive appendix on the pathetic attempt, as Posidonius saw it, which ended in catastrophic disaster, to seize Delos and its treasure, commanded (and you can see Posidonius' eyebrows rising as he fleshes this out) by the shady bibliophile Apellicon, off to war as if he were attending a public festival, while Athenion fed the silly Athenians on barley in quantity fit for poultry.

No more is heard of Athenion. The trouble is that nothing at all is heard of Athenion apart from this passage, and this is a problem which must be faced because it is germane to my argument. Everyone else—Appian, Strabo, Plutarch (in several places), Pausanias—mentions only Aristion as tyrant of Athens.[19] So scholars have divided between Unitarians, who believe that there was only one tyrant Aristion, and Posidonius was confused, and Separatists.[20] Now the Separatists are certainly right.[21] Apart from the unmistakable detail of the Posidonian account, the clinching argument for separatism is based on comparing Posidonius' narrative with that of Appian, *Mith.* 28, on Aristion. Athenion arrived back alone in Athens after his embassy, at a time when Mithridates had just completed his military conquest of Asia. After establishing himself as tyrant at Athens, he sent the ill-fated expedition to take Delos and its treasure. Aristion, however, an Epicurean incidentally, was on the coat-tails of Archelaus when he captured Delos while Mithridates was besieging Rhodes. After the capture of Delos, he was sent back to Athens with the Delian treasure and two thousand troops, with which he made himself tyrant of Athens. We have two pieces of jigsaw which fit into each other, giving a succession of two tyrants. They may be contaminated, but they cannot be conflated or identical.

But this raises two complementary questions: why does the

[18] e.g. by Jacoby, *FGrH* 87, *Komm.* p. 187; Wilamowitz, *Sitz. Berlin* 1923, 43; Touloumakos, *Philol.* 110 (1966) 140 f.

[19] See above n. 16.

[20] Unitarians: Casaubon, Mommsen, Geyer (*RE* s.v. Mithridates, xv. 2171), Reinhardt, Laffranque, Nicolet. Separatists: Wilamowitz, Jacoby, Ferguson, Deininger, Badian (hesitantly), Theiler, Sherwin-White.

[21] For detailed argument, see Kidd [5] vol. II (ii), F 253 fin., *Athenion and Aristion.*

other evidence not mention Athenion at all? And why did Posidonius give so much space and prominence to Athenion? For the first there is a clue in Strabo IX. 1. 20: 'The incidence of the Mithridatic War established tyrants [in the plural] over the Athenians; by far the most powerful one, Aristion, who oppressed the city, was caught and punished by Sulla after the siege.' It was Aristion whose advent overshadowed the initial bungling, who was in power through the decisive events from 88 BC to the fall of the city in 86, who was linked with Archelaus in the Greek campaign, and above all with Sulla. Any brief account of the Greek campaign (Appian), or of the siege of Athens (Pausanias), or of Sulla's campaigns (Plutarch), especially if derived from Roman sources, would concentrate entirely on Aristion, who was the important tyrant, as Strabo says, not Athenion. In fact, Athenion enjoyed an ephemeral tyranny of a few weeks, soon forgotten because superseded by more important events and people.

Why then did Posidonius single him out for such a vivid historical portrait? The whole character of presentation and tone surely indicates that he must have believed that it was Athenion for all his brief and apparently unimportant, because unsuccessful, career who nevertheless started off the people of Athens on a course from which by the time he was succeeded they could not withdraw; a course which inevitably was to end not only in a reign of terror, but in the eventual capture and humbling of a once proud and enlightened state. But he probably took the case of Athenion not simply as an initial antecedent cause, but as an obvious illustration and warning of the principal or determining cause of disaster, the uncontrolled πάθη in human political behaviour arising out of a combination of the silly greedy mob of Kekropids and a leader whom he regarded as a fifth-rate philosopher on the make. This relationship between ruler and ruled surfaces elsewhere in the fragments.[22] The deliberate overpainting in strong colours results in a striking picture of tyranny, its causes and results, as the reverse of the philosopher king or statesman. The choice of incident and its dramatization betray a moralist's view of historiography, where the relation of events may for a time be

[22] See Kidd [5] vol. II (i), F 60, F 57, F 58, F 66, F 67D; II (ii), F 252, F 263, F 284.

side-tracked for an examination of the moral behaviour and conditions which cause them. As such, the case of Athenion was edifying; but not simply as a moral exemplar in the style of Plutarch.[23] The fundamental difference between Plutarch and Posidonius is that the latter was seeking to trace causal explanation, as opposed to presenting exemplars.

I now want to step briefly sideways. Posidonius had a psychological view of history quite different from that of Polybius, who did not believe that men's actions are the consequence of their nature, as Posidonius did. Polybius thought that, on the contrary, in most cases men act and speak against their own nature, because they are determined by the circumstances of the situation, or by the influence and advice of their friends.[24] Posidonius disagreed. He believed that we are ourselves solely responsible for our mind and character.[25] Our friends are of our own making. So it is no surprise to find evidence of some preoccupation with the characters of leading statesmen and rulers. On the one hand, we have the virtuous Scipio on his eastern embassy, supported by Panaetius;[26] on the other, the effeminate Ptolemy Physcon[27] supported by the awful parasite Hierax, erstwhile accompanist for transvestite burlesque shows,[28] or his gross son Alexander, supported in his turn by two attendants to enable him to shit.[29] But what about ethnology, underlined by Athenaeus? In some ways this is still more interesting. Ethnography has a long pedigree of course, and seems at this point to have become fashionable again. But was Posidonius merely indulging in another intellectual fad, or is it integral to his historical perspective? I want to suggest that for Posidonius ethnology was a principal form of historical explanation, necessarily linked to and demanded by his philo-

[23] e.g. Plut. *Demetr.* 1. 1–6.

[24] Polyb. IX. 22. 9–23. 9.

[25] F 169; Kidd [217] 19–21.

[26] F 254.

[27] F 58.

[28] F 56.

[29] F 77. I now incline to Capps's emendation ἀποπατεῖν in l. 7, which is more in tune with Posidonius' forthright line in searing sarcasm. Cicero (*Off.* I. 159 = F 177, T 107) complained of Posidonius' use of disgusting examples. It did not dim his admiration for Posidonius' style, nor prevent him from attempting to persuade Posidonius to write up his consulship (T 34).

sophical system of moral aetiology in the field of human action and events.

In VII. 292–3 (F 272 EK) Strabo gives a detailed account of the popular debate raging on the cause of the Cimbrian migrations, which ended in the Cimbrian Wars. The Cimbrian invasions and migrations were certainly fully dealt with in the *History*. Strabo, at some length, probably from Posidonius, lists and criticizes the usual explanations for the cause that set the Cimbri off on their marauding way from Jutland, namely the inundation in some form of their homeland from the sea. No, said Posidonius, with Strabo's full approval, the real cause was the piratical and nomadic nature of the Cimbri themselves. There is no sign that Posidonius denied that bad flooding of some kind may have occurred, which may have acted as a kind of antecedent cause, but the real cause or explanation for the historian of the behaviour of the Cimbri lay in their own character.[30]

We can take this further in the extended fragment from Athenaeus VI. 233d–234c (F 240a EK), reporting Posidonius on gold. Posidonius gave a row of examples of the apparent corrupting effect of gold. The Spartans, forbidden to import gold, acquired it by underhand means, and deposited it with the Arcadians, which led to enmity. After the cases of Lysander and Gylippus, he turned to the Celtic tribe, the Scordistae: they will not have gold in their country, so they plunder for silver and do terrible things for it. His conclusion is explicit (F 240a. 40–45 EK):

> It is not precious metal that is the cause of such behaviour, but impiety and greed which ought to be banished, not gold; if they banished gold and silver, they would sin for bronze and iron, and if these were banned, they would fight for the bare necessities of life.

Now this is pure Posidonian philosophy. Gold and wealth are 'indifferents';[31] it is greed and the lust for gold that is *πάθος* and vice. Or, as Posidonius would put it, the attitude of the

[30] There is an apparent contradiction to this theory in Strabo II. 102 = F 49. 303–5. But the full argumentation in F 172. 1–36 is too explicit and must be accepted as the controlling evidence for the principal cause. I am therefore inclined to emend F 49. 304 f. to . . . *ἐκ τῆς οἰκείας* ⟨*οὐ*⟩ *γενέσθαι κατὰ θαλάττης ἔφοδον* [*οὐκ*] *ἀθρόαν συμβᾶσαν*. For full discussion, see Kidd [5] vol. II (i), F 49D (2), 303–5; II (ii), F 272. 1–36.

[31] Sen. *Ep.* 87. 31–40 = F 170. For analysis and discussion, see Kidd [217].

Scordistae betrays a confusion between relative and absolute natural propensities (οἰκειώσεις) in a human being.[32] The theme of the corruption of wealth and luxury was widespread, of course, in contemporary literature. But any author or historian who implies that it was the principal cause of corruption does not derive from Posidonius. The theme also patently runs through the whole of his *History*, but is linked to and derived from the historical explanation of ethnology, and the ethical one of πάθη, which Posidonius in one place[33] startingly says is the linch pin of all ethical enquiry.

This concept of ethnology as explanation in historical argument very occasionally in unguarded reporting slips through the chinks unexpectedly in some other historical fragments. It is one of Posidonius' main arguments against the popular view that the notorious treasure of the Tectosages was plunder from Delphi (F 273 EK). That is not so, said Posidonius: the god-fearing character and customs of the people show that it must have been locally amassed.[34] An odder example is his explanation of proper names not from popular philological etymology, which was common among the Stoics too, but from ethnology. He derives the Cimmerian Bosporus from the Cimbri,[35] the Ἄβιοι from the Thracian ethnography,[36] and the Ἐρεμβοί from his ethnography of the Mesopotamian peoples.[37] But usually our reporters of Posidonius seem blissfully ignorant of the historical significance of his ethnographies. The Celtic ethnography is a case in point; quite a lot of snippets from that ethnology turn up,[38] but entirely devoid of historical context: Athenaeus is merely concerned with food, drink, and remarkable traits; Strabo, who blames Posidonius for over-addiction to aetiology,[39] sticks to geographical interest, and Diodorus records ethnography for its own sake. This is the superficial froth of Posidonius' brew. For Posidonius, ethnography was not

[32] Frs. 160, 161, and Kidd [5] vol. II (ii) on them.

[33] F 30.

[34] See Kidd [5] vol. II (ii), F 273 for the analysis of Posidonius' version against accounts such as that of Timagenes.

[35] Kidd [5] vol. II (ii), F 272. 34–6.

[36] Kidd [5] vol. II (ii), F 277a. 41 ff.

[37] Kidd [5] vol. II (ii), F 280. 19–24.

[38] e.g. Frs. 67, 68, 69, 73, 274.

[39] F 49. 357–62.

merely descriptive; ethnology was rather a key for historical explanation, related to his philosophy. As an individual's actions can only be understood through his psychology as revealed by his behaviour, so ethnology supplied evidence for the psychology of the group.

I have been careful to use the term '*historical* explanation'. I think that Posidonius regarded ethnology as an *αἰτία* within the art of history, as scientific hypotheses and theories were regarded by him as quasi-explanatory or subordinate within the sciences, but not the ultimate *αἰτίαι* which are the province of and imposed by philosophy.[40] Ethnology after all is allied to and supported by parallel enquiries on the same plane, such as human geography, environment, and physiognomy. Indeed, it is clear from the end of Strabo's account of *Περὶ ὠκεανοῦ* in Book II (F 49 EK fin), that in this work also, where Posidonius was engaged in human geography as a natural growth from astronomical zones, or the interrelation of celestial and terrestrial phenomena, ethnography was an explanatory tool.[41] *On Ocean* (*Περὶ ὠκεανοῦ*), which is one of the lost works I would most like to recover from antiquity, is a parallel work to the *History*. Neither of them is philosophy, that is to say, natural philosophy or ethics. Final explanation in aetiology can only come from philosophy; in the case of history, from the philosophical study of psychology and *πάθη* in the field of ethics. But Posidonius was interested not only in ultimate or principal causes in the Stoic sense, but in the whole chain of intermediate causation right the way through. That is why he was known throughout the ancient world for *τὸ αἰτιολογικόν*. But we are an integrated part of the whole world that we live and act in, a world that is to the Stoic an organic unity. Posidonius took this seriously, so not only were the sciences a necessary if subordinate part of the study of the whole, but so too was history.

I should like to point out that I have only been attempting to broach one aspect of Posidonius' *History*, the possible philosophical springs. I am aware that this can distort. It seems to have been also a genuine history of his time, containing a mass of vivid detail of facts, deeds, and phenomena, much of which he attempted indefatigably to confirm or discover for himself in

[40] F 18.

[41] See Kidd [5] vol. II (i), F 49. 309–56; cf. II (ii), F 169. 84 ff. on physiognomy.

his travels. It was rhetorical and deliberately trenchant in style, but it was not an evangel or protreptic to philosophy (a work he wrote separately anyway).[42] He was after the truth in his own lights, and criticized other historians including Polybius[43] for biased reporting. He was clearly interested in recording as well as explaining, for much of the detail is so minute as to be there for its self-contained interest and information. But the composition of the whole canvas, as I suggest, is another matter. I only wish we had it.

42 Frs. 1–3.

43 F 271, F 271A, F 225.

# 3
# Antiochus of Ascalon

JONATHAN BARNES*

## I. PREFATORY

ANTIOCHUS of Ascalon was a very great man indeed. Scholarch of the Athenian Academy and intimate of Roman senators, he determined the course of philosophy and influenced the history of nations. His writings are lost; but they can be read at one remove in numerous texts whose authors were too coy to mention his name—in the pages of Cicero and Sextus, in the essays of Arius Didymus and Albinus, in the letters of Seneca, in the miscellanies of Clement of Alexandria, in the late Greek commentaries on Aristotle. As an historian of philosophy, Antiochus fixed the character and form of his subject. As a philosopher, he revived Platonism and thus prepared the way for the dominant philosophy of the later Imperial period.

So, at any rate, several scholars have supposed.[1]

There is excellent evidence for Antiochus' personal eminence. Cicero, who spent six months in his company (*Brut.* 315), describes him as 'nobilissimus et prudentissimus philosophus' (ibid.), as pre-eminent in *ingenium* and *scientia* (*Luc.* 4), as 'prudens et acutus et in suo genere perfectus' (*Leg.* I. 54), as 'politissimus et acutissimus omnium nostrae memoriae philosophorum' (*Luc.* 113). So persuasive was he that he almost seduced the Epicurean Atticus from the pleasures of the Garden (*Leg.* I. 54), and he charmed Cicero 'with the flow and grace of his discourses' (Plut. *Cic.* 4. 1). No doubt that is what earned him his nickname of 'the Swan' (Steph. Byz. s.v.

* Parts of this paper were read to the Seminar in Oxford, parts to the Herodoteans at Cambridge: I am grateful to both audiences for their helpful comments. I am also especially indebted to Miriam Griffin for her valuable comments on earlier drafts.

[1] See esp. Theiler [72] 34–55 (on p. 51 Theiler concludes that Antiochus was 'the ἀρχηγέτης of the school tradition which culminated in Neoplatonism'). This essay has had a vast influence. The fullest recent account of Antiochus' thought, in Dillon [73] 52–113, is much indebted to Theiler; see also Donini [99] 73–81.

*'Ασκάλων*). In addition, he had the mildest of characters (Cic. *Luc.* 11).

Yet such general commendations do not establish or explain the stature which Antiochus assumes in many modern histories. More than thirty years ago, Georg Luck, who collected most of the *testimonia*,[2] warned against the temptation to elevate Antiochus into a 'counter-Posidonius'.[3] The warning was timely. It may be doubted that Luck himself took sufficient heed of it. He asserts, for example, that Panaetius had 'a powerful influence' on Antiochus;[4] yet there is no evidence that Antiochus had ever read Panaetius. He asserts that 'Lucullus was certainly not without influence over Antiochus—anyone who lives so long in the company of an outstanding master of intellect, spirit and power, becomes another man';[5] yet this is pure fantasy. He asserts that Eudorus, the Middle Platonist, was Antiochus' pupil;[6] yet no text associates the two men. He asserts that Antiochus re-introduced Plato's Ideas into philosophy and construed them as thoughts in the mind of God;[7] yet the assertion is without textual foundation.

Any attempt to reconstruct Antiochus' thought requires fantasy and imagination. But fantasy must be responsible to the evidence, and imagination must acknowledge one sobering fact: we do not know much about Antiochus.

## 2. LIFE

### (i) *Apprenticeship*

He came from Ascalon in Syria.[8] According to Cicero (*Tusc.* v. 107) he was one of several philosophers who lived permanently abroad, never returning to his native city once he had left it.

The date of his birth is not recorded. We first meet him in the company of Philo of Larissa. Philo was born in 161/0 and

[2] Luck [241]—Luck was a pupil of Theiler. Luck's collection of texts has now been supplanted by Mette [22].

[3] Luck [241] 11, echoed by Donini [99] 73.

[4] Luck [241] 14.

[5] Luck [241] 17.

[6] Luck [241] 27.

[7] Luck [241] 30 (see below, Appendix E).

[8] Strabo, xvi. 759; Plut. *Brut.* 2. 3; Ael. *VH* xii. 25; Steph. Byz. s.v. *'Ασκάλων*.

elected scholarch of the Academy in 110/9. In 88, when Mithridates besieged Athens, he left the city along with numerous other distinguished men and removed to Rome (Cic. *Brut.* 306). He died a few years later.[9]

It is unlikely that Antiochus reached Athens before 110: several texts associate him with Philo,[10] but none connects him with any earlier Academic scholarch. Probably he did not join the Academy until Philo was in charge. He is said to have spent an unusually long time as Philo's follower (Cic. *Luc.* 69). If he came to Athens in about 110 at about the age of 20, then he was born in about 130. But no text gives his age on coming to Athens.

Augustine and Numenius say that he was also a pupil of the Stoic Mnesarchus.[11] Modern scholars add that he was a student of the Stoic Dardanus; they recall that he was a compatriot of the Stoic Sosus, with whom he retained cordial relations; and they tell a pleasant romance. As a young man, Antiochus was urged to come to Athens by his friend Sosus, who had preceded him to the city. There he studied with Sosus under the Stoic pupils of the mighty Panaetius and the learned Diogenes of Babylon. Stoicism entered his soul and moulded his philosophical character. And his juvenile perambulations in the Porch explain all that is remarkable in his subsequent intellectual career.[12]

Sosus came from Ascalon (Steph. Byz. s.v. Ἀσκάλων), and he was a pupil of Panaetius (*Ind. Stoic.* LXXV. 1–2). Since Panaetius died in 112/11, Sosus probably arrived in Athens before Antiochus. It is true, too, that the fellow-citizens kept up some sort of acquaintanceship[13]—many years later Antiochus named a

[9] On the date of Philo's death (84/3) see Glucker [71] 100 n. 11; Dorandi [238]. It is not known whether Philo ever returned to Athens. The *testimonia* to Philo are collected in Mette [22]; see also K. von Fritz, 'Philon (40)', *RE* xix (1938), 2525–44.

[10] August. *Acad.* II. 15; III. 41; Numen. fr. 28 des Places = Euseb. *Praep. Evang.* XIV. 9. 4.

[11] August. *Acad.* III. 41; Numen. fr. 28 des Places = Euseb. *Praep. Evang.* XIV. 4. 4. For Mnesarchus see K. von Fritz, 'Mnesarchos (5)', *RE* xv (1932), 2272–4.

[12] The story is largely accepted even by the normally sceptical Glucker [71] 14 n. 4, 28 n. 52.

[13] But note that according to *Ind. Stoic.* Sosus *ἐν Τεάνῳ διέτριψεν καὶ μετήλλαξεν* (i.e. Teanum Sidicinum in Campania, according to Rawson [94] 22–3), and if that is right then it is not clear how closely he and Antiochus will have kept in touch.

work after Sosus. But there is no evidence that Sosus introduced Antiochus to the Stoa.

The connexion with Dardanus depends on a sentence in Cicero's *Lucullus*, the context of which will concern us later:

> quid eum [sc. Antiochum] Mnesarchi paenitebat? quid Dardani? qui erant Athenis tum principes Stoicorum. (*Luc.* 69)

Cicero might mean: 'Why did he change his mind about Mnesarchus and Dardanus?'. If so, then he implies that Antiochus had in the past been a pupil—or at least an admirer—of Mnesarchus and of Dardanus.[14] But this translation does not fit the context particularly well,[15] and the Latin more probably means: 'Why did he not find Mnesarchus and Dardanus satisfactory?'.[16] Hence we need not believe that Antiochus studied under Dardanus.

Even if Cicero's text does not establish Stoic teachers for Antiochus, Augustine and Numenius remain. I see no good reason to dismiss their evidence.[17] In any case, two things are indubitable. First, the young Antiochus will have studied Stoicism *in the Academy* if he did not do so in the Porch—for most of the Academy's philosophical energy was expended in its long battle with Stoicism. Secondly, even if Antiochus was once a *pupil* of Mnesarchus, we may not infer that he was ever a *follower* of Mnesarchus. Historians of philosophy frequently assume that if X studied under Y then X must have shared the philosophical views of Y. The assumption is insidious. But it is palpably absurd. Without it the pretty story of Antiochus' apprenticeship falls apart.

We do know that Antiochus had once shared Philo's views (Cic. *Luc.* 69). At some point he broke with Philo and gained fame for his sharp attacks on his old master. According to Cicero, he had 'studied these views [sc. Academic scepticism] with Philo for a long time—indeed, it is generally agreed that

[14] So (I assume) e.g. Glucker [71] 28 n. 52 and Dillon [73] 53 n. 2. Observe, though, that Glucker takes Mnesarchus to have been an *early* teacher, while Dillon thinks a *late* period fits the evidence equally well.

[15] Had Cicero meant that Antiochus was an ex-pupil of the Stoics, he might have asked 'Why did Antiochus not *return* to the Stoa?' rather than 'cur non se *transtulit* . . . ad Stoicos?'. And we should expect *paenituit* rather than *paenitebat*.

[16] I am indebted to James Irvine for help with this point.

[17] *Pace* von Fritz, 'Mnesarchos (5)', 2273; cf. Dillon [73] 53.

no-one has ever studied them for longer' (ibid).[18] Cicero may be exaggerating. But let us guess that Antiochus remained in the Academy as a docile Philonian for some ten or fifteen years.

### (ii) *The Middle Years*

In 88 Philo left Athens. It is often assumed that Antiochus left with him.[19] No text says so.[20] John Glucker has argued that Antiochus did *not* leave Athens, on the grounds that he did not learn the contents of Philo's Roman lectures until copies were brought to Alexandria.[21] But Antiochus could have left Athens with Philo—and then have left Rome before Philo gave his lectures. In truth nothing can be affirmed here: Antiochus was probably in Athens until 88; and in the autumn of 87 we meet him in Alexandria in the company of Lucullus. How and when he moved from Athens to Alexandria we do not know.

'Cum Alexandriae pro quaestore essem, fuit Antiochus mecum': so Lucullus, according to Cicero (*Luc.* 11). Alexandria was the setting for the most celebrated episode in Antiochus' career, the 'Sosus affair'. The philosophical aspects of the business will occupy us later. Here chronology is the concern.

We are tolerably well informed of Lucullus' activities.[22] Quaestor in 88 or 87, he was sent by Sulla to Greece. In 87/6 he was instructed to collect a fleet, and he visited Crete, Cyrene, Egypt, Syria, and Rhodes. From then until 80 he was occupied in the Aegean and in Asia. He returned to Rome and the aedileship in 79.

For how much of this time was Antiochus with him? The only direct evidence is Cicero's reference to their being in Alexandria together—and it is unlikely that Lucullus spent more

[18] 'haec ipsa quae a me defenduntur et didicit apud Philonem tam diu ut constaret diutius didicisse neminem et scripsit . . .': the sentence is elliptical—with *didicisse* should we supply (*a*) *haec apud Philonem*, or (*b*) *apud Philonem*, or (*c*) *haec*, or (*d*) nothing? Most scholars implicitly opt for (*c*), taking Cicero to mean that no-one had studied Academic scepticism longer than Antiochus had.

[19] e.g. Luck [241] 14; Dillon [73] 54.

[20] There is no reason to date to 88 the embassies referred to in *Ind. Acad.* xxxiv (below, n. 25).

[21] Glucker [71] 21. The rest of Glucker's story is fantasy: 'It is not unlikely that Antiochus escaped ⟨from Athens⟩ to Sulla's camp and met Lucullus there' (381).

[22] References in vol. ii of T. R. S. Broughton, *The Magistrates of the Roman Republic* (New York, 1952); cf. e.g. M. Gelzer, 'Licinius (104)', *RE* xiii (1927), 376–414.

than a few weeks there in his fruitless negotiations with Ptolemy. We hear nothing more of Antiochus until 79, when Lucullus was back in Rome. But Cicero also says that Lucullus 'had Antiochus with him when he was quaestor' (*Luc.* 4); he writes of a close and friendly acquaintance between the two men; and he refers to their frequent philosophical conversations. Plutarch calls Antiochus the *φίλος καὶ συμβιωτής* of Lucullus (*Luc.* 42. 3; cf. Ael. *VH* XII. 25). All this clearly presupposes a longer companionship than the few days in Alexandria. It is tempting to suppose that Antiochus remained in Lucullus' entourage while he was in the East: Cicero says that Lucullus studied philosophy 'pro quaestore aliquot annos' (*Luc.* 4), and the *aliquot anni* were perhaps passed in Antiochus' company.

Glucker believes that Lucullus found in Antiochus an informal 'political adviser', a Greek who knew Asian Greeks and who could help him in his delicate dealings with the natives:

> . . . during all these operations [sc. in 87–85], Antiochus, as his adviser and go-between in the Greek east, must have been indispensable to him, and would hardly have left his side. He would be especially valuable to Lucullus once he moved east of Egypt and nearer Antiochus' native parts, and it is inconceivable that Lucullus would leave him behind in Alexandria when he was having his dealings with the Syrian coastal cities.[23]

The story has an inherent plausibility. But what evidence is there that Antiochus ever functioned as a political adviser?

Aelian perhaps means to imply that Antiochus offered Lucullus practical as well as philosophical aid.[24] Plutarch asserts that on the death of Sulla Antiochus urged Cicero to devote himself to public affairs (*Cic.* 4. 5). The *Index Academicorum* seems to state that Antiochus 'went on embassies . . . both to Rome and to the generals in the provinces'.[25] We know nothing about the embassies. The reports in Aelian and Plutarch are of

[23] Glucker [71] 91–2; cf. 21–7 for elaboration and support of the hypothesis. (When Glucker says that it is 'inconceivable' that Lucullus would have left Antiochus in Alexandria, he is wrong: it is perfectly *conceivable*.) On philosophical advisers see further Rawson, below, p. 237 ff.

[24] Lucullus *'Αντιόχου . . . ὤνητο τοῦ 'Ασκαλωνίτου* (Ael. *VH* XII. 25): the remark is vague, but the context suggests more than purely philosophical benefit.

[25] See *Ind. Acad.* XXXIV. 36–9: . . . *πρεσβεύων* [. . . *πρό*]*ς τε 'Ρώμην καὶ πρὸς τοὺς ἐν ταῖς ἐπαρχίαις στρατηγούς, κἀξ ὑστέρας κτλ*. For the text see Dorandi [238] 115.

doubtful value. We may suspect—but we may not claim to know—that Antiochus was Lucullus' political adviser. On the other hand, we do have good reason for believing that he was his house philosopher. And he may, of course, have fulfilled both functions.

These are not minor questions about Antiochus' biography. They bear directly on a major problem in the history of Platonism. Many scholars have assumed that Antiochus spent some considerable time in Alexandria in the 80s. They have affirmed that an Antiochian School of philosophers was founded there. And they have maintained that this School eventually brought about a great change in the direction of philosophy; for it is the Alexandrian pupils of Antiochus, foremost among them Eudorus, whom we should regard as the ultimate originators of Neoplatonism.[26]

Much could be said about this notion from a philosophical point of view.[27] The historical facts can be stated briefly: there is no evidence that Antiochus ever stayed more than a week or so in Alexandria,[28] no evidence that he founded a School there, no evidence that Eudorus was his pupil. Antiochus' Alexandrian School is a figment of modern scholarship.[29]

### (iii) *Maturity*

In 79 Cicero visited Athens and listened—for six months—to Antiochus (*Brut.* 315). Antiochus was then lecturing in the Ptolemaeum (*Fin.* V. 1).

Antiochus is often supposed to have become scholarch of the Academy, διάδοχος to Philo. It is noteworthy that Cicero never refers to him as scholarch; and it might be thought odd that a head of the Academy should have lectured in the Ptolemaeum.[30] But two texts in the *Index Academicorum* suggest the

[26] See Glucker [71] 90–1, with references to the modern literature.

[27] See, recently, Dörrie [74] 477–83; Tarrant [247] 115–26. On the crucial question of Antiochus and the Forms see below Appendix E.

[28] *Pace* Theiler [72] 39: 'Antiochus himself had taught for a long time in Alexandria: Cic. *Luc.* 11 f.' The text does not say this.

[29] So, convincingly, Glucker [71] 90–7.

[30] Dörrie, [74] 547, thinks that Antiochus lectured in the Ptolemaeum because the Academy was in ruins; but *pace* Dörrie I find no evidence that the Academy was destroyed in 88/6 (see Glucker [71] 242). However that may be, note that Charmadas had

ascription of a scholarchate to Antiochus. The first states clearly enough that Aristus, Antiochus' brother, *τὴν διατριβὴν αὐτοῦ διεδέξατο* (xxxv. 2–3): it is certain that *αὐτοῦ* refers to Antiochus, and it follows that Antiochus had a *διατριβή*. It does not, however, follow that he led a School (for the term *διατριβή* need not imply any institutional paraphernalia[31]) nor does it follow that he led the Academy (indeed the *αὐτοῦ* in *ἡ διατριβὴ αὐτοῦ* might suggest a private affair of Antiochus' own rather than the established Academy). The second text has been produced by the most recent scrutiny of the papyrus. At xxxiv. 34 the word *διεδέξατο* can now be discerned. The subject of the verb can only be Antiochus, and it is hard to think that the object of the verb can have been anything other than the Academy. In that case we must read: '⟨Antiochus⟩ took over ⟨the Academy⟩'—and the *Index* does after all make Antiochus an Academic scholarch.[32]

The question is important for the history of the Academy as an institution, less important for the story of Antiochus. For it is certain that Antiochus was, and was called, an Academic; that he always regarded himself as an adherent to the Academic philosophy; and that for some years he was a member of the Academic institution (whatever exactly such membership involved). It matters less whether he was ever titular head of the School, or inherited Plato's knives and forks.

However that may be, he did not reside permanently in Athens. 'Eum [sc. Antiochum] secum et quaestor habuit et post aliquot annos imperator' (Cic. *Luc.* 4) Lucullus was consul in 74 and took command against Mithridates. He was busy in the East for six or seven years. In 69 he defeated Tigranes at Tigranocerta. In 67 he was replaced and in 66 returned in temporary disgrace to Rome.[33] For at least some of this time Antiochus was with him. Maybe he was a 'political adviser'—but

---

lectured in the Ptolemaeum (*Ind. Acad.* xxxii. 8–9, but the text is uncertain), and so, in 123/2, had Zenodotus the Stoic (*IG* II$^2$ 1006—if the Zenodotus referred to is the Stoic mentioned at D.L. vii. 30). On the location of lectures see Glucker [71] 235 n. 29; on the library in the Ptolemaeum see M. N. Tod, 'Sidelights on Greek Philosophers', *JHS* 77 (1957) 132–41, at p. 137.

[31] On *διατριβή* see Glucker [71] 162–6: 'class' or 'seminar' is one common meaning of the word.

[32] See Dorandi [238] 115.

[33] The chronological details are complex: see e.g. Broughton (above, n. 22) i. 106–8.

again no text says so and Cicero expressly asserts that the two men talked philosophy together (*Luc.* 61).

According to Cicero, they were together in Syria. In all probability Antiochus was present also at Tigranocerta: he referred to the battle ἐν τῇ περὶ θεῶν γραφῇ in terms which suggest an eye-witness (Plut. *Luc.* 28. 8; cf. *Suda* s.v. Λούκουλλος). The *Index Academicorum* adds further information: 'he died in Mesopotamia in the service of Lucius Lucullus' (XXXIV. 39–42). Cicero too implies that he died in the East (*Luc.* 61). The date must have been 68 or 67.

## 3. INFLUENCE

### (i) *Pupils*

The *Index Academicorum* contains at XXXIV. 6–16 a list of pupils: Iollas of Sardis, Menecrates of Mitylene, Mnaseas of Tyre, Polus of Acragas, Melanthius, and Lysimachus. These men are usually supposed to have been pupils of Antiochus. But the text is broken, the names mean nothing to us,[34] and in any case it now appears unlikely that the list was attached to Antiochus.[35] But at XXXV. 4–10 the *Index* does refer to pupils of Antiochus—who 'though very busy, had many hearers'. There are named Aristus, Antiochus' brother; Aristo and Dio of Alexandria; and Cratippus of Pergamum. Cicero too refers to Aristus, Aristo, and Dio, and he adds Heraclitus of Tyre (*Luc.* 12). Aristus took over Antiochus' διατριβή (*Ind. Acad.* XXXV. 2–3). He became φίλος καὶ συμβιωτής of Brutus (Plut. *Brut.* 2. 3). Cicero visited him in Athens in 51 (*Att.* V. 10. 5). Dio was murdered in Rome in 57 while on an embassy from Alexandria (e.g. Cic. *Cael.* 23–4). Aristo deserted the cause and turned Peripatetic (*Ind. Acad.* XXXV. 10–16). So too did Cratippus (ibid).[36] Heraclitus was not

[34] See Glucker [71] 99–100, with footnotes.

[35] See Dorandi [238] 115, who confirms the puzzling *Μαίκιος* at XXXIV. 3, and whose διεδέξατο at XXXIV. 34 (see above) presumably came near the *beginning* of the *Index*'s account of Antiochus (which must, therefore, have been extremely brief).

[36] For Aristo see I. Mariotti, *Aristone d'Alessandria* (Bologna, 1966); Moraux [75] i. 181–93 (but note the doubts at 182); for Cratippus, ibid. 223–56; for Aristus and Dio see the references in Glucker's indexes. (Glucker, [71] 96, says that Dio too became a Peripatetic, and he cites *Ind. Acad.* XXXIV. 7–9 in support. But this text refers to Cratippus and Aristo.)

an Antiochian: he adhered to the New Academy and frequently disputed with Antiochus (Cic. *Luc.* 11).[37]

It would be naive to assess the importance of a philosopher by the number and fidelity of his pupils. But by this measure Antiochus scores poorly.

More impressive are the Roman connections. First, Lucullus. His association with Antiochus during his two tours of the East has already been mentioned. And it is possible that he had met Antiochus earlier, as a young man in Athens.[38] In his *laudatio* Cicero says 'maiore studio . . . philosophiae deditus fuit quam qui illum ignorabant arbitrabantur' (*Luc.* 4) and 'delectabatur mirifice lectione librorum de quibus audierat' (ibid.). Plutarch's *Lucullus* includes similar praise: no doubt his source is Cicero. The *Lucullus* is Book II of the first version of Cicero's major study of Academic scepticism. The second version, the *Academici*, changed the personnel, Varro replacing Lucullus.[39] Cicero explained that '*παρὰ τὸ πρέπον* videbatur, quod erat hominibus nota non illa quidem ἀπαιδευσία sed in iis rebus ἀτριψία' (*Att* XIII. 16. 1)—as he put it in another letter on the same topic, Lucullus was not *philologus* (*Att* XIII. 12. 5).[40] Glucker concludes that 'Lucullus the Philosopher is a creation of Cicero'.[41]

Cicero's dialogues are not historical records: 'nosti morem dialogorum' (*Fam* IX. 12. 5, on the 'events' described in the *Academici*). And we should not imagine that Lucullus had ever argued with the command and subtlety displayed by his homonym in the *Lucullus*. Nor need we dispute Cicero's charge of ἀτριψία: Lucullus presumably had no sophisticated interest or professional competence in philosophy.[42] But it does not follow

[37] Heraclitus has been identified with the 'Heraclides' of Diogenes Laertius IX. 116 and thus turned into a Pyrrhonian (see Glucker [71] 109 n. 38). The identification is gratuitous.

[38] See below, Appendix A.

[39] For the complex and rapidly changing history of the work see the texts and discussion in Plasberg's Teubner edition of the Academic books, pp. iii–x. Note that Cicero first thought to replace Lucullus, Catulus, and Hortensius by Brutus and Cato: the idea of introducing Varro came later, from Atticus.

[40] Cf. *Att.* XIII. 19. 5; and note *Luc.* 7, which disingenuously anticipates—and denies—the charge that the *dramatis personae* of the dialogue did not in reality understand the things which Cicero puts into their mouths.

[41] Glucker [71] 27.

[42] Ἀτριψία is not ignorance but lack of expertise (the word is apparently a ἅπαξ, but compare the common use of τετριμμένος in the sense of 'expert'). Note, too, that Catulus and Hortensius were replaced along with—and for the same reason as—Lucullus;

from this—and we have no reason to assume—that Lucullus' interest in philosophy is a Ciceronian fiction. Cicero allows that he was πεπαιδευμένος. The *laudatio* surely exaggerates, but we need not suppose that it invents. And it is worth referring to Lucullus' celebrated library, which contained works of Aristotelian and Stoic philosophy.[43]

Cicero himself was a more profound student. He records his pupillage with Antiochus (*Brut.* 315; *Nat. D.* I. 6; *Fin.* V. 1), and he asserts their mutual love (*Luc.* 113; cf. *Acad.* 13, 43).[44] Note that friendship and admiration do not imply philosophical assent: Cicero was no Antiochian.

Quintus Cicero also heard Antiochus (*Fin.* V. 1), and so did the young Lucius Cicero (ibid. V. 1, 6).

Next, Varro. He too had listened to Antiochus (*Acad.* 12), and unlike Cicero he was persuaded (*Att.* XIII. 12. 3; 16. 1; 19. 3; *Fam.* IX. 8. 1). That is why Varro became the spokesman for Antiochus in the *Academici*—Cicero worried that Varro might not relish his role (*Att.* XIII. 25. 3), but he did not fear that Varro might have any *philosophical* scruples.

Another pupil was M. Pupius Piso, who spent several months with Antiochus (*Fin.* V. 8) and is made to call him *familiaris* (*Fin.* V. 75). Piso also studied with Staseas of Naples, the Peripatetic (ibid.).[45]

Atticus heard Antiochus and found him charming—but not quite charming enough to seduce him from the Epicurean Garden (*Leg.* I. 54; *Acad.* 14).

Then there is Q. Lucilius Balbus, the Stoic spokesman in *De Natura Deorum*, to whom Antiochus sent one of his books (*Nat. D.* I. 16).[46]

Finally, Cicero reports that Brutus was an Antiochian (*Tusc.* V. 21; *Fin.* V. 8; *Att.* XIII. 25. 3).[47] But Brutus was the friend of

---

yet Catulus had been the advocate of philosophy in the dialogue named after Hortensius.

[43] See Cic. *Fin.* III. 7–9 (cf. Plut. *Luc.* 42. 1; Isid. *Etym.* VI. 5. 1)—see Rawson [94] 40.

[44] See also the fragment of a letter to Pansa: 'de Antiocho fecisti humaniter; quem quidem ego semper dilexi meque ab eo diligi sensi' (Nonius 509. 14–16 M; Priscian, XV. 13). But the MSS of Nonius read *Antio*; and Priscian, who reports *Antiocho*, only preserves the first four words. Cf. Plut. *Cic.* 4. 1; anon. *Vir. Illust.* 81. 2.

[45] For Staseas see Hobein, 'Staseas', *RE* iii A (1929), 2153–8; Moraux [75] i. 217–21.

[46] See below, p. 63.

[47] He wrote a Latin work on philosophy (*Acad.* 12—see Reid [112] ad loc.), presumably in Antiochian vein.

Aristus, and it is unlikely, on chronological grounds, that he knew Antiochus himself.[48]

Antiochus was befriended by some influential Romans, and he no doubt influenced some important Romans. What form this influence may have taken we do not know. Some (as I have said) have conjectured that Antiochus was a political adviser, a philosophical *éminence grise* behind the practical men of the Senate. Others may suggest that Antiochus' ethical teaching had its effect on the minds and policies of the Roman ruling class. There is little evidence for either of these suppositions. We do know, on the other hand, that Antiochus taught and talked about *philosophy*; and our evidence suggests that the Romans listened to him because he was a philosopher and admired him because he was a philosopher.

Several eminent Romans appear to have thought that philosophy was an interesting topic in its own right—a pleasant *divertissement* from the arduous life of politics, or even an indispensable part of the culture of an educated man.[49] Scholars and historians sometimes write as though such notions were intolerably naïve, as though it were absurd to believe that senators could possess intellectual interests and obligatory to discover more subtle motives for their known associations with philosophers. Philosophers may be forgiven for finding this attitude odd. Some men do find philosophy—even the more abstract and abstruse portions of philosophy—interesting and engaging. Some modern statesmen—even some monarchs—have betrayed a weakness for the subject. For my part, I see no reason to doubt that Cicero and his friends associated with Antiochus not, or not merely, for his political *aperçus* or his moral authority but rather for his prowess in the traditional and technical sport of philosophizing.

### (ii) *Writings*

We hear of four works. In addition, Cicero says that in his early

[48] See Glucker [71] 112 n. 50; but *pace* Glucker Plutarch does not imply that Brutus knew Antiochus personally.

[49] Not that *all* educated Romans shared this enlightened view—witness Cicero's defences of his philosophical activity (esp. *Fin.* 1. 1–2; *Luc.* 5–6). See Griffin, above, pp. 11–18.

years Antiochus wrote 'most acutely' in defence of Philo's views (*Luc.* 69); that he wrote *locis pluribus* on the relation of virtue to happiness (*Tusc.* v. 22); and that he wrote on Carneades' criticism of Chrysippus' views on grief and consolation (*Tusc.* III. 59).

His last book was perhaps the *Περὶ θεῶν* (Plut. *Luc.* 28. 8), which referred to the battle of Tigranocerta. The title is our only clue to its contents.[50]

Cicero refers to 'liber Antiochi nostri qui ab eo nuper ad hunc Balbum missus est' (*Nat. D.* I. 16). The dramatic date of the *De Natura Deorum* is 77 or 76. If Cicero is accurate, Antiochus' book was composed shortly before 77. It is commonly said that the work was dedicated to the Stoic Balbus.[51] But *missus* need imply no more than use of the post office.[52] As for the content of the book, it maintained, apparently on a general front, that 'the Stoics and the Peripatetics agree in fact and disagree in words' (ibid.).[53]

Sextus refers to a *Κανονικά* in at least two books, and he preserves the only fragment of Antiochus to have survived (*M.* VII. 202).[54] The title suggests a work on 'canonics' or epistemology. (The term *κανονική* is primarily Epicurean; but it is not exclusively so, and it would be unwarranted to infer that the *Κανονικά* was mainly concerned with Epicurean epistemology.)[55] Some have held that the *Κανονικά* was an early work, since it contains

[50] Dörrie, [74] 453–4, thinks that the book treated the victory at Tigranocerta as a miracle, i.e. as evidence (against the sceptical Academy) for the providence of the gods. The texts do not suggest this: they say that Tigranocerta was a great *battle*, not (*pace* Dörrie) a great *victory*. No doubt the *Περὶ θεῶν* discussed theological issues; but I am not persuaded by Dillon ([73] 89–90) that we may see Antiochus' views on divination behind Cic. *Div.* I or his views on 'demonology' in Varro (August. *CD* VII. 6). (Dillon is a circumspect scholar who does not indulge in fancy flights of *Quellenforschung*; but of his 44 pages on Antiochus' philosophy, 22 are by my reckoning dubiously Antiochian.)

[51] e.g. Dillon [73] 59.

[52] *OLD* gives 'dedicate' as one of the senses of *mittere* (*ad*). But *mittere*, when used of a book, certainly does not *always* mean 'dedicate'; and the examples cited in *OLD* do not seem to show that the word *ever* has this sense.

[53] See below, p. 79. The book 'sent to Balbus' has been identified, unpersuasively, with the *Sosus* and with the *Περὶ θεῶν*. We know nothing about it beyond Cicero's brief reference.

[54] Cumont [237] suggested that Antiochus of Athens, the astrologer (see e.g. Hephaestion Thebanus, II. 1. 5; 10. 9), should be identified with our Antiochus. In that case, we possess a number of astrological essays by Antiochus. But to my knowledge noone has accepted Cumont's implausible suggestion (cf. e.g. Luck [241] 19–20).

[55] See Gisela Striker, *Κριτήριον τῆς Ἀληθείας* (Göttingen, 1974) 16 n. 1.

no critique of scepticism.[56] Others think that it was a late work, since in it Antiochus criticizes Asclepiades from a Stoic standpoint.[57] But we have no idea whether or not the *Κανονικά* contained any criticism of scepticism; and we have no reason to think that it criticized Asclepiades from any standpoint.

Finally, there is the *Sosus*. The sole reference to it (Cic. *Luc.* 12) tells us that it was written *contra suum doctorem*, i.e. against Philo, and in particular against Philo's 'Roman books'. Cicero implies that it was written quickly, perhaps in 86. Since Cicero uses the singular, *liber*, it is almost certain that the *Sosus* consisted of a single book.[58] It was surely named after Antiochus' Stoic compatriot. It was probably a dialogue, in which case Sosus must have been a speaker. Maybe Heraclitus of Tyre and Antiochus himself were the other *personae*.[59] We know something about the content of the *Sosus*—but that is better reserved for the next section.

### (iii) *Quellenforschung*

Antiochus has been sighted behind numerous later texts. In most of these cases scholars have been beguiled by will-o'-the-wisps. If we restrict ourselves to the positive evidence we shall find that two authors come into account: Cicero and Sextus.

The fragment preserved by Sextus reads thus:

> ὅτι γὰρ ἐγένοντό τινες τὸ τοιοῦτο ἀξιοῦντες προὖπτον πεποίηκεν Ἀντίοχος ὁ ἀπὸ τῆς Ἀκαδημίας ἐν δευτέρῳ τῶν Κανονικῶν ῥητῶς γράψας ταῦτα:
>
> ἄλλος δέ τις, ἐν ἰατρικῇ μὲν οὐδενὸς δεύτερος, ἁπτόμενος δὲ καὶ φιλοσοφίας, ἐπείθετο τὰς μὲν αἰσθήσεις ὄντως καὶ ἀληθῶς ἀντιλήψεις εἶναι, λόγῳ δὲ μηδὲν ὅλως ἡμᾶς καταλαμβάνειν.
>
> ἔοικε γὰρ διὰ τούτων ὁ Ἀντίοχος τὴν προειρημένην τιθέναι στάσιν καὶ Ἀσκληπιάδην τὸν ἰατρὸν αἰνίττεσθαι. (*M*. VII. 202)

Scholars have gone to town on the *Κανονικά*. It is now orthodox to believe that it was the main source for Sextus' doxography on the criterion of truth in *M*. VII.[60]

[56] So Luck [241] 53; Mette [22] 57.

[57] So Dillon [73] 68.

[58] See Glucker [71] 392 n. 5.

[59] Glucker [71] 417–19.

[60] This was argued for at length by Hirzel [110] iii. 493–524; cf. e.g. Theiler [72] 55 n. 1; Tarrant [247] 89–114, and [246]; Sedley, in Barnes *et al.* [29] 265–6.

I do not believe that the *Κανονικά* lies behind Sextus' doxography. The arguments for the hypothesis are frail. On the other side, Sextus refers to the work once explicitly (and once implicitly, at VII. 162, where Antiochus is again invoked on a point of detail): he thus implies that Antiochus was *not* his regular copy-text. Perhaps Sextus is being disingenuous, or perhaps he is confused. But as matters stand we have no reason to reject the plain implication of his references to Antiochus. Moreover, as Sextus says, the sole fragment 'refers riddlingly' (*αἰνίττεσθαι*) to Asclepiades. Riddling reference is neither appropriate to nor likely in a doxographical text. There is no good reason for seeing more than two sentences of Antiochus in Sextus' writings.

Cicero is a different matter; for 'there is hardly a philosophical work in the Ciceronian corpus in which the influence of Antiochus as a source . . . has not been upheld by some modern scholar or scholars at some time or other'.[61] If we look more closely, however, we find direct evidence for Antiochian influence in two works only: *De Finibus* V and the Academic books.

At the beginning of *Fin.* V Lucius Cicero inquires after the views of the Old Academy and the Peripatos 'de finibus bonorum'. Piso is the man to expound them:

> quod et Staseam Neapolitanum multos annos habueris apud te et complures iam menses Athenis haec ipsa te ex Antiocho videamus exquirere. (*Fin.* V. 8)

Piso rises, and Brutus is asked to judge 'satisne videatur Antiochi complexa [sc. Piso's *oratio*] esse sententiam' (ibid.). At the end of his speech Piso repeats that he was drawing on the views of Antiochus and Staseas (V. 75).

What do these texts tell us? Only, and precisely, that Piso's speech is intended to represent the views of Antiochus. It does not follow that Antiochus was Cicero's *source*[62]—except in the trivial sense that if I represent X's views then X is my ultimate source. We can suppose that *Fin.* V tells us something about Antiochus' views: we should not suppose that we are reading

[61] Glucker [71] 391. For a brief history of attempts to find Antiochus in Cicero see Mette [22] 27–9.

[62] See e.g. M. Giusta, *I dossografi di etica* i (Turin, 1964), 74–100, whose theory is inadequately dealt with by Glucker [71] 55 n. 148.

Antiochus in Latin translation, nor even that Cicero is paraphrasing a work of Antiochus.[63]

That the Academic books rest in part on Antiochus is equally certain. Cicero explicitly remarks that he is representing Antiochian views at *Luc.* 10, 12, and 49 (cf. 98), and at *Acad.* 14.[64] Glucker argues that about half the Academic books were taken from Antiochus, and he believes that Cicero did little more than translate Antiochus' Greek. For the latter belief he relies on two passages in Cicero's letters: the notorious *ἀπόγραφα* confession of 21 March 45 BC (*Att.* XII. 52. 3), and a text in *Att.* XIII. 19. 5 (29 June 45), which is 'almost an echo of the *ἀπόγραφα* statement'. He argues that the *ἀπόγραφα* statement refers specifically to the first version of the Academic books: 'the *Lucullus* is—on Cicero's own admission—an *ἀπόγραφον*'. Thus in *Luc.* we read manicured translations of Antiochus.[65]

I shall not add to the literature on the *ἀπόγραφον* passage: the text is crucially corrupt, the reference is uncertain, and above all the tone of Cicero's words—urbane irony or honest confession?—is unclear.[66] But *Att.* XIII. 19. 5, which explicitly refers to the *Lucullus*, requires brief consideration. Speaking of the Lucullan speeches in *Luc.* which he intends, on Atticus' suggestion, to transfer to Varro, Cicero remarks:

> sunt enim vehementer *πιθανά* Antiochia, quae diligenter a me expressa acumen habent Antiochi, nitorem creationis nostrum—si modo is est aliquis in nobis.

Varro should be content with the role, because the Antiochian material is persuasive: it combines the *acumen* of Antiochus with the *nitor* of Cicero.

Cicero is not confessing that he has translated Antiochus. His point is not that the *content* is Antiochus' and the *language* his own. Rather, he insists that Antiochus' *acuity* (his logical prowess), partnered by his own *elegance* (his rhetorical prowess), make an unsurpassably persuasive pair. This does not imply that the work was an *ἀπόγραφον*, and we have no evidence for thinking that it was. Moreover, in *Att.* XIII. 13. 1 (24 June 45),

[63] Note that the references to Antiochus at *Fin.* V. 14 and 16 indicate that he was not Cicero's sole or direct source. (See below, n. 70.)

[64] Cf. *Att.* XIII. 12. 3; 16. 1; *Fam.* IX. 8. 1.

[65] See Glucker [71] 406–14 (my citations are from 414 and 412).

[66] See Barnes [107].

Cicero plainly indicates that the revised *Academici* are no mere parroting of Greek works: 'the books have turned out—unless I am deceived by that common failing, self-love—better than anything of their kind, even in Greek'.

It remains true, of course, that *Luc.* and *Acad.* provide us with invaluable information about Antiochus' views. But how much of them is Antiochian? and in particular, how much derives from the *Sosus*?[67]

The one explicit reference says that the *Sosus* was written 'contra' Philo (*Luc.* 12). Scholars suppose that some or all of Lucullus' speeches in *Luc.* derive from the *Sosus*. Cicero pretends that his source was Lucullus' memory—his 'divina memoria rerum' (*Luc.* 2)—of a long disputation at Alexandria (*Luc.* 12, cf. 63).[68] We need not believe this—and we are surely not intended to. However that may be, Cicero indicates that his main source was *not* the *Sosus*; for he has Lucullus explicitly remark that 'ea pars [sc. istius disputationis] quae contra Philonem erat praetermittenda est' (*Luc.* 12), and Lucullus says this only a few sentences after he has characterized the *Sosus* as being 'contra Philonem'. This surely means that the *Sosus* does not stand behind any of Cicero's argumentation. The Antiochian material in Lucullus' speeches has a different source or sources. We might think of Antiochus' later writings (or indeed of Cicero's memory of his lectures in Athens). But we have no need to fix on any single 'source':[69] Cicero was thoroughly familiar with Antiochus' views, and he was surely quite capable of producing an Antiochian speech without copying it from a written text.[70]

In the *Academici* Varro refers to 'quae contra Philonis Antiochus scripserit' (14), and he accepts Cicero's invitation to

[67] The fullest recent discussion is in Glucker [71]. He holds that *Acad.* 15–42 and *Luc.* 13–39 derive from the *Sosus*, and that *Luc.* 40–60 derives from a later work of Antiochus. (*Luc.* 64–146 comes from Philo's lost reply to the *Sosus* [see below]; and the lost *Catulus* derives in part from the *Sosus* and in part from Philo's Roman books.) See [71] 419 for a summary of Glucker's views.

[68] Cf. *Luc.* 61, which adds that Lucullus had heard the same arguments from Antiochus years later in Syria.

[69] With the general references to Antiochus contrast the precise references to Clitomachus at *Luc.* 98 (Book 4 of the *Περὶ ἐποχῆς*) and 102 (the work addressed to Lucilius).

[70] Note also the references to Antiochus at *Luc.* 29 and 49: these seem to suggest that the speech as a whole does not derive directly from Antiochus (see above, n. 63).

remind him of 'et ista et tota vetus Academia'. Varro's speech at *Acad.* 14–42 thus conveys, *inter alia*, the contents of the *Sosus*. But there is no reason to think that the whole of Varro's argument was drawn from the *Sosus*—or even from Antiochus.

We have one further source of information about the *Sosus*, namely Cicero's account of the '*Sosus* affair'. Consideration of this may be postponed for a few pages.

## 3. ANTIOCHUS AND PHILO

### (i) *The Conversion*

Antiochus began his philosophical life as an Academic sceptic, a follower of Philo in his Carneadean phase; and he adhered to that persuasion for 'many years' (Cic. *Luc.* 63, 69). He then changed his mind: Cicero implies that the change was both sudden and radical—that it was a 'conversion'.[71] Some said that he changed 'gloriae causa', that he wanted to have followers called Antiochians (Cic. *Luc.* 70; cf. Plut. *Cic.* 4. 2; August. *Acad.* II. 15). Plutarch thinks that he may have been 'moved by the evidence of the senses' (*Cic.* 4. 2). Cicero guesses that he was unable to withstand the philosophical attacks on Philo's Academy, which was epistemologically isolated (*Luc.* 70).[72] Plainly Cicero did not really know why Antiochus converted: neither, then, shall we.

When did he convert? The date of the '*Sosus* affair' is known: late 87. Should we take the *Sosus* affair to mark Antiochus' conversion, his break with Philonian scepticism? Scholars have usually assumed so.[73] But it is noteworthy that *Luc.* 11–12, which describes the affair, does not mention Antiochus' conversion (Cicero makes no reference to Antiochus' philosophical stance before he came to Alexandria); and conversely, *Luc.* 69–70, which describes the conversion, makes no reference to the *Sosus* affair.

[71] See *Luc.* 64 and 69. Dillon says: 'it is far more likely that [the change] was the result of a gradually growing dissatisfaction' with Academic scepticism ([73] 53). Should we prefer Dillon's hunch or Cicero's testimony?

[72] Note that *non sustinere* at *Luc.* 70 echoes 18: Cicero matches *Philo*'s alleged reason for his Roman innovations against *Antiochus*' alleged reason for abandoning scepticism. The *non sustinere* is as much as literary artifice as an historical conjecture.

[73] See e.g. Dillon [73] 53; Mette [22] 57.

Cicero gives the impression, then, that the conversion and the *Sosus* affair were two separate events. The impression is confirmed by Cicero's account of the conversion. For, as I have said, he expresses himself puzzled by it:

quis enim iste dies inluxerit quaero qui illi ostenderit eam quam multos annos esse negitavisset veri et falsi notam? excogitavit aliquid? eadem dicit quae Stoici. paenituit illa sensisse? . . . (*Luc.* 69)

Had the Roman books caused the conversion, Cicero would have had no reason to puzzle: Antiochus changed, he could have said, because of Philo's lectures. He does not say this—and we may infer that he did not think that the conversion was caused by the 'Roman books'. The text continues:

cur non se transtulit ad alios, et maxime ad Stoicos? . . . quid eum Mnesarchi paenitebat? quid Dardani? qui erant Athenis tum principes Stoicorum.

If Cicero is right, the conversion took place when Mnesarchus and Dardanus were the Stoic leaders.[74] It is implied, too, that the conversion took place in Athens. Since Antiochus studied scepticism for an unusually long time, we should perhaps think of a date in the nineties for the event.[75] The dates of Mnesarchus and Dardanus are not secure, but they are compatible with this suggestion.[76]

[74] See Glucker [71] 15–21—but he misses the significance of Cicero's puzzlement.

[75] Cicero's statement 'idem haec non acrius accusavit in senectute quam antea defensitaverat' (*Luc.* 69) might seem to cause a problem. In the 90s Antiochus will have been in his thirties: how, then, can Cicero say that he turned to attack Philo 'in his old age'? Has Cicero slipped? Is he exaggerating wildly? No: he says not that Antiochus *converted* in his old age but that he attacked Philo in old age—and we need not infer that these senile attacks were the first he essayed.

[76] The chronology is obscure. We know that Dardanus was successor to Panaetius, who died in *c.* 110 (*Ind. Stoic.* LIII. 5–7); that Mnesarchus *vigebat* in 110 (Cic. *De Orat.* I, 45); and that both Dardanus and Mnesarchus had been pupils of Diogenes of Babylon (*Ind. Stoic.* LI. 4–7). Now Diogenes is generally supposed to have died some years before 150 (but after 155, when he was one of the three ambassadors to Rome). Hence Dardanus and Mnesarchus cannot have been born much later than 175. Hence at the proposed time of Antiochus' conversion they would both have been in their late seventies or early eighties. This is physically possible; but it might be thought unlikely.

But the argument which leads to this unlikely conclusion is shaky at two points. (i) Our only evidence for the death of Diogenes is indirect. The dramatic date of Cicero's *De Senectute* is 150. In it a character refers to Diogenes in such a way as to imply that he was dead (*Sen.* 23). Hence Diogenes was dead by 150. (Cf. e.g. Glucker [71] 19 n. 18.) How much weight will this bear? Was Cicero such a stickler for accuracy that we can rely on the incidental implications of his dramatic dates? I doubt it. Perhaps Diogenes

We can perhaps go further. Cicero implies that the conversion was not immediately followed by a 'transfer' to another School: 'cur non se transtulit ad alios?' The institutional defection came, according to Cicero, 'after he had begun to get an audience of his own' (*Luc.* 69). So we should infer that Antiochus remained in the Academy while disagreeing with Philo: the intellectual conversion preceded the institutional divorce.[77] When and where did the divorce take place? It *could* have been in Alexandria after the *Sosus* affair. But I see nothing against the hypothesis that it occurred in Athens some time before 88.

After a decade or more of Philonian scepticism, then, Antiochus changed his philosophical allegiance. What new position did he assume? Before turning to that question, let us suss out the *Sosus*.

### (ii) *The* Sosus *Affair*

In 87, when Antiochus was with Lucullus in Alexandria, two books by Philo—the 'Roman books'—came into Antiochus' hands. They made him angry: he could not believe the views they expressed were Philo's—he had never heard anything like them from any member of the Academy. But Heraclitus, though he too found the contents idiosyncratic, recognized the work as Philo's, and the Selii and Tetrilius Rogus[78] confirmed that the two books were copies they had taken from the Roman lectures.[79] A long discussion of the philosophical issues followed—and Antiochus' own views were eventually written up in the *Sosus*.

---

lived into the 140s. (ii) It seems often to be supposed that a man will only become a pupil of a philosopher at the age of 20 or so. The supposition is false: Philo, for example, came to Athens at the age of 24, having already studied for eight years in Larissa with Callicles, the friend of Carneades (*Ind. Acad.* XXXIII. 5–11: text in Dorandi [238] 114); and a quantity of epigraphical evidence suggests that people started on philosophy young (see Tod (above, n. 30) 140). Thus we might imagine that Dardanus and Mnesarchus were born in about 160, or even a little later: in the 90s they may have been in their thriving sixties.

[77] So Sedley [244] 70, *contra* Glucker [71] 19–20. But this may seem to press Cicero's text too hard. 'Was Cicero such a stickler for accuracy . . . ?'

[78] Lucullus styles them 'mei familiares, docti homines, P. et C. Selii et Tetrilius Rogus': the names are otherwise unknown, and various emendations (see Reid [112] ad loc.)—none of them illuminating—have been proposed.

[79] They are no doubt the *libri* which Cicero himself had heard delivered as lectures: *Acad.* 13.

So Cicero, our only source (*Luc.* 11–12). Most scholars suppose the story to be true, thinking that Cicero perhaps took it from the *Sosus* itself.[80] Whether or not all the details are historical, we may surely believe that in Rome in 87 Philo lectured on Academic topics; that Antiochus found the thoughts he expressed heretical; and that the *Sosus* was Antiochus' (first) reply to the Roman books. What made Antiochus angry?[81]

Philo's Roman books are lost. Their argument was rehearsed in Cicero's *Catulus* (*Luc.* 12)—but that is also lost. Hence we are in no position to reconstruct Philo's Roman views in any detail. But at least two theses were certainly maintained in them.

First, Philo held the historical thesis that there had been only *one* Academy: the tradition from Plato to himself was, doctrinally as well as institutionally, continuous and unbroken (*Acad.* 13). How did Philo envisage this unbroken tradition? We have some indirect evidence.[82] For since Philo maintained the unity of the Academy, he must have supposed that his own Roman views had also been Plato's views. And of those views we know one.

Secondly, then, Philo advanced a philosophical thesis about epistemology and the criterion of truth. The issue is intricate and controversial. Again, the main text is in Cicero's *Lucullus*: it refers explicitly to the *nova quaedam* of Philo against which Antiochus argued—and hence to Philo's Roman books:

When Philo advanced some novel views, because he could hardly withstand the attacks on the intransigence of the Academics, he was plainly mistaken (as the elder Catulus argued) and in addition (as Antiochus showed) he landed himself in the very position he feared. For when he denied that anything can be known (that is how we render *καταληπτόν*) if what is known must be an impression of the sort

[80] E.g. Luck [241] 14; Glucker [71] 14 n. 5; Dillon [73] 54.

[81] I do not know why Dörrie [74] 452 supposes that the Roman books were written explicitly *against Antiochus*.

[82] Glucker [71] assembles the few texts which seem to bear on the Roman books and cites a number of these as testifying to Philo's conception of Plato (see 65–6, 69–70). Now in fact only one of these texts presents a view about Plato, namely the view that Plato was a thorough Sceptic: 'nihil adfirmatur, . . . de omnibus quaeritur, nihil certi dicitur', etc. (*Acad.* 46). The passage occurs in Cicero's speech. He has been introduced as the partisan of Arcesilaus (43), he is supposedly offering the standard Arcesilaan view of things, and as Glucker has shown, Arcesilaus and his followers construed Plato as a sceptic ([71] 31–47; cf. Ioppolo [70] 40–54). We must not attach the view expressed at *Acad.* 46 to the renegade Philo.

Zeno defined (the term 'impression' for *φαντασία* was made familiar enough by yesterday's conversation), namely an impression so stamped and sealed from that from which it came that it could not be from something from which it had not come (we say that Zeno's definition is absolutely right—for how can anything be grasped if you openly admit that what is known and apprehended is of a sort which could actually be false?)—when Philo attacks and rejects this sort of impression, he rejects the criterion of the known and the unknown, from which it follows that nothing can be known. (*Luc.* 18)

The paragraph is condensed and artfully clumsy. But it emerges clearly, first, that Philo *rejected* Zeno's definition of knowledge, and secondly, that he *accepted* that some things can be known. By rejecting the reigning account of the nature of knowledge, he thought that he could rescue knowledge from the attacks of the sceptic. And on this very point Antiochus finds fault: Philo cannot *both* reject the Stoic definition *and* reject scepticism.

The Stoic definition of knowledge, or *κατάληψις*, presents formidable problems of interpretation. Our longest text suggests something like the following account.[83]

(i) *Κατάληψις* is assent to a *φαντασία καταληπτική*, an 'apprehensive impression'. I know something—e.g. I know that the table is polished, just in case I assent to an apprehensive impression that the table is polished.

(ii) An apprehensive impression is a sort of *true* impression. If I know that the table is polished, then it must seem to me *truly* that the table is polished.

(iii) An apprehensive impression must be caused by a real object (it must come *ἀπὸ ὑπάρχοντος*). It must not be a mere matter of luck, say, that it seems to me that the table is polished: the table itself must bring it about that it seems to me that the table is polished.

(iv) Moreover, the impression must be 'stamped and sealed' by the object in accordance with its own features. It must, in other words, be because the table is polished that it seems to me that the table is polished.

(v) Finally, the impression must be such that it could not have come from any other source: had the table not been

[83] See Sext. Emp. *M.* VII. 247–52; cf. e.g. *M.* VII. 152, 402; *P.H.* II. 4; III. 241–2; Cic. *Luc.* 18, 77 (see Hülser [3] frs. 329–41).

polished, then it could not have seemed to me that the table was polished.

There is much that is disputable and much that is unclear in these five propositions. Nevertheless, I shall simplify matters yet further, and say that, according to the Stoic definition:

X knows that *P* just in case

(1) it truly seems to X that *P*, and

(2) it is because *P* that it seems to X that *P*, and

(3) were it not the case that *P*, then it would not seem to X that *P*.

This schema does not purport to represent the nuances of the Stoic theory. It does purport to convey what is philosophically important in the Stoic account—and what was deemed philosophically vulnerable by its Academic enemies.

For the Academic attack centred on clause (3) in the definition:

> They say that they reject this one element: that something true can appear in such a way that what is false could not appear in the same way. (*Luc.* 33)

Cicero is speaking of the Carneadeans (cf. Sext. Emp. *M.* VII. 402); but we can properly generalize the point: the Academics found especial difficulty with clause (3) in the definition of knowledge. And Philo's epistemological breakthrough—his *nova quaedam*—consisted in his rejection of that clause. In other words, Philo's thought was this: Suppose I truly believe that *P*, and it is because *P* that it seems to me that *P*: then I know that *P*. Perhaps it would have seemed to me that *P* even if it had not been the case that *P*. But that possibility does not invalidate my claim to knowledge; for it is no part of the concept of knowledge that I *could not have been* misled—it is enough that I *have not been* misled.

Cicero's implicit account of Philo's Roman epistemology is supported by Sextus:

> Philo and his followers say that, according to the Stoic criterion, i.e. apprehensive impression, things are indeed unknowable, but according to the nature of the things themselves they are knowable. (*P.H.* I. 235)

The passage is opaque, but scholars who puzzle over it often obscure its straightforward meaning: if you stick to the Stoic criterion, you will know nothing; but in fact knowledge is not unattainable—for the Stoic criterion should be rejected.

Thus Philo was a dogmatist: he held that, in truth, things can be known.[84] But we should not infer that this dogmatism was in itself the novelty of the Roman books which so shocked Antiochus. For Antiochus was by now a dogmatist himself: he would have welcomed rather than deplored a dogmatic Philo.

Then what were the shocking novelties of the Roman books? I suggest that the chief *philosophical* novelty was not the return to dogmatism but rather the explanation of how such a return might be possible; that is to say, it was Philo's discovery that the Stoic definition of knowledge should be rejected. Consequently the chief *historical* novelty of the Roman books was the claim that this epistemological view had been the view of Plato and the Old Academy. According to Philo, Plato was indeed a dogmatist; but he did not accept—he did not anticipate—the Stoic definition of knowledge. Even Arcesilaus and Carneades were dogmatists (cf. Cic. *Luc.* 12). True, they vehemently argued for ἀκαταληψία; but their arguments were directed, explicitly and exclusively, against the Stoic conception of κατάληψις[85]—and once this conception is rejected it can be seen that the Academy's attack on κατάληψις was in reality never an attack on knowledge itself.[86]

We know that Antiochus rejected both these features of

[84] Numenius reports, in his contorted style, that Philo was originally an adherent of Clitomachus: 'but as time passed and their suspension of judgement became insipid through familiarity, he preserved no constancy in his thoughts and was converted by the vividness and congruity of his impressions [ἡ τῶν παθημάτων . . . ἐνάργειά τε καὶ ὁμολογία]' (fr. 28 des Places = Euseb. *Praep. Evang.* XIV. 9. 4). (Compare Plutarch's explanation of Antiochus' conversion: εἴτε καμπτόμενος ὑπὸ τῆς ἐναργείας καὶ τῶν αἰσθήσεων . . . (*Cic.* 4. 2).) Cicero first heard Philo in Rome (*Brut.* 306) and he learned from him the standard New Academic method 'de omnibus rebus in contrarias partes disserendi' (*Tusc.* II. 9). This might suggest that Philo was still advocating scepticism in Rome. But the *in contrarias partes* method is not an exclusively sceptical practice (cf. e.g. *Fin.* V. 10). Two other hard texts are discussed below in Appendices B and C.

[85] So e.g. August. *Acad.* III. 41. But there the point is tied to Augustine's notion that the sceptical Academy surreptitiously preserved an esoteric and dogmatic Platonism (see below, Appendix B).

[86] The view developed here is close to that of Brochard [66], which has recently been endorsed by Glucker [71] (see esp. 74). I differ from Brochard and Glucker on some important details, notably in the philosophical interpretation of Philo's Roman epistemology; but it is not worth annotating the points of disagreement.

Philo's Roman books. He held that the Academy had changed its epistemological position: the Old Academy had been dogmatic, the New Academy sceptical. And he believed that he, and not Philo, was recalling the Old Academy. For he also held that the Stoic criterion of knowledge could not be rejected:[87] Philo's revised criterion of knowledge was a sham, and his new dogmatism was in fact scepticism under a false name. Antiochus himself embraced the Stoic criterion and insisted that the Stoics had adopted it from the old tradition of the Academy and the Peripatos.

Two further texts must be taken into account. First, *Luc.* 32–3. Here Cicero distinguishes two groups of Academics: members of the first group simply say that there is no knowledge, that the world is not such as to be known by us. Members of the second group say that, although nothing can be known, it does not follow that everything is *incertum*; for the *probabile* will still give us a criterion of action and of judgement. It is plain, I think, that the two groups represent Arcesilaus and Carneades. Thus the Carneadeans—according to Metrodorus and Philo, whose interpretation Cicero is here following[88]—say that they reject one thing only, viz. that truths can present themselves in a way in which falsities cannot.

But does this not mean that the Carneadeans rejected the third clause in the Stoic definition of knowledge, so that the Carneadean view is exactly the view which I have ascribed to Philo and claimed to be the great novelty of his Roman period? It is undeniably similar to Philo's view. But then this should cause no surprise; for Philo claimed that his own Roman view had been the standard view of the Academy—and hence that it had been the view of Carneades too. Antiochus accused Philo of innovation: Philo himself claimed to be following the unbroken Academic tradition. Nonetheless, there is a significant distinction to be drawn between the view which I have ascribed to Philo and the view which our text ascribes to the Carneadeans.

[87] Antiochus insisted on retaining the Stoic definition of knowledge (Cic. *Luc.* 18) and in particular its third clause (*Luc.* 22, 23, 27, 33, 34, 36, 44, 57, 58; cf. 77, 84, 99, 101, 113; *Fin.* v. 76).

[88] Glucker, [71] 77 n. 220, thinks rather of the Clitomachian interpretation on the grounds that the text only implies that *probabile* is a guide to action. But the text explicitly says that the second group treat *probabilia* both as a practical and as a theoretical *regula*.

The difference can best be stated in terms of the following three propositions:

(1) The definition of knowledge requires the third Stoic clause.

(2) The condition stated in the third clause can never be met.

(3) There is knowledge.

Plainly these three propositions are mutually incompatible. Carneades and Philo both accept (2). Carneades therefore rejected (3). Philo—and this was his Roman innovation—rejected (1). (Antiochus, of course, rejected (2).)

The second text is *Luc.* 112, where Cicero explicitly states that the Peripatetics did not incorporate the third Stoic clause into their definition of knowledge. (The same point is made at *Fin.* v. 76.) Philo, then, was reverting in his Roman books to a Peripatetic account of knowledge. Yet it is Antiochus, as we shall see, who claimed to be following the old Academico-Peripatetic line in epistemology. But this should not worry us. We must suppose that at *Luc.* 112 and *Fin.* v. 76 Cicero is giving us the *Philonian* view of the Peripatetics. Since Philo maintained the doctrinal unity of the Academy, he may well have ascribed his own definition of knowledge to the Peripatetics as well as to Plato. Antiochus will not have accepted the ascription. On the contrary, the ascription will have been one of the features of the Roman books to which he objected.[89] In his view, the Old Academy and the Peripatos had subscribed (no doubt only implicitly) to what was to become the standard Stoic analysis of knowledge, including its controversial third clause.

### (iii) *Philo's Reply?*

Did Philo reply to the *Sosus*? Only one text bears explicitly on the issue, and it is puzzling:

> But the old arms were taken up again: Philo resisted him [sc. Antiochus] until he died, and our Tully destroyed all that remained of him, unwilling that anything he had loved should in his lifetime fall or be corrupted. (August. *Acad.* III. 41)

[89] Note that at *Luc.* 113 Cicero emphasizes *against Antiochus* that the Old Academy and the Peripatos rejected the third clause of the Stoic definition.

The remark about 'our Tully' has provoked much comment, and it has, I think, been misunderstood.[90] 'Omnes eius reliquias Tullius noster oppressit': *eius* refers to Antiochus (not to Philo); and *oppressit* means 'squashed', 'destroyed' (not 'suppressed').[91] Augustine is adverting to Cicero's patronage of the New Academy and to his defence of scepticism, in the Academic books, against the attacks of Antiochus.

The remark about Philo has been taken to suggest a lively debate: Philo defended his Roman views against the *Sosus*, and Antiochus, who continued to attack Philo 'in senectute' (Cic. *Luc.* 69), did not let the battle slacken. That story may be true. But it is not the story Augustine tells. According to Augustine, Philo resisted Antiochus 'arreptis iterum illis armis': he took up his old arms again. The old arms must, in the context, be the defensive weapons of scepticism; and Augustine can only mean that Philo, having thought that the siege was over and that the standard of dogmatic Platonism could safely be raised, realized that he must once more adopt the old sceptical tactics: Platonism had to wait for Plotinus before it could again be openly taught. We may well doubt the truth of Augustine's report, which is the final chapter of his idiosyncratic history of the Academy.[92] But the text admits of only one interpretation, and it cannot be taken to imply that Philo defended his Roman views against Antiochus.[93]

My account of these epistemological maneouvres has been laborious and contorted. In summary form, this is how the history went. First, from 110 to about 95, Philo and Antiochus harmoniously maintained the Carneadean scepticism of the New Academy. In the nineties, Antiochus converted from scepticism to a form of dogmatism; a little later he left the institutional framework of the Academy. His philosophical position did not change thereafter. Philo remained sceptical. We may suspect, but we have no evidence to show, that he felt himself gradually drawn towards a form of dogmatism. However that

[90] Glucker, [71] 84–87, offers an extraordinarily ingenious explanation.

[91] See e.g. Cic. *Fam.* x. 20. 3: 'qui reliquias huius belli oppresserit . . .'

[92] See Appendix B.

[93] A second text—see Appendix C—probably refers to the Philonian Academy in the period after the Roman books. But this text contains no hint of any continuing dispute between Philonians and Antiochians.

may be, in Rome he came to realize that the Stoic definition of knowledge was not mandatory: he dropped the third clause, explicitly proclaimed the possibility of knowledge, and became a thorough-going dogmatist. And so (unless we believe Augustine) he remained to the end of his life.

## 4. PHILOSOPHY

### (i) *Syncretism*

To what did Antiochus convert? What was his philosophical position after the break with Philo and the New Academy?

So far as we know, he did not style himself an 'Antiochian'; nor will he have spoken, as some doxographers do, of a Fifth Academy.[94] On the contrary, he regarded himself as reviving the Old Academy: 'vetus Academia revocata est' (Cic. *Luc.* 70, cf. 11); Antiochus 'moved back from the new house to the old' (*Acad.* 13).[95] The Old Academy was the Academy of Plato and his immediate successors, up to the scholarchate of Polemo. It is not attested that Antiochus read Plato's works, but we may surely suppose that he did.[96] It is attested that 'Antiochus particularly approves of Polemo' (Cic. *Luc.* 131; cf. *Fin.* v. 14).[97] When our texts speak of a revival of the Old Academy, we should not at once imagine a revival of what *we* tend to think of as Platonism.[98]

Antiochus is also said to have converted to Stoicism: 'eadem dicit quae Stoici' (Cic. *Luc.* 69; cf. 67); 'erat quidem si perpauca mutavisset germanissimus Stoicus' (ibid. 132); he was 'Stoicus

[94] E.g. Sext. Emp. *P.H.* I. 220, 235; [Gal.], *Hist. Phil.* 3; Euseb. *Praep. Evang.* XIV. 4. 16. Cf. Glucker [71] 344–6.

[95] Cf. Plut. *Luc.* 42. 3; *Brut.* 2. 3. Thus Varro, an Antiochian, is a follower of the Old Academy: Cic. *Acad.* 7.

[96] See e.g. Luck [241] 23–4. For knowledge of Plato's dialogues in the sceptical Academy see Glucker [71] 35–47.

[97] See e.g. Dillon [73] 57–9: he regards Polemo as the central figure in Antiochus' version of the Old Academy. But in fact we know little enough about Polemo's views: see Gigante [19].

[98] Dörrie, [74] 466–8, asserts that the *veteres* whose views Antiochus sought to revive did not include Plato himself: the 'Old Academy' was the Academy of the first generation of Plato's successors, not the Academy of Plato. (Hence there can be no question of Antiochus' having prepared the way for Neoplatonism.) But this is implausible in itself; it goes against the intention of most of the relevant texts; and it conflicts with the explicit statements of e.g. Cic. *Luc.* 15, *Acad.* 33, and Sext. Emp. *P.H.* I. 235.

perpauca balbutiens' (ibid. 137). 'Antiochus brought the Stoa into the Academy, so that they actually said of him that "he does Stoic philosophy in the Academy"' (Sext. Emp. *P.H.* I. 235).[99] Real Stoics were not always impressed—Diodotus did not accept his views (Cic. *Luc.* 115), nor did Balbus (*Nat. D.* I. 16).[100] But it seems clear that Antiochus thought of himself as a champion of the Porch.

Yet how can he have professed himself both an Old Academic and a Stoic? 'He tried to show that the doctrines of the Stoics are to be found in Plato' (Sext. Emp. *P.H.* I. 235). For 'our friend Antiochus holds that Stoicism should be considered an emendation of the Old Academy rather than a new school of thought' (Cic. *Acad.* 43).[101] Nor was that all: 'Antiochus thinks that the Stoics agree with the Peripatetics in substance and dispute only over terminology' (*Nat. D.* I. 16). If Stoicism and the Peripatetic philosophy are the same, that is because the Peripatetics really belong to the Old Academy: 'as you have heard Antiochus say, there are numbered among the Old Academy not only those who are called Academics—Speusippus, Xenocrates, Polemo, Crantor, and the rest—but also the old Peripatetics, of whom Aristotle is the chief' (*Fin.* v. 7).[102]

Thus Antiochus was a syncretist:[103] there is one true philosophy, and it is the philosophy of Plato and the Academy, of Aristotle and the Lyceum, of Zeno and the Porch.

If we peer more closely at the texts, they will seem to describe somewhat different forms of syncretism. Most often it is said that Zeno *holds the same views as* the Academy, while differing in words (*Luc.* 15; *Leg.* I. 54; *Nat. D.* I. 16; cf. *Acad.* 37). It is also said that Zeno *corrects* the Academy (*Acad.* 37, 43). And again, that Zeno *attacks* the Academy (*Acad.* 7). But we should not try to make anything of these differences. All Cicero's formulations

[99] Cf Numen. fr. 28 des Places = Euseb. *Praep. Evang.* XIV. 9. 4; Plut. *Cic.* 4. 2; August. *Acad.* III. 41; *CD* XIX. 3. Note too that Cicero's reply to Lucullus' Antiochian speech takes the form of an attack on Stoicism.

[100] See Luck [241] 45–6.

[101] Cf. e.g. *Acad.* 35, 37; *Luc.* 15; *Leg.* I. 54.

[102] Cf. *Fin.* v. 14; *Luc.* 131; and Varro's remarks at *Acad.* 17, 18, 22.

[103] 'Syncretism' and not 'eclecticism' is the word: Antiochus did not think of himself as selecting the choicer morsels from each of three rival philosophies and constructing a new system from them; he meant to accept (almost) all the doctrines of the apparently diverse philosophies, claiming that they were to be envisaged as partners rather than as competitors.

are intended to convey a single picture of Antiochus' syncretical interpretation: although Zeno overtly attacks the Academy, and corrects it on some points, his innovations are primarily terminological and in substance his philosophy is the same as that of Plato and Aristotle.[104]

Antiochus' syncretism may strike us as bizarre: how could anyone possibly combine Plato and Aristotle and Zeno? The oddity of the business is not to be explained by invoking the precedent of Panaetius; for even if Panaetius was φιλοπλάτων καὶ φιλοαριστοτέλης (*Ind. Stoic.* LXI. 2), he did not assert the identity of the three philosophies. Nor is the oddity substantially mitigated by the fact that Antiochus recognized disagreements of various sorts within the schools.[105]

Moreover, the syncretism may seem worse than odd: it may seem a cheat. For Antiochus explicitly recognizes that, in ethics for example, Zeno disagreed with the Academico-Peripatetic point of view on a number of crucial issues (*Acad.* 38–9); and Varro, in expounding the views of the Old Academy, must argue *contra Stoicos* (*Acad.* 7).[106] Was Antiochus disingenuous about his syncretism? Or was Cicero obtuse and false to his teacher when he reported his views?

We may summon up a more sympathetic idea of Antiochus' position if we attempt to look at his intellectual background through his own eyes rather than through ours. *We* tend to think of Hellenistic philosophy in terms of the four great and rival Schools: the Stoa and the Peripatos, the Garden and the Academy. The doctrinal differences which divide these Schools, and their own idiosyncratic characters, are central to our understanding of the age.

To Antiochus things looked different. The Lyceum was intellectually dead: there were three Schools, not four. Two of the three were the same as two of our four: the Stoa and the Garden. And there was no doubt that *they* were rivals. Third came the Academy—but the Sceptical Academy, the Academy of Arcesilaus and Carneades, which in Antiochus' eyes (as in

[104] For the problem raised by Cic. *Luc.* 16 see Appendix D.

[105] See e.g. Cic. *Fin.* v. 12, 14; *Acad.* 33–4.

[106] For Cicero's own objections to the syncretism see *Luc.* 132 ('est enim inter eos non de terminis sed de tota possessione contentio'), 137, 143.

ours) had little to do with the Academy of Plato and his first followers.

How, then, would Antiochus have thought of the old followers of Plato and of Aristotle? They could not, *pace* Arcesilaus, be construed as proto-sceptics. Equally plainly, there is no taint of Epicureanism in their writings. On the other hand, they seem to have much in common with the Stoics: no doubt, as Antiochus insisted, there were important differences between Zeno and Aristotle and between Zeno and Plato; but these differences must have seemed trifling—indeed they *were* trifling—when compared to the differences between Zeno or Aristotle on the one hand and Epicurus or Arcesilaus on the other.

In short, in the early part of the first century BC Antiochus' syncretism will have seemed both true and illuminating. In logic, the struggle of the time was between scepticism and science; in physics, the tussle concerned a mechanistic atomism on the one side and teleology and a material continuum on the other; in ethics, there was a duel between virtue and pleasure. In each of these great battles the Old Academics and the Peripatetics stood shoulder to shoulder with the Stoics: Plato, Aristotle, and Zeno formed a philosophical triumvirate defending the republic of knowledge and virtue against the barbarian attacks of sceptics and voluptuaries.[107] Antiochus was aware of this. He saw it, not without justification, as the essential feature of the philosophy of his day. His enthusiasm may have led him to exaggerate his thesis (and the relatively gross texture of our sources may hide the nuances of his views); but that should not obscure the important insight which lies behind Antiochus' syncretism.

### (ii) *The Parts of Philosophy*

Varro's speech at *Acad.* 14–42 is largely Antiochian in

[107] For a very clear statement of this idea see Cic. *Leg.* I. 37–8: he will be satisfied with principles which are accepted not by everyone (that is impossible) but by those *qui omnia recta atque honesta per se expetenda duxerunt*, i.e. by the Old Academy, the Peripatos, and the Stoa—the Epicureans are to remain apart in their gardens, and the New Academics are asked to keep silent. The division of philosophical opinion here is precisely the one which underlay Antiochus' syncretism. (But at this point in the *De Legibus* Cicero does not mention Antiochus.)

inspiration. It runs like this. First, Socrates turned philosophy to ethics, and introduced a thorough-going scepticism (16).[108] Then Plato dogmatized, and his Academic and Peripatetic successors maintained his dogmatic attitudes (17–18). The dogmatic philosophy had three parts, and Varro describes in turn its ethics (19–23), its physics (24–9), and its logic (30–3). After Aristotle, various differences and dissensions arose (33–5), but Zeno, the founder of Stoicism, reworked the old philosophy: Varro describes his 'corrections' in ethics (35–9), in physics (39–40), and in logic (40–2).

Thus Antiochus, as we should have expected, discussed each of the three traditional parts of philosophy (cf. *Luc.* 116).[109] We know little about his views on physics.[110] He held, traditionally enough, that physics is relevant to ethics; for in order to know ourselves we must know the whole of nature (*Fin.* v. 44). But if we may judge from Cicero's remarks at *Luc.* 29, the subject played a minor role in Antiochus' system.

*Λογική* included what we call logic and the ancients termed *διαλεκτική*, namely the science of argument and inference. We know that Antiochus taught Cicero logic (*Luc.* 98), and that the logic he taught was Stoic (ibid. 97)—indeed Antiochus was a Chrysippean in the matter (ibid. 143). Like the Stoics, Antiochus argued against the Epicurean claim that some disjunctions of the form '*P* or not-*P*' are false (ibid. 97); like Zeno, he thought that it was important to be trained in the study of fallacies (ibid. 46); and in general he adopted the Stoic view that logic was a means of discovering truth by the use of proofs or *ἀποδείξεις* (ibid. 26–7; cf. *Acad.* 32). There is no evidence that Antiochus had any original views in logic—and none that he had any knowledge of Peripatetic logical theory.[111]

[108] Contrast *Luc.* 15, where Socrates is an (ironical) dogmatist.

[109] Dillon [73] notes that Antiochus followed the standard tripartition of philosophy, and he takes *Acad.* 19 to suggest that 'Antiochus preferred the order Ethics–Physics–Logic' (63). But at *Fin.* v. 9 the parts are listed in the order physics, logic, ethics.

[110] Antiochus' physics is discussed by Dillon [73] 81–8: he argues that in important points it prefigures Middle Platonism (and he also urges that much of Cicero's *De Fato* expresses Antiochus' views). There is an alternative account in Dörrie [74] 472–7: he argues that the physics is almost pure Stoicism, and that it has nothing in common with Platonic metaphysics.

[111] I doubt Dillon's view that Cicero's *Topica* is Antiochian in origin ([73] 103–4).

According to Antiochus 'there are two things of the greatest importance in philosophy: the judgement of truth, and the determination of the good; no-one can be wise unless he is aware both of the beginning of knowledge and of the end of desire, unless he knows whence he is to begin and whither he is to journey' (Cic. *Luc.* 29). Epistemology and ethics were thus the two chief elements in Antiochus' philosophy; and, as we shall see, epistemology was in a sense prior to ethics.

### (iii) *Epistemology*

For Antiochus' epistemology the main source is Lucullus' speech (see also *Acad.* 30–3). After a historical introduction (13–18), the speech divides into two parts, the first of which is primarily constructive (19–39) and the second largely negative (40–60). Lucullus ends with a brief peroration (61–2). The negative part summarily expounds the chief Academic arguments against κατάληψις and offers equally summary refutations. The structure of the positive part is not always clear; but it begins with a short exposition of 'Old Academic' epistemology (19–22). I shall restrict my attention to these sections.

We begin with the senses: their canons, *indicia*, are so 'clear and certain' that we could not ask for anything better from God. Of course, not *everything* is as it seems; but if the senses are 'healthy and strong, and they have no obstacles and impediments', then their reports are true (19). Moreover, skill and practice can refine them further—observe what happens to the eyes of painters and the ears of musicians (20, cf. 56).

But by themselves the senses only warrant judgements of the form 'There's something *F* there' (where '*F*' is a perceptible predicate, like 'red' or 'round' or 'rough') (cf. Sext. Emp. *M.* VII. 162, 344). By employing our minds too, we can identify individual objects and say '*That* is *F*'; and then we can develop complex predicates, enabling ourselves to say, e.g., 'That is a horse'. Later still, we can say such things as 'A horse is a quadruped with a flowing mane', and thus ground our ἐννοίαι or *notitiae*, which in turn form the foundation of science and inquiry (21).

There are some odd features, philosophically speaking, in this concise account. But the account can reasonably be called

Peripatetico-Stoic.[112] It is, I might add, no more thin or feeble than the little essays in epistemology which are found in Aristotle's writings.

In its Antiochian context, the account must seem to raise two particular questions. First, why should it be tied to the Stoic definition of *κατάληψις*, and in particular to the third clause of the definition? Secondly, how can the account guarantee the availability of Stoic *κατάληψις*? how can it evade sceptical objections?

Neither question, as far as I can see, receives an interesting answer. As to the first question, Antiochus held that the third clause in the Stoic definition was required by the very concept of knowledge: you cannot know anything if you might be wrong about it; knowledge, as Plato and Aristotle had also said, is *ἀναμάρτητος* and *ἀμετάπτωτος*. There is—and there need be—no *special* connexion between Antiochus' epistemological story and the definition of *κατάληψις*. The epistemology is tied to the definition only in the weak sense that *any* satisfactory epistemology must be tied to the (true) definition of knowledge.

As to the second question, Antiochus holds that we do possess knowledge; that knowledge must satisfy the third clause in the definition; and that our path to knowledge is in fact the one which his epistemology maps out. It follows from these propositions that the epistemology *will* secure something which satisfies the third condition. But Antiochus does not, in the texts which survive, offer any explanation of *how* it can satisfy it.[113] Perhaps he felt no need for an explanation—perhaps he thought that his arguments against Academic scepticism were all that could or should be offered in defence of his anti-sceptical position.

We might wonder, finally, whether we should accept the third clause in the Stoic definition: Antiochus insisted on it—was he right? Was Philo's innovation an error or an advance? Antiochus' surviving argument for the retention of the third clause is simple:

[112] Dillon concludes that the epistemology is 'taken over wholesale from the Stoics' ([73] 69). As far as I can see, the theory, as we find it in *Luc.*, is no more Stoic than Peripatetic.

[113] But see Sext. Emp. *M.* VII. 162–3, where a hint of an anti-sceptical argument might be detected.

How can anything be grasped if you openly admit that what is known and apprehended is of a sort which could actually be false? (*Luc.* 18, cf. 36)

On the basis of evidence *E*, I claim to know that *P*. (It looks to me as though there's a snake in the corner—and I assert that there is a snake in the corner.) Can I in these circumstances admit that, even given *E*, not-*P* is possible? No: if, given *E*, not-*P* is still possible, then, given *E*, for all I know it may be the case that not-*P*. But if for all I know it may be the case that not-*P*, then I do not know that *P*. (Even if it looks to me as though there's a snake in the corner, it is still possible that there isn't one there. Hence for all I know, there isn't a snake in the corner. Hence I do not know that there is a snake in the corner.)

That, I take it, is the argument. It can be paraphrased as follows. Suppose that:

(1) On the basis of *E*, X knows that *P*

Suppose, secondly, that the third clause of the Stoic definition is rejected, and hence that:

(2) Possibly both *E* and not-*P*

Now from (2) we are invited to infer that:

(3) Given only *E*, for all X knows it may be the case that not-*P*

—and (3) conflicts with (1).

That is the argument which Antiochus gave in support of the Stoic definition and against Philo's Roman view. Philo would have rejected it. In effect he would have denied that (3) follows from (2). And I do not think that (3) does follow from (2). For (2) asserts that it is *logically* possible, or consistent to suppose, that *E* should hold and *P* fail to hold; while (3) asserts that it is *epistemically* possible for *X*, or consistent with all *X* knows, that *E* should hold and *P* fail to hold. At the moment, everything suggests to me that I am sitting at my table in my room in Balliol. I know that all these suggestions *could* be misleading, and that it is logically compatible with them that I am in fact lounging on a truckle-bed in an opium den in Hong Kong. But I do not, and I should not, infer that *for all I know* I am in Hong Kong. Thus (3) does not follow from (2). Philo (so far as this argument goes) was right.

(iv) *Ethics*

Piso's speech at *Fin.* v. 9–74 is preceded and followed by references to Piso's two teachers, Staseas the Peripatetic and Antiochus. But Cicero goes out of his way, both at v. 8 and at v. 75, to stress the Antiochian origins of the speech: Staseas gave things a somewhat different twist. We should not doubt that the speech is intended to express the views of the converted Antiochus.[114]

The speech is introduced to give an account of Peripatetic ethics, and Piso begins by referring to the 'Peripateticorum disciplina' (9).[115] A little later he remarks that 'our Antiochus seems to me to adhere most scrupulously to the views of the ancients (*antiqui*), which he teaches to be common to Aristotle and to Polemo' (14). As for the Stoics, 'since they took everything over from the Peripatetics and Academics, they offer the same theories in different words' (22). At the end of the speech the remark about the Stoics is repeated:

> They did not take one or two things from us, but adopted the whole of our philosophy. And just as other thieves change the marks on the things they have taken, so they, in order to use our opinions as their own, have changed the names which are, as it were, signs of the things. (74)

But in this later section Aristotle and Theophrastus appear in a somewhat different light—at least, they are named first among those who 'snatched pieces' from the system Antiochus has described (74): they are not its originators.

It is thus not wholly plain what the system purports to be: an Academic-Peripatetic construction later stolen and renamed by the Stoics? or an Academic construction later renamed by the Stoics and pillaged by the Peripatetics?

The speech itself begins by stressing the importance of ascertaining the *summum bonum*, the standard to which everything else is referred (15). By way of the *divisio Carneadea*, 'which our Antiochus is always happy to use' (16), we come to the

[114] For Antiochus' ethics see also *Acad.* 19–23. There is another important text, omitted from Luck's collection and only fragmentarily printed in Mette's, viz. August. *CD* xix. 3: Augustine purports to report what Varro said 'auctore Antiocho' on Old Academic ethics.

[115] See also *Fin.* v. 54; *Att.* xiii. 19. 4.

'ancient' view that the τέλος consists in the *prima naturae* conjoined with *honestas* (16–23). The argument then turns to the content of the *prima naturae*, and outlines the fundamental notions of self-love and of living *secundum naturam* (24–33). There follows a discussion of the two-fold nature of man, body and soul (34–45), and the different perfections of each part are described and commended (46–64). Finally Piso discusses the place of 'external goods' in moral theory (65–74, cf. *Tusc.* v. 22–3).

The speech presents something which can decently be called an ethical system, and many elements in it are indeed Peripatetico-Stoical. (So, for example, the thesis of the ἀντακολουθία of the virtues: 67.) But some parts of the system may strike us as peculiarly Aristotelian—for example, the emphasis on the supreme value of knowledge (48–54) or the conception of man as a political animal (66).[116] Other parts are, from our point of view, quite un-Aristotelian—for example, the repeated appeal to 'the cradle' (e.g. 24, 55, 61), an appeal which united the Epicureans and the Stoics but which controverts a fundamental tenet of Aristotelianism.[117] Again, the system appears to contain a novelty or two, notably the characteristic insistence on 'degrees' of happiness and on the distinction between *beatus* and *beatissimus* (71, 81; cf. III. 43; *Acad.* 22; August. *CD* XIX. 3). As historians we must be inclined to regard Antiochus' ethics as an eclectic construction: although Antiochus promises to unify Stoic, Academic, and Peripatetic theories, in fact he selects different ideas from the different systems.

But Antiochus certainly regarded himself as a syncretist and not as an eclectic. How could he have done so? How, for example, could he have hoped to show that Zeno's ideal of ὁμολογουμένως ζῆν was identical—or at any rate consonant—with Aristotle's ideal of θεωρία? or that the cradle argument was compatible with Aristotelianism? We possess one illustration of Antiochus' method: it appears at *Fin.* v. 88–92, it is

[116] Cf. *Luc.* 132–4 for aspects of Antiochus' ethics that were thought to be inconsistent with Stoicism.

[117] Note esp. *Fin.* v. 55: 'quamquam enim vereor ne nimius in hoc genere videar, tamen omnes veteres philosophi, maxime nostri, ad incunabula accedunt'. On all this see Jacques Brunschwig. 'The Cradle Argument in Epicureanism and Stoicism', in Schofield and Striker [30].

alluded to at *Nat. D.* I. 16 and at *Acad.* 37, and it is most clearly described in Cicero's *De Legibus.* Cicero claims, in Antiochian fashion, that the differences between the Old Academy and the Stoa are mainly verbal. Atticus asks him if he shares Antiochus' views on the matter, and Cicero gives a guardedly affirmative reply. Then comes the Antiochian attempt to reconcile the Stoa and the Academy:

> Had Zeno, like Aristo of Chius, said that only what is *honestum* is good and only what is *turpe* is evil and that all other things are absolutely on a level, it not making the slightest difference whether they are present or absent, then he really would differ from Xenocrates and Aristotle and from Plato's school, and there would be a dispute between them about a point of capital importance, namely the whole way one should live. But in fact while the ancients held that honour is the highest good, he holds that it is the sole good; and similarly they hold that dishonour is the highest evil, he that it is the only evil—and he calls riches and health and beauty advantageous rather than good, and poverty and illness and pain disadvantageous rather than bad. Hence he holds the same view as Xenocrates and Aristotle but he does not use the same words. (*Leg.* I. 55)

Antiochus thus reconciles Zeno with the Academy by claiming that there is no real difference between saying that X is the greatest among several goods and saying that X is the sole good among several things which are advantageous. The Stoic distinction between the good and the valuable, or between what is ἀγαθόν and what is προηγμένον, is merely a matter of terminology.[118]

The reconciliation may seem not unreasonable. Certainly, the Stoic distinction is at first sight puzzling, and modern readers are sometimes tempted to dismiss it in precisely the Antiochian way. But of course the matter is more complicated than this: the Stoics themselves thought that the distinction between the good and the valuable was both real and of the last importance; and Balbus professed himself astonished that Antiochus could confound differences in degree with differences in kind (*Nat. D.* I. 16). We do not know how Antiochus attempted to show that the distinction was merely terminological. Indeed, we do not know whether he tried to *show* it at all,

[118] For the distinction see e.g. Long and Sedley [1] 354–9.

whether he was concerned to achieve scholarly or historical exactitude. For his syncretism claimed not only to interpret the ancients but also to propound a true system of ethics, and we may suspect that the latter aim was more important to Antiochus than the former.

I end with a small point. If knowledge is to be a central component of the *summum bonum*, then it surely must be attainable by us. And Antiochus in fact explicitly maintains that 'nature has perfected the mind no less than the body, equipping it with senses suitable for apprehending things and requiring little or no augmentation for their maturation' (*Fin.* v. 59). The ethical system thus presupposes a dogmatic epistemology. In itself, this is scarcely surprising; but it underlines the fact that the two major parts of Antiochus' philosophy were necessarily linked one to the other.

## 6. CODA

Antiochus of Ascalon was a very great man indeed?

Institutionally, he reached the summit of his profession: he was probably scholarch of an Athenian School, probably of the Athenian Academy. But his School did not last, and it was not his pupils who prepared the way for Neoplatonism.

Politically, he numbered Roman senators among his friends. He was admired and esteemed by great men. But he was renowned as a philosopher, and we need not believe that he had any particular influence over the political events of his time.

He had an effect on later philosophical writers, and his ideas lie behind certain Ciceronian texts. But the large claims which *Quellenforschung* has made on his behalf are unproven and improbable.

Those scholars who have inflated his reputation have usually, and paradoxically, decried his intellectual claims. They deny that he was a first-rate philosopher. They opine that his views are 'much more a product of robust common sense than of strict philosophical analysis'.[119]

But here I will take issue with the inflationists. They judge by

[119] Dillon [73] 105, 73.

inappropriate canons. Antiochus did not purport to be an innovatory thinker: on the contrary, his main philosophical effort was expended on syncretism—on collecting and collating, fitting and polishing, combining and assembling old arguments and old doctrines. Innovation is one mark of intellectual grandeur, but it is not the only mark. A syncretist may properly claim that he does no small service to his subject: and if Antiochus' philosophy is to be assessed at all, it must be assessed as the work of a syncretist.

We can hardly hope to judge the subtlety or success of Antiochus' particular syncretistic endeavours: our evidence is imperfect, and what we possess is at best abbreviated paraphrase. But we can perhaps say something about the general merits of Antiochus' project. And were I composing a *laudatio Antiochi*, I might begin in this vein:

> He learned his philosophy in an age of scholasticism. The Schools were engaged in esoteric bickering, unintelligible to the layman and unprofitable to the discipline. His vision pierced the dust of the present and he discerned the clear, clean shape which philosophy had shown in the past. He had the insight to grasp what was essential, the courage to ignore the accidental. If his syncretism was false in detail, it conveyed a general truth—and a truth pertinent to his day. For when the Athenian Schools were battered by external enemies and fractured by internal squabbles, he was prepared to publish a plain and conservative system of philosophy—and to commend his system to the rulers of the world.

## APPENDIX A

### Plutarch, *Luc.* 42. 3

A controversial passage in Plutarch's life of Lucullus requires consideration:

> *φιλοσοφίαν δὲ πᾶσαν μὲν ἠσπάζετο* [sc. Lucullus] *καὶ πρὸς πᾶσαν εὐμενὴς ἦν καὶ οἰκεῖος, ἴδιον δὲ τῆς Ἀκαδημείας ἐξ ἀρχῆς ἔρωτα καὶ ζῆλον ἔσχεν, οὐ τῆς νέας λεγομένης, καίπερ ἀνθούσης τότε τοῖς*

Καρνεάδου λόγοις διὰ Φίλωνος, ἀλλὰ τῆς παλαιᾶς, πιθανὸν ἄνδρα καὶ δεινὸν εἰπεῖν τότε προστάτην ἐχούσης τὸν Ἀσκαλωνίτην Ἀντίοχον, ὃν πάσῃ σπουδῇ ποιησάμενος φίλον ὁ Λεύκολλος καὶ συμβιωτὴν ἀντετάττετο τοῖς Φίλωνος ἀκροαταῖς, ὧν καὶ Κικέρων ἦν καὶ σύγγραμμά γε πάγκαλον ἐποίησεν εἰς τὴν αἵρεσιν.... (*Luc.* 42. 3)

The text has been discussed at some length by Glucker, who argues that it is muddled and unreliable; and he explains its confusions by supposing that Plutarch is compressing a Latin source which he has imperfectly understood ([71] 380–90).

There are two main difficulties. First, Plutarch implies that Lucullus took up with Antiochus at a time when the New Academy, in its Carneadean form, was flourishing under Philo. The date is not specified, but it must be in the 90s when Philo was still teaching New Academic doctrine at Athens and Antiochus had already broken with him. But, according to Glucker, 'Lucullus could not have met Philo in Athens—by the time he arrived there, Philo was already in exile' (380). Now it is true that Lucullus could not have met Philo in Athens *after 88*. But why could he not have done so on an earlier visit to Athens?

Cicero says that Lucullus devoted himself to philosophy 'nec vero ineunte aetate solum sed et pro quaestore aliquot annos et in ipso bello' (*Luc.* 4). The phrases *pro quaestore* and *in ipso bello* advert, I assume, to the years 87–80 and 74–67, during at least parts of which Antiochus was in Lucullus' company. *Ineunte aetate* refers to an earlier period, unspecified elsewhere in the *Lucullus*: perhaps, as Plutarch implies, Lucullus went to Athens as a young man and there studied philosophy with Antiochus? (If Cicero's *Luc.* is Plutarch's main or sole source for Lucullus' philosophical career, then Plutarch's ἐξ ἀρχῆς may simply be a translation of Cicero's *ineunte aetate*.)

The second difficulty concerns the phrase ὃν ... ἀντετάττετο τοῖς Φίλωνος ἀκροαταῖς. (Editors accept Reiske's ἀντετάττε; but see Glucker [71] 383 nn. 12 and 14.) Glucker takes the phrase to mean that Lucullus established Antiochus as a rival scholarch in opposition to Philo and his followers. But this is a historical absurdity; hence Glucker conjectures that ἀντετάττετο represents the Latin *anteposuit*: Plutarch's source said that Lucullus 'preferred' Antiochus to Philo, and Plutarch misunderstood the verb.

There is a better solution. Ἀντιτάττειν in the middle is normally intransitive, and so it can be taken in our text: ὅν is governed by the participle ποιησάμενος and not by the finite verb ἀντετάττετο. The sense is this: 'Having made Antiochus his friend and companion, Lucullus went into battle against Philo's followers, who included Cicero.' And that is surely what Plutarch meant to say; for it is precisely what purportedly happens in Cicero's *Lucullus*. (On this point I find that I have been anticipated by C. P. Jones, 'Plutarch, Lucullus 42, 3–4', *Hermes* 110 (1982) 254–6, who gives convincing Plutarchan parallels for the proposed construal of ὃν . . . ἀντετάττετο.)

## APPENDIX B

### Augustine, *Acad.* III. 41

Augustine's history of the Academy (*Acad.* III. 38–41) is based upon the fantastical premiss that the Academics, beseiged by Zeno and his followers, defended themselves by keeping the true Platonic doctrines hidden and professing a scepticism which was purely tactical. After Carneades' death the attacks diminished and the defenders could relax.

> Thus Antiochus, a pupil of Philo—Philo, who was, I think, a most distinguished man, had already begun as it were to open the gates (for the enemy were retreating) and to recall the Academy to the authority and the laws of Plato (though Metrodorus too had earlier tried to do so . . .)—Antiochus, as I had started to say, who had been a pupil of the Academic Philo and the Stoic Mnesarchus, found the old Academy empty of defenders and carefree in the absence of enemies: he insinuated himself in the guise of a supporter and fellow-citizen, introducing some poison or other from the ashes of Stoicism with which he violated the shrine of Plato. (III. 41)

Thus according to Augustine, while Antiochus was first advancing his new dogmatic philosophy, Philo had already shown himself in dogmatic dress. This might be taken to indicate that Philo had moved to dogmatism *before* the Roman books were out—perhaps during his last years in Athens before the exile. But first, Augustine's text is highly coloured, and the bias against Antiochus (whom Augustine has just called a *faeneus Platonicus*) is patent. We should not believe everything Augustine says. And secondly, the text describes an episode in Augustine's idiosyncratic and incredible history of the Academy—it is tied to his idea that the New Academy preserved an esoteric dogmatism. Everything about the story must be suspect.

## APPENDIX C

### Photius, *Bibl.* 212, 170 a 14–22

In his *Πυρρώνεια*, Aenesidemus contrasted his own Pyrrhonian scepticism with the sham scepticism of the Academy to which he had once belonged:

> Members of the Academy—especially of the present Academy—sometimes actually subscribe to Stoic doctrines, and if the truth be told they are evidently Stoics fighting Stoics. . . . they determine many things firmly and say that they dispute only about apprehensive impressions. (Photius, *Bibl.* 212, 170 a 14–17, 20–2)

Aenesidemus claims that the Academics are inconsistent: they persist in denying *κατάληψις* and yet they commit themselves to any number of dogmatic opinions: *τὸ γὰρ ἅμα τιθέναι τι καὶ αἴρειν ἀναμφιβόλως, ἅμα τε φάναι κοινῶς ὑπάρχειν ἀκαταληπτά, μάχην ὁμολογουμένην εἰσάγει* (170 a 30–2—*ἀκαταληπτά* is Hirzel's emendation of the transmitted *καταληπτά*: Glucker [71] 117 n. 67, has a more complicated proposal, but Hirzel's is simple and gives the right sense). He cannot be referring to Antiochus and his followers; for they did not fight with the Stoics. The reference is surely to Philo—and to the Philo who rejects the Stoic criterion while professing a form of dogmatism. (Aenesidemus claims to find this position inconsistent. It is not—and we might therefore wonder if he really is thinking of Philo. Perhaps there were some other Academics who did maintain an inconsistent position? But this is highly improbable. Aenesidemus is writing polemically—and his polemic is easily understood as directed against the dogmatic Philo.)

What is the date of all this? The chronology of Aenesidemus is a matter of long dispute. Various pieces of evidence can be arrayed, but one text must have primary importance. According to Photius, who had read Aenesidemus' *Πυρρώνεια*, the work was dedicated *τῶν ἐξ Ἀκαδημείας τινὶ συναιρεσιώτῃ Λευκίῳ Τοβέρωνι, γένος μὲν Ῥωμαίῳ, δόξης δὲ λαμπρῷ ἐκ προγόνων καὶ πολιτικὰς ἀρχὰς οὐ τὰς τυχούσας μετιόντι* (*Bibl.* 212, 169 b 32–5). The man must be L. Aelius Tubero, a friend of Cicero's, who ascribes philosophical interests to him (*Lig.* 21). Tubero may have been expected to achieve the highest honours, but so far as we know he did not. He served as a legate in Asia in 60 BC. If we assume that he was then in his thirties (a reasonable but by no means a mandatory assumption), then he will have been born in the first decade of the first century. Since the *Πυρρώνεια* was dedicated to him as he set out on the *cursus honorum*, it can hardly have been written earlier than the seventies. Even if Tubero served as a a legate at a relatively late age, the book cannot have been written before 85.

Thus we may believe that shortly after Athens had been liberated, Tubero and Aenesidemus were fellow-students in the Academy. Whether or not Philo had returned from Rome, the official Academic view was the one Philo had expressed in his Roman books. The Stoics were still the formal enemies, but the Academy itself was, in an ordinary sense of the term, dogmatic. The position disgusted Aenesidemus. He broke away and attempted to re-establish a rigorously sceptical philosophy.

## APPENDIX D

## Cicero, *Luc.* 16

Of Arcesilaus Cicero writes:

> Arcesilas Zenoni ut putatur obtrectans nihil novi reperienti sed emendanti superiores immutatione verborum . . . (*Luc.* 16)

The text is generally and easily understood as follows:

> Arcesilaus, it is thought, objects to Zeno on the grounds that he discovered nothing new . . .

Thus Cicero is ascribing to Arcesilaus the Antiochian thesis of the essential unity of the Stoa and the Old Academy. And since Cicero in this passage is giving *Antiochus*' version of the history of the Schools, we must suppose that Antiochus thought himself to be following the syncretism of Arcesilaus. But that is impossible. Arcesilaus construed Plato as a sceptic: he cannot have regarded Zeno as an Academic. And we have no reason to think that Antiochus was so ill-informed that he thought Arcesilaus had taken Plato for a dogmatist.

The solution is to construe *reperienti* in a concessive rather than an explanatory sense: it should be tied to *ut putatur* and not to *obtrectans*. The sense is then this:

> Arcesilaus objects to Zeno, as it is thought—though in fact Zeno discovered nothing new . . .

According to Antiochus, in other words, Arcesilaus' arguments are thought to be directed against the Stoics. This is a mistake, for the Stoics discovered nothing new. In point of fact, Arcesilaus' arguments—whatever *he* thought of them—are directed against the Old Academy.

## APPENDIX E

## Antiochus and Plato's Forms

We know that Antiochus gave a brief account of the function of Ideas in Plato's epistemology (Cic. *Acad.* 30), and observed that Aristotle had exploded the theory (ibid. 33). It is plain that the ἰδέαι or *species* to which Antiochus refers are Forms or Ideas in the standard Platonic sense. They have a function in the epistemological system described at *Acad.* 30–2. This is called the *forma prima* of the Old Academic philosophy: it is not the perfected form, to which Antiochus himself subscribed—and in the account of Antiochus' epistemology in *Luc.* the Forms are not even mentioned. It seems clear, then, that Antiochus' interest in the Forms was purely historical: they had a role in the philosophical drama from which the system of the *veteres* derived; but they had no role in the derived system itself.

Theiler [72] nonetheless argued that Antiochus was responsible for the reintroduction of the Theory of Forms into serious philosophy; among recent scholars Dillon [73] and Donini [99] have followed him. But their arguments are, I think, frail. Donini [99] 95, says that 'Cicero's text, *Acad.* 33, requires us to recognize that Antiochus is (mildly) hostile to Aristotle's criticism of the Forms, and hence that for his part he accepts the Platonic doctrine'. I can see no trace of hostility, however mild, in the text. Dillon accepts Theiler's ascription to Antiochus ([72] 17) of the famous text on beauty at Cicero, *Orat.* 8; Donini relies heavily on the testimony of Seneca, *Ep.* 58. and 65. But there are no adequate grounds for seeing Antiochus behind these passages. In the Preface to the second edition of *Die Vorbereitung*, Theiler explicitly says that his claim about the Forms finds positive support in no ancient text. He is right.

Dillon also offers a general argument:

> If Antiochus is . . . prepared to talk about Ideas, as, indeed, being a professed Platonist, he could hardly help doing, the conclusion seems unavoidable that he identified them with 'cognitive perceptions', the objects of knowledge in the Stoic system ([73] 93).

It is the first part of the quotation which matters here. (I will not ask how Antiochus could have identified Forms with φαντασίαι καταληπτικαί. Nor will I quibble over the word 'Platonist'—though it is perhaps true and perhaps important that Antiochus regarded himself as an Academic rather than as a Platonist.) Why suppose that every Platonist—or rather, every Academic—must have accepted the theory of Ideas? Did Arcesilaus? Did Carneades? Did Philo? We may think—perhaps wrongly—that the Theory of Ideas is the centre-piece of Platonism, the core and essence of Plato's philosophy. But did Antiochus think so? As far as we know, he did not: Aristotle disposed of the Forms, and the philosophical system which remains when they are removed is still, in Antiochus' eyes, the Academic system. Antiochus did not feel the need to 'interpret' the Ideas in Stoic terms; he did not believe in the Ideas; and he knew that you could be a loyal Academic while rejecting the Ideas. (Cf. Sedley, below, pp. 99–100.)

# 4
# Philosophical Allegiance in the Greco-Roman World

DAVID SEDLEY*

AT the risk of over-generalization, I shall be claiming in this paper that in the Greco-Roman world, especially during the Hellenistic and Roman periods, what gives philosophical movements their cohesion and identity is less a disinterested common quest for the truth than a virtually religious commitment to the authority of a founder figure. More specifically, I shall try to illustrate how this kind of loyalty can look when put into practice, using the earliest datable instance known to me, from the writings of the first-century BC Epicurean Philodemus. I accept that there may be individual professed school-adherents who break this pattern. But the pattern itself must be appreciated before the nature of any such exceptions can be understood.

## I. IPSE DIXIT

There is a familiar contrast between the well-regimented Epicureans, all but enslaved to their sect's official doctrines, and the emancipated, freebooting Stoics, all of them busy disagreeing with each other.[1] This characterization does scant justice to either school. Both groups equally were ruled by a set of

* I am grateful to a number of people at the Oxford Seminar whose comments on that occasion helped me, and in particular to Professor P. A. Brunt and to Miriam Griffin, who made me think harder about, respectively, Ariston and Seneca. I have no idea whether they will think the result any improvement. I am also grateful for extremely helpful written comments supplied by Jonathan Barnes, Myles Burnyeat, William Jordan, Francesca Longo Auricchio, Peter Roots and Richard Sorabji.

[1] This characterization of the two schools goes back at least to Numenius (*ap.* Euseb. *Praep. Evang.* XIV. 5. 3–4). Seneca, *Ep.* 33. 4, is sometimes taken to make the same contrast (cf. Griffin, above, p. 16, n. 27); but, as I understand it, the discussion there concerns not doctrinal authority, but the more literary question of which authors it is legitimate to plunder for quotations. On this the Stoics and Epicureans did indeed differ in the way Seneca says.

canonical texts. For the Epicureans, these were the writings of Epicurus himself and of his three leading co-founders, Metrodorus, Hermarchus, and Polyaenus. For the Stoics, they were the works of their founder Zeno of Citium. It was every bit as unthinkable for a Stoic to criticize Zeno, or to question his authority, as it was for an Epicurean to show such disrespect to Epicurus. Of course, the Stoics were constantly at loggerheads with each other. But as often as not what they were quarrelling about was the correct way to interpret and expound the views of Zeno.[2] I can think of no instance in which any of Zeno's successors in the school is reported as ever suggesting that Zeno had been *wrong* about anything. On the other hand, no Stoic seems to have thought twice before attacking the views of the school's greatest leader, Chrysippus.

There is just one real difference between the schools, so far as their adherence to authority is concerned. Epicurus and his colleagues had set out the system in massive detail, leaving room for their successors to indulge in only occasional disagreements about the school position on important issues. (We shall be examining one such case in the next section.)[3] Zeno, by contrast, seems to have been an inspirational rather than a systematic teacher, leaving vast areas of unclarity about his teachings for his successors to illuminate, and much virgin territory, including logic, for them to colonize. As a result, his heirs had as much scope for innovation and for disagreement among

[2] Examples are: the disagreements between Cleanthes and Chrysippus as to what Zeno had meant by *φαντασία* (Sext. Emp. *M.* VII. 227–41), and whether he had believed in a unity or a plurality of virtues (Plut. *Mor.* 441A–C; 1034C–E; cf. Long and Sedley [1] sect. 61); and the independent attempt by virtually every Stoic from Cleanthes to Posidonius to encapsulate the precise meaning of Zeno's formula for the ethical end, *ὁμολογουμένως ζῆν* (cf. Long and Sedley [1] sects. 63–4). Cf. also the attempts by later Stoics to vindicate Zeno's much mocked theological syllogisms (see M. Schofield, 'The syllogisms of Zeno of Citium', *Phronesis* 28 (1983) 31–58); and Chrysippus' defence, in his work *On Zeno's proper use of terminology*, of Zeno's ethical paradoxes (D.L. VII. 122).

[3] Other disagreements include those about the grounds for hedonism, and about the basis of friendship (Cic. *Fin.* I. 31, 66–70). For some further instances, see Philodemus, *Πρὸς τοὺς* [?, (ed. F. Sbordone, *Philodemi Adversus* [*sophistas*], *e papyro Herculanensi 1005* (Naples, 1947) ); Longo Auricchio and Tepedino Guerra [250], which also includes discussion of the notoriously problematic distinction between 'genuine' and 'sophistical' Epicureans at D.L. X. 26. Philodemus, it should be added, supplies plenty of evidence (e.g. in the *De signis*) that in his day Epicurean theories had been expanded and updated to meet contemporary challenges from the Stoa and elsewhere.

themselves as they could reasonably require, while still remaining (as each undoubtedly saw himself) scrupulously loyal to the founder.

It would, I think, be safest to say that it was only after a founder's death that his teachings were likely to become truly canonical. There is no reason to think that either Epicurus or Zeno was seen as above criticism in his own lifetime and within his own circle of philosophical friends and pupils. Among Epicurus' immediate pupils there was a degree of philosophical independence which, if slight by most standards, was striking for a later, traditional Epicurean like Philodemus.[4] And it is hard to see how the deviant early Stoic Aristo of Chios can have presented his insistence on the absolute and literal indifference of moral intermediates as anything other than a disagreement with Zeno.[5] Here the likely explanation is that at this formative stage of Stoic philosophy it was Socrates who still loomed for both Zeno and Ariston as the great authority figure.[6] It is difficult at the best of times for a living philosopher to achieve the infallibility of a dead saint.

The history of the Academy is not dissimilar. Plato ran a school in which a healthy degree of dissent was in evidence. Although the theory of Forms was in some sense school doctrine—at least to the extent that Aristotle in his Academic phase could write of it as what 'we' Platonists say[7]—Aristotle himself felt free to reject it, as did Speusippus and others. Whether Speusippus, during his period as Plato's successor, tried to represent his philosophy as authentically Platonic, is hard to say on the evidence available. But at least in subsequent generations there is every reason to believe that all Academics presented themselves as loyal to Plato's thought, on *some* interpretation of what that thought amounted to. Fortunately Plato's writings were open to an immense range of interpretations, so that the same succession of loyalists could comfortably include

[4] See Philodemus, *De libertate dicendi* fr. 6; *De Epicuro* II (P. Herc. 1289), 6. III (texts and discussion in D. Sedley, 'Epicurus and the Mathematicians of Cyzicus', *Cronache ercolanesi* 6 (1976) 23–54, pp. 27–8 and 46, and in Angeli [12] 50).

[5] See A.-M. Ioppolo, *Aristone di Chio e lo stoicismo antico* (Naples, 1980), especially 152 ff.

[6] This is powerfully argued by A. A. Long, 'The Hellenistic view of Socrates', *CQ* 38 (1988) 151–71.

[7] *Met.* 990a33–993a10.

both the system-building Xenocrates and the sceptical dialectician Arcesilaus.

The glaring exception to all this is the Peripatos. Although Aristotle's close collaborator and successor Theophrastus evidently saw his aim as a continuation and extention of Aristotle's projects, his own successor Strato was a highly independent physical theorist who cannot by any stretch of the imagination be represented as a committed Aristotelian, and who did not even manage to retain for the school the manuscripts of Aristotle's own works. It is perhaps then no coincidence that from the beginning of Strato's headship (267 BC) the school rapidly declined in importance, virtually vanishing as a philosophical force in the remainder of the third century.[8] It re-emerged only in the course of the second century under the headship of Critolaus, who appears to have reverted to a form of orthodox Aristotelianism. And it was arguably only with the belated establishment of a set of canonical school texts by Andronicus in the late first century BC that Aristotelianism was able to become once again a major presence on the philosophical stage. Thus the Peripatos' fall from prominence under Strato only serves to re-emphasize the indispensable cohesive force exerted by a school's commitment to its scriptures. Without them, there was no school.

Under the Roman Empire the large centralized schools gave way to individual teachers with their small groups of adherents, but the role of loyalty to scriptures remained integral to the philosophical enterprise.[9] To meet the demand, the forgery industry gathered pace, and innumerable epistles of Socrates, Diogenes the Cynic, Aristotle, and others came into circulation. For the vast majority of thinkers in this period, however, the revered text was either that of Plato, commonly regarded as divine, or of course the Old and/or New Testament, which were taken to represent, most prominently, the authority of Moses and St. Paul respectively. Even a double allegiance, such as to Plato *and* the Bible, was not uncommon.

The rules of the game admit of further refinements. One

[8] On this decline, see Lynch [77].

[9] For the character of philosophical groups in this period see especially Glucker [71]. The role of loyalty to tradition and texts in ancient Platonism is well brought out in Dörrie [74] esp. 16–32.

twist is that acknowledged forerunners of one's primary authority could themselves bear secondary authority-status. Thus Platonists could revere Socrates or Pythagoras, and Stoics could if they wished revere Plato or Socrates—as they increasingly did. Indeed, the antiquity of a doctrine was itself standardly advertised as one of the grounds for expecting it to be true, so that if one could show one's own tradition to be older than that of a rival school this in itself lent it additional authority. A nice example is the dispute about the pedigree of the identity puzzle known as the Growing Argument, over which the Stoic Chrysippus spilt much ink.[10] The Academics pointed out that the gist of it was already to be found in Plato.[11] Opponents of the Academy could counter that Plato himself had filched it from Epicharmus.[12] The Academics conceded this,[13] but found salvation in the tradition that Epicharmus was himself an associate of the Pythagoreans,[14] Pythagoras being an acknowledged forerunner of Plato's. Thus the puzzle could be ascribed to Pythagoras, and so reappropriated to the Academic tradition.

So far I must have given the impression of trying to reduce ancient philosophy, as practised from the fourth century BC down to the sixth century AD, to a rather mindless enterprise, in which the *ex cathedra* pronouncements of long-dead saints counted for more than open-minded inquiry and debate. This is by no means the correct consequence to draw. The role of scriptural authority was to provide a philosophical movement with a *raison d'être* and a framework within which it could preserve its cohesion *while* continuing to inquire and debate. At one extreme, we have the Epicurean school, whose scriptural framework was, for reasons I have described, rather rigid and

[10] Cf. D. Sedley, 'The Stoic criterion of identity', *Phronesis* 27 (1982) 255–75, and texts in Long and Sedley [1] sect. 28. What follows is somewhat speculative, to the extent that it cannot be proved that all the moves and countermoves originally occurred in the order given here.

[11] Anon. *In Plat. Theaet.* LXX. 9–12.

[12] Alcimus (date uncertain, unless he is the 4th-cent. BC Sicilian historian of that name) *ap.* D.L. III. 9–11; Chrysippus *ap.* Plut. *Mor.* 1083 A.

[13] Pl. *Theaet.* 152 E; anon. *In Plat. Theaet.* LXXI. 12 ff.; Plut. *Mor.* 1083 A.

[14] Anon. *In Plat. Theaet.* LXX. 5–9; LXXI. 12. In [27] 76, I have likewise suggested that the Dialectical school of Diodorus chose as its 'founder' Clinomachus, a figure of the early or mid 4th cent., partly in order to establish the priority of its own logical tradition over the competing traditions of the Academy and Peripatos.

well-defined. But at the other extreme there were the sceptics of the New Academy, and, from the first century BC on, the Pyrrhonist sceptics. For Academics like Arcesilaus and Carneades, Plato's sanction was contained in the dialectical methodology and spirit of open-ended debate energetically pursued in his Socratic dialogues. Far from committing them to any fixed doctrines, the Platonic scriptures encouraged them to shun anything so intellectually stultifying. Their first-century BC successors in the Academy could even, with a touch of paradox, invoke Socrates and Plato as providing authority for the practice of never relying on authority.[15] Likewise Pyrrhonists could invoke Pyrrho as their patron saint merely because, as portrayed by his pupil Timon, he had embodied in his own life the detached tranquillity to which their debates represented a means. The Stoics, as I have described them, fall somewhere between these two extremes.

The strongest point that should be made in defence of ancient philosophers is that they did not make it their practice to treat a founder's authority as sufficient proof of a tenet. (In Cicero's eyes, it was only the Pythagorean sect that stooped to that.)[16] That their founder was unfailingly right they never doubted. But much of their energy went into finding the arguments to *prove* him right.

My object, then, has been not to devalue ancient philosophical schools, but to warn against a temptation to assimilate their ways to those of a modern philosophy department, forgetting the additional self-imposed constraints under which they operated. Even a movement ruled by scriptural authority, whether this be the Bible or the writings of Marx, can throw up

[15] Cic. *Nat. D.* I. 10–12; cf. *Luc.* 8–9, 60; *Tusc.* V. 83; Galen, *Opt. doctr.* I. 40 K ( = Long and Sedley [1] 68 V). Some Neoplatonists (e.g. Olymp. *In Gorg.* 214. 13–25) cited *Alc. I* 114 E 7–9 and *Phd.* 91 C 1–2 as Plato's authorization for Aristotle's departure (if any) from Platonic authority. Cf. Tarán [254].

[16] Cic. *Nat. D.* I. 10, plus numerous parallel passages catalogued by Pease [323] i. 149–50; Cicero never makes the same allegation against any other school, not even the Epicureans. K. Popper, 'Back to the Presocratics', in his *Conjectures and refutations* (London, 1963), repr. in D. J. Furley and R. E. Allen (eds.), *Studies in Presocratic Philosophy* i (London, 1970), 130–53, sect. XI, regards the Pythagoreans as the only authority-bound Presocratic school. This may be right, if only because there perhaps were no other Presocratic 'schools' in any recognizable sense. (Even Cratylus the 'Heraclitizer' felt able to criticize Heraclitus on at least one point, Arist. *Met.* 1010$^a$10–15.)

a brilliantly original thinker, and Plotinus' achievement as a card-carrying Platonist is in no way inferior to those of Aquinas and Lukács within their own respective movements.

## 2. PHILODEMUS

Philodemus of Gadara is, or should be, a figure of considerable interest to historians of ancient thought.[17] Scarcely a leader of opinion, he is nevertheless, one may speculate, a typical *teacher* of Epicureanism, spreading his school's gospel at the intersection of the Greek and Roman worlds. For much of the last half century of the Roman Republic he taught Epicureanism in the Naples region, where he was respected by Roman intellectuals as an authority on the subject.[18] Thanks to the volcanic accident which preserved remnants of his library for us in a suburban villa at Herculaneum, we can gain a variety of insights into his philosophical outlook.

Philodemus had studied Epicureanism in Athens around the beginning of the first century BC, under the then scholarch Zeno of Sidon, and his own brand of Epicureanism tries to be scrupulously faithful to Zeno's interpretations of the master's doctrines. This illustrates an aspect of school loyalty not touched on in the previous section (once again inviting obvious analogies with institutionalized religion): a school member's response to the texts he reveres, although it may in a few instances (as many have suspected in the case of Lucretius) be a direct one, is more likely to be mediated and shaped by his own living teacher. Indeed, in Philodemus' philosophical texts the debt to his master is greater still, for some of them are really just his writing up of the lecture notes he took at Zeno's classes in Athens. His book *On frankness* (*Περὶ παρρησίας*), which itself deals with the topic of master–pupil relationships, is marked below the title as being *ἐκ τῶν Ζήνωνος σχολῶν*, that is,

[17] The long-standing neglect of Philodemus has been energetically countered by work in Naples over the last eighteen years, especially with the succession of articles on him in *Cronache ercolanesi*, and with Marcello Gigante's pioneering [135].

[18] Cicero, as a speaker in his *De Finibus* II. 119 (dramatic date 50 BC), refers to Philodemus and his colleague Siro as 'optimos', 'doctissimos', and 'familiares', and implies that he would consult them on difficult doctrinal matters. This should be taken more seriously than the points which Cicero scores off him in the *In Pisonem*, as a way of hitting at Philodemus' patron Piso.

probably, based on notes 'from Zeno's classes', as is at least one other work, of uncertain content. Some others show clear dependence on Zeno, especially *On signs*, which is a report of a debate on scientific method between Stoics and Epicureans in the late second century BC. Philodemus simply reproduces his own notes on Zeno's lectures, plus those of his fellow pupil Bromius, who (as he makes clear in col. XIX) had attended a different set of Zeno's lectures from himself, appending for good measure the Epicurean Demetrius of Laconia's very similar account of the same debate, possibly based on a published work by Demetrius. Not only Zeno's arguments, but also the Stoic ones to which they are rejoinders, are known to Philodemus from those classes in Athens: he himself has no direct acquaintance with the opponents, and no personal involvement in the debate. We cannot know whether all, or most, of Philodemus' doctrinal texts are of similar status and provenance (apart from the *Rhetorica*, to which we will turn shortly), but it seems not over-bold to suggest that many of his works should be thought of as in some ways comparable in content to Arrian's transcripts of Epictetus' teaching. He may even have deliberately concentrated on those topics on which Zeno himself had lectured but never published.[19]

There is not even any solid evidence to suggest that these works of Philodemus were themselves, strictly speaking, published. They may well have been produced purely for teaching purposes. At least, no doctrinal treatise by Philodemus is ever cited in any ancient source.[20] What he was demonstrably

[19] To judge from the fragments more or less reliably ascribed to Zeno by Angeli and Colaizzo [11] Zeno wrote (fr. 12) on physics, ends, grammar, ἱστορία, proverbs, diction, the use of poetry, and piety; (fr. 27) on geometry; and perhaps (fr. 28) on women. Of these topics, only 'piety', 'diction' (cf. Phld. *Rhet.* I. 156. 10–14 Sudhaus), and to some extent 'the use of poetry' match known works by Philodemus. In the *Rhetorica*, written in support of Zeno's views on rhetoric (see below), Philodemus tells us explicitly (II a. LIII. 12–13—see below, n. 31) that Zeno had not himself published the views.

[20] Strong correspondences have been noted between works of Philodemus and later works by others: e.g. between *Piet.* 3–17 and Cic. *Nat. D.* I. 25–41, see H. Diels, *Doxographi Graeci* (Berlin, 1879), 529–50; and between his *De musica* and Sext. Emp. *M.* VI, see Gigante [38] ch. 7. Direct influence is clearly one possible explanation of these resemblances; but another is the existence of a common source. In the case of the *Rhetorica*, Cavallo, [262] 63–4, distinguishes papyri containing working drafts of individual books from others containing the definitive edition. I am not sure how much, if anything, can be inferred from this about the work's public circulation. But for an attempt to establish the influence of the *Rhetorica* on Sextus Empiricus, see Longo Auricchio [260].

known for in the literary world was, first, his rather elegant poetry (on non-philosophical themes), which is mentioned by Cicero,[21] and which survived antiquity through the regular manuscript tradition; and second, his works of philosophical historiography, of which many fragments have survived through the Herculaneum library. Of these, his *Σύνταξις τῶν φιλοσόφων* is cited by Diogenes Laertius (x. 3). And his *Περὶ τῶν 'Επικούρου τε καί τινων ἄλλων πραγματεῖαι μνημάτων*, 'Studies of documents concerning Epicurus and some others',[22] looks very much like an original piece of biographical research, assembling data about the lives and characters of individuals from the collected and dated letters of the early Epicureans. Indeed, could his labelling the work as 'Philodemus' *πραγματεῖαι . . .*' be precisely his way of indicating that this is (for once) his own original work? A book of uncertain authorship which Philodemus had in his library (PHerc 176)[23] puts together letters proving the great humanity and kindness of the early Epicurean master Polyaenus—he was nice to children (fr. 5 col. XXIII), and even to Stoics (fr. 5 col. XXIV)—and that Philodemus himself developed this portrait in some published work is strongly suggested by the report in Diogenes Laertius x. 24: 'Polyaenus was a man of integrity and kindness, as the circle of Philodemus say.' His biographical techniques, so far as they can be gleaned from his fragments, are scholarly, and if his literary reputation in antiquity was more that of a biographer (and poet) than that of a philosopher, this may have been quite just. It is, at least, easy to see why an Epicurean working in Italy might be nervous of developing doctrinal ideas for himself, in isolation from the current climate of thought in the Garden at Athens, and why secondary literary activities like philosophical biography should be for him the much less hazardous option.[24]

One of the school concerns of which Philodemus' library can afford us a glimpse is that of establishing the canon of Epicurean authorities. Four founding members were traditionally

[21] Cic. *Pis.* 70–1.

[22] For text, see Spina [14].

[23] Text in Vogliano [10] 21–55. According to Cavailo, [262] 44, 57, 60, the papyrus is probably of the 2nd cent. BC—too early to be by Philodemus himself.

[24] One work which scarcely fits my descriptions so far is his *On the good king according to Homer* (ed. Dorandi [16]). I am inclined to agree with Murray [142] that this work falls altogether outside Philodemus' philosophical activities.

accorded canonical status: Epicurus, Metrodorus, Hermarchus, and Polyaenus, a group known collectively as *οἱ ἄνδρες*,[25] which I would tentatively translate 'the Great Men'. Their works were not all handbooks of doctrine; some, such as at least parts of Epicurus' *On nature*, represented rather the actual process of working out, debating, and refining the details of the system. It is unlikely that they always wrote with an eye to the future canonical status of their words, and it would be surprising if the result had not been occasional divergences of view. When their texts achieved canonical status in subsequent generations, much tidying up remained to be done. The business of establishing a reasonably consistent and authoritative canon out of their works had at least three discernible aspects.

One of these (with obvious biblical parallels) was the branding of certain works as apocryphal. At least, Philodemus speaks of someone, usually taken to be his master Zeno, who questioned the authenticity of a number of works attributed to Epicurus, Metrodorus, Polyaenus, and Hermarchus.[26] It is, I think, no coincidence that it should be precisely these four—the four authoritative founding fathers—who are singled out for such treatment. If works by, or attributed to, other leading members of the school, such as Idomeneus or Polystratus, seemed to clash with the official party line, that would pose no threat to the current orthodoxies, but such a situation could hardly be comfortable when it came to the infallible four. At any rate, we shall shortly hear of Philodemus turning one of Zeno's verdicts of inauthenticity, that on Polyaenus, *Against the orators*, to just the sort of purpose I have indicated.[27]

The second kind of activity is one of textual scholarship. Inevitably, there were individual cruces in the canonical works. Epicurus and his colleagues might have slipped up with an

[25] See Longo Auricchio [251]. The fuller title is perhaps [*το*]*ῖς ἀν*[*δρ*]*άσιν κ*[*αθ'*] *οὓς* [*φι*]*λοσοφοῦμεν* (art. cit. T 24).

[26] Zeno fr. 25 in Angeli and Colaizzo [11].

[27] I hope this diagnosis will not seem excessively cynical. Naturally I am not questioning Zeno's sincerity in believing these texts to be apocryphal, but it is dangerous to assume that such judgements are examples of nothing more than disinterested scholarship on his part. Zeno has been applauded (wrongly, in my view) by some modern scholars for questioning the authenticity of Epicurus' *Letter to Pythocles*. In this instance we simply cannot know whether there were other astronomical works in the canon with which it was out of step, and hence whether Zeno's doubts were motivated by anything more than disinterested scholarship.

invalid or incoherent argument, or an assertion which seemed at odds with their usual position or with the truth; or a text might be genuinely corrupt. Thus in Philodemus' library we find a work (PHerc 1012) by Demetrius of Laconia, a respected Epicurean contemporary of Zeno of Sidon, discussing just such cruces.[28] Demetrius discusses the precise text of Epicurus, *Kuriai Doxai* 3, comparing MS readings (col. XXXVIII), a passage in which Epicurus apparently gave an incoherent description of the motion of minimal magnitudes (XLVIII–L), and one in which Epicurus located the rational mind in the chest (cols. XLII–XLVII), a view which had accorded with medical opinion in his own day but which was now out of date, thanks to advances in anatomical research. (This last is a reminder of a familiar problem in many religious orthodoxies—how to square biblical texts with modern science.) Demetrius' own preferred methods of solution cannot easily be extracted from the fragments, but he makes it clear that some, including Zeno, were ready to posit scribal errors in such cases.

A third difficulty to be confronted was that Epicurus himself had said explicitly that some of his own and his colleagues' earlier work had been mistaken—a prominent theme in the fragments of Book XXVIII of his *On nature*.[29] Here there was no choice but to exclude the discredited texts from the canon. We learn from Philodemus that these Epicurean juvenilia were classed under the title *τὰ ἀρχαῖα* or *τὰ ἀρχαϊκά*,[30] 'the early works'; and he concedes that they contain mistakes.

So far I have tried to outline the Epicureans' attitude to their scriptural authorities. But far more can be learnt by looking more closely at one text in which these attitudes and methods are brought to bear on an actual problem. Philodemus' *Rhetorica* is a work in at least six books, composed over many years in the mid first century BC.[31] Book II, although not a mere

[28] See Puglia [264].

[29] Ed. Sedley [9].

[30] Philodemus, *De Stoicis* XI. 4–22; see Dorandi [75]. In the papyrus of Epicurus, *De Natura* XXVIII, below the title there appear the words ] ṭῶν ἀρχαίωṿ [ . In my edition (see previous note) I followed Vogliano's conjecture ἐκ] ṭῶν ἀρχαίωṿ [, 'from the old exemplars', but I am now more inclined to see here the remains of a phrase meaning roughly 'concerning the early works'.

[31] For the date, see Gigante [136] 19. S. Sudhaus' valuable Teubner edition (*Philodemi Volumina Rhetorica*, 2 vols. plus supplement (Leipzig, 1892–6) ) is now superseded, for Books I and II, by Longo Auricchio [13], which I shall be following except where I

transcript of Zeno's lectures, has as its central aim to vindicate, against a rival view current within the school, Zeno's interpretation of the early Epicureans' policy on rhetoric, namely that Epicurus' condemnation of rhetoric as not a proper expertise (τέχνη) applied only to political and forensic rhetoric, and not to 'sophistic' rhetoric. That is, that while applied rhetoric, as a means of persuading the public, is a quite unmethodical enterprise in psychology, the literary exercise of model speech writing, as once taught by the Sophists at Athens, is a proper discipline. 'Sophistic' rhetoric is, as Philodemus makes fairly explicit, equivalent to what was more frequently called 'epideictic' rhetoric, and it has rightly been observed that what the Epicureans have in mind is in effect the art of prose writing.[32] Clearly Epicurus *could* have thought this to include techniques which it might even be respectable for a philosopher to acquire for use in non-oratorical contexts—he does, after all, employ its artifices himself in his ethical writings—and Zeno was no doubt concerned to justify his own cult of an elegant lecturing style,[33] as well, conceivably, as seeing advantages for pupil recruitment in putting such a discipline as prose writing on the school curriculum. In line with a long tradition of debate starting from Plato's *Gorgias*, showing rhetoric to be a genuine expertise (rather than, say, a mere knack) was accepted as a necessary, though not a sufficient, condition of its respectability.

In evaluating the arguments on both sides of the debate, it is advisable to start out with a healthy degree of agnosticism as to which party, if either, is in the right. It is certainly not enough to reason that since Philodemus constantly affirms his strict Epicurean orthodoxy he *must* be telling us the truth. One thing that goes without saying in such a dispute is that both parties consider themselves scrupulously loyal to Epicurus, and that

---

indicate a divergence. I shall use 'II a' for the part of *Rhet.* II preserved in PHerc 1674, and 'II b' for the part preserved in PHerc 1672. In my translations, words enclosed in angle brackets, ⟨ ⟩, are guesses as to the sense of what is lost in lacunae. Some of the relevant portions of this text are usefully gathered and discussed in Longo Auricchio [261]; cf. also [250]. For the relation of the *Rhetorica* to the ancient debate to which it contributes, see especially Barnes [256]; Isnardi Parente [259] esp. 385 ff.; Angeli [255] 73–5. These last two include some particularly salutary remarks on Philodemus' and his immediate Epicurean opponents' respective interpretations of the evidence.

[32] See Hubbell [258] 255. Cf. Ferrario [257]; Angeli [255] 74; Longo Auricchio and Tepedino Guerra [250] 30–1.

[33] According to Cic. *Nat. D.* I. 59, Zeno spoke 'distincte, graviter, ornate'.

each brands the other as heretical. And the very existence of this bitter dispute makes it inherently unlikely that there was a single simple answer to the question what the Epicurean founders had thought about the technical standing of sophistic rhetoric. Indeed, Philodemus implicitly concedes that most of what the founders had written about rhetoric had concerned not the sophistic branch but the political (II a. XXXIV. 28–31).

As a matter of fact, there are at least *three* different positions at stake, although they are not all given equal space in Philodemus' discussion. (1) Of the three branches of rhetoric, Zeno and Philodemus held that the political and the forensic were not τέχναι, but that the sophistic was. (2) Philodemus' main opponents in this work, one of whom had written a rejoinder to Zeno's view, held that no rhetoric was a τέχνη. (3) The work *Against the orators*, ascribed to Polyaenus, treated all rhetoric without distinction as a τέχνη (II a. XXII. 34–XXIII. 14); this same view perhaps influenced Bromius, Philodemus' friend (as he calls him, II a. XXXIV. 13–15) and fellow pupil at Zeno's school, who discussed only the political branch, and called it a τέχνη (II a. XXXIV. 11–31). But position (3) does not receive very extended treatment:[34] Philodemus is more than happy to endorse Zeno's dismissal of the work by 'Polyaenus' as inauthentic (II a. XXIII. 7–11; cf. above). There may even have been good scholarly grounds for the dismissal—we cannot know. But an ulterior motive is not far to seek.

We can now join the text in Book II of the *Rhetorica*, at the point where Philodemus undertakes to cite chapter and verse in favour of the Zenonian position:

But now let us move on to showing that it is not the case that while we call sophistic rhetoric an expertise the founders of our sect say the opposite;[35] and that it is not just we, but they too, who call political

[34] Bromius is criticized at II a. XXXIV–XXXVI. It must be borne in mind that to hold position (3) is not necessarily to approve of any, let alone all rhetoric. When Epicurus called forensic rhetoric a κακοτεχνία (fr. 51 Usener), he may have meant that it is a phoney τέχνη, but equally he may have meant that it is a real τέχνη (with methodical principles, etc.), but a morally bad one. This ambiguity itself illustrates the kind of difficulty faced by Epicureans hoping to squeeze too much theoretical content out of their school scriptures.

[35] At II a. XLIII. 28 Usener read ἡμεῖς ⟨μέν⟩. With or without the supplement, I take the interpretation implied by Usener to be right, and I translate accordingly. At II a. XLIII. 35–6 I read (with Gomperz) οὐχ ἡμεῖς, ἀλλὰ κἀκεῖ|νο⟨ι⟩.

rhetoric a kind of research and observation developed by practice. I shall cite the texts and the expressions by which Zeno thought these points were made clear.

Well, what would one make of the fact that in his *On rhetoric* Epicurus continually speaks of 'the schools of rhetoric', and 'the abilities produced by the schools', and in addition 'the elegant output of the schools', and that he says also 'their discipline', and 'the instructions and precepts about argument, enthymemes and the rest', and so on? (II a. XLIII. 26–XLIV. 19)

In II a. XXXVIII Philodemus has cited a general definition of a *τέχνη*: it uses universal principles and produces regular results; and in what follows, this is treated as boiling down to 'method'. In the current passage, it is evidently *teachability* that he is using as a criterion, on the ground that nothing unmethodical could be teachable; it would be, at best, a knack picked up by trial and error, as Philodemus here claims political rhetoric to be.

It is hard to see how the evidence adduced in this first argument can help Philodemus' case. Epicurus' terminology here may be, as it were, in quotation marks, describing the rhetorical schools as they present themselves to the world, in which case it would tell us nothing of his own attitude to them. But even if it does represent Epicurus' own view of them, it is unfortunately at least as favourable to position (3) as to position (1), since, as far as one can tell, he is speaking about rhetoric in general, without distinguishing any one branch.

Philodemus now turns from Epicurus to Hermarchus:

But Hermarchus also, in some letter to Theopheides written in the archonship of Menecles [=267/6 BC], is of the same opinion. (II a. XLIV. 19–23)

There follows, at II a. XLIV. 23–IL. 19, a long and fragmentary retort of Hermarchus to a text of the dialectician Alexinus which attacked the useless pedantries of sophistic rhetoricians but conceded that rhetoric could be useful too. The significance of Hermarchus' reply, for Philodemus' purposes, apparently consists in the fact that at least once (II a. XLVII. 17–18) he spoke of *ῥητορικὴ τέχνη*. Even Philodemus apparently realizes, at the end, that the passage has not done much to strengthen his case, for his sole comment on it is:

I have cited the full context as well in case anyone is keen to have it too; I realize that it will be seem to have been written about a different topic, not the one in hand. (II a. IL. 19–27)

He finally moves on to Metrodorus:

Metrodorus too, in *On poems* I, seems to imply[36] clearly enough the view that sophistic rhetoric is an expertise. (II a. IL. 27–33)

What follows, at II a. IL. 33–LI. 29, is a set of excerpts from Metrodorus' work, in which he speaks several times of a rhetorical τέχνη and 'the τέχνη of Thrasymachus or some other of them' (II a. L. 14–16), implying, in Philodemus' eyes, that sophistic rhetoric is an expertise.

Philodemus now concludes his survey:

Such then are the passages which we can cite as a result of our study, passages which avoid both the loose sense [i.e. of τέχνη: as explained in cols. XLI–XLII] and the sense which implies that what is being spoken of is the sophistic precepts (which are themselves also, by an equivocal usage, called *technai*), as will be known by anyone who has attended with understanding even to the actual texts we have cited, but more so by one who has absorbed the entire writings of the Great Men. (II a. LI. 29–LII. 10)

Here he has correctly reminded us of the complication that τέχνη can be used in a loose or 'catachrestic' sense for almost any acquired capacity—we can call someone an 'expert flatterer', for instance, without seriously implying that he has mastered some methodical discipline. It is indeed a rather obvious challenge to Philodemus' argument that the texts which he cites from the 'Great Men' may be using τέχνη in some such loose way. He himself is quite confident that this would be a misreading. But he offers no solid basis for his confidence, beyond the intuitive feeling for the precise meaning of these texts which years of study have taught him. In short, he has become so used to reading the authoritative texts in a certain way that he cannot see how they could be read differently. He has so far shown no real ability for *arguing* an interpretation of a text.

[36] παρεμφαίνειν: to 'indicate incidentally', hence to 'imply' rather than to state explicitly. Cf. Chrysippus' use of the word at *SVF* ii. 895; also Polybius XII. 24. 2. The same sense seems quite likely at Philodemus, *Piet.* 18. 19–20.

So much for Philodemus' appeals to chapter and verse. The tone now becomes more personal as he begins to unmask his opponents:

Some of those currently working in Rhodes write that while they were teaching, in Cos and again in Rhodes, on the theme that rhetoric is not an expertise, in each of these cities some people recently arrived from Athens said that they were taking a position which conflicted with that of the Great Men, by being over-complacent that it is not an expertise. And in Cos one of them [i.e. one of those recently arrived from Athens], when asked where this view is made clear, replied that one place was in the *Symposium* and another in the *On modes of life*;[37] while the other one replied that he could not say where, but that he knew that those who taught in Athens took this view about the sophistical branch. These same claims, they say, were trumpeted in Rhodes too, by one of those recently returned from Attica, who told them not to begrudge the rhetoricians the possession of an expertise.

Now this person darkly hinted to be working in Athens and to hold this opinion is our own Zeno. He had never written on the subject, but that did not prevent the person from writing a rejoinder to him. (II a. LII. 11–LIII. 14)

It is now that we begin to see one of the factors that have prompted Philodemus to write this work. For once he is not merely preparing a textbook on Zeno's brand of Epicureanism for his pupils in Italy, far away from the true hub of philosophical activity in Athens. The unnamed Epicurean's written rejoinder to the views Philodemus and others had learnt from Zeno in Athens has given him a rare chance to engage directly in a current controversy.

It is interesting to notice that Zeno's thesis about rhetoric was by no means the established orthodoxy, or even generally known. Epicureans working in the east Aegean region had only just received news of it. And those who had picked it up when attending the school in Athens were fairly hazy about the textual warrant being offered for it. Even more interesting, the unquestioning loyalty of all parties to Epicurus and his co-founders has no counterpart in the Rhodian Epicureans'

[37] The titles of these two works are inside square brackets here, but they are supplied by the editors on the basis of the later passage II a. LVII. 22–3 (itself restored with the help of the parallel text in PHerc 1672), translated on p. 114 below.

attitude to the current head of the school[38]—for they can hardly have failed to recognize him and his immediate circle as the primary reference of the expression 'those who taught in Athens'. The scholarch has no aura of papal infallibility, and is as open to attack as any other member of the school suspected of heretical views. Philodemus' own unswerving loyalty to Zeno, we must conclude, stems from Zeno's standing as his teacher, rather than as official scholarch.

Philodemus now launches his rejoinder to the Rhodes opponent, whose very name is apparently so distasteful to him that he avoids mentioning it:

In his treatise he conducts himself in a variety of ways, saying that of the theme that rhetoric is an expertise he has found not so much as a trace, while of the theme that no branch of it is expert he has found innumerable indications; and he undertakes to prove this. Whatever errors this philosopher seems to me to make in his rejoinder I shall not hesitate to document in detail, and to share in the puzzlement of our and his mutual friends. But for the time being I shall mention the actual points which would seem to bear on the present investigation, not laboriously (for I cannot persuade myself that what is obvious[39] requires proof), nor again in a conjectural way, but in a way which is sufficient to refute him.

Well, in setting out what are to be the headings under which the argument demonstrating his thesis will proceed, he states his belief that the circle of Epicurus and Metrodorus did not allow that either the political or the forensic or the panegyric [treated for present purposes as equivalent to 'sophistic'] branch of rhetoric involves expertise, but said that the political and forensic branches require rehearsal, practice, and a sort of empirical research, while the panegyric branch, they said, consists in rehearsal, practice, and habituation at a certain kind of speaking, without practical research. Moreover, he expresses the view that according to the Great Men it is totally impossible for there to exist an expertise of persuading mobs;

[38] For Zeno as scholarch, see Angeli and Colaizzo [11] 49–50. For an interesting account of the respective roles of school founders and living teachers, cf. Nock [253] ch. 11.

[39] Conjecturing ὃ φ[ανερόν—οὐδ'] ἔṭ[ι at II a. LIV. 8 (ὀφ[ειλούσης,] ἔṭ[ι Longo Auricchio). I had better give my own text for the whole of II a. LIV. 4–15, since in addition to this conjecture I have altered the punctuation found in Longo Auricchio's edition at several points: οὐ πρ[ο]ṣκαρτ[ε][ρ]ητι|κῶς—οὐδὲ γὰρ μὰ τὸν Κύ|να δεῖται, καθ[ά]περ ἐμ̣αυ|τὸν ἐγὼ πείθω, συναγ[ω]|γ[ῆ]ς ὃ φ[ανερόν—οὐδ'] ἔṭ[ι σ]το|χαστικῶς, αὐ[τά]ρκως δὲ | πρὸς διακοπήν. ἐκτιθεὶς | τοίνυν δι' ὧν ὁ λόγος αὐ|τῶι προελεύσεται κε | φαλαίων ὁ τọ̀ π̣[ρ]οκε[ί]με|νον [ἀπ]οδεικṿ[ύω]ν, φησὶν τοὺς (κτλ.)

and that it is their doctrine also that the aforementioned rehearsal, practice, and experience do not produce persuasion always or for the most part, and that it sometimes turns out that non-rhetorical discourses are more persuasive than rhetorical ones. (II a. LIII. 15–LV. 11) . . . and that even if, hypothetically, someone does have an ability which always persuades the many, this is the cause not of goods but of great evils.

And having, as he believes, established each of these points, he thinks that he has multiply and exhaustively demonstrated that those who declare that either all of rhetoric or a branch of it involves expertise are taking a position against Epicurus.

For my part, I am amazed also at the pupils of the 'man teaching in Athens', one of whom expressed the belief that rhetoric had been written about in the *Symposium* (if one should believe those philosophers who speak about philosophers unfairly [i.e. the Rhodes opponent may have misreported him]), while the other said that he did not know where Epicurus and his circle say it. So the disciples, or judges, were not attentive to what they were taught, any more than the Rhodian who writes that to this very day he has not been able to hear from anybody where it is said. (II a. LVI. 3–LVII. 4) . . . ⟨He could have got the answer⟩ from the school of Zeno, who lives in Athens, not in Persia. However, in order to save him his long search and inquiry from many sources, I can say that it is not in the *Symposium* nor in the *On modes of life*, nor do we tell him to search for a pebble in the ocean, but that the texts and expressions in which we say it is made clear that sophistic rhetoric is an expertise are the ones we have cited. Even if these are shown to be lengthening our verdict, there is still a need for them to be set out, for all who follow our philosophy. (II a. LVII. 13–36)

Skipping a minor argument and some very fragmentary text, we can resume at a point where the opponent is being quoted as basing his case on a passage from a dialogue by Epicurus.[40]

Epicurus . . . portrays Idomeneus, after the words 'Let him speak frankly . . . to you', as being asked to forgive his [referring to a young

[40] For the most recent text of II b. X. 21–XI. 3, see Angeli [12] 63. But I cannot agree with what seems to have been the unanimous view since Sudhaus (*Philodemi Volumina Rhetorica*, 2 vols. plus supplement (Leipzig, 1892–6) i. xxxiv; and 'Exkurse zu Philodem', *Philologus* 54 (1895) 80–92), that the passage comes from Epicurus' *Symposium*. Philodemus has already told us (II a. LVI. 18–27) that rhetoric was not discussed there; and Athenaeus (177 b, 187 b; cf. Usener [8] 56–65 for these and further testimonia on the dialogue) makes it clear that all the guests portrayed in the *Symposium* were Epicurean philosophers—which the young man in the present fragment evidently is not.

man who is present] youthful presumption, and adding the following (and I quote):

'It's amazing if you have not been in any way prevented because of your age, as you would yourself say, from greatly exceeding in rhetorical ability all those men who, by comparison with your youth, are old and renowned. . . . It's amazing, as I say, if you have not been in any way prevented because of your age from being foremost in rhetorical ability, which seems to depend on a great deal of practice and habituation, while it is possible to be prevented because of age from worldly understanding, whose cause would seem to be knowledge rather than practice and habituation.'

Because of this . . . they say that the whole of rhetoric would, by being such as he[41] declares it to be, result from practice and habituation, and not even a single branch of it . . . from expertise; and[42] they claim to see him clearly explaining, distinguishing in addition what will be the result of knowledge and what of practice and habituation. . . . ⟨The argument is that if⟩ that which is hard to master because it is unmethodical can be acquired by a young man, much more can that which comes through knowledge, since that is gained by method and universal principles. But if ⟨rhetoric⟩ or any branch of it is an expertise, the argument would become nonsensical, by going as follows: 'If that which comes about by method is not prevented from being acquired by a young man, much more is this true of that which comes about by method.' Moreover no one will claim that he is picking out the political and forensic branches: he explicitly says 'rhetoric', and in reply to a sophist who professes to possess all the branches. Hence, if it does not come out thus, Epicurus will[43] have made absurd use of the inference. (II b. X. 27–XII. 10)

Here at last we have something recognizable as an analysis of a philosophical argument. In common with some modern analytic interpreters of Plato, the Rhodian opponent (like Philodemus himself in the sequel) interprets only the letter of the text, making no allowance for any element of humour or irony. His last words, incidentally, prove that he is appealing not to the authority of the dramatic speaker Idomeneus, who although a distinguished early Epicurean was not one of the

[41] i.e. Epicurus, or (what here amounts to the same thing), Idomeneus. The sense seems to require *ἀπọφαί[ν]⌜ε⌝|ται* at II b. XI. 16–17, rather than Sudhaus' *ἀπọφαί[ν]ọ[ν]|ται*.

[42] At II b. XI. 20–3 I restore and punctuate as follows: *τέχνηι· καὶ σαφῶς τ[ιθ]έασι | θε[ωρ]εῖν ἐγδιδάσκει`ν´ πρọσ|διαστέλλοντα ποῖά τ' ⌜ἔ⌝[σ]|ται (κτλ)*.

[43] I would prefer *ἔστ[αι]* to *ἐστ[ι]* at II b. XII. 9, and it appears consistent with the spacing shown in the Naples apograph (see Longo Auricchio [13] 178).

infallible four, but rather to that of Epicurus, whose spokesman Idomeneus is taken to be. The opponent's argument is impressively clear and to the point. But (after a short lacuna) Philodemus has a neat rejoinder:

⟨We reply: if⟩ it is the doctrine, as indeed it is, that ⟨sophistic⟩ rhetoric is an expertise, but an expertise which also requires a good deal of practice and habituation—for it is neither impossible nor ruled out by the Great Men that some kinds of knowledge should additionally need a good deal of practice and habituation—how do these considerations make Epicurus' argument nonsensical? And good heavens, let someone show us how,[44] if the political form or branch of rhetoric needs a good deal of practice and habituation, but the sophistic branch needs only knowledge, the argument comes out as silly. For it is not, as he claims, an argument like this, 'If that which arises by method is found in the young, much more will this be true of that which comes about by method', but one like this: 'If that which is acquired *not purely* by method, etc.' (II b. XII. 31–XIII. 11)

Shortly afterwards, following a lacuna, we seem to find Philodemus addressing a subsidiary point of interpretation:

. . . If it [the word 'seems'] was added by way of hesitation and conjecture, ⟨note that⟩ he retained it as applying not just to rhetoric but also to practical wisdom, adding 'seems' there as well. And clearly we will take the 'seems' as applying also to the political branch, which they everywhere trumpet to be without expertise. Also, the persuasiveness of the argument would be supplied not from a contentious premise but from an agreed one. (II b. XIII. 32–XIV. 7)

If I understand this correctly, Philodemus is here rejecting an alternative defence of the Zenonian position, which would consist in conceding the opponent's reading of the argument, but observing that, when Epicurus makes his speaker imply that rhetoric in general is no τέχνη, his words are qualified with a hesitant use of 'seems': '. . . rhetorical ability, which seems to depend on a great deal of practice and habituation'. Philodemus himself must be taking 'seems' to represent 'is evidently', or 'is thought to be'. His three grounds are: (1) 'seem' is immediately afterwards used in the clause about 'worldly understanding', which no Epicurean could regard as questionable; (2) the premise in question is *undoubtedly* true of at least one

[44] At the end of II b. XIII. 4, I place a comma instead of a question mark.

branch of rhetoric, the political; and (3) the premises of arguments should be agreed, not controversial. Although all these points could do with further discussion, it is pleasing to see how well Philodemus gets to grips with detailed textual interpretation here and in his previous rejoinder, once he has an opposing interpretation in his sights. This contrasts very favourably with his rather lame use of the passages which he earlier quoted as confirming the Zenonian view. On that occasion, it seems that he was so habituated to reading the texts in the Zenonian way that he simply could not see the need to argue his interpretation.

At this point we can leave Philodemus' text. What has emerged from it, I think, is that both Philodemus and his opponent are learned and discerning readers of their school's canonical texts, but that each is probably trying to squeeze out of them a more precise theory of rhetoric than their authors ever intended: when it comes to a direct confrontation, neither interpretation can be proved.

Finally, it must be stressed that this activity of appealing to scripture occupies only a small part of Philodemus' *Rhetorica*. Absolute though his commitment to Epicurus is, it never enters his head that winning the battle over scriptural interpretation is a way of obviating the need to argue his own case on its merits.

## 3. EPILOGUE

What we have seen is—in an unusually articulated form—the kind of reverence for ancient texts which underlies all the main philosophical movements in the Greco-Roman world. At the very end of antiquity, Simplicius' veneration of Plato is not really different in kind from Philodemus' veneration, some six centuries earlier, of Epicurus.

Nor need this be dismissed as a quaint attitude providing no more than a picturesque backdrop to the real philosophical investigations that went on in the schools. It is integral to their whole way of conducting those investigations. This can be illustrated with an aspect of the story to which I have paid little attention so far, the influence of Aristotle. In the early first century BC it occurred to the Academic Antiochus that there was a continuous Platonist tradition to which Aristotle, among others, could be counted a contributor; and thereafter it became a commonplace for Platonists to present Aristotle as their ally, a more or less loyal[45] expounder of at least part of Plato's thought. Thus it was that Aristotelianism could come to be part of the very fabric of philosophy throughout the Roman imperial period. But before Antiochus introduced this subtle variant on the old pattern of loyalty,[46] no leading Hellenistic school acknowledged Aristotle as a forerunner. Consequently, there was simply no motive for Stoics, Epicureans, Academics, or Pyrrhonists to seek out Aristotelian authority for their doctrines. It has always been a struggle for modern scholars to accept how extraordinarily little notice the Hellenistic philosophers apparently took of Aristotle,[47] in view of his immense importance to the subsequent history of philosophy. I would suggest that the primary explanation lies in the nature of ancient school allegiances.

Do Roman philosophers conform to the pattern I have sketched? In general, they do. There is no more eloquent statement of the kind of reverence I have been describing than Lucretius' hymn to Epicurus in his proem to Book III. In Cicero's philosophical dialogues his spokesmen for the various schools do not seem to diverge from the norms as I have described them. And there is no reason to doubt that even Cicero saw himself as a loyal Platonist, despite wavering between different brands of Platonism.[48]

[45] The degree of authority accorded to secondary figureheads of this type varies, but it normally falls short of infallibility. See e.g. Simplicius, *In Cat.* 7. 27–9 on Aristotle, 'nor . . . should one strive to prove him totally and utterly infallible, as if one had joined his sect'.

[46] Cf. Barnes, above, ch. 3.

[47] This issue has been brought into the open by Sandbach's important and controversial monograph [58]. I would not myself deny that Hellenistic philosophers did sometimes take notice of what Aristotle had said, but in general I share Sandbach's doubts about extensive influence. In Epicurus' case, I would locate the main 'debt' to Aristotle not in any doctrinal influence but in his subtle replies to Aristotle's criticisms of Democritean atomism (cf. Long and Sedley [1] sects. 5, 9, and 11); and this was for him probably a case of living up to his *own* school loyalties, since we know that in his formative years he called himself a 'Democritean' (Plut. *Mor.* 1108 E–F).

[48] Cf. Cic. *Acad.* 13. This question is interestingly explored in Dörrie [74] sects. 25–31, with commentary; but, in view of such texts as those cited in n. 15 above, Dörrie's insistence on the uniqueness of Cicero's stance, and his denial to him of the label 'Platonist', seem to me exaggerated: Cicero clearly regards his open-minded methodology as faithful to the New Academy of his own day. Cicero has often been called an 'eclectic':

But I must end with a puzzling exception. Seneca is a self-proclaimed Stoic, yet seems to pride himself on disavowing reverence for his school's founder. He makes it plain that for him Zeno's authority is neither a necessary nor a sufficient condition for his acceptance of an argument or doctrine.[49] He is prepared to make fun of a bad Zenonian argument; and, while conceding that the normal practice of the Stoics is to try to make even these arguments come out true, he pointedly refuses to join in the game.[50] How is this to be explained? Could it be that Roman philosophers did sometimes feel themselves less straitjacketed than their Greek counterparts by their school allegiances? Has Seneca's Stoicism somehow been infected by the brand of Academic philosophy (see section 1 above, with n. 15), espoused at times by Cicero, which makes non-reliance on authority the chief tenet of Platonism. Or is he simply *sui generis*? Others may be better equipped to pursue these questions than I am. But I hope at least to have laid the groundwork for such an inquiry by outlining the normal style of ancient philosophical allegiance, so that, when any such exceptions do come to light, we can see just how exceptional they really are.[51]

---

the issue of eclecticism is one I have not addressed directly, but the implication of my whole argument has been that (apart from the curious individual called Potamo, D.L. 1. 21) no ancient philosopher is an eclectic. The complex allegiances of such alleged eclectics as Posidonius and Cicero comply well enough with the rules for loyalty to a single tradition, as I have outlined them. Against the familiar picture of Diogenes of Apollonia as 'eclectic', see A. Laks, *Diogène d'Apollonie*, Cahiers de Philologie 9 (Lille, 1983) xxix ff. and 93. Even Lucian's Demonax (cf. Griffin, above, n. 25), for all his apparent eclecticism (*Demon.* 5), looks very much like a committed Socratic of some kind (especially ibid. 62), perhaps comparable to Epictetus in his range of loyalties.

[49] Cf. *Otio* 3. 1; *Vit. Beat.* 3. 2; *Ep.* 33. 11; 45. 4; 80. 1.

[50] *Ep.* 82. 8–9, 19; 83. 8–17. *Ep.* 33. 4, 'non sumus sub rege', is sometimes taken to claim philosophical independence of Zeno for *all* Stoics, but see n. 1 above.

[51] Other questions worth pursuing, but not pursued here, include: (1) How far are philosophical allegiances actually religious? Why, for instance, do the Platonists and Epicureans, but not the Aristotelians and Stoics, develop religious cults of their founders? (2) What happens when a philosopher, e.g. Carneades in the Academy, acquires a degree of authority which begins to rival that of the movement's founder? (3) How far do school allegiances in medicine differ from the pattern for philosophy? (4) What part did the phenomena I have described play in the forgery of Pythagorean, Socratic, Platonic, etc. texts? There are leads on some of these, and further questions, in the excellent chs. 1–5 of Meyer and Sanders [252].

# 5

# Lucretius and Politics

D. P. FOWLER*

THE original title of this paper was 'Lucretius and the *language* of politics', and I formerly devoted more space to illustrating the concordances between Lucretius' language and that of contemporary political discourse, as seen in the writings largely of Cicero and Sallust and as analysed in the well-known study of Hellegouarc'h.[1] As I now spend more time talking of propositions than of words, I have abandoned the fashionable linguistic turn. Nevertheless, I should wish to retain something of the original orientation. When we interrogate a poem like the *De Rerum Natura* to discover the attitude to politics it embodies, we cannot simply assemble from it a selection of sentences explicitly dealing with the subject and string them together to answer our question. It may well be that this is never good methodology for any text, but it fails more spectacularly for a dense literary work.[2] The words are more important and their interpretation more difficult. I make no excuse therefore for retaining some of the nit-picking obsession with mere words which distinguishes literary scholars from their more adult colleagues.

Let me begin however with facts, or rather their absence.[3] We know next to nothing about Lucretius' life; Latin scholars remain more gullible about ancient biography than their Greek counterparts,[4] but as with all the Republican and

* I am most grateful for corrections and comments to Peta Fowler, Alessandro Schiesaro, and Martin F. Smith.

[1] Hellegouarc'h [302].

[2] Cf. *CR* 34 (1984) 45–52.

[3] What follows is brief and dogmatic; there is some further detail in Fowler [269] ch. 1.

[4] Cf. M. Lefkowitz, *The Lives of the Greek Poets* (London, 1981) viii: 'virtually all the material in all the lives is fiction'. J. Fairweather, 'Fiction in the Biographies of Ancient Writers', *Ancient Society* 5 (1974) 234–55, and 'Traditional Narrative, Inference, and Truth in the Lives of Greek Poets', *PLLS* 4 (1983) 315–69, offers useful analyses of some of the types of fiction employed.

Augustan poets the first step to understanding their chronology is to discard the biographical tradition. We do not know where Lucretius came from, nor what his social status was. The one secure datum is Cicero's famous letter to Quintus in February 54 BC which mentions with praise the combination of *ars* and *ingenium* in 'Lucretii poemata'.[5] This is naturally taken to refer to a recent work, and certainly there is no reason to suppose the *De Rerum Natura* was not published[6] in late 55 or early 54. Whether the work is finished or not, and in consequence whether we are to think of posthumous publication, are not easy questions to answer, but it is at the very least substantially complete and the date of intended publication, if that is important, cannot have been very different from the time when the work actually appeared. It is addressed to one Memmius; we are only given the family name. It is laid before him 'studio ... fideli' (I. 52), and Lucretius declares that he is induced to write his poem by 'sperata voluptas | suavis amicitiae' (I. 140–1). This is the language of literary patronage, though not only of literary patronage: it is quite wrong to draw sweeping conclusions from these phrases about Lucretius' status or to deny that Epicurean friendship, the entry of Memmius into the Epicurean community, is also in question.[7] Memmius' services are said to be required by the state, and he is therefore an active politician. In these circumstances and at this date, it is difficult for the reader to take the reference to be other than to C. Memmius L. filius, the praetor of 58 and luckless consular candidate in 54.[8] It was common to 'dedicate'

[5] *QFr.* II. 10(9). 3 = 14. 3 Shackleton Bailey (who well explains ad loc. the sense of Cicero's words, greatly mauled by critics).

[6] I hope to defend elsewhere my use of the term 'published', by which I mean something not essentially different from modern publication. The description of Lucretius declaiming his work in the public baths given by Wiseman [296] 37–8, might politely be said to be underdetermined by the facts. On the date, note Fellini's discussion, [284], of possible polemic in Lucretius against Cicero's *De consulatu meo*, which appeared in 60.

[7] Cf. Wiseman [296] 35–6, and his earlier [295] 35. On the language of dedication to a patron, see especially C. W. Macleod, 'Catullus 116', in his *Collected Essays* (Oxford, 1983) 181–6, at 185.

[8] *RE* Memmius 8; good sketch in Boyancé [279]. For the complicated events of 54, see Cic. *Att.* IV. 17. 2, and E. S. Gruen, 'The Consular Elections for 53 B.C.', in J. Bibauw, *Hommages à Marcel Renard* (Brussels, 1969). The only problem with the identification is I. 42 'Memmi clara propago': there is no eponym of the *gens Memmia* as there is of the *gens Claudia* when Manilius talks of 'Claudi magna propago' (I. 796). One might wonder if a young man was being addressed as his father's son, and think of the

works of literature to politicians on their attaining public office; perhaps Lucretius anticipates. The later letter of Cicero[9] to this Memmius asking him not to pull down Epicurus' house in Athens is no objection; that Memmius is not already an Epicurean is presupposed by the *De Rerum Natura* and nothing forces us to imagine that the poem brought about a successful conversion.[10] One might even wonder whether it was the *De Rerum Natura* which Cicero refers to when he talks of the 'offensiuncula' caused to Memmius by the 'perversitas' of some Epicureans, but this is no more than conjecture.[11] Certainly, however, there is a mismatch between work and addressee, and Memmius might well find uncongenial the view of political life displayed in the *De Rerum Natura*. This will worry only those who take a narrow view of the possible relations between 'patron' and 'poet' in the Republican period.

It is becoming a commonplace of modern scholarship that the *De Rerum Natura* is a political work, and like most commonplaces this is more true than false.[12] The poem addresses the ills of contemporary society and suggests a solution for them in Epicurean philosophy. It has often seemed unusual that an Epicurean work should be so involved with the political world, but recent work has stressed the social message of Epicureanism from the time of the founder on.[13] Some of the details of this message are still in dispute, however, and a brief sketch of the Epicurean attitude to politics is a necessary prelude to any examination of the political stance of the *De Rerum Natura*.

The essence of Epicurus' position is well known, and easily summed up: do not take part in politics,[14] live unknown.[15] This

---

younger C. Memmius, who was tribune in 54 and prosecuted Rabirius. But this is not enough to direct the reader away from the more famous politician, and *clara* supports the traditional identification.

[9] *Fam.* XIII. 1. 3–4 = 63. 3–4 Shackleton Bailey, on which see Griffin, above, pp. 16–17.

[10] *Desciscere* (I. 103) refers to the future, and is in any case hypothetical. If Memmius knew the truth only about the gods, it is likely that the fear of death would make him desert, but Lucretius is going to tackle that fear as well.

[11] Cf. M. F. Smith's introduction to the revised Loeb, p. xlvii.

[12] Cf. especially Nichols [272] 17–20, and the fervid advocacy of Minyard [271] 33–70.

[13] Cf. Philippson [49]; Müller [41]; Goldschmidt [39]; Long [46].

[14] D.L. X. 119 = fr. 8 Usener, from *Περὶ βίων* Book One: on the likely content of that work, see Liebich [140] 104–18, especially 107–10.

[15] Fr. 551 Usener.

was one of the school's most notorious tenets, attacked by Cicero in the opening of the *De Re Publica* and in the *In Pisonem*, by Plutarch at the end of the *Adversus Colotem* and in the little work *An recte dictum sit latenter esse vivendum.*[16] The application of the rule can be traced in all periods of the school's history, but I offer three examples. First, two passages from Epicurus' letters to his disciple Idomeneus, referred to by Seneca in the course of his own attempt to dissuade Lucilius from political life:[17]

Let me cite the example of Epicurus' letter to Idomeneus, written when the latter was an agent of royal power, engaged in great affairs. Recalling Idomeneus from a life of vain show to secure and certain glory, Epicurus wrote: 'if it is love of glory which touches you, my letters will make you more famous than all the things you court and because of which you are courted.' Did Epicurus lie? Who would know of Idomeneus if Epicurus had not inscribed his name in his correspondence? All those *megistanes* and satraps and the king himself from whom Idomeneus' title was being sought, all are buried by deep oblivion.[18]

Read Epicurus' letter to Idomeneus on this subject, in which he tells him to put all his efforts into escaping, and to hurry before some greater force intervenes to take away the liberty of withdrawing. He adds that of course nothing should be attempted unless the time and circumstances are right; but when the long-awaited occasion comes, Idomeneus must, says Epicurus, leap up and be off. Anyone who wants to make the break must not relax, but there is every hope of being able to extricate ourselves from even the most difficult situation, so long as we neither hasten before the right time nor stay idle when it comes.[19]

Idomeneus was the recipient of a number of letters from Epicurus, including the famous one written on the latter's deathbed.[20] The two passages referred to by Seneca presuppose that Idomeneus is involved in political life in the service of some king; context, chronology, and historical background are

[16] Cic. *Rep.* I. 1–12; *Pis.* 53–63; Plut. *Mor.* 1124 D–1127 E; *Mor.*, especially 1129 B–D. For the tradition of attacks on the precept, see De Lacy [118] 52–5. For Cicero's *De Re Publica* as an 'anti-Lucrèce', see Andreoni [225].

[17] The context in the sequence of letters 19 to 22 is important, as also the relation to Seneca's own position: see the detailed discussion in Griffin [146] 315–66.

[18] *Ep.* 21. 3 = fr. 132 Usener = fr. 55 Arrighetti = Idomeneus F 13 in Angeli [12].

[19] *Ep.* 22. 5–6 = fr. 133 Usener = fr. 56 Arrighetti = F 14 Angeli [12].

[20] D.L. x. 22 = fr. 138 Usener = fr. 52 Arrighetti = F 23 Angeli [12].

obscure,[21] but Epicurus is clearly encouraging Idomeneus to avoid political involvement. Whether he did so we cannot say, but there is ascribed to him a work *On Demagogues* which earned him a place in Jacoby's *Fragmente der griechischen Historiker*.[22] That contained an attack on the great Athenian political heroes of the past such as Themistocles, Pericles, and Demosthenes; the genre is a familiar one as Jacoby notes, its most famous representative being Theopompus in Book Ten of the *Philippica*.[23] It is wrong however to situate the work solely in an anti-democratic historiographical tradition. A. Angeli in her edition of the testimonia to Idomeneus goes so far as to claim that *On Demagogues* is the work not of the Epicurean but of a namesake, and she does not include the fragments in her collection. But such attacks on politicians have a philosophical dimension, as readers of Plato's *Gorgias* will not need to be reminded, and the demolition of the reputations of the famous was a favourite Epicurean tactic. I have no doubt that Angeli was wrong, and that *On Demagogues* should be restored to the Epicurean Idomeneus.

My second example of the school's antipathy to politics, comes from the peroration of Plutarch's reply to Colotes, in the course of which he quotes two fragments of Epicurus' companion Metrodorus:[24]

They mention politicians only to laugh at them and to destroy their reputations. They say, for instance, that Epaminondas had only one good thing about him, and that a 'wee' one (using the Boeotian dialect word); they call him 'ironguts', and ask what made him walk across the Peloponnese rather than sit at home with a little felt cap on his head—by which they mean, I suppose, that he would have been better off devoting his life to looking after his belly. And it is worth remembering what Metrodorus wrote in his work *On Philosophy*, when burlesquing the state: that 'some wise men in their prodigality of conceit have such a clear vision of the function of the state that when they talk about ways of life and virtue they get carried away with the same desires Lycurgus and Solon had'. Was it then conceit, and prodigality of conceit, to think that Athens ought to be free and Sparta well-

[21] For a review of the evidence, see Angeli [12] 43–7.

[22] *FGrH* 338.

[23] Cf. W. R. Connor. *Theopompus and Fifth-Century Athens* (Cambridge Mass. 1968), especially 19–76.

[24] *Mor.* 1127 A–C = fr. 560 Usener = Metrodorus frr. 31–2 Körte.

ordered, that young men should not be arrogant, that we should not have children by prostitutes, that law and justice should rule our cities and not money, extravagance, and brutal lust? These are the things Solon desired. Metrodorus adds the following piece of abuse: 'Therefore it is right to laugh a truly free laugh, at all mankind, but especially at these Lycurguses and Solons'. In fact, Metrodorus, this is not a free man's laughter, but that of a badly brought-up slave . . .

As R. Westman points out,[25] Plutarch is misconstruing Metrodorus, who is not attacking actual lawgivers at this point but philosophers who imitate them, like Plato, Zeno, and Diogenes in their ideal states.[26] But the context shows that the attitude to real statesmen is no different. Metrodorus indulges in Democritean laughter as he looks down on his deluded fellow-men with a serenely indifferent smile. The wise man is free: they are not. These are themes that recur in Lucretius.[27]

My final passage is a well-known one, quoted by Momigliano in the short review (of Farrington's *Science and Politics in the Ancient World*) which is still the most stimulating treatment of Epicurean political theory.[28] It comes from the end of the first book of Philodemus' *De Dis* (PHerc 26 XXV. 22–37), as edited by Diels:

But I think I have said enough about the disturbance which comes from the gods, and I have done what I can to persuade the man of good character to stay outside of these endless disturbances; and so to free himself from evils which are hard to deal with, and to gain for himself goods of great importance; to consider himself alone a real man, and to look down on the others as if they were gnats—not only the insignificant, but also the rich private citizens, the famous political office-holders, those afire with treacherous disease (?), when he sees the opponents throwing away the affairs of Rome into the hands of one man, Antony . . .

[25] Westman [304] 213–14.

[26] Bignone [34] i. 598, ii. 56–8, saw Plato and 'early Aristotle' as the main targets; B. Einarson and P. H. De Lacy in the Loeb ad loc. think of Diogenes' *Republic* because of the ironic phrase δαψίλεια τύφου, 'prodigality of conceit'. Zeno's *Republic* is said to be an early work (cf. Baldry [62] 5) and so cannot be ruled out.

[27] See below on the opening of *De Rerum Nat.* II. For Democritus' laughter, see A 21 Diels/Kranz (despite 'Demokrates' B 107a); Courtney on Juvenal 10. 28–30; R. Philippson, 'Verfasser und Abfassungszeit der sogenannten Hippokratesbriefe', *RhM* 77 (1928) 293–328, at 317–20, who also collects the passages on Epicurean laughter: cf. especially Polystratus, *De Irr. Cont.* XXX. 7–14, pp. 127–8 Indelli.

[28] Momigliano [47] 153 = 383.

Because of the apparent mention of Antony, this has excited much discussion about context and date.[29] Unfortunately, Diels's text of the *De Dis* is very unreliable: 'kaum eine Zeile gibt, die ohne Fehler ist' according to the current editor K. Kleve,[30] and he has pointed out that the presence of Antony here is very dubious.[31] But even without Antony's name the attitude of Philodemus is plain: once more a philosophic pity and contempt for those caught up in political life, τῶν ἐπιφανεστάτω[ν ἐ]ν δυνάμεσι πολ[ι]τικαῖς. This may not always have been Philodemus' attitude, but here at the end of the *De Dis* he is fully in harmony with the traditions of the school.

There are however some qualifications of the basic message mentioned in some of our texts, and they deserve particular attention because of their possible relevance to Lucretius' position in the *De Rerum Natura*. First, a passage of Plutarch's *De Tranquillitate Animi* (465 F = Epicurus fr. 555 Usener):

> Not even Epicurus thought men who were in love with fame and honour (τοὺς φιλοτίμους καὶ φιλοδόξους) should lead a quiet life, but they should indulge their nature by taking part in politics and public life, because they are constitutionally more likely to be disturbed and corrupted by inactivity, if they do not attain what they want. But he is a fool to encourage to take part in public life not those who are most able but those who cannot live a quiet life . . .

This is a surprising statement, since we expect the pursuit of fame and glory, *philotimia* and *philodoxia*, to be attitudes of mind that Epicureanism completely removes. The philosophy is in general an intellectualist, Socratic one: once the truth is grasped, 'all the tempest of the soul is dispersed' (Epicurus, *Ep. Men.* 128) and the desire to go wrong is removed with its cause.[32] It is true that in *De Rerum Natura* III. 307–22 Lucretius admits that *doctrina* cannot completely remove natural proclivities like irascibility and timorousness, but these seem to be affections of a different order to love of glory and fame, and

[29] See most recently Grimal [95].

[30] [139] 89.

[31] See Dorandi [16] 28 n. 22; Gigante [136] 28. I avoid with relief discussion of the phrase τὴ[ν ὑ]π̣ουλό[τητ' ἐκ]και[ό]ντων (and wager £5 that it will no longer be there when Kleve publishes his edition).

[32] I am aware that this is a controversial statement and that apparent counter-evidence is not hard to seek: I hope to return to the question elsewhere.

Lucretius claims that the traces left are so small 'that nothing hinders our living a life worthy of gods' (III. 322). It is hard to see how the life of a politician actively pursuing glory could be so described by an Epicurean. As always, we sorely miss the context of Epicurus' remarks. We do not know whether this one comes from a monograph or a letter, and it is possible that the sentiment represented a hypothetical concession; if anyone was so constituted, he would have to pursue a political life, but normal people are not like that. It is a common tactic of those authors who polemically quote Epicurus to present a μέν clause without its answering δέ. Nevertheless, one can see how a concession like this could be congenial to some Roman Epicureans.

A second and more significant qualification is mentioned by Cicero and Seneca: the wise man will not take part in politics 'extra quam si eum tempus et necessitas coegerit' (Cic. *Rep.* I. 10), 'nisi si quid intervenerit' (Sen. *De otio* 3. 2 = Epicurus fr. 9 Usener).[33] That is, sometimes political conditions will be so extreme that the Epicurean wise man will act (to which Cicero objects that this action will be ineffectual unless the wise man has studied political theory, something Epicurus enjoins him not to do). Context is again missing, and we can only guess at what sort of emergency might be envisaged as justifying a political act. There are also problems with integrating this injunction into the main body of Epicurean ethics. The wise man will be happy in the brazen bull of Phalaris, so why should, say, a politically authoritarian regime concern the individual?[34] We might look to the doctrine of Epicurean friendship; the wise man will die for a friend, and might *a fortiori* be expected to take part in politics, for example, to protect an Epicurean community from destruction. The problems here are considerable, and

[33] Cf. I. Dionigi ad loc. in his edition of the *De Otio* (Brescia, 1983), pp. 198–9. The exact form of the quotation in Seneca may be influenced by the contrast with the maxim Seneca ascribes to Zeno, 'accedet ad rem publicam nisi si quid impedierit'; that is however a translation of a maxim ascribed in D.L. VII. 121 to Chrysippus' *Περὶ βίων*.

[34] Cf. Epicurus fr. 601 Usener; Ardizzoni [45] 88–90; Nisbet on Cic. *Pis.* 42. Note Philodemus, *De morte* XXXIV–XXXV with Momigliano [47] 154 = 383. Long [46] 286, on the other hand suggests that even the Epicurean 'needs assurances that he or she will not be molested by wild animals, subjected to the privations and continuous torture, it may be, of a concentration camp, or living in an environment where vandalism, assault, mockery, and other forms of psychological pressure are the order of the day'. This perhaps suits Epicureanism in some moods, but not the philosophy at its most austere.

take us right to the centre of the difficult question of Epicurean αὐτάρκεια.[35] But as has often been observed, this doctrine of 'emergency action' could provide a motivation for an Epicurean like Cassius.[36] Whereas the first concession might provide an excuse for normal political action, this might justify a 'heroic' existential choice, say, to kill a tyrant. Such heroic rhetoric was of course well established in the Greek tradition of tyrannicide.[37] The maxim may also provide a context for Lucretius' statement at I. 41–3 that 'neither can I concentrate on my task with untroubled mind in this bad time for our country,[38] nor can the noble offspring of Memmius in such circumstances be wanting to the common weal'. While the poem is composed/read Lucretius asks Venus for peace; as things stand, the times are such that he cannot concentrate on his writing nor Memmius abandon political life. The logic here is not straightforward: it seems that we are to suppose that the prayer is granted, that peace is temporarily established, and that Lucretius can calmly write the *De Rerum Natura* and Memmius read it. But the allegory of the address to Venus demands that the achievement of the plea be achieved by the reading of the *De Rerum Natura* and the reader's conversion.[39] Converted to Epicureanism, the reader will cease the civil strife which prevents Lucretius from calmly writing the work of conversion! Nevertheless, the doctrine of 'emergency action' might justify the actions of a Lucretius as well as of a Memmius.[40]

[35] See Long [46], especially 301–8; P. Mitsis *ap.* Long, 305 n. 22.

[36] Cf. Momigliano [47] 151–5 = 379–5, and e.g. M. Bringmann, comments on Long [46] 321–2. Shackleton Bailey (on Cic. *Fam.* XV. 17. 4 = his 214. 4) makes the important point that Cassius did not *convert* to Epicureanism in 46, and there are of course many doubtful identifications in Momigliano's prosopography. But I am here concerned with potentiality, not actuality (discussed by Griffin, above, pp. 29 ff).

[37] Cf. H. Berve, *Die Tyrannis bei den Griechen* (Munich, 1967) ii. 742.

[38] It is significant that *patriai tempore iniquo* seems to be not a formal political phrase but an educated colloquialism: cf. *TLL* vii. 1. 1641. 6 ff. By contrast *nec . . . communi desse saluti* strongly recalls political language: the phrase *communis salus* occurs 39 times in Cicero's speeches according to Merguet (cf. especially II *Verr.* IV. 140; *TLL* iii. 1970. 76 ff.), and Cicero is always talking of 'not betraying the Republic, the Roman people' etc. (*cf. Cat.* IV. 18; *Red. Pop.* 18; *Phil.* III. 34; Plancius *ap. Fam.* X. 21. 3; Lepidus *ap. Fam.* X. 34. 2; Pollio *ap. Fam.* X. 33. 5; Brutus *ap. Fam.* XI. 9. 2, all from 43 BC; *TLL* v. 1. 788. 5 ff.). Cf. Wiseman [295] 32–3.

[39] Again brief and dogmatic: more elsewhere.

[40] See below. For a recent attempt to find a place for philanthropic philosophic exposition in Epicurean ethics, see Long [46] 306–8. Diogenes of Oenoanda frs. 1–2 is of course an important parallel; in part the 'emergency' for him was his approaching

The third concession to the injunction μὴ πολιτεύεσθαι needs the most discussion. Although Plutarch (*Adv. Col.* 1126E) says that no Epicurean has ever been an adviser to kings, in the list of things which the wise man will and will not do in Diogenes Laertius' life of Epicurus (x. 121b) we are told that the wise man 'will pay court to a king, if occasion demands', and links between Epicureans and various Hellenistic monarchs can be traced.[41] Colotes dedicated the work to which Plutarch devotes the *Adversus Colotem* to a Ptolemy, probably Philadelphus, and perhaps not unconnectedly at the end of his work praised kingship:[42]

Those who established laws and customs and the rule of kings and magistrates in cities brought human life into great security and peace, and freed men from chaos. If someone takes all this away, we shall live the life of wild beasts, and men will all but devour each other when they meet.

Plutarch, however, points out that other Epicurean statements on kingship are less favourable (*Adv. Col.* 1125C–D):

But who are the men who nullify, abolish, and totally destroy these things? Is it not those who withdraw themselves and their companions from the state? Is it not those who say that the crown of an undisturbed mind is incomparably greater than the highest command? Is it not those who declare that to be a king is a mistake and an error, and write in these very words that 'we must tell in what way a person may best observe the purpose of life, and how someone will not in the first place willingly approach public office'? And further that 'there is no need then to be a saviour of the Greeks or to be crowned by them for wisdom, but to eat and drink, Timocrates, with pleasure and without harm to the flesh'?

It is not difficult to see how these statements might be reconciled, as R. Westman has again shown.[43] An Epicurean would not be a king, with all the disturbances of office, but he might be glad that there was a king preserving the peace, and might

---

death, but his motivation is complex. On the wider issue of Epicurean recruitment, see Frischer [37] 49–50, 67–86; for a possible instance of an Epicurean taking 'emergency action' on behalf of his city, cf. the embassy of the Pergamene Apollophanes to Rome noted by J. and L. Robert, *RÉG* 71 (1958) 198.

[41] Cf. Momigliano [48]; Grimal [95] 262–3; Angeli [12] 87–8.

[42] On the passage see most recently Grimal [95] 261, and Long [46] 291–2.

[43] [304] 201–6.

well prefer a benevolent monarchy to a democracy, since in the latter he would be continually pestered by people like Pericles reminding him of his civic duties: 'ut satius multi iam sit parere quietum | quam regere imperio res velle et regna tenere' (*De rerum nat.* v. 1129–30). It could be objected that this is the morality of the freebooter:[44] kings are a good thing, but one would not wish one's daughter to marry one. But early Epicureanism, like early Christianity, presupposes that its supporters will be a minority in a hostile world. If everyone was an Epicurean things would be different; no kings, and no laws, since a community of the wise would not need them.[45] But as it is, monarchy might be the easiest system to live with, and if circumstances required action—the second concession—it might well be right μόναρχον ἐν καιρῷ θεραπεύειν.

It has recently been argued however by M. Gigante and T. Dorandi that the Epicureans had a more positive attitude to kingship.[46] Attempting to find a context for Philodemus' *On the Good King according to Homer*, they discuss a number of fragments, most of which unfortunately involve problems of text. They connect the injunction to pay court to kings ἐν καιρῷ with the preceding statement in Diogenes Laertius Book Ten, which states in the manuscript text that the wise man χρηματίσεσθαι, ἀλλ' ἀπὸ μόνης σοφίας ἀπορήσαντα (121b). Bailey translates this, 'He will be ready to make money, but only when he is in straits and by means of his philosophy', and this is the commonest translation, though W. Schmid tried to interpret ἀπὸ μόνης σοφίας as 'secundum scientiae doctrinas' ('solo secondo i principi della filosofia', Arrighetti).[47] Gigante suggested reading εὐπορήσαντα for ἀπορήσαντα, translating the maxim 'il sapiente cercherà di procurarsi i mezzi per vivere, ma attingendoli dalla sola filosofia';[48] that is, money-making for the wise man is not seen as emergency act but as normal practice (εὐπορήσαντα going closely with ἀπὸ μόνης σοφίας). Connecting this with the following fragment on courting kings, Gigante and Dorandi then see the wise man as obtaining his income by instructing

[44] Cf. Plut. *Mor.* 1127A, 'they enjoy the advantages of society without contributing to them'.

[45] Cf. fr. 530 Usener; on Epicurean utopianism, see below.

[46] Gigante and Dorandi [299]; Dorandi [16] 22–32.

[47] Doxography in Arrighetti's apparatus, Gigante and Dorandi [299] 484.

[48] *Diogene Laerzio, Vite dei Filosofi*[2] (Rome/Bari, 1976) 439, 574 n. 94.

kings: 'in cambio del progresso morale che può conseguire un monarca, il saggio può ricavare i mezzi di vita oltre alla gioia.'[49] This is ingenious, but the emended εὐπορήσαντα is redundant and the connection suggested between the maxims overelaborate. Keeping the manuscript ἀπορήσαντα there is a link with ἐν καιρῷ in the following maxim: both detail things the wise man will not normally do but may be forced into by circumstances. The Gigante interpretation is at best not needed.

In two other passages Gigante and Dorandi are rather on the side of the manuscripts against excisions in the vulgate texts. The manuscript version of *Kuriai Doxai* 6 runs:

ἕνεκα τοῦ θαρρεῖν ἐξ ἀνθρώπων ἢ (ἦν Usener) κατὰ φύσιν ἀρχῆς καὶ βασιλείας ἀγαθόν, ἐξ ὧν ἄν ποτε τοῦτο οἷος τ' ἦι παρασκευάζεσθαι.

As Bailey points out (ad loc.), this would have to mean 'To secure protection from men the advantage of rule and kingship is a natural blessing, by which you may be able to attain this end'. The syntax of ἀρχῆς καὶ βασιλείας is very awkward, however, and the phrase is normally excised as a gloss on ὧν. Gigante and Dorandi wish to keep the phrase,[50] but, syntax aside, it seems unlikely that Epicurus would have declared rule and kingship to be natural goods. The following *Kuria Doxa* criticizes those who think that they can obtain security by becoming famous, and Lucretius inserts his translation of this into the context of the struggle for power within a city.[51] Even if one could find a form of words which enabled ἀρχῆς καὶ βασιλείας to be retained,[52] the maxim would have to be taken as a counterfactual. *If* rule and kingship provided security, there would be nothing wrong with them but, as *Kuriai Doxai* 7 shows, they do not. There is however a lot to be said in terms of simplicity for the deletion of the phrase.[53]

Two fragments are ascribed by Usener to Epicurus' *On*

[49] Gigante and Dorandi [299] 486 (linking also the following fragment in D.L.).

[50] Cf. Barigazzi [297] I. 79–82 (best defence of the syntax, with καί for ἤ instead of Usener's ἦν); Long [46] 324.

[51] *De Rerum Nat.* V. 1120–6; see below. *Kuriai Doxai* 7 should not be interpreted in a positive sense: cf. Long [46] 324, in reply to Gigon.

[52] Cf. Bailey [265] ad loc.

[53] ἐξ ὧν represents πάντα ἐξ ὧν and so can probably stand as the subject of ἦν (ἀγαθόν is nominal, 'a good', not 'good').

*Kingship*. The first records Epicurus' advice to kings to avoid literary symposia, an injunction apparently contradicted by Philodemus in *On the Good King according to Homer*.[54] The second is Plutarch's complaint that the Epicureans:

*γράφουσι περὶ πολιτείας ἵνα μὴ πολιτευώμεθα, καὶ περὶ ῥητορικῆς ἵνα μὴ ῥητορεύωμεν, καὶ περὶ βασιλείας ἵνα [μὴ] φεύγωμεν τὸ συμβιοῦν βασιλεῦσι.*

they write about politics to prevent us taking part in political life, and about rhetoric to stop us engaging in it, and about kingship to make us [not] flee the court of kings.[55]

The *μή* in the final member of Plutarch's tricolon is usually excised as an intrusion from the first two members; the negative idea the sequence requires is already present in *φεύγωμεν*. Gigante and Dorandi point out the contrast with Diogenes Laertius X. 121b on courting kings, and suggest keeping the *μή*: the Epicureans did *not* wish the wise man to flee the company of kings. However, it is hard to see how Plutarch could have regarded such a view as paradoxical or horrific, and if the point was in the apparent self-contradiction by the Epicureans he would surely have drawn this out more explicitly. The contradiction of Diogenes Laertius X. 121b is lessened by the presence there of *ἐν καιρῷ*; as Westman remarks, 'daß man etwas vermeiden soll, schließt nicht aus, daß man es unter besonderen Umständen tun kann'.[56] Plutarch's reference is probably not to the *On Kingship* but to the letters to Idomeneus mentioned earlier, which precisely encourage him to flee the court.

Finally, a passage of Lactantius' *Divinae Institutiones*, from a section where Lactantius is attempting to show that Epicurus 'ut ad se multitudinem contrahat, adposita singulis quibusque moribus loquitur'; that is, he tried to be all things to all men, so that for example a weak man was told pain is the greatest evil, a brave one that the wise man is happy even under torture

[54] Fr. 5 Usener = 9 Arrighetti (Plut. *Mor.* 1095 C); Phld. *Hom.* XX. 9 ff. Dorandi. Murray [141] 173 n. 41, noted the contradiction: Gigante and Dorandi [299] 492 (cf. Dorandi [16] 37), claim that the relationship between the passages is merely 'di difficile determinazione'.

[55] Fr. 6 Usener (Plut. *Mor.* 1127 A, immediately before Metrodorus frs. 31–2 Körte quoted above).

[56] [304] 205.

(III. 17. 2–5). Lactantius' final example concerns Epicurus' attitude to kingship:

*qui claritati ac potentiae studet, huic praecipitur reges colere, qui molestiam ferre non protest, huic regiam fugere.*[57]

It would be consistent with Lactantius' rhetoric for the combination of these two injunctions to be his own,[58] but Gigante and Dorandi may be right in seeing them as combined already in Epicurus.[59] I would see this again however as an instance where all the emphasis falls on the δέ clause. If someone wants fame and power, let him court kings, but the true Epicurean will not have such desires, and will know that kingship brings disturbance. It is as if someone said, 'If all you are really interested in is money, by all means rob a bank, but if you do not fancy spending twenty years in gaol, do not take to crime'. The maxim is clearly related to the passage of Plutarch's *De Tranquillitate Animi* discussed above which contained Epicurus' first concession to political life. Both fragments would fit well into a sequence in, say, a letter to Idomeneus, in which the addressee was told to pursue a political life if he really had to, but to become a true Epicurean if he wanted real happiness and freedom from disturbance.

When one deals with these tiny fragments shorn of their context, nothing is certain. But the case for a positive view of kingship in Epicureanism seems to me not yet to have been made out. This leaves us with the problem of Philodemus' *On the Good King according to Homer* and its relation to orthodox Epicureanism; perhaps we have no alternative but to return to Murray's view of that treatise as not in essence an Epicurean work.[60] Nor can we see Lucretius' address to Memmius in the *De Rerum Natura* as in a tradition of Epicurean 'advice to the great'; the relation of message and addressee remains problematic, though the scepticism about power that we shall see the work contains is less anomalous than it would be if the Epicurean attitude to kingship were more favourable. I now turn

[57] *Div. Inst.* III. 17. 6 = Epicurus fr. 557 Usener.

[58] Cf. Usener ad loc.

[59] [299] 494.

[60] [141] 165; [142]. My agreement with Dorandi in *CR* 36 (1986) 81–5, on the Epicurean context of the work was over-hasty: I hope to return to the question of the date and occasion elsewhere.

to the *De Rerum Natura* itself, beginning with those texts which most concern themselves with political life.

First, the description of the 'edita doctrina sapientum templa serena' which opens Book Two:

> sed nil dulcius est, bene quam munita tenere
> edita doctrina sapientum templa serena,
> despicere unde queas alios passimque videre
> errare atque viam palantis quaerere vitae,
> certare ingenio, contendere nobilitate,
> noctes atque dies niti praestante labore
> ad summas emergere opes rerumque potiri. (II. 7–14)

The elevation of the wise man is important: the philosophers are continually described as 'looking down from above on the life of those below',[61] but Lucretius is also stealing one of the central metaphors of the political world, the climb through the lower offices to the pinnacle of success, 'making it to the top'. The imagery on which Lucretius draws for his citadel of serenity is complex,[62] but one element is perhaps the view of unphilosophic men as like insignificant ants, scurrying about their tiny tasks: so Philodemus in the passage of *De Dis* quoted above seems to talk of 'looking down on everyone else as gnats' (though it has to be said that the phrase κ]αταφρ[ο]νήσοντα [π]άντων [ὡς σ]έρφ[ων is again just the sort of Greek which tends to disappear when the papyrus is put under the microscope in Naples). The description of the unphilosophic hurly-burly[63] is full of the clichés of politics: *niti*, *labore*, *emergere*, and expecially *rerum potiri* are common in political discourse,[64] and

[61] Pl. *Soph.* 216 C (after *Od.* XVII. 485–7 on the gods).

[62] e.g. the citadel of philosophy (cf. Nisbet and Hubbard on Hor. *Carm.* II. 6. 21; Lyne on *Ciris* 14–17; Gruber on Boeth. *Cons.* I. 3. 13), the flight of the mind (cf. P. Courcelle s.v. *Flügel* (*Flug*) *der Seele*, *RAC* 8 (1972) 29–65), the mount of virtue (cf. West on Hes. *Op.* 287–92; Lucian, *Nec.* 4, *Hermot.* passim); and much else.

[63] Common in 'diatribe': cf. e.g. Dio Chrys. 13. 13; Marc. Aur. *Med.* VII. 48, with Farquharson ad loc.; Lucian, *Charon* 15, with Anderson [176] 16–17; as a protreptic topos Iambl. *Protr.* p. 13 Pistelli. Important Latin examples from the satiric tradition are Lucilius 1228–34 Marx, and Varro, *Eumenides* and *Endymiones* (cf. Cèbe on his fr. 160).

[64] *Niti*: Cic. *Planc.* 67; Sall. *Iug.* 4. 7, etc. *labor*: Hellegouarc'h [302] 248–51, 478; D. Lau, *Der lateinische Begriff LABOR* (Diss. Munich, 1975), 122; Vretska on Sall. *Cat.* 2. 5 *emergere*: *TLL* V. 477. 58 ff *rerum potiri*: Caelius ap. Cic. *Fam.* VIII. 14. 12; Cic. *Rosc. Am.* 70; *Cat.* II. 19; *Att.* X. 8. 4, etc.; Koestermann on Tac. *Ann.* I. 5. 4; R. Syme, *Tacitus* (Oxford, 1958) i. 412. With *niti* and *labor*, cf. the discussion of *ponos* in L. B. Carter, *The Quiet Athenian* (Oxford, 1986) 11. Carter's first chapter contains much of interest on the Greek roots of the language of glory.

even *noctes atque dies* is pointed. Ancient, like modern, politicians boasted that they never slept; Cicero tells L. Papirius Paetus in a letter of 43 that 'my days and nights are passed in one sole care and occupation—the safety and freedom of my countrymen'.[65] Lucretius however inserts this insomnia not into a tradition of heroic selflessness but into that of the moralists' attacks on the disturbed nights of the careworn.[66] Line 11 is particularly significant for Lucretius' view of contemporary politics. In 'certare ingenio, contendere nobilitate', *ingenio* is the watchword of the *novus homo*, *nobilitate* that of the established ruling class.[67] Lucretius encapsulates the strife within the aristocratic élite between those inside and those outside the circle of light. Both parties toil in vain: they will never really 'make it', never really 'get to the top', because only *sapientia* can lead men up to the citadel.

In the prologue to Book Three—linked to that of Two by the repetition of II. 12–13 = III. 62–3—Lucretius is concerned with the effect on men's lives of the fear of death. Though the passage has been criticized as based on an implausible and possibly un-Epicurean psychology, there are in fact Epicurean parallels to what Lucretius says and the role assigned to the fear of death is perfectly in harmony with the Epicurean analysis of human motivation.[68] We should remember that Lucretius is not analysing men's conscious thoughts but their hidden drives, revealed only in extreme circumstances; it is no objection to say that politicians do not all the while have death on their minds. He offers two reasons why he has to treat the fate of the soul and the fear of death at length. In the first place, though non-Epicureans often boast of being free of any fear of death, because their beliefs are not rationally based they give way in the face of adversity.[69] His example is a criminal fleeing into exile:

[65] *Fam.* IX. 24. 4 = 362. 4 Shackleton Bailey (his translation).

[66] Cf. Nisbet and Hubbard on Hor. *Carm.* II. 11. 8; 16. 15; Boeth. *Cons.* IV. 2. 28.

[67] Cf. Cic. *Sest.* 136 'vosque adulescentes, et qui *nobiles* estis . . . et qui *ingenio* ac virtute nobilitatem potestis consequi'.

[68] See especially Konstan [40] 11–34. Cf. also P. Shorey, *CPh* 7 (1912) 353–5; Perret [291]; Desmouliez [282]; Pianezzola [292] 617–9; Schmid [294] 137–53; Barrigazzi [297].The most important Epicurean parallel is Porph. *De abst.* I. 54. 2–3 = Epicurus fr. 458 Usener.

[69] Cf. Polystratus, *De irr. cont.* X. 27 ff. Indelli (compared already by Heinze).

extorres idem patria longeque fugati
conspectu ex hominum, foedati crimine turpi,
omnibus aerumnis adfecti denique vivunt,
et quocumque tamen miseri venere parentant
et nigras mactant pecudes et manibus divis
inferias mittunt multoque in rebus acerbis
acrius advertunt animos ad religionem. (III. 48–54)

This could be true of any criminal in any country at any time, but the details assimilate the picture to contemporary Rome. In particular the phrases *foedati crimine turpi* and *omnibus aerumnis adfecti* exactly pervert legal terminology. Strictly it is a *iudicium* which is *turpe*, and the man found guilty is *adfectus* with a *poena* or *supplicium*.[70] Here, as often at Rome, the accused is seen as fleeing before he can be officially condemned, but he is yet punished by the *aerumnae* of exile. The Epicurean point is insinuated that even the man who escapes formal punishment cannot really get away with—or from—his crime. We do not know whether Lucretius' description would have brought to mind for his readers any particular figure; I can think of no plausible candidate. But they would surely think here of an exiled *politician*, since a political trial is by far the likeliest reason for a Roman to go into exile. The description thus anticipates the picture Lucretius offers of political life in the following lines 59–86, where the reader discovers that if the man had really freed himself from the fear of death he is unlikely to have had to flee before a *crimen turpe* in the first place.

In 59–86 Lucretius gives the second reason for his extensive treatment of the soul and death in Book Three. The fear of death is the root cause of the fight for wealth and power which leads directly to the horrors of contemporary politics; terrified of death men try to cling on to 'life', reified as the security of wealth and the bright lights of political success. Their pursuit of these unnatural and unnecessary objects of desire can never satisfy, but leads them further into a paradoxical syndrome of misery, which can be represented graphically as in my figure. In Book Two Lucretius exposed and subverted the central political metaphor of ascent, and here the opposition between

[70] *Turpe iudicium: TLL* vii. 2. 612. 52 ff., e.g. Cic. *Flacc.* 10 'turpi iudicio condemnatus' *supplicio etc. afficere: OLD* s.v. *afficio* 4 b.

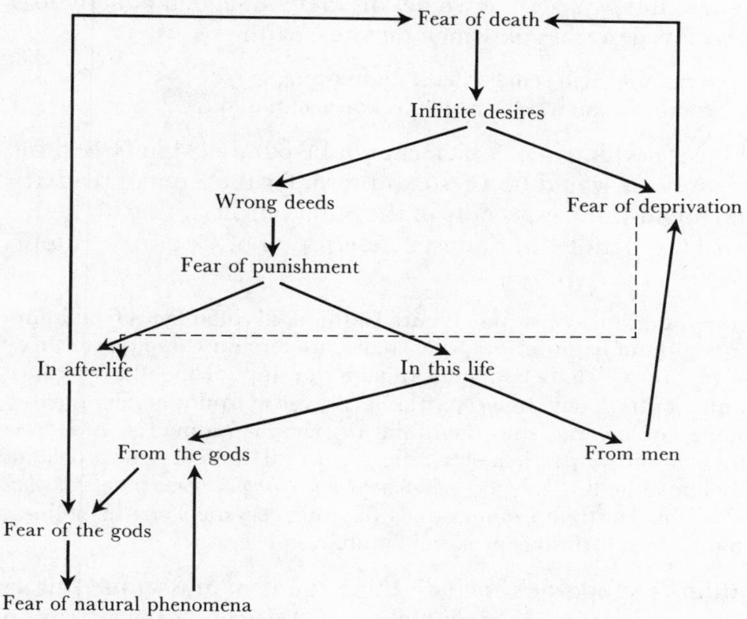


the light of success and the dark obscurity of failure receives the same treatment. In conventional thought, the successful politician is again Olympian, raised on high in the regions of light, while the ordinary man lies unseen in the turbid darkness. But to Lucretius the politician is blind (59), a paradigm of unphilosophic man, like a child in the night (87–90); the ultimate paradox of the pursuit of bright fame is 'vitae . . . odium lucisque videndae' (79–80), a hatred of light. The moralizing traditions into which the passage inserts itself are again complex, and a purely 'Roman' reading would be reductive,[71] but the presence of contemporary political language is not hard to seek: clichés like *caeca cupido*, *socios scelerum atque ministros*, *rem conflant*, *incedit*, *caeno*, the commonplace abstracts of political hyperbole like

[71] Much is owed, for instance, to the Hesiodic stance of accumulating vivid descriptions of contemporary (or coming) crimes: cf. *Op.* 176–9, 180–201, and note how Catullus 64. 397–406 and Vergil *G.* II. 503–12 combine Lucretius and Hesiod. Hes. *Op.* 176–7 is alluded to in *De Rerum Nat.* III. 62–3 = II. 12–13.

*pudorem* and *pietatem*.[72] Two details may be singled out. In 70–1 Lucretius describes how men pursue wealth:

sanguine civili rem conflant divitiasque
conduplicant avidi, caedem caede accumulantes.

There is nothing here which cannot be paralleled in Greek, but *sanguis civilis* would be a resonant term for the Roman reader,[73] who might think especially of the Sullan proscriptions. There is a striking parallel in Sallust's description of Catiline's entourage (*Cat.* 14. 1–3):

in tanta tamque conrupta civitate Catilina, id quod factu facillimum erat, omnium flagitiorum atque facinorum circum se tamquam stipatorum catervas habebat. nam quicumque inpudicus adulter ganeo manu ventre pene bona patria laceraverat, quique alienum aes grande conflaverat, quo flagitium aut facinus redimeret, praeterea omnes undique parricidae sacrilegi convicti iudiciis aut pro factis iudicium timentes, ad hoc *quos manus atque lingua periurio aut sanguine civili alebat*, postremo omnes quos flagitium egestas conscius animus exagitabat, ii Catilinae proxumi familiaresque erant.

Catiline's supporters include those 'quos manus atque lingua periurio aut sanguine civili alebat'. E. Wistrand drew attention to a tendency in Latin political rhetoric to talk hyperbolically of disgrace in the courts as death and murder, and suggested that the reference in Sallust was not to banditry but to 'men who make their living out of ruining their fellow citizens through false-swearing and forged documents'.[74] This thesis certainly cannot be accepted without reservation: questions of Latinity aside, it is important to note that Sallust's model in this passage[75] is Theopompus' account of Philip's followers (*FGrH* 115 F 225), and the reference there to men who are 'murderers by nature' is clearly not metaphorical. In the *De Rerum Natura* the meaning is of course made clear by *caedem caede*

[72] *Caeca cupido: TLL* iii. 44. 30 ff., e.g. Cic. *Pis.* 57 *socios scelerum atque ministros*: Hellegouarc'h [302] 88 nn. 5–6; *TLL* viii. 1003. 68 ff., e.g. Cic. *Phil.* XII. 17 *rem conflant:* Reid on Cic. *Sull.* 13, e.g. *Sest.* 66 *incedit: TLL* vii. 1. 853. 70 ff., e.g. Sall. *Jug.* 31. 10 *caeno:* A. Otto, *Die Sprichwörter und sprichtwörtlichen Redensarten der Römer* (Leipzig, 1890) 63, e.g. Cic. *Vatin.* 17, 23 *pudorem* and *pietatem*: Hellegouarc'h [302] 283, 276–9, e.g. Cic. *Cat.* II. 25.

[73] *TLL* iii. 1216. 27 ff., e.g. Cic. *Phil.* II. 71.

[74] *Sallust on Judicial Murders at Rome* (Göteborg, 1968) 23.

[75] Cf. K. Büchner, *Sallust*[2] (Heidelberg, 1982) 329; McGushin ad loc.

*accumulantes*, but it is to Lucretius' point if the reader initially takes *sanguine civili rem conflant* more loosely and vaguely. Judicial 'murder' becomes real murder with dispiriting ease.

Sallust and Catiline are perhaps relevant also to 74–7:

> consimili ratione ab eodem saepe timore
> macerat invidia ante oculos illum esse potentem,
> illum aspectari, claro qui incedit honore,
> ipsi se in tenebris volvi caenoque queruntur.

That political life is inevitably the subject of *invidia* or *φθόνος* is not a novel thought, and as if to underline this Lucretius' metaphor in *macerat* is not a Roman cliché but an adaptation of the common Greek use of *τήκω* with *φθόνος*.[76] Philodemus in his *Rhetoric*[77] singles out envy as the great disadvantage of political life, 'most hostile to friendship and most productive of enmity'; Lucretius returns to the subject in V. 1125–9. It is instructive however to compare Lucretius' description with part of Catiline's great speech in Sallust (*Cat.* 20. 7–8):

> nam postquam res publica in paucorum potentium ius atque dicionem concessit, semper illis reges tetrarchae vectigales esse, populi nationes stipendia pendere; ceteri omnes, strenui boni, nobiles atque ignobiles, volgus fuimus sine gratia, sine auctoritate, iis obnoxii, quibus, si res publica valeret, formidini essemus. itaque omnis gratia potentia honos divitiae apud *illos* sunt aut ubi *illi* volunt; nobis reliquere pericula repulsas iudicia egestatem.

Apart from the general resemblance of thought between the two passages, there is one stylistic trick in common, the *illum* . . . *illum* of *De Rerum Natura* III. 75–6 and the *illos* . . . *illi* in Sallust.[78] In Lucretius the repetition conveys 'the ambitious man's obsession with his rival' (Kenney ad loc.), and in Sallust too *gratia*, *potentia*, *honos*, and *divitiae* are seen as being in *their* hands or where *they* want them to be. Of course the resemblance between the two passages functions for the reader of the *Catiline* as a pointer back to the context in the *De Rerum Natura*; Catiline unconsciously shows himself to be one of Lucretius' bitter madmen. But the sentiment is not an implausible one, and it does the modern reader of Lucretius no harm to be reminded that

[76] Cf. Pfeiffer on Callim. *Aet.* fr. 1. 8.

[77] *Rhet.* II. 158 ff. Sudhaus.

[78] Cf. Cic. *Off.* II. 44, though that is less obviously parallel.

the Catilinarian 'conspiracy' was less than a decade in the past when the poem was published, and that memories of it must inevitably have conditioned the poem's reception.

The most direct reference to contemporary political life comes in the allegorical interpretation of Sisyphus in II. 995–1002:

> Sisyphus in vita quoque nobis ante oculos est
> qui petere a populo fascis saevasque securis
> imbibit et semper victus tristisque recedit.
> nam petere imperium quod inane est nec datur umquam,
> atque in eo semper durum sufferre laborem,
> hoc est adverso nixantem trudere monte
> saxum quod tamen e summo iam vertice rursum
> volvitur et plani raptim petit aequora campi.

Again we meet Lucretian subversion of the metaphor of the climb to fame, and there are other resemblances to the prologue to Book Two. Sisyphus is perhaps present there too as an 'implicit myth'.[79] The *fasces* which are the goal of every Roman politician—though no-one would *say* they were his goal[80]—become merely a burden, and power rolls away back to the Campus which is its source. As David West pointed out in his discussion of this passage,[81] although the primary reference is to failure (*victus tristisque recedit*) even a successful Roman politician only held office for a year. The stone always rolls back to the Plain, and even the successful candidate never receives true *imperium*. In this passage of dense allegory one term stands out, *imbibit*. This is conspicuous precisely because it does not cohere with the major metaphors of the description.[82] The evidence is not strong, but this could be a political cliché;[83] if so, it derives its force from its lack of poetic coherence. It is the ambitious hack's own word. There is also, however, an Epicurean point.

[79] On the term 'implicit myth', see R. O. A. M. Lyne, *Further Voices in Vergil's Aeneid* (Oxford, 1987) 139–40. The politicians strive night and day to 'get to the top': but Odysseus is also present in II. 12–13, since *emergere* suits a swimmer, cf. *Od.* V. 388–9, with Prop. III. 12. 32.

[80] *Petere fasces* is a perversion of the normal *petere consulatum*, etc. On the *pulchros fasces saevosque securis* cf. *De Rerum Nat.* V. 1233–5.

[81] [275] 100–2.

[82] The other occurrence of *imbibo* in the *De Rerum Nat.* is VI. 72; note there *delibata* (70) and *respuis* (68).

[83] Cf. Cic. *Quinct.* 27; Livy II. 47. 12.

The Epicurean classification of desires[84] drew a contrast between those whose satisfaction involved the physical ingestion of substances into the body (natural and necessary) or at least a variation of the state of the sense organs (natural but not necessary), and those whose satisfaction was impossible because they involved nothing real (unnatural and unnecessary). So at the end of Book Four Lucretius contrasts the natural and necessary desires for food and drink and the natural but unnecessary desire for sex with the unnatural and unnecessary passion of love:

> nam cibus atque umor membris assumitur intus;
> quae quoniam certas possunt obsidere partis,
> hoc facile expletur laticum frugumque cupido.
> ex hominis vero facie pulchroque colore
> nil datur in corpus praeter simulacra fruendum
> tenuia; quae vento spes raptast saepe misella.
> ut bibere in somnis sitiens cum quaerit et umor
> non datur, ardorem qui membris stinguere possit,
> sed laticum simulacra petit frustraque laborat
> in medioque sitit torrenti flumine potans,
> sic in amore Venus simulacris ludit amantis . . . (IV. 1091–1101)

The Sisyphan politician 'drinks in' an object which is *inane* and never granted: the use of a verb which normally refers to the satisfaction of a real desire points the inanity.

If III. 995–1002 contain the most explicit reference to contemporary Roman politics, the most extensive treatment of the political world in general comes in the account of the rise of civilization in Book Five. To be dogmatic about a much discussed passage,[85] Lucretius' account seems to be structured around a division between an early stage where society developed naturally under the promptings of nature, and a later

[84] I follow Diano's account of Epicurean pleasure as expounded in his famous exchange with Bignone: see his [35] 23–66, 67–128. This has been much assailed, most recently by J. C. B. Gosling and C. C. W. Taylor, *The Greeks on Pleasure* (Oxford, 1982) 365–96, and G. Giannantoni, 'Il piacere cinetico nell'etica epicurea', *Elenchos* 5 (1984) 25–44: I think Diano's theory survives these criticisms, and remains the most important contribution to Epicurean ethics in modern times: argument (perhaps) elsewhere.

[85] For bibliography on the whole *Kulturgeschichte* see Furley [227] 1 n. 1; there is an excellent survey in Manuwald [230]. On the specifically political aspects, see most recently Long [46] 309–11. I recapitulate here some material published for a different audience in *Omnibus* 10.

one where man's reasoning played a decisive role. The discussion of specifically social developments is split between these stages and is not continuous. Nevertheless, a five-stage analysis of social development is clear:

(1) Man is *durus*, lives outdoors, and has no marriage nor any kind of law (925–1010).
(2) Houses, fire, and marriage lead to *amicitia* between neighbours (1019–20) who form a *foedus* (1025).
(3) Men who *ingenio . . . praestabant et corde vigebant*[86] (1107) become kings and create cities (1109); they distribute property on the basis of beauty and strength (1110–11) until wealth becomes more important (1113–16).
(4) The rich desire power and fame as a safeguard for their wealth[87] (1120–2) and in the resulting strife the kings are overthrown and a state of anarchy results (1141–2).
(5) Eventually magistrates and laws are introduced by some men (1143 *partim*) because mankind is *defessum vi colere aevum* (1145).

As Momigliano noted,[88] this is a more complicated account than we find in the only other Epicurean text of any length on the subject, the summary of Hermarchus' views given in Porphyry's *De Abstinentia* (I. 7–12 = Hermarchus fr. 24 Krohn). In that account there are only three stages, anarchy, social contract, and the intervention of legislators. Similarly Colotes contrasts a preceding state of anarchy with the peace brought by 'those who appointed laws and customs and established the government of cities by magistrates and kings'.[89] By contrast, Momigliano claimed, 'to Lucretius, magistrates and laws, not kings are able to ensure durable peace'. Thus Momigliano

[86] Cf. Hermarchus *ap.* Porph. *De abst.* I. 8, contrasted with Polybius VI. 5. 7 by Goldschmidt [39] 289 n. 5. The Epicurean kings excel in intellect, not bodily strength; contrast Grimal [95] 261, though he is talking of a later stage. Cf. also Cic. *Rep.* II. 24.

[87] It is tempting to take *opulenti* in 1122 as meaning '*by being* wealthy', that is, it is their wealth which is to assure them of a *placidam . . . vitam*. But the men are already wealthy (1113–16); what they need now is security to enjoy their wealth, and they seek this in glory and fame. T. Cole, *Democritus and the Sources of Greek Anthropology* (Ann Arbor, 1967) 75 n. 11, is wrong to say that 'monarchy . . . is the result of the attempt on the part of individuals to guarantee themselves security': monarchy precedes the competitive phase.

[88] [47] 157 = 388.

[89] See above, p. 129.

concluded that the *De Rerum Natura* was favourable to the politics of the Republic and likely to encourage men to stand against the sort of domination represented by Caesar.

We should be careful not to assume that Hermarchus and Colotes represent the whole of the Epicurean theory of the development of law. In each case the context of the argument might justify a compression of the different stages of development. But Momigliano is quite right that the account in the *De Rerum Natura* is more complicated than the other versions we have. It is also true that a social contract theory of law as held by the Epicureans will tend to be opposed to absolutism;[90] and there is an important difference between Lucretius' account and those of non-Epicurean thinkers who have a similar pattern of development from the family to the city. In Plato's post-deluge state in the *Laws* and in Aristotle's *Politics* kingship is already present in the earliest developments as a natural progression from the authority of the father in the family.[91] The *padre* is the prototype of the *padrone*. By contrast, in Lucretius' account kings only begin to appear at the start of the stage of development where man's reasoning about his development is becoming important.

Nevertheless, Momigliano's analysis requires some modification. The development from kingship to anarchy parallels those theories which see a degeneration in the progress of society through the different polities, an idea already implicit in the *Republic* but finding its most developed expression in Polybius.[92] In contrast to these, Lucretius' account is optimistic; anarchy is not permanent, nor does the cycle begin again with monarchy, but constitutional government by magistrates results. But the description of the breakdown of kingship in 1113–42 is full of the language of contemporary Roman politics,[93] and the

[90] Cf. Denyer in [44]—though note the special case of Hobbes. Long [25] 70, and Goldschmidt [39] 240 n. 1, rightly point out the differences from Rousseau, but this does not prevent us continuing to use the term 'social contract' for the Epicurean theory.

[91] Pl. *Leg.* 676 A ff.; Arist. *Pol.* $1252^{b}19$ ff.

[92] Cf. Walbank on Polybius VI. 4. 7–9, 14.

[93] e.g. *sectam: OLD* s.v. 1 b, e.g. Cic. *ad Brut.* I. 3a (4) *claros atque potentis: TLL* iii. 1274. 7 ff., e.g. Sall. *Cat.* 38. 1 *quietum: OLD* s.v. 3 a, e.g. Caesar *ap.* Cic. *Att.* x. 8b. 2; Cic. *Comment. Pet.* 9; Sall. *Hist.* I. 55. 26 *regere imperio*: famously Verg. *Aen.* VI. 851, and often thought Ennian, but the allusion may be to Lucretius; and cf. Cic. *Rep.* II. 15; Sall. *Iug.* 18. 2; Hor. *Carm.* III. 4. 48; Livy I. 7. 8 *sudent*: Cic. *Sest.* 139; *Fam.* III. 12. 3 *ambitio*: Hellegouarc'h [302] 208–11 *faecem: TLL* vi. 1. 171. 11 ff.

injunction of 1131–5 explicitly indicates that the struggle for *imperium . . . ac summatum* is still continuing in Lucretius' day:

proinde sine incassum defessi sanguine sudent,
angustum per iter luctantes ambitionis;
quandoquidem sapiunt alieno ex ore petuntque
res ex auditis potius quam sensibus ipsis,
nec magis id nunc est neque erit mox quam fuit ante.

The *summus honor* which men seek would suggest above all the consulship for Lucretius' readers,[94] and the whole description is obviously parallel to the accounts of contemporary political strife already examined. For Polybius Rome's mixed constitution enabled it to stand outside of the cycles of decline he expounded; Lucretius associates present realities with his period of degeneration.

Moreover, it has often been observed that Lucretius' account alludes to the history of Rome itself. A period of regal power is followed by republican magistracies and laws. The Roman elements are particularly clear in 1136–9:

ergo regibus occisis subversa iacebat
pristina maiestas soliorum et sceptra superba,
et capitis summi praeclarum insigne cruentum
sub pedibus vulgi magnum lugebat honorem.

The throne, the sceptre, and the crown are the three most important of the regal insignia Rome derived from Etruria,[95] the one missing element, the purple robes, appearing later (v. 1418–29). It has also been suggested that *superba* alludes to Tarquinius Superbus and perhaps *pristina* to Tarquinius Priscus.[96] But there is an important difference between Lucretius' account and the traditional Roman one. In the history of Rome, the Republic followed directly on the expulsion—not the murder—of the kings, and there is no intervening period of anarchy.[97] In the *De Rerum Natura*, however, magistracies and

[94] Cf. Hellegouarc'h [302] 385; note 1123 *summum*, 1125 *summo*, 1127 *summa*, 1138 *summi*, 1141 *summam*, and the ironic coinage *summatum* in 1142.

[95] Cf. Dion. Hal. III. 61. 1; IV. 74. 1; L. Bonfante Warren, 'Roman Triumphs and Etruscan Kings: the changing face of the triumph', *JRS* 60 (1970) 49–66.

[96] Cf. Snyder [274] with D. A. West's review, *CR* 32 (1982) 25–7, at 27.

[97] It is true that Cicero and Sallust can describe the early days of the Republic as particularly turbulent (cf. Cic. *Rep.* I. 62, with Büchner ad loc.; Sall. *Hist.* I fr. 11 Maurenbrecher). But Lucretius' picture of a time when there were no magistrates at all is much more extreme.

constitutional government come into being only because the human race is 'tired of living in violence'. They are a refuge from something worse, not an ideal state of human society, and Lucretius' imagery reflects this: like an animal worn out by living in the wild, mankind 'sponte sua cecidit sub leges artaque iura (1147).[98] The metaphor is continued in the following lines (1151–60): in established society crime itself 'enmeshes' (*circumretit*) the criminal with fear. The law-abiding are of course free of this constriction, but the tone of the passage shows that if law is a saviour for men it is a harsh and forbidding one.[99] A constitutional republic imperfectly realized and beset by the evils of ambition might be preferable to anarchy or straight tyranny. But it is not enough of an ideal to form the object of 'magnanimous enthusiasm', to misuse a phrase of Momigliano's. Lucretius is no more a republican by principle than Epicurus was a monarchist. What matters for the Epicurean is the chance to lead a quiet life; human societies are very imperfect instruments for attaining this end, but one has to do the best one can.

So far I have examined those passages of the *De Rerum Natura* whose subject matter is most obviously connected with contemporary Roman politics. There is however another area where the poem draws heavily on political discourse and one that cannot be neglected in an examination of the stance of the work towards politics. This is the area of what G. Cabisius has called 'social metaphor', the use of metaphors from political life for the physical processes of the Epicurean universe.[100] This is a device which goes back to the origins of Greek philosophy and can be traced in most ancient scientific systems; it is by no means absent from modern science.[101] The role the metaphors play

[98] Cf. Tac. *Ann.* III. 28 'acriora ex eo vincla' used as an epiphonema by P. Brunt. *Social Conflicts in the Roman Republic* (London, 1971) 156. For a comparison of Tacitus' account with Lucretius', cf. d'Eufemia [283].

[99] Cf. Cole (op. cit. n. 87) 77. Goldschmidt, on the other hand, stresses that in Hermarchus' account (Porph. *Abst.* I. 7) there is 'une vision plus large et plus optimiste de la loi: la plupart des hommes obéissent spontanément à la loi, parce qu'ils y trouvent la garantie . . . de leur interêt bein entendu' ([39] 289 n. 2). Lucretius is not 'un-Epicurean' here, but the emphasis is his own.

[100] Cabisius [280]. Cf. Sykes Davies [281] 36–38; Kenney [266] 33.

[101] Cf. for the pre-Socratics especially G. Vlastos, 'Equality and Justice in Early Greek Cosmologies', *CPh* 42 (1947) 156–78 = D. J. Furley and R. E. Allen, *Studies in Presocratic Philosophy* i (London, 1970) 56–91; 'Isonomia', *AJP* 74 (1953) 337–66, at 361; C. Kahn, *Anaximander and the Origins of Greek Cosmology* (New York, 1960) 192–3; and the full discussion in G. E. R. Lloyd, *Polarity and Analogy* (Cambridge, 1966) 210–32.

varies between systems, and in some versions the link between the physical and social worlds will be such as to constitute more than simply an analogy (as for instance in Stoicism). But even where the two spheres are kept formally apart the uses made of social metaphor are likely to affect the reader's view of society as well as of physics. To many ancient writers the striking thing about Epicurean physics was the absence of a divine ruler; it all looked very democratic. The point is made explicitly by the Christian writer Dionysius of Alexandria:[102]

But if no ruler laid upon the atoms any word of command, or selection, or ordering, but of their own accord they directed themselves out of the great tumult of their flow, and crossed the great mêlée of their collisions; and it was not by the guidance of god (as Homer says) that like was attracted to like but they themselves ran together and gathered in groups, recognizing their kin; then the democracy of the atoms must have been truly amazing, friends shaking hands and embracing, hurrying to set up home together. Some of them presumably rounded themselves off of their own accord into that great luminary the sun, to make day, while others flared up into many pyramids, it may be, of stars, to crown the whole heaven; and others again must have taken station around to make the heaven firm at random, and to arch over the ether to enable the luminaries to ascend, while the confederacies of the ordinary atoms chose their own dwellings and divided up heaven by lot into houses and habitations for themselves.

The anti-theological context is important: Lucretius continually stresses the way the atoms act like free agents in forming their *concilia* in order to eliminate any notion of divine control:[103]

quae bene cognita si teneas, natura videtur
libera continuo dominis privata superbis
ipsa sua per se sponte omnia dis agere expers. (II. 1090–2)

The analogy is so frequent that Lucretius has to remind the reader that it is only partial: it must not be thought that the atoms are really animate:

nam certe neque consilio primordia rerum
ordine se suo quaeque sagaci mente locarunt

[102] *Ap.* Euseb. *Praep. Evang.* XIV. 25. 9.
[103] Cf. Masson [270] i. 126–7; Boyancé [267] 111 n. 4.

nec quos quaeque darent motus pepigere profecto,
sed quia multa modis multis mutata per omne
ex infinito vexantur percita plagis,
omne genus motus et coetus experiundo
tandem deveniunt in talis dispositaras,
qualibus haec rerum consistit summa creata. . . . (I. 1021–8)

Pursuing the metaphor, however, Lucretius talks not of the laws of nature but of *foedera*, 'compacts'.[104] The behaviour of the atoms is not governed by an external law laid down by a divine ruler but is controlled by pacts they have freely entered into. In this respect atomic society is strongly republican, and the metaphors suggest a favourable view of the cohesive force of social institutions.

There are however complications. If god is dethroned, his place is taken by *Natura*.[105] Nature does all the things god would otherwise do, and Cabisius suggests that the world of atomic compounds is not in fact entirely one of pacts between equals:[106]

> Strictly speaking, the *foedera* are not pacts made among the atoms themselves; they apply only to atoms when they have formed a *concilium*. Then, like men who have banded together in a society, the atoms are bound to specific aims and interests that result from the identity of the group as a whole. The other party to the agreement is *natura* whose position of superiority is suggested by the possessive in the phrase *foedera naturai*.

But though there is a sense in which the atoms and Nature are the parties to the pact, the genitive in *foedera naturai* is not simply possessive. The pacts the atoms make *are* nature, constitute the natural process. Although opponents constantly misconstrued the Epicurean use of *Physis* and *Natura*, in the end

[104] Cf. I. 586, II. 302, V. 310, 924, VI. 906–7, V. 57–61. As Long points out, [303] 81, 'Lucretius is playing on the meaning of *foedus* as both something concrete—a bond or union of atoms with congruent shapes—and the more abstract notion of law; contra, Reich [301] 125. See also Heinze on III. 416.

[105] See especially Sallmann [273], with W. Schmid's review in *Gnomon* 39 (1967) 464–95, at 489–93. Of the older bibliography, Merrill [288] is still worth consulting. More recently, see Berns [278] 480–3, and E. Zellmer, *Die lateinische Wörter auf -ura*² (Frankfurt, 1976) 212–30, 231–9. Cf. also Pease on Cic. *Nat. D.* II. 81; R. M. Grant. *Miracle and Natural Law in Greco-Roman and early Christian Thought* (Amsterdam, 1952) 3–18; A. Pellicer, *Natura, étude sémantique et historique du mot latin* (Paris, 1965).

[106] [226] 113.

there is of course no figure over and above the atoms and the void.[107] Lucretius personifies Nature as a dramatic device to polarize the conflict between theism and Epicureanism and to wean the reader away from belief in a providential deity, but it is a device the reader must eventually discard. The role assigned to *Natura* has no obvious lessons for the reader's view of society and does not affect the basic picture of freely co-operating atoms. Other elements perhaps do. Once the atoms have entered into their pacts, their behaviour is controlled: as A. A. Long has stressed, the Epicurean universe is one of order and stability.[108] The Epicureans delighted in turning back on their opponents the accusation that without a controlling god there would be cosmic anarchy: on the contrary, if the gods did interfere in the world, they could act with the arbitrary whimsy of tyrants and nothing would be certain.[109] The *foedera naturai* determine the stability and order of the world. Nevertheless, there is a sense in which the pacts of nature are more precarious and less perfect than immutable divine decrees. Apart from the gods in the *intermundia*, no compound lasts forever. Eventually the harmonious motions of the constituent atoms become so disturbed that the compound falls apart. No pact is truly eternal. From this point of view the atoms in a compound are also at war, a civil war:[110]

> hoc etiam magis haec animum te advertere par est
> corpora quae in solis radiis turbare videntur,
> quod tales turbae motus quoque materiai
> significant clandestinos caecosque subesse. (II. 125–8)

Modern writers often talk of the dance of the atoms; it is perhaps significant that Lucretius' metaphors are more harsh.

What are the implications of this for the Lucretian view of political life? I would suggest again that it implies a realistically sceptical view of social institutions. Without the *concilia* of the atoms and the *foedera naturai* there would be no world, but the

[107] Criticisms: cf. Sen. *Ben.* IV. 7. 1; Min. Fel. XIX. 8; and the equivalent fate of Strato of Lampsacus (frs. 32–9 Wehrli, cf. Pease on Cic. *Nat. D.* I. 35). For a classic demonstration that the claim that natural process *is* divine action is an empty one, see 'Epicurus' in chapter 11 of Hume's *Inquiry*.

[108] [303].

[109] Cf. I. 159–214, V. 87–8, etc.

[110] On the political language, see Cabisius [280] 116.

order they bring is not eternal. Even the world will one day fall apart. The political institutions of Rome are better than anarchy, but they are imperfect, and the wise man will avoid getting involved in them unless he has to. To be a little anachronistic (but not much[111]), like the 'radicals' in the 50s BC Lucretius has no time for the pomp and empty glory of Roman political life, the ideal and goal of a Cicero. But like the 'conservatives' he sees the opposition to this as motivated by no more than psychological aberration, greed, and envy ultimately grounded in the fear of death. He is concerned with the state of Rome, but the solution is a personal one: everyone should become an Epicurean. Or perhaps we cannot even go as far as that. Such a social solution—the conversion of the world—is suggested by Cassius in the famous letter in which he gives his reasons for becoming an Epicurean (*Fam.* XV. 19. 2), and we now know from a new fragment of Diogenes of Oenoanda that Epicureans did speculate in detail about what the world would be like if everyone were converted:[112]

> . . . then truly the life of the gods will pass to men. For all things will be full of justice and mutual love, and there will come to be no need of fortifications or laws and all the things which we contrive on account of one another. And with regard to the necessaries derived from agriculture, as we shall have no farm-labourers—for indeed we shall all plough and dig and mind flocks and divert rivers and watch . . .— . . . And such activities will interrupt the continuous study of philosophy for needful purposes; for the farming operations will provide us with the things which our nature wants.

As Long points out, such speculation may help to provide a motive for the exposition of Epicureanism: 'the prudent Epicurean will want his neighbours to share his commitment to justice; i.e. to perceive the utility of the social contract'.[113] And that is one element in the allegory of Venus and Mars in the prologue to the *De Rerum Natura*: if men became Epicureans,

[111] Cf. Grimal [95] 269.

[112] Diogenes of Oenoanda NF 21, published by M. F. Smith, *Thirteen New Fragments of Diogenes of Oeoanda*, Denkschriften der öst. Akad. der Wissenschaften, phil.-hist. Klasse 117 (Vienna, 1977) 21–5 (his translation). Cf. Barigazzi [298], Long [46] 314–15. Diogenes' belief that Epicureanism will one day triumph is shown by his use of the future indicative: see Smith on NF 21. I. 6.

[113] [46] 302.

they would stop killing each other and bring peace to the world.[114] But in many ways the *De Rerum Natura* seems still focused upon individual salvation, how an individual Epicurean might survive in a hostile world. And the answer is the same as it has always been: stay away from politics.

This attitude to political life is widespread in modern democracies, not of course as a reasoned philosophical belief but as a cynicism towards the political process. It is usually treated as a problem, to be solved either by persuasion that politics does not deserve the cynicism[115] or more radically by changing society. It would be a bold person who would argue that the Epicurean position is simply correct. But it will not do to dismiss it with loose talk of politics being a natural activity, or inescapable, or necessary for the full development of the person: all such arguments re-define 'politics' away from the institutional reality. It is less easy than it looks to argue that, say, standing for parliament is other than the manifestation of a psychological aberration.

[114] See above, p. 128; cf. v. 42–8, vi. 19–34, etc.

[115] Cf. e.g. B. Crick, *In Defence of Politics* (London, 1962, 1982).

# 6

# Cicero on Stoic Moral Philosophy and Private Property

JULIA ANNAS*

## I

IN Book III of the *De Officiis* Cicero is discussing cases where what is morally right appears to conflict with what is advantageous. In the course of this he retails some examples and the conflicting treatment of them by two heads of the Stoic school, Diogenes of Babylon and Antipater of Tarsus. Both of these were long since dead: Diogenes was a pupil of Chrysippus, and one of the members of the famous embassy to Rome of the three leading Athenian philosophers in 155 BC; Antipater was Diogenes' pupil, as was Panaetius, whose work *On Duties* Cicero is following, as he tells us, in the first two books of *De Officiis*.

These examples are very striking, and, even though Cicero carefully says that Diogenes' position is not that one should do what one admits to be morally wrong, most readers find Diogenes' position on the issues notably repellent.

First let us look at the passage, parts of which we shall come back to in detail.

> But, as I said above, cases often arise in which advantage may appear to conflict with being moral; so we should give them some attention, to see whether advantage is in open conflict with being moral or can be reconciled with it. They are problem-cases of the following kind. Suppose, for example that a good man has brought a large cargo of grain from Alexandria to Rhodes. At Rhodes there is scarcity and famine, and produce is extremely expensive. He knows that several other merchants have set sail from Alexandria—indeed on the voyage he has seen their ships laden with grain making for Rhodes. Should he tell this to the Rhodians, or by keeping quiet sell

* An early version of this paper was read to the Oxford Seminar. I am grateful to the audience, and to the Herodoteans in Cambridge, to whom a revised version was read in 1986. I am also grateful for written comments to Jonathan Barnes (twice), Miriam Griffin and Anthony Long.

his own cargo for as much as he can get? We are supposing him to be a wise and good man; we are asking about the deliberations and considerations of a person who would not conceal this from the Rhodians if he judged this to be wrong, but is wondering whether it might not really be wrong. (50)

In cases of this kind Diogenes of Babylon, a great and serious Stoic, consistently decides one way, his pupil Antipater, a brilliant man, the other. Antipater thinks that all should be disclosed, so that the buyer should not be unaware of anything whatsoever that the seller knows. Diogenes thinks that the seller must tell of any defects, insofar as this is legally prescribed, but otherwise merely act without trickery, and, since he is selling, aim to sell for as much as he can get. 'I have imported it, put it on sale, my price is no higher than the others'—perhaps even less when the supply is greater—who is wronged?' (51)

Antipater's speech begins on the other side: 'What do you mean? You ought to act in the interests of your fellow humans and serve human fellowship; that is the law under which you were born, and the principles of nature you contain, which you should obey and follow, are that your advantage should be the common advantage and conversely the common advantage yours. Will you still conceal from your fellow humans what relief and what plenty are at hand?' Diogenes will perhaps reply as follows: 'It is one thing to conceal, another not to tell. I am not now *concealing* anything from you, if I am not telling you what the nature of the gods is and what the final good is, which would be a lot more use to you to know than a drop in the price of corn. But it is not the case that I *have* to tell you whatever it is advantageous to you to know.' (52)

'Oh yes you do', Antipater will say, 'if you remember at all that there is such a thing as fellowship among humans joined together by nature.' 'I do remember that,' Diogenes will say, 'but surely that fellowship is not such that no-one has anything of their own? If that is so, no-one has anything to *sell*, only to give away.' You see that in the whole of this dispute no-one says this: 'Although this may be wrong, still I will do it, because it is advantageous.' Rather one side says that it is advantageous without being wrong, and the other side, that it is precisely because it is wrong that it should not be done. (53)

Suppose that a good man is selling a house because of some defects which he knows of, but of which others are unaware. It is unsanitary, though held to be healthy; people are not aware that maggots are appearing in all the bedrooms, and that it is built of bad timber and about to collapse. No-one knows this but the owner. I ask: if he does not tell the buyers this, but sells them the house for a great deal more than he expected to get for it, has his action been unjust or improper? (54)

'Yes indeed,' says Antipater. 'What is the difference between refusing to show the way to someone who is lost (for which the sanction at Athens is public curses) and allowing the buyer to be carried away and through mistake rush into great loss? It is even worse than not showing the way; it is knowingly leading another into error.'

Diogenes objects: 'He didn't force you to buy, did he, when he didn't even urge you to? He advertised it for sale because he didn't like it; you bought it because you did. People who advertise a country house for sale as "sound and well built" are not thought to have deceived other people, even if the house is neither sound nor rationally built. How much less so those who have merely not praised their house. Where the buyer can use his own judgement, what deception can there be on the seller's part? We do not have to stand by everything we say—do you think we should stand by what was *not* said? What could be more stupid than a seller's reciting the faults of the object he is selling? What could be more absurd than the owner ordering the auctioneer to announce, "An insanitary house for sale!"?' (55)

So this is how in some doubtful cases the one side defends being moral, while the other speaks of advantage in such a way that not only is it morally right to do what appears advantageous—it is even wrong not to do it. This is the dispute which often appears to arise between advantage and being moral. And it ought to be settled; we did not set these cases out merely to raise the problems, but to disentangle them. (56)

My view, then, is that the grain merchant should not conceal the facts from the Rhodians, nor the house seller from the buyers. Not any case of keeping quiet is concealing—concealing is when you know something and try for your own benefit to keep people in whose interests it is to know it, unaware of it. Who fails to see what this kind of concealing is like, and what kind of person does it? Certainly no open, straightforward, sincere, just or good person. Rather someone shifty, sly, cunning, deceitful, malicious, an inveterate trickster. How can it be advantageous to submit oneself to all these words of blame, and many others beside? (57)

He [Hecato] further asks whether a wise man who has unknowingly accepted forged coins as good ones, would, when he recognized this, pass them on, if he owes someone, as good ones. Diogenes says yes, Antipater no, and I prefer to agree with him. If someone is selling wine that is going off, and knows it, ought he to say so? Diogenes says that he does not have to, Antipater says that a good person would do it. These are, so to speak, the Stoics' controversial points of law. In selling a slave, should one speak of his faults—not those which if you fail to disclose them could render the sale legally void, but these: he is a liar, a gambler, a thief, an alcoholic? One thinks that you should say these things, the other not. (91) If someone is selling gold thinking it is bronze, will the good man point out to him that it is gold, or will he buy for one denarius what is worth a thousand? It is already clear what I think, and what the debate is between the philosophers I named. (92)

## II

Before we discuss a passage in Cicero's philosophical works, it is orthodoxy to ask what source he is following. The passage certainly reads as though Cicero had read works by Diogenes and by Antipater, and is discussing their views on that basis. This is not, however, the scholarly consensus, for the following reason: the second passage comes from a section where Cicero has begun by discussing cases taken from a later Stoic, Hecato, a pupil of Panaetius. After discussing examples from Hecato Cicero says that he, Hecato, asks a question, and then goes on to Diogenes and Antipater. Scholars have tended to follow Hirzel in inferring, firstly, that the Diogenes–Antipater debate was constructed by Hecato and taken over from there by Cicero, and, secondly, that the same must be true of the first, longer passage.[1]

Neither inference is sound. From the fact that Cicero gives the replies of Diogenes and Antipater to a question raised by Hecato, it scarcely follows that he cannot have read Diogenes and Antipater for himself. Those who assume this have to dismiss *De Finibus* I. 6 where Cicero says that, although

[1] Hirzel [110] ii. 726 and 733–4: 'Daß die erste Erörterung der zwischen Diogenes und Antipater schwebenden Controverse, die an der Hand einzelner Fälle (49 ff.) gegeben wird, aus derselben Schrift Hekatons genommen ist wie die zweite unterliegt wohl keinem Zweifel.' Cf. Holden [311] xxix: 'Again, it would appear that he had never even seen the writings of Diogenes and Antipater, but had learned their views at second hand, if we may judge from his mode of quotation, by which he unconsciously reveals to us the fact that he had never read them himself. . . .' After concluding that the later passage derives from Hecaton, Holden adds, 'But if Cicero in this one instance knew Diogenes and Antipater only indirectly through Hekaton, it may be taken for granted that this is the case where he quotes them for the first time without naming Hekaton.' The Budé edition concurs in the view that Cicero's sources are not direct—pp. 47–8 of *Cicéron, Les Devoirs*, ed. M. Testaud, Paris, 1970. Von Arnim oddly prints the contents of the first, but not the second interchange in his *Stoicorum Veterum Fragmenta* as fragments of Diogenes and Antipater, perhaps implying that the second but not the first passage should be ascribed to Hecato.

Chrysippus was pretty comprehensive, we still read Diogenes, Antipater, Mnesarchus, Panaetius, and many others, especially Posidonius. Hecato is not even mentioned. In any case, even if Cicero were dependent on Hecato in the second passage, it would not in the least follow that he was so dependent in the earlier one. And, since the point of both passages is the same (as far as Diogenes and Antipater are concerned), bringing Hecato in makes no difference.

Cicero certainly writes as though he were constructing the debate himself. 'Diogenes will *perhaps* reply . . .', he says at 52, and we find future tenses throughout, rather than the present tense of reporting. And in general, before we start dissolving Cicero into his sources it is always a good idea to look first and see what he actually says; to reconstruct his sources from his philosophical use of them, not *vice versa*. In what follows, I shall assume that the discussion, and what I take to be two major mistakes in it, are Cicero's. But if he *is* slavishly copying a single source, then what I say will transfer to his source, and apply to Cicero only in so far as he transmits that source.[2]

## III

Most of us are rather shocked by what Diogenes appears to be saying here. Sandbach says, fairly mildly,[3] 'Diogenes believed that one should pass on a false coin that one has received and sell without remark a thieving slave or wine that had turned sour. We should perhaps side with Antipater, who took the other view.' Holden, a nineteenth-century editor of the *De Officiis*, puts things in a more forthright and Victorian way: Diogenes, he says, 'openly justified fraud and imposition.'[4] It

[2] Dyck [308] argues that Posidonius should be seen as the sole philosophical source for Book III. But Dyck is surely too quick in claiming that Cicero 'surely never looked at a book by either' Diogenes or Antipater (see above). And he rejects even Hecato as a direct source on the grounds that 'Cicero uses a source favorable to Antipater's humanism'; this relies on what I shall argue to be a wrong view of the debate. Pohlenz [313], on whom Dyck draws for the latter point, argues that Cicero is dependent on Hecato and others through the medium of Athenodorus of Tarsus; this depends on over-interpretation of *Att.* XVI. 11.

[3] Sandbach [57] 128.

[4] Holden [311] xxvi. Compare Pohlenz [313] who speaks of Diogenes' 'Egoismus' and 'Profitmoral' (291); Diogenes 'die egoistische Klugheit soweit wie möglich als sittlich rechtfertigt' (290); 'die Art, wie er namentlich im zweiten Falle [the dry rot] die

certainly looks as though Diogenes was not a very nice man, certainly not someone from whom you would buy a house—at least, not without first hiring a good lawyer and a good surveyor. Commentators have been encouraged in this view by what Cicero says later (56) when he says that not to tell someone what is in their interests is not the act of a person aiming at virtue, but rather of a 'shifty, sly, cunning, deceitful, malicious, inveterate trickster'.[5]

There is something odd here. We know that there are people who will knowingly sell you a house riddled with dry rot (or termites or whatever the local equivalent is) but they are not, at least not usually, professors of moral philosophy. Even if they are, they don't write in their moral philosophy books that that is how it is morally right to behave. Everything else we know about Diogenes presents him as highly respected, highly respectable, and, above all, highly orthodox; his developments of Stoic doctrines are not innovations so much as developments firmly within the lines laid down by Zeno.[6] Even Cicero calls him (51) 'a great and serious Stoic'. It is simply good method, then, to avoid turning him into a defender of outrageous views if we can.

## IV

A clue may come from some of the examples; for they turn up in another famous context, the notorious second speech 'against justice' delivered by Carneades in Rome in 155 BC. A man can sell an unhealthy house, or an untrustworthy slave, to an innocent buyer; or buy gold at the price of bronze or silver at the price of lead from an innocent seller. If he tells the other person

Verantwortung für die Schädigung auf den Benachteiligten abschob und zwischen *kruptein* und *sigan* (*celare* und *tacere*) schied, bedeutete eine bedenkliche Laxheit und Spitzfindigkeit' (269).

[5] I take this splendid phrasing from the translation by Higginbotham [310].

[6] Diogenes' redefinition of the Stoic *telos* has been claimed as a radically new departure, but this is wrong. As often, a sensible view on this was put forward by Bonhöffer [305] and then ignored by scholars until recently. See, however, Long [306]. The article by Striker [307] also shows clearly how Diogenes' and Antipater's new definitions of the *telos* can be read as ingenious attempts to defend the orthodox view against criticism, not as new departures. (Even Bonhöffer, though, is defensive and uncharacteristically evasive about the *Off.* III passage.)

the relevant facts he will perhaps be admired for his honesty, but can hardly be said to be acting in his own interests. Cicero reported these cases in the account of Carneades' speech he gives to Philus in *De Re Publica* III.[7] Is Diogenes then responding to Carneades' criticisms by claiming that Stoicism can accommodate what look like very unwelcome cases? I think not, for several reasons. Firstly, the use of striking examples on its own proves nothing about dependence, or a felt need to meet the point of the first user of the example. Striking examples develop a life of their own. Take the sheriff tempted to allow an innocent person to be lynched to avoid a riot. This example is on the face of it a problem for utilitarianism, according to which the sheriff should (morally) go ahead. This example has cropped up innumerable times in utilitarian and anti-utilitarian literature since its introduction, and has been claimed to support a number of distinct positions. A future historian of philosophy would be rash to conclude that a person using it must be trying to meet the claim of the writer who introduced it—who was in fact J. J. C. Smart, a utilitarian. Carneades' speech was clearly a source of good examples—soon after in one of our sources we also find the two drowning men and the plank, taken up and discussed by Hecaton (see *De Officiis* III. 90)[8] in a context quite different from the problems exercising Diogenes and Antipater.

Secondly, Carneades' speech was not, as far as we can tell, anti-Stoic. Rather, it was an attempt to argue against Plato and Aristotle; Chrysippus seems to be dismissed as having nothing relevant to say about justice, only word-splitting.[9] It was also about justice, not about problems of moral rightness and advantage in general; again, there is no clear application to the problems of *De Officiis* III. Of course it is possible that the Stoics may have felt a special need to protect themselves against Carneades' attacks; but it is not clear why they should do so from the fragments of the speech that we possess. It is more likely that the examples themselves sparked discussion beyond

[7] They are preserved for us in Lactantius, *Inst. Div.* v. 16. 5–8.

[8] *Inst. Div.* v. 16. 10.

[9] *Inst. Div.* v. 14. 3 ff. for the reference to Plato and Aristotle; Cic. *Rep.* III. 8 for the reference to Chrysippus: 'nam ab Chrysippo nihil magnum nec magnificum desideravi, qui suo quodam more loquitur, ut omnia verborum momentis, non rerum ponderibus examinet.'

their original context. Since there is no direct reason to think of Carneades' speech as anti-Stoic, there is no reason why Diogenes should have felt called upon to show that the Stoics could accommodate Carneades' examples and to show how and why these sellers and buyers could be considered good Stoics. We shall see why he should discuss examples like these; but we do not have to suppose that what he was doing was directly meeting Carneades. Finally, if we do, we have to ascribe to him a view both implausible and unpleasant, one which has understandably drawn contempt from Cicero onwards. As I have said, we have good reason to avoid ascribing such a view to an orthodox Stoic.

## V

When we read the passage, we notice that there is a striking discrepancy between the concerns of Diogenes and those of Antipater. It is not the case (as some accounts of the passage suggest) that they are agreed on the question, 'Ought one to do this?'—to which Diogenes says, 'yes', and Antipater, 'no'. Rather, Diogenes' concern throughout is with whether or not you *have* to do it ('necesse, non necesse', 52, 91). Antipater, however, concentrates on what a good person would do ('viri boni', 91). Indeed, in 91 these concerns are juxtaposed: 'Non necesse putat Diogenes, Antipater viri boni existimat.' Now to say that a good person would do something is in no way to contradict the claim that it is not something he *has* to do. And this suggests that Diogenes and Antipater are focusing on rather different aspects of the matter.

I think that this is fundamentally right, although the opposition as it is set up in 91 does not quite capture the point. At the end of 52 Diogenes denies that he *has* to (*necesse*) tell someone what is in their interests. Antipater is made to reply, 'Yes, you do have to'—'Immo vero necesse est'. So at least once they are represented as differing on exactly the same point. The words 'Immo vero necesse est', however, are absent from one family of manuscripts, and could easily be a gloss. Even if they are a gloss, however, it is clear that here Antipater is represented as directly denying exactly what Diogenes affirms; so whether he uses the *word necesse* does not determine matters.

Whatever the form of words used, it is clear that Diogenes is not talking directly about what you ought or ought not to do in the way that Antipater is. Antipater is throughout pointing to the *duties* which each person has, according to Stoic theory. If one lives in agreement with nature, one will live according to rational principles which hold for all humans endowed with reason, and which thus can be said to create a fellowship and kinship of all rational beings which can grasp them and live according to them. One is thus said to have duties to all humans ('hominibus consulere debeas', 52). I shall call this the notion of *moral duty*.

In these passages Diogenes is not concerned with this at all; he is thinking of people not in so far as they are akin by virtue of the shared rationality that enables them to grasp the principles of living in agreement with nature, but in so far as they are selling and buying, activities which give rise to certain *legal obligations*.

There are of course important features shared by moral duties and legal obligations; they are both, for instance, examples of *what we ought to do*, and the *words* 'duty' and 'obligation' can be unforcedly applied to both. But two differences are important here, especially the latter. Firstly, a legal obligation is *enforceable*; it has public and institutional sanction, and penalties attach to not keeping it. A moral duty, by contrast, has (normally) no such sanction, only the individual's conscience; and certainly the kind of duties Antipater is talking about have no legal backing.

Secondly, a legal obligation on my part creates a legal *right* on your part that I keep to it. You have a right against me that I tell you what I am legally obliged to tell you about the house I am selling you. By contrast, if I have a moral duty involving you, you do not (typically) have a right against me that I do that duty. You certainly do not have a legally enforceable right against me. You can take me to court if I don't tell you what I am legally obliged to do about the house, but you cannot take me to court, or otherwise enforce a right against me that I be, say, generous to you. If we nowadays do say that you have a right here, what we mean is a moral right, and I agree with the scholarly consensus that in ancient moral philosophy there is no notion clearly answering to our concept of a moral right, not, at least, of a moral right of this form.[10] Antipater, then, is concerned with our moral duties; Diogenes, with our legal obligations, and particularly with the rights on the part of others which these create. This distinction makes immediate sense of the passage, and of the alleged controversy.

In the corn merchant case, Antipater insists that the merchant has a moral duty to tell the customers that there are other ships on the way. For clearly it is their interests to know this, and Antipater stresses that the interests of others give rise to moral duties to further those interests. As a rational being I grasp the principle that I should respond to the needs and interests of other humans; a moral duty arises from the fellowship established by nature between humans. Diogenes, on the other hand, points out that the seller, while he is under a legal obligation to declare any defects in what he is selling, is under no legal obligation to sell it at the price most in the buyer's interests. And so he does not *wrong* anyone in selling for as much as he can get; for the customers have no right that he sell at a price which is in their interests, and thus no right to the information that would lower the price. The seller is not violating the buyers' rights, then—there is no *iniuria*, since no *ius* is violated—though admittedly he is failing to further their interests. Diogenes is not asking whether he ought morally to further their interests; nor is he claiming that he has fulfilled his moral duty by acting in a way which merely does not violate their rights; he is merely asking if any right has been violated here, to which the answer is, 'no'; there is no *iniuria*.

In discussing this case, Diogenes makes two interesting points. One is the distinction between *concealing* and *not telling*. This seems to Cicero merely an irritating quibble, which he belabours in 57: concealing, he says there, is not telling people something which it is in their interests to know, when doing this is in your interests (*emolumenti tui*). This, he declares, is low and unworthy. However, he has got the distinction wrong. 52 makes it clear that for Diogenes concealing is not telling what someone has a right to know, whereas not telling is merely not

[10] I do not here go further into the question of what the *structure* of rights is. I take it as just common sense that A can have a legal right against B that B do something; whether A can have moral rights of this form, and, if so, what they are, is the subject of much controversy.

telling someone something which the person has no right to know, even if it is their interests to know it. Nothing could be more in your interests to know than the truths of Stoic philosophy, but you have no *right* to know these, so if I fail to tell you them I am not telling you what it is in your interests to know; but I am not *concealing* anything from you, since you have no right to know it. What is in *my* interests is neither here nor there. Cicero's indignation is based on a misunderstanding.

We do not know what the Greek verbs were which Diogenes used, and which Cicero translates here as *celare* and *tacere*, so it is hard to judge how plausible the distinction originally was.[11] However, it is of interest that in both major discussions Diogenes makes a point which is in some way linguistic; he was interested in what we now call philosophy of language and wrote extensively on logic, grammar, and linguistic matters.[12] The other interesting point here is that Cicero represents Diogenes as being quite aware of the kind of point that Antipater is represented as making. In 53 he claims to be aware of what I have called moral duty, based on the natural bond between all humans. Still, he goes on to ask, is this to *exclude* people's owning anything? If so, there will be no selling, only giving away. He is clearly right; if moral duty is just to override or nullify legal obligations, then it makes a nonsense of the very notions of legal obligation and rights. If the seller is motivated to do everything he can to further the interests of the customers, then although this is morally admirable (and nice for the customers) it can scarcely be thought of as *selling*. Rather it would be a rejection of the whole institution of selling. Diogenes thus seems aware of the essential distinctness and independence of his concerns and those of Antipater.[13] The discussion of the second example—the house with the Roman equivalent of dry rot—

[11] Pohlenz [313] 269, identifies them with *kruptein* and *sigan* (see above, n. 4). This seems plausible, though Pohlenz cites no grounds.

[12] Cf. von Arnim [2] iii, Diogenes 17–26 ('Logica'). Much of this is preserved in the account of Stoic philosophy in D.L. vii.

[13] This is ignored by e.g. Reesor [54] 24–5, who takes Antipater's position to be that the 'higher principle of morality must be obeyed by the individual regardless of the laws of a particular state', whereas Diogenes is taken to hold that 'moral virtue was simply obedience to existing regulations'. It is clear that Diogenes recognized the existence of both; nothing follows from what we have in these passages as to his view on their relation.

reveals the same positions on both sides. Antipater says that in letting your buyer incur this loss you are failing in your moral duty towards him. It is like refusing to tell someone the way when they are lost. This is, of course, a different matter from legal obligation; there is no legal obligation to tell someone the way either, and a lost tourist has no right to demand it from me. The (alleged) fact that people who fail to tell people the way are publicly cursed at Athens shows only that at Athens such people are regarded as reprehensible (and bad for the tourist trade?); it does not show that they have, or are thought to have, violated anyone's rights. And the further claim, that selling the house with dry rot to the unsuspecting buyer is worse than refusing to tell the way, for it is like deliberately sending someone in the wrong direction, is a claim about the morally low level of the seller's character and intentions; but again it is scarcely relevant to the question of whether or not the buyer's *rights* are violated. If they are not, the seller has violated no legal obligation, and the goodness or badness of his intentions is not what is in question.

Diogenes' answer is slightly odd. We are not, he says, held to everything that we *do* say—for example, to the truth of an advertisement. Still less can we be held to what we do not say. Presumably the idea of not being held to what we do not say is the same as what we have already seen: no-one can complain if you do not tell them something, as long as it is not concealing, i.e. not telling someone something that they have a right to know. Here it is supported by the claim that we are not always held to the truth of what we do say. How can this, however, support the point about concealing and not telling? Plausibly the point is this: in not telling you may be violating no legal right, and so failing in no legal obligation, even if someone is thereby misled, and you know it—just as in certain forms of positive declaration you may be violating no right, and so failing in no legal obligation, even though someone is thereby misled, and you know it. The example of this offered is that of advertising. Diogenes says that when I advertise my tumble-down house I fail in no legal obligation if I call it 'well built'. Why? The assumption seems to be that advertisements are by common convention regarded as declarations which are not to be believed, so that if someone believes me actually to mean that the house is well built I am not guilty of deceiving him; rather he is 'guilty' of mistaking the convention.[14]

Is it true that we do not so much as expect advertisements to tell the truth? In modern societies there is usually some form of Trades Descriptions Act, showing that we do not share this assumption. It is less likely, however, that Diogenes' interest here is in passing off unsound houses than that it is in the linguistic matter of there being forms of words which look like truth-communicating declarations but are not in fact treated as such. An advertisement, for Diogenes, seems to be a claim which is not, or not primarily, an attempt to say something true. In an advertisement the primary intention is not to communicate truth but to sell the product. Suppose, for example, that I tell you earnestly that Persil washes whiter. My intention is to get you to believe that Persil washes whiter; but while conceivably this could be my only, disinterested intention it is more likely that it is subordinate to the intention to get you to buy Persil. Someone who thought that the claim that Persil washes whiter was only, or essentially, a truth-communicating activity would have missed the point.

We know that the Stoics were interested in forms of words that had propositional content but were not straightforwardly statements, and Diogenes' interest in advertisements makes sense in this context. Diogenes can be faulted, however; for even if we recognize an advertisement as primarily an attempt to get us to buy the product and only secondarily an attempt to say something true, it does not at all follow that we do not regard it as an objection to an advertisement that it in fact says something false. That is what a lot of lawsuits are about; the matter is complicated. What is odd here, however, comes from Diogenes' too hasty claim that we do not fault a clearly recognized advertisement for falsity, rather than from his interesting point that we do not regard it as primarily an attempt to state the truth.

[14] Holden [311] in his note on this passage quotes *Digest* XVIII. I. 43: 'ea quae commendandi causa in condicionibus dicuntur, si palam appareant, venditorem non obligant, veluti si dicat "servum speciosum", "domum bene aedificatam"'. Diogenes may thus be straightforwardly appealing to a point in Roman law. However, he does not here say anything corresponding to the crucial 'si palam appareant'; and even if he has the law in mind it is also plausible that he should be interested in the more general principle behind it.

The additional point, however, does not really add anything to what has gone before: you are not violating the buyer's rights just by not telling him what it is in his interests to know, and leaving it up to his judgement. And, once again, we are not given the faintest reason to think that Diogenes said that this kind of not telling is what you morally ought to do, or that doing this exhausts what your moral duty is. For moral duty is one thing, legal obligation another; if I publicly announce that my house has dry rot, I may be acting in accordance with my grasp of the principles of what actions are in agreement with nature, and conformable to the kinship of all rational humans; but I am not acting very much like someone with something to *sell*.

The four later examples are easily seen to fit what has been said hitherto. The sellers whose buyer is at a disadvantage and the buyers whose seller is at a disadvantage are all cases where A fails to tell B something which B has no right to know, although it is clearly in B's interests to know this. Antipater says that A has a moral duty to tell B the relevant facts; Diogenes says that A has no legal obligation to tell B, since B has no right against A that A tell him.[15] Antipater is concerned throughout with our moral duties, Diogenes with our legal obligations and rights. What Cicero fails to see is that these concerns are in no way antithetical. The debate he has constructed is a spurious one, since the alleged opponents are not talking about the same thing.

Cicero has in fact badly misunderstood Diogenes' position. This emerges in two ways. Firstly, it is clear from the conclusion that he thinks that Diogenes' position is at the top of a slippery slope. If you blame those who keep quiet about the dry rot, he says in 58, what of those who actually mislead? And he goes on to give, doubtless from his lawyer's experience, shock-horror stories of people who misled buyers about the advantages of houses, or concealed defects. (Then, as now, the buying and selling of houses seems to bring out the absolute worst in people.) So he is thinking of Diogenes as defending a kind of disingenuousness which is not only dislikeable, but can slide

[15] Merely possessing a forged coin was illegal (see M. H. Crawford, *The Roman Republican Coinage* (Cambridge, 1974) i. 561); so passing it on was not just an offence against the public good, but put the other person in jeopardy.

into outright fraud. But we have seen that this is wrong; there is no slippery slope. On the contrary, Diogenes' position, which focuses on doing what you are legally obliged to, precisely counters any such slide. The seller should obey the laws about sale (51). Not telling someone something which they do not have a right to know has nothing in common with defrauding people. Cicero entirely misses this point. Later in 67 he says that if Marcus Cato was right in his judgement that a seller should, legally, declare all faults in the house, then the corn seller, and the owner of the house with dry rot, were wrong not to say what they knew. But this does not touch Diogenes; he casts no doubt on the idea that you should do what you are legally obliged to do.

Secondly, Cicero throughout constructs a contest between Diogenes and Antipater, giving points to the latter. But we have seen that they are not in opposition. There is no reason for either to reject what the other says. Indeed, we have seen that Diogenes recognizes moral duties, but insists that there are legal obligations as well, which are not nullified by moral duties; they are distinct. Diogenes can perfectly well accept that although the house owner is not legally obliged to tell about the dry rot, he may do so out of moral duty. And Antipater can perfectly well absorb the idea that as well as moral duties to all humans we also have legal obligations to our buyers and sellers. In fact Antipater wrote extensively on social institutions such as marriage, so he can hardly have been unaware of the philosophical relevance of legal rights and obligations. And since Diogenes and Antipater were both respected and orthodox heads of the Stoa, we should probably conclude that each of them dealt with both moral duty and legal obligation. Cicero has created a non-existent conflict by putting together Diogenes' views on the latter and Antipater's views on the former.

## VI

From this passage, however, we do not find out anything about Antipater's view on legal obligation; we get from him only orthodoxy about moral duties. It is from Diogenes that we get an interesting glimpse of a view that recognizes both and makes some kind of moral room for legal obligations. Can we be more precise as to what kind of moral room, and what kind of theory Diogenes held?

Two interpretations of Diogenes' position, as it is visible here, are possible. On the *weak* interpretation, Diogenes recognizes legal obligations as distinct in kind from moral duties, but argues that this kind of claim is *compatible* with moral duty. On the *strong* interpretation, Diogenes thinks that legal obligations themselves have a kind of moral worth; following them counts as a kind (an indirect kind) of moral duty. The strong interpretation would give Diogenes a two-level theory of a familiar kind: one aims to do one kind of thing, but achieves this aim indirectly, by doing something else the doing of which achieves the first kind; one is thus no longer motivated by the original aim, but achieves it by aiming at something else. The weak interpretation merely rejects *conflict* between legal obligation and moral duty, but does not give legal obligations themselves any kind of value that contributes to achieving a moral goal.

Diogenes' words in 53 may well suggest the strong interpretation, giving him a view which would go as follows: Yes, we are morally bound to consider the welfare of others equally with our own. But it would be inept to go about this directly, nullifying in the process institutions like buying and selling and their associated laws. We are more likely to achieve our end if we respect legal obligations instead of always directly performing our moral duty; for having institutions and legal rights and obligations is a better way, overall, of bringing it about that all achieve the moral aim.[16] However, Diogenes' overall concern, as far as we can see from the passages, does not seem to be the positive one of promoting the doing of moral duty more effectively; it seems limited to the negative tasks of pointing out that moral duty must make room for legal obligations, and that there are cases where no wrong has been done, no right violated, even though the agent has not done as much as moral duty might require. This impression, of course, may be due to the selection that Cicero, who does not grasp Diogenes' position, has provided for us; we are in the common position of inferring a position from a source whose nature hinders our search. I do not think, in fact, that we can ascribe either view

[16] I shall not here go into the merits and (I think insoluble) problems of two-level views, about which there is considerable modern discussion.

definitely to Diogenes; partly because the evidence is not determinate enough, and partly because on this point the Stoics do not seem ever to have had a very definite theory.

Stoic political theory became notorious for the picture of the ideal state in Zeno and Chrysippus, in which social and political life would reflect the moral fact that most existing social institutions are merely conventional. Of course it is hard to interpret the fragments of these works, which have come to us through hostile sources, but it seems as though in a world where people acted on moral reasons and did their moral duty, most current social and political institutions would not exist. On the other hand, Chrysippus at least defended some institutions, notably private property, though in just what context we do not know.[17] In *De Officiis* III. 42 Cicero quotes Chrysippus to the effect that life is like a race; one should compete with others and try to win; all that is ruled out is tripping up the opponent and other foul play.[18] More notably, at *De Finibus* III. 67 Cicero quotes Chrysippus as claiming that, just as in a theatre the space is public, but I can rightly be said to own the seat which I have paid for, so in the world at large the fact that everything is common is compatible with people's owning things.[19] This

[17] Kargl [52] 18, claims that since Zeno's notorious *Republic* abolished private property, 'sicherlich gehen wir nicht fehl mit der Annahme, daß Chrysipp seine Verteidigung des Privatbesitzes, die uns Cicero de fin. III, 20 berichtet, im Gegensatz zu Zeno und von dessen gegenteiliger Ansicht ausgehend gehalten hat'. Kargl never attempts to reconcile this with his repeated insistence that private property is inconsistent with the ethical and political theory of *all* the early Stoics (cf. 28 ff.). Indeed, Chrysippus' *Republic* was just as notorious as Zeno's, and for the same reasons, so this alleged change of attitude needs some explanation. Unless we are to discount Cicero's report here entirely, the only reasonable conclusion is that all the early Stoics combined the view that ethically we are all equal and that in ideal conditions politics would reflect this fact, with the recognition that in the world as it is legal claims (especially property claims) have a valid hold on us. Thus they are not committed to being political revolutionaries; but neither are they committed to being political reactionaries.

[18] Cicero mentions this approvingly, failing to see that it is effectively the same view as Hecato's, which he abuses. On Cicero's own attitude, see below, sect. VII.

[19] 'Sed quemadmodum theatrum cum commune sit, recte tamen dici potest eius esse eum locum quem quisque occupavit, sic in urbe mundove communi non adversatum ius quo minus suum quidque cuiusque sit.' 'C'est-à-dire qu'il y ait un droit de propriété', J. Martha, *Cicéron: Des terms extrêmes des biens et des maux*, II. 45, Budé. There are limits to the aptness of the theatre seat as an analogue for private property (pointed out to me by Jonathan Barnes). I do not have the right to destroy the seat I have paid for, nor to sit in it naked. However, I do not have unqualifiedly the right to destroy, at least, things which are clearly private property (an irreplaceable natural wonder, a work of art), nor to sit naked in my own garden; other factors are involved.

thought is echoed in a passage of Epictetus.[20] The theatre ticket is in some ways a good analogy for private property. My 'ownership' of a seat is temporary, based on convention, transferable, and in no way dependent on my moral worth. Nonetheless, if I have paid for my opera ticket I will rightly not put up with your trying to occupy my seat on the grounds that since we are all equal as rational humans there are just as good grounds for you to sit there as for me (perhaps even better if you are more musical). But the analogy with the box-office fails to tell us what we want to know about the moral status of private property; is it merely a concession to unideal human nature, or could it itself have some moral worth of an indirect kind?

It is frustrating that Cicero's account of Diogenes' position should leave us in the dark on this crucial point. But it is possible, of course, that Diogenes himself was not very clear on it either. We certainly do not find much more clarity here from his pupil Panaetius, who arguably touches on this issue.

Cicero's account of the virtues in *De Officiis* I is probably close to Panaetius, and the account there given of justice, which initially seems merely odd, can be taken as an attempt to bring together questions of moral duty and of legal obligation, as I have characterized these. For without any warning, or argument, justice is treated as a single virtue consisting of two distinct parts—justice proper (*iustitia*) and benevolence (*beneficentia*, *benignitas*, *liberalitas*, *benevolentia*). Although I cannot argue it properly here, I think it can be shown that justice proper is concerned with what we could call matters of legal obligation and rights,[21] while benevolence is concerned with

[20] *Diss.* II. 4. Epictetus inveighs against an adulterer who offers a specious defence of his behaviour by claiming, as an expert scholar, that women are by nature common to all. Epictetus does not reject the assumptions that women are property, nor that property is really common to all; he merely points out that women though by nature common property have already been assigned by 'the lawgiver'. He offers the adulterer an ironic analogy (9): 'Well, isn't the theatre the citizens' common property? So go there when they are seated, if it seems to you a good idea, and throw someone out of his seat.'

[21] Justice proper (I. 20–41) covers rights arising from property or from agreements; hence it covers rules of (properly declared) wars and treatment of (open) enemies. Central is the discussion of *fides*, keeping your contracted word; Cicero emphasizes that once you have done this, the other party has rights, and it is not all right to break your word just because it is to your disadvantage, or even because you discover that the other party is less admirable than you thought. This virtue extends to proper treatment of others within rules or conventions you have accepted, even in circumstances where it is

moral duties which we have towards others as fellow human beings.[22] These are summarily brought under a single virtue; it is simply presumed that they do not conflict, and nothing is said as to either's being an indirect means to the other's end. Cicero complains that Panaetius did not treat of possible conflict between the virtues; he also failed to consider the possibility of conflict within his strikingly disjunctive account of justice.

Only Hecato, Panaetius' pupil, seems clearly to hold some version of the stronger position. Cicero at *De Officiis* III. 63 reports from Hecato's books on appropriate action:

> A wise person should look after his family property, doing nothing contrary to customs, laws and institutions. For we do not wish to be rich just for ourselves, but for our children, relatives and friends, and especially for our country. For the means and resources of individuals are the riches of the state.[23]

This looks like a straightforward two-level justification. Private property is not just compatible with using one's money to benefit others; it is presented as an effective way of doing just that, of achieving the morally desirable end and thus having some derivative moral worth itself.

Still, we have no reason to think this part of a *general* justification of legal obligations and rights on Hecato's part.[24] The

---

most tempting to break them (hence the stress on war). It seems odd that in 41 Cicero adds behaviour to slaves; but here he is recommending that we treat them *as though* by explicit *contract*—'uti ut mercennariis, operam exigendam, iusta praebenda'.

[22] Benevolence (42–60) is concerned with the areas where you are not bound by others' rights. It is not simply the moral duty of treating all equally—Cicero starts (50–52) from the fundamental Stoic idea that by nature we are all equal and akin by virtue of our shared rationality, but either he or Panaetius restricts our duties here in two ways. They cover only what we can do without making things worse for ourselves. And there is considerable stress on the *differentiation* of our duties to friends, parents, fellow-citizens, etc. The passage is reminiscent of Hierocles' 'circles of affinity', except that Panaetius (or Cicero) in deference to Roman sensibilities puts duty to the Fatherland above all else.

[23] 'Sapientis esse nihil contra mores, leges, instituta facientem habere rationem rei familiaris. Neque enim solum nobis divites esse volumus, sed liberis, propinquis, amicis maximeque rei publicae. Singulorum enim facultates et copiae divitiae sunt civitatis' (*Off.* III. 63).

[24] He does say, however, at *Off.* III. 90, that you should put duty to a treasonable parent above duty to the state, because the attitude of doing this is conducive to having a good state: 'ipsi patriae conducit pios habere cives in parentes'. But he also adds that if you are forced by circumstances to a choice (which it is permissible to avoid as long as you can) then you should choose the state.

Stoics seem, in fact, to have been somewhat vague about just what kind of status legal rights and obligations had in their moral and political theory.

Another point on which they are surprisingly uncommitted is *which* legal obligations are either a means to, or merely compatible with, achieving our moral end. For some laws and institutions are unjust; some legal rights are such that it would be immoral to press them. The Stoics pay remarkably little attention to this problem. When Cicero (that is, presumably Panaetius at this point) talks of the origin of property rights at *De Officiis* I. 21, we find that, although he is very sure that people have just entitlements to what is theirs, he has no criterion for deciding whether an entitlement is just.[25] And at *De Officiis* II. 81–3 Cicero, telling the story of Aratus of Sicyon, approves of Aratus, who, restoring fifty-year-old property claims, rejected a single principled solution and instead dealt with the matter in a wholly pragmatic way.[26] Surprisingly, the Stoics seem to have no clear theory as to which existing institutions can be morally justified. They seem to share this attitude with modern two-level utilitarians. Holding a highly revisionary moral theory, they are, when they do compromise with the real world, too ready to use their theory to accommodate existing institutions just the way they are.

[25] *Off.* I. 21: 'Things are not private by nature, but become so either by long occupation—e.g. people who have at some point entered vacant territory, or by conquest—e.g. people who have acquired them by war, or by law, pact, agreement, lot.' Cicero then stresses the right of people to keep their entitlements. But he has given us no theory of just *acquisition* of these entitlements. We have some *un*just acquisition (conquest), some just *transfers* (law, purchase). Only occupying vacant territory can be just acquisition. Note also the way that all these are thrown together, as though the nature of the original acquisition were not crucial. See also the next note.

[26] *Off.* II. 81–3. Aratus restored, in a *coup*, the exiles from a previous *coup* fifty years before. He did not just restore the original owners, on the grounds that since fifty years had passed the estates had been in other hands a long time and were now even held, often, by people who had acquired them by just transfer. Instead he proceeded on no single principle, sometimes restoring the exile but compensating the current owner, sometimes leaving the owner and compensating the exile. This was a sensible pragmatic solution; like many such, it is illogical. After one, or five, years he would have restored the exiles to the estates from which they had been expropriated. After fifty, he accepted that their claim was still just, yet also accepted that time alone had conferred some legitimacy on the current owners' claims. If Cicero's praise for this procedure derives from Panaetius, then the Stoics had no single consistent principle here.

## VII

I have argued that Cicero is badly mistaken in his interpretation of Diogenes. He fails to see that Diogenes is concerned with legal rights and obligations, and recognizes that these are distinct from moral duties. As a result, he wrongly takes Diogenes to be denying the orthodox moral claims that Antipater puts forward. We might excuse this by the plausible supposition that Diogenes' own position was probably not very clear; we have seen that neither his predecessors nor his successors as heads of the Stoa did much better, with the possible exception of Hecato. However, Cicero makes an exactly parallel misinterpretation of Hecato also, in a clearer context. Hecato, as we have seen, says (*De Officiis* III. 63) that private enterprise is fine, if it is legal. Cicero says disapprovingly that Hecato could not endorse generosity such as that of a Q. Scaevola who paid for a house more than the seller asked. But of course Hecato could, and probably did. He would say that Scaevola had no legal obligation to do it, since the seller had no right that Scaevola pay what was most in the seller's interests; but Scaevola's moral duties were distinct from, and not exhausted by, his legal obligations, and he acted morally and deserves praise.

Recognizing Cicero's mistake here should not lead us to a patronizing judgement that he was stupid, or unphilosophical. Cicero's philosophical works show a sharp mind; but sometimes he is insufficiently critical of a position or an argument which he finds obvious. We would do better on the whole to refrain from criticizing too sharply a fault we are all prone to.

Cicero does, however, appear to make another mistake which looks somewhat stupid. Having set up a spurious debate between Diogenes and Antipater, he then appears to range himself on the wrong side. Nobody could be a stronger supporter of the institution of private property than Cicero. And yet instead of seeing natural allies in Diogenes and Hecato he abuses them and lines up with Antipater, whom he takes to overrule private property in the name of our moral duty to act in the interests of other people equally with ourselves. We know that Cicero himself hardly believes this. And it is especially unfortunate that he has just, in *De Officiis* II, especially 72–85, passionately defended private property. Is Cicero confusedly speaking with two voices?

I think not. We must not forget that Cicero often sees himself as an Academic—that is, a sceptic. Even if his scepticism is a moderated, late-Academic kind, it remains true that in none of his philosophical works does he put forward arguments (as opposed to incidental remarks) for a position which represents what he, the individual Marcus Tullius Cicero, thinks. He puts forward arguments pro and con various theses; within the dialogues he sometimes defends some positions against others, but he always reminds us that he does so as an Academic, defending a position which seems viable, but uncommitted as to its being the truth of the matter. On a matter as crucial and difficult as the nature of our final good he is even to be found arguing on opposing sides at different times, explaining this by his Academic habit of defending what seems most convincing at the time. (Compare *De Finibus* IV with *Tusculan Disputations* V.)

*De Officiis* I and II are based on Panaetius and put forward Stoic ideas—yet in II. 7–8 Cicero reminds us that *he*, unlike Panaetius, writes not as a Stoic, convinced of the truth of these ideas, but as an Academic, trying them out and arguing for them but not committed, despite their plausibility, to their being the truth. So when in Book III he launches out on his own, we should take him seriously, especially as he repeats the point at III. 20: he is not giving his personal position. Despite the Roman examples and the often-stressed fact that the book was written at an emotional time in his own life, it does not straightforwardly express a position of his own. It is an attempt on the part of an Academic to work out *in Stoic terms* the solution to the *Stoic* difficulty that Books I and II have raised. Cicero is doing the job himself, but doing it in Stoic terms, for after all it would be pointless for an Academic to solve a Stoic problem in un-Stoic terms (just as it would be pointless to attack a Stoic position in un-Stoic terms). Both could only be done by relying on your own substantial position, which would then have to be defended in turn. Cicero, as a good Academic, and no doubt also by temperament, has no such substantial position.

Cicero's solution is not a subtle one. He just restates standard Stoic orthodoxy: virtue always overrides any other kind of value. Private property may be a good thing, but still it is, in Stoic terms, an indifferent: it can never conflict with virtue since it is always overridden by it. Or, as Cicero standardly puts it, since only virtue benefits, the only benefit we get from doing something virtuously comes from the virtue; getting any other value adds nothing comparable, and without virtue any other kind of value is of no real benefit. Cicero merely insists strongly on the orthodox line, and in the process misinterprets Diogenes and Hecato as quibblers at best, dubious at worst. Even if he were to get their position straight, however, it is hard to see how Cicero's type of approach could provide an adequate answer to the issues of legal rights and obligations which arise from Chrysippus to Hecato. For the Stoics seem to have tried, however hesitantly and unsatisfactorily, to make moral room for legal rights and obligations. A seller who proceeds on the principle of *caveat emptor* is not responding to the needs and interests of all others, as it is his moral duty to do; but it is also true that he is not *wronging* anyone—where no *ius* is violated, there is no *iniuria*. And this is a relevant point, which is simply not answered or in any way illuminated by repeating the old point that there can be no conflict between virtue and any other value, since virtue is always overriding. Cicero stresses that the problem is not how to solve a conflict, but how to grasp the situation in the light of all relevant considerations so that we can see that there is no real conflict. But this, though true, leaves us no further forward with cases like the corn-seller and the house with dry rot. If we read these passages with an eye only to the orthodoxy repeated by Antipater, we are left with a moral theory and little idea of how to apply it in the real world in which there are established institutions like those of buying and selling. And that was the problem that Diogenes and others (including quite possibly Antipater in other works) were at least trying to attack. Cicero's orthodox but unsatisfactorily crude solution tells us something about Cicero—or rather, about how he argues as an Academic. It also tells us something about the continuing struggle the Stoics had, especially after contact with the Romans, to keep their moral and political theory consistent and free from major revisions, and yet to bring it nearer to real life by making it more realistically and usefully applicable in the actual world.

7

# Philosophy and Religion in the Late Republic

P. A. BRUNT

FROM the second century BC Greek culture was increasingly imbibed by the Roman élite. Many of them thus became familiar, or at least superficially acquainted, with Greek philosophic ideas, partly through the medium of instruction in Greek rhetoric, which had a more practical value for those who followed a political career. It was members of the élite who filled the great priesthoods at Rome and were responsible for the maintenance of the state cults. Scholars have commonly held that in the late Republic these cults were increasingly neglected, that traditional beliefs on religious matters were weakening, and that the attempt made by Augustus to restore the old religion was artificial and had little permanent effect. The critiques of Greek religion, explicit or implied in the various philosophic doctrines on theology, which applied more or less to Roman religion too, have been adduced as part of the explanation of this supposed development, by reason of their influence on the élite, if not on the masses. Carcopino, for instance, had no doubts on this; in a chapter entitled 'L'affaiblissement de l'esprit romain', he traced the malign impact both of Greek myths and of Greek philosophy on the minds of Romans. As the elder Pliny put it (*NH* xv. 19), the Greeks were 'omnium vitiorum genitores'. My purpose here is not to inquire how far, if at all, the old Roman religion was really in decay, but whether and to what extent Greek philosophic theories could have had the supposed effect. For these theories we naturally have to go back to what survives of the works of the Greek thinkers who commanded most influence in Rome, and in my judgement the occasional references in writings of the imperial period to the relation between philosophical doctrines and modes of worship are valid indications of the views that Cicero and his contemporaries may well have held, though of course no two individuals necessarily perceived it in exactly the same way.[1]

Romans were certainly conscious that philosophic teaching was at variance with inherited religious practices and beliefs. For example, Varro (as we know through St. Augustine) followed an unidentified Greek thinker in distinguishing three types of theology, three ways of giving an account of the divine: mythical, natural, and political. Mythical theology was purveyed by the poets, natural by the philosophers, and political in the laws and civil customs of the state. Of course the poets told and interpreted the myths in various ways, the theories of the philosophers were diverse, and each people had its own gods and cults, though often ready enough, and none readier than the Romans, to equate their own with foreign deities or to borrow from other peoples; still in Cicero's epigram 'sua cuique religio, nostra nobis' (*Flac.* 69).[2]

[1] In this general survey I abstain from learned annotation, and may refer readers to standard works on the various philosophies mentioned. For the relationship of Epicureanism and Stoicism respectively to traditional religions see esp. Festugière [36] ch. 4, and Zeller [23] 318 ff. Stoic theology rests on Stoic physics, on which Sambursky [56] is helpful. On the supposed decline of Roman religion see Wissowa [318] 70–103, and Latte [315] 264–311; Liebeschutz [316] chs. 1 and 2, is more reserved, and others seem now disposed to challenge the once orthodox theory of decay. I am impressed by some but not all of the evidence adduced in its support, and by the fact that religion obtrudes so little, if at all, in the correspondence of Cicero and in the writings of Sallust, Caesar, and his continuators; on the other hand Cicero appeals fairly often to religious beliefs in his speeches. I have discussed the particular religious attitudes of Marcus Aurelius and shown that they were not exactly the same as those of Epictetus, of all Stoics known to us the closest to Marcus, in [171].

[2] August. *CD* VI. 5: 'tria genera theologiae dicit esse, id est rationis quae de dis explicatur, eorumque unum mythicon appellari, alterum physicon, tertium civile. . . . Deinde ait: "Mythicon appellant, quo maxime utuntur poetae; physicon, quo philosophi; civile, quo populi. . . . Primum . . . quod dixi, in eo sunt multa contra dignitatem et naturam immortalium ficta.' (Cf. IV. 27: 'primum genus nugatorium dicit esse, quod multa de diis fingantur indigna') '. . . Secundum genus est . . . de quo multos libros philosophi reliquerunt, in quibus est dii qui sint, ubi, quod genus, quale est; a quodam tempore an a sempiterno fuerunt dii; ex igni sint, ut credit Heraclitus, an ex numeris, ut Pythagoras, an ex atomis, ut ait Epicurus. Sic alia, *quae facilius intra parietes in schola quam extra in foro ferre possunt aures*.' Cf. IV. 27: 'Secundum genus (dicit) non congruere civitatibus, quod habeat aliqua supervacua, aliqua etiam quae obsit populis nosse', e.g. 'non esse deos Herculem, Aesculapium, Castorem, Pollucem; proditur enim ab doctis quod homines fuerint et humana condicione defecerint' and 'quod eorum qui sint dii non habeant civitates vera simulacra, quod verus Deus nec sexum habeat nec aetatem nec definita corporis membra'. Augustine comments: 'expedire igitur existimat falli in religione civitates', since Varro himself wrote that 'hi qui populis instituerunt

Varro held explicitly that the state was prior to its (political) religion, which was its creation, just as a picture is the creation of the painter.[3] He described the Roman religion, its priesthoods, sacred places, public games, public and private rituals, and its gods classified as *certi*, *incerti*, and *selecti*, in the sixteen books of his *De Rebus Divinis* (August. *CD* VI. 3). His aim was to teach 'why we should supplicate each god and what we are to ask from each' and for this purpose to establish the function and power in any particular matter that each god possessed; just as you needed to know who was a doctor if you were in want of medical attention, so it was necessary to understand that Aesculapius was the god of healing; it would be senseless to ask Liber for water or the Nymphs for wine.[4] He thought this necessary as some old forms of worship were in danger of neglect; they had to be rescued, as Anchises had saved the Penates in the sack of Troy.[5] In some cases he was too late: he had to

simulacra, et metum dempserunt et errorem addiderunt' (IV. 9, cf. 31; but note VII. 5). For the tripartite theology see also Aetius, *Plac.* 6; Plut. *Mor.* 753 B–F; Tert. *Ad Nat.* II. 8. 15; Euseb. *Praep. Evang.* IV. 1.

[3] *CD* VI. 4: 'Iste ipse Varro propterea se prius de rebus humanis, de divinis autem postea scripsisse testatur quod prius extiterint civitates, deinde ab eis haec instituta sint', adding 'sicut prior est pictor quam tabula picta, prior faber quam aedificium, ita priores sunt civitates quam ea quae a civitatibus instituta sunt'. IV. 31: 'Nonne its confitetur non se illa iudicio suo sequi quae civitatem Romanam instituisse commemorat ut, si eam civitatem novam constitueret, ex naturae potius formula deos nominaque eorum se fuisse dedicaturum non dubitet confiteri? Sed iam quoniam in vetere populo esset, acceptam ab antiquis nominum et cognominum historiam tenere, ut tradita est, debere se dicit, et ad eum finem illa scribere ac perscrutari ut potius eos magis colere quam despicere *vulgus* velit.' Thus he made plain 'multa esse vera, quae non modo *vulgo* scire non sit utile, sed etiam, tametsi falsa sunt, aliter existimare populum expediat'. Augustine remarks that the *ludi* were part of the civic religion and gave currency to the mythical religion (IV. 26; VI. 5 f.) which was also reflected in the imagery of the gods; the mythical and civic religions were not distinct (VI. 7).

[4] In his *De Rebus Divinis* (August. *CD* VI. 1) Varro systematically showed 'quod sit cuiusque munus et propter quid cuique debeat supplicari' (VI. 9); cf. VI. 1: 'quare cuique deo supplicandum esset, quid a quoque esset petendum' (by the citizens, esp. the public rites which the priests must know and administer, VI. 5); cf. IV. 22: 'quoniam nihil prodest, inquit, hominis alicuius medici nomen formamque nosse, et quod sit medicus ignorare. Ita dicit nihil prodesse scire deum esse Aesculapium, si nescias eum valetudini opitulari atque ita ignorare cur ei debeas supplicare'; by learning 'quam quisque deus vim et facultatem ac potestatem cuiusque rei habeat, . . . poterimus scire quem cuiusque causa deum advocare atque invocare debeamus, ne faciamus, ut mimi solent, et optemus a Libero aquam, a Nymphis vinum'.

[5] VI. 2: 'cum vero deos eosdem ita coluerit colendosque censuerit ut in eo ipso opere litterarum suarum dicat se timere ne pereant, non incursu hostili, sed civium neglegen-

devote a book to the *di incerti* about whom he could at best resort to conjectures (VII. 17). Cults too had vanished. For instance, the religious calendar included a festival in honour of Furrina, who had once had a *flamen*, but even her name was now known to few (*Ling*. VI. 19). He singled out twenty gods as select, Augustine could not see on what principle. Most of them corresponded to the Greek Olympians (Apollo had actually been imported), but Genius, Sol, and Luna also appeared among them (*CD* VII. 2 f.).

The Roman gods were in fact innumerable, some of them having no characteristics but that of being the divine power immanent in some natural object or process or in the actions, relationships, and attributes of men, like Victoria, Concordia, Fides, Libertas. These personifications as well as gods like Jupiter or the Lares were given images in human shape. The images in their shrines were for the more sophisticated worshippers symbols of their power, but no doubt Christian critics were right that many, supposing the divinity to be immanent in the image, revered sticks and stones. At any rate the gods were conceived as having the form of men. Long ago Xenophanes had ridiculed this conception. If horses could make works of art, they would represent the gods like horses; if there was any divinity, it was 'all eye, all mind, all ear' (12–14; 19 f. Diehl). Most philosophers concurred, though the Epicureans adopted the anthropomorphic view, which Cicero thought ludicrously inappropriate to their notions of the kind of life that their gods lived (*Nat. D.* I. 92 f.). Varro himself wrote that those who had set up images had subtracted awe and added error to religion (above, n. 2). He supposed that the Romans had had none in the first 170 years of their history, and suggested that their religion would have been purer if there had been no change (August. *CD* IV. 31), even though anthropomorphic representation of the gods might symbolize the truth that the divine notion was the intelligence also present in man (VII. 5). Varro himself accepted, perhaps from Antiochus of Ascalon, a Stoicizing theology; god was the world-soul, but was also individuated

tia [cf. *Ling*. VI. 19 for Furrina] de qua illos velut ruina liberari a se dicit et in memoria bonorum per eius modi libros recondi atque servari utiliore cura quam . . . Aeneas de Troiano excidio penates liberasse praedicatur'.

in visible forms and in the human soul; as for the Roman gods he could give only his opinions without feeling any certitude. It was his purpose to preserve traditional practices rather than correct them.[6]

Once Roman gods had been identified with Greek and imaged by artists working in the Greek tradition, it must have been harder for Romans to free their minds from the Greek myths told of them. They had no myths of their own (their native poetic imagination had found early expression in the pseudo-historic legends of old Rome), but they became familiar with the Greek tales by their contacts with Greek cities in Italy and beyond the seas and as a result of immigration from those parts; moreover, these tales were given currency in Roman drama, performed in the games which were themselves religious institutions of the state. Augustine consequently insisted that the mythological religion was imbedded in the civic: religion of the theatre was that of the state (above, n. 3). The representations of the conduct of gods propagated in these myths had again been regarded as false and pernicious by moral philosophers since Xenophanes: 'Homer and Hesiod have ascribed to the gods all that is reproach and blame in the world of men, stealing and adultery and deceit' (10 Diehl). On this count Plato had banned much Greek poetry from his ideal city. Varro too had decried mythical theology for the same reason, yet he did not propose any censorship. Perhaps after all it did not matter much. It was only essential that the cults be kept up; if the right ritual was followed, it was immaterial how the votary conceived the god he worshipped. 'Religio, id est cultus deorum', as Cicero said.[7]

The cults themselves comprised no moral teaching. None the

[6] Philosophically Varro held 'deum esse animam mundi . . . et hunc ipsum mundum esse deum', but the four elements 'animarum esse plenas, in aethere et aere inmortalium, in aqua et terra mortalium'; thus the heavenly bodies were visible gods in the aether, and the air was full of gods perceived by the mind, called heroes, Lares, and Genii (August. *CD* VII. 6); the highest form of *anima* is intelligence; 'hanc partem animae mundi dicit deum, in nobis autem genium vocari' (VII. 23). Conjecturally Varro drew on Antiochus, as for ethics (XIX. 3). Varro on the 'select gods' (cf. VII. 2): 'de diis populi Romani publicis, quibus aedes dedicaverunt eosque pluribus signis ornatos notaverunt, in hoc libro scribam, sed ut Xenophanes Colophonius scribit, quid putem, non quid contendam, ponam. Hominis est enim haec opinari, dei scire'; on the *di incerti* he had even more doubts.

[7] August. *CD* IV. 27; Cic. *Nat. D* II. 8.

less social morality was thought to be linked with belief in the gods; take that away, said Cicero, and worship will be neglected, piety and religion will disappear, and then, (who knows?) good faith, human solidarity, and justice. Citizens should be imbued with the conviction that the gods were beneficent rulers of the world and observed the character and conduct of men; the sanctity of oaths depended on this, and many were deterred from crime by fear of divine punishment.[8] 'It is in the interest of society', Diodorus wrote, 'that fear of the gods should be deeply embedded in the minds of the people; few men practise justice from personal virtue; the mass of mankind are kept from wrong-doing by the penalties of the law and of divine retribution'; the passage is extracted from his account of the first Sicilian slave revolt, which demonstrably derives from Posidonius, and Posidonius also praised the reverence for the gods and justice towards men shown by Romans in the good old days, perhaps suggesting that the two qualities went together. Plutarch had read that Numa's religious institutions tamed the primitive ferocity of the Romans. Polybius too held that it was terror of divine anger that kept the multitude in check at Rome and produced that singular good faith in Romans that was hardly to be found among his own countrymen.

He seems to think that it was punishment in a future life that was feared. That may well have been a misconception. The official religion inculcated no such terror. According to the experts there is no evidence in the cults themselves or in funeral monuments for any widespread Roman belief in personal survival after death; the *di parentes* or *di Manes* were revered only as a collectivity of ancestors until the late Republic, when tombstones begin to show that the individual soul of the departed could be treated as living; even then, naturally enough, it was not depicted as enduring the agonies of Hell. In Greece there seems to have been more popular belief, though it was far from universal, both in individual survival and eternal punishment, and it was perhaps because of the strength of this feeling at Athens that Epicurus was concerned to show that it had no foundation. The passion with which Lucretius dilates on this

[8] *Nat. D.* I. 4; cf. 14, 63; *Leg.* II. 15 f.

theme might suggest that in his own experience the fear of torments in an after-life was the chief mode in which religion aggravated human misery. We might speculate on the possible penetration of Greek ideas, notably Pythagorean, in this as in so many other spheres. Cicero could refer to popular opinion about the sufferings of the dead. But in the very same book he says that not even old wives entertained them, and elsewhere he suggests that Epicureans were seeking to dispel apprehensions which hardly any felt but themselves. The only alternatives he personally considered were total extinction and everlasting blessedness.[9]

Divine vengeance in this life was another matter. In taking an oath you invoked it on yourself in the event of perjury, which was not a secular crime: 'dis iniuriae dis curae' (cf. Cic. *Leg.* II. 22). In some civil suits one party might tender an oath to the other; who swore the oath won the case.[10] But a litigant sure of the justice of his cause might be wary of giving so easy an escape to an unscrupulous adversary; it does not appear that the procedure was in common use. Magistrates and *iudices* had to swear that they would act properly. Soldiers swore obedience to their commanders; still desertions and mutinies occurred; whole armies in civil wars went over to the other side. In 44 all the senators swore to protect Caesar;[11] eighty of them, it is said, helped to kill him. Still, we must remember how many Christians who believed in Hell-fire have committed mortal sins, quite deliberately. We cannot be sure that religious fears did not tend to make men true to their oaths. And conceivably cults of Jupiter Fidius or Fides or Honor and Virtus had some morally strengthening effect.

Perhaps there was a more subtle connection between the civic religion and social morality felt but not clearly articulated by Cicero, Polybius, and Posidonius. The cults were part of the

[9] Diod. XXXIV. 2. 47 (Posid., cf. *FGrH* 87 F 59; Malitz [222] 138 ff.); Plut. *Num.* 8; Polyb. VI. 56 and Walbank ad loc. Romans and after-life: see e.g. Jocelyn Toynbee, *Death and Burial in the Roman World* (London, 1971) 85 ff.; for the Greeks: K. J. Dover, *Greek Popular Morality* (Oxford, 1973) 61 ff. Cic. on Epicurean fears: *Nat. D.* I. 86. Note *Tusc.* I. 36 f., 48, 111.

[10] M. Kaser, *Das römische Zivilprozeßrecht* (Munich, 1966) 197 ff. Plato had wished to forbid oath-taking by litigants, since it meant that half of them were forsworn, as they believed that the gods were non-existent, indifferent, or venal (*Laws* 948 C).

[11] Weinstock [317] 223–7.

structure of a hierarchical society. If their validity were questioned by the masses, who could say how far questioning might then extend? To Cicero, and to other members of his class, the official religion, controlled as it was by men of the highest station, themselves engaged in politics, afforded useful devices for frustrating what they were pleased to call popular sedition; Cicero is perfectly open on this, and in fact exaggerated its utility.[12] But I doubt if political expediency so narrowly conceived was the basic reason why they thought that, whatever errors in the civic religion they might intellectually discern, it must be sedulously maintained. It was rather perhaps that if the common man ceased to respect the gods in the forms that tradition prescribed he might become no less disrespectful of all other traditional prescriptions of law and custom, and of the unthinking compliance with moral standards that they inculcated. Those who were versed in philosophy might be able to give reasons for belief in a god or gods, though not necessarily gods as they were commonly represented, and, perhaps independently, for observance of moral law and respect for social organization; the masses could not do so, and it was therefore important that they should believe without reason in what had been determined by ancestral wisdom. Subvert this reverence for tradition in any way, and all might be lost. At any rate, as will be seen, they were all prepared to conform to official religion with whatever *arrière-pensées*, if only to set an example to the less enlightened. 'Expedit esse deos, et ut expedit, esse putemus'. Ovid's epigram is not quite apposite. What was needed was a maxim that 'it is expedient that men should believe in the gods, and as this is expedient, let us act as if it is true.'

To philosophers the fear of the gods which was supposed to be the basis of popular morality was wholly or partly misplaced. Epicureans denied, and sceptics doubted, that the gods intervened in human affairs at all. Like Plato, the Stoics held that they would punish wickedness, but no great emphasis seems to have been placed on this doctrine; the gods were

[12] *Leg.* II. 30–3, cf. *Div.* II. 42 f., 70, 75; often in speeches when belabouring Clodius' limitation of the practice of *obnuntiatio*; in fact Bibulus' resort to it in 59 had been unavailing, and it is impossible to cite any case in which religious obstruction of 'seditious' proposals which had strong popular backing had been successful.

beneficent, and fear of them was the mark of superstition; as Varro put it, the superstitious man fears the gods as enemies, the religious man reveres them as parents.[13] The Stoics did indeed regard theology as the foundation of ethics, since the end for man could be defined both as living virtuously and as living in conformity with nature, in which the divine reason was everywhere immanent.[14] However, Cicero could expound Stoic ethics in *De Finibus* III without the least allusion to the Stoic doctrines on physics of which theology was a part, though in his Stoicizing account of the divine natural law in *De Legibus* he too had asserted that nature was the basis of justice and all the social virtues, as well as of the pious worship of the gods, which he calls pure religion (I. 43, 60). The penalty for wickedness that he envisages is the anguish of a guilty mind (I. 40), coupled with posthumous infamy (II. 43 f.); he is hardly much concerned here with the mental attitudes of the vulgar. In *De Officiis* II *pietas* and *sanctitas*, which must comprise acts of worship, are recommended 'to propitiate the gods'; in the context this implies that their favour is requisite for worldly success. But Cicero does not enlarge on this, nor discuss piety as a virtue and the obligations it would entail. We cannot be sure how far this reflects the attitude to religion of Panaetius, whom he was mainly following.[15] Certainly Panaetius deprecated the construction of new temples as mere prodigality (ii. 60).[16]

The cults of course involved beliefs such as were within the

[13] August. *CD* VI. 9. To Romans it often means addiction to foreign religious practices. I quoted some Stoic opinions similar to Varro's in [171] 16 f. On *superstitio* R. Freudenberger, *Das Verhalten gegen die Christen im 2 Jahrhundert* (Munich, 1967) 189 ff. has useful material. Cf. *SVF* iii. 394, 408 f., 411, treating superstition (δεισιδαιμονία) as a species of fear, an irrational emotion; Sen. *Ep.* 95. 47–50: 'errat si quis (deos) putat nocere nolle: non possunt'. But punishment of the wicked (no doubt conceived as a benefit to mankind) was allowed them, cf. Plut. *Mor.* 1050 E, Hierocles *ap.* Stob. *Ecl.* II. 181 f. (ed. Wachsmuth), though Plut. *Mor.* 1040 A–C finds contradictions in Chrysippus' views on the subject. Some Stoics held that the gods visited the sins of the fathers on descendants. *Nat. D*, III. 90. However, the meagreness of the evidence may suggest that divine retribution was not important in Stoic theology.

[14] Plut. *Mor.* 1035 B–C, cf. Epict. *Diss.* II. 14. All standard accounts of Stoic ethics discuss its connection with their theology. It is very marked in Epictetus.

[15] Other Stoics treated piety as that species of justice which is proper to our relations with the gods, *SVF* ii. 1017; iii. 264; no Stoic treatise on it is known, and Cicero does not mention it in his discussion of justice in *Off.* I.

[16] Like Cicero (II. 57) Panaetius may also have condemned as wasteful expenditure on games, viewing them as mere entertainments and not as religious institutions.

faculty of the simplest understanding. Our ancestors, says Cicero, handed down to us belief in the existence of gods, i.e. of the particular gods whom they worshipped.[17] The rituals also presupposed that these gods could be induced to give aid or might be provoked into doing harm to men. Cicero insists over and over again that to those who held that they did not concern themselves with human affairs prayers and offerings were futile. Why should I say of a god 'propitius sit' if he could not be *propitius* to anyone?[18] Now before reaping his crops the Roman farmer would offer a sow to Ceres to procure her blessing and another after the harvest in gratitude for her aid; there were also prayers and sacrifices to Janus, Jupiter, and Juno. Cato preserves the formulae (*Agr.* 134); for example, the suppliant begged Janus to be 'volens propitiusque' to himself, his children, *domus*, and *familia*. His treatise on agriculture is full of similar instructions. Sometimes the worshipper vowed a specified offering in return for a specified favour. Votive offerings were debts to be discharged: 'votum solvit libens merito', as innumerable inscriptions put it. Local communities and the state itself had similar rituals for the collective good. The magistrates were the intermediaries of the state with the gods, performing the essential functions of honouring and propitiating them with supplications and sacrifices. They were also supposed to have methods of assuring themselves that the actions they proposed to take had divine sanction and of expiating signs vouchsafed to them of divine disapproval. All this of course implied that there were gods able and ready to affect human affairs, who responded to invocations by particular names, could be influenced by the honours paid to them, and gave indications by which their will could be divined, and that there were special skills accessible to men for interpreting these indications, and for procuring their favour or averting their

[17] *Nat. D.* I. 5, 43; III. 5, 11. The distinction taken over by S. R. F. Price, *Rituals and Power* (Oxford 1984) 8, from Sperber between two kinds of knowledge (a word apparently not used in any lexical sense), 'encyclopaedic' and 'symbolic', was naturally unfamiliar to Greeks and Romans; in philosophic discourse propositions of the kind, 'gods exist' and 'gods care for mankind', were clearly taken to be 'encyclopaedic' (a bizarre term), i.e. susceptible of demonstration or refutation or doubt on rational grounds, and philosophers clearly supposed that ordinary men understood them in the same way (cf. *Nat. D* III. 63).

[18] *Nat. D.* I. 3, 14, 115 ff., esp. 124. Cf. Epict. *Diss.* I. 22. 15: we hear men saying 'what have I to do with Zeus when he can't help me?'

wrath. (One such skill, with which Varro, as we have seen (n. 4), was much concerned, was that which identified the particular god amidst their almost infinite number whom it was best or necessary to approach in each particular contingency.) The Romans considered themselves pre-eminent in these skills. It was not, said Cicero in the senate, by their superiority in numbers, valour, or any human excellence that they had conquered so many other peoples, but by surpassing them in *pietas*, *religio*, and the wisdom that consisted solely in comprehending that everything was ruled and determined by the will of the gods. This was doubtless a very ancient notion, first documented for us in 193 BC, which Augustine still had to rebut at enormous length in the fifth century AD.[19] No doubt many Romans thought their success sufficient proof of the efficacy of their cults and of the truth of the underlying beliefs.

Now all such beliefs were rejected or questioned by philosophers. The very diversity of philosophical views since Thales, noted by Cicero and others who discussed the matter, was thought disturbing to popular faith; it gave colour to the sceptical contention that nothing could be known about gods.[20] Few thinkers were outright atheists, as Cicero says,[21] but Epicurus was not the first to make the gods indifferent to human fortunes; Plato suggests that this opinion had become widespread in Greece. In his view it was still more common, and worse, for men to think that the gods were ready to grant favours, even to wrongdoers, in return for gifts. He derided the principles of 'do ut des' and 'do quia dedisti', which underlay the Greek and also the Roman practices of sacrifice and votive offerings, as reducing piety to a sort of trade between the gods and their worshippers.[22] Hierocles would assert that the judgements of gods are constant, unaffected by human intercessions,[23] but other Stoics admitted their efficacy, like that of divination; such

[19] Cic. *Har. Resp.* 18 f. Cf. *SIG*$^3$ 601 (193 BC); August. *CD* IV. 3 and often.

[20] *Nat. D.* I. 25–41. cf. August. *CD* VI. 5 (Varro); Sext. Emp. *PH* III. 2–12, 218–28; *M.* IX. 13–194.

[21] *Nat. D.* I. 2, 63; Sext. Emp. *M.* IX. 51 speaks of a great number—wrong, but cf. n. 32.

[22] *Laws* 885 D, 948 C; cf. *Euthyphro* 14 C, cf. Origen, *c. Cels.* II. 13 on Peripatetics.

[23] Stob. *Ecl.* I. 63 f. (Wachsmuth), but cf. n. 15 and Marcus VI. 44.

human actions could have their necessary place in the causal chain, if the 'lazy argument' (*SVF* ii. 956–8) is fallacious. Anthropomorphism was generally repudiated by philosophers who adopted the most exalted conceptions of the divine, alien to popular beliefs and practices. Euhemerus, whose theory Ennius had made familiar to Romans, contended that all the gods were dead men of past power and distinction; Stoics thought it proper to recognize divinity in past benefactors of mankind whose virtues assured their souls of survival, but Epicureans could contend that worship of dead men was destructive of true religious veneration.[24]

All these contradictions led Cicero to conclude that an inquiry into the true nature of the divine was 'essential to the regulation of religious observance' ('ad moderandam religionem necessaria'). In the sequel he refrains from examining any doctrines but those of the Epicureans and the Stoics, together with the sceptical critiques of their doctrines produced by the Academy, notably by Carneades, of which he himself was now an avowed follower.[25] Though he translated the *Timaeus*, he feels no need to examine the Platonic doctrine of the divine *demiourgos* and the created gods, nor that of the unmoved mover of Plato's *Laws* and Aristotle's teaching. We may conclude that it was the theories of the Garden, the Porch, and the Academy that had most currency in contemporary Rome.

The Epicureans, who claimed to prove the existence of anthropomorphic gods, assigned them a life of undisturbed tranquillity; in Tennyson's imitation of Lucretius they—

[24] *Nat. D.* I. 119 (Euhemerus); I. 38, II. 60–2 (Stoics, who cannot have held, as suggested, that Hercules etc enjoyed *aeternitas*, cf. Plut. *Mor.* 1051 F; 1075 A–C).

[25] *Nat. D.* I. 10–13. By contrast in *Leg.* I. he expounds in his own person, and without giving room for opposed views or expressing any dubiety, a Stoic or Stoicizing theology, which is also implied by interlocutors in *Rep.* (e.g. III. 33; VI. 13), though without his own personal and explicit assent: moreover, there the theological doctrines were incidental to the main theme. Both works were composed, and *Rep.* was published, in the 50s, but *Leg.* was perhaps never finished (though more was written than we possess), and it is not in the list of his published treatises in *Div.* II. 2–4 (early 44). The agnosticism or sheer disbelief in divination shown in that work (below, p. 193) is in flagrant contradiction with *Leg.* II. 32 f. It seems most probable that when he set himself in 46 to the systematic study and exposition of philosophical problems he reverted to the Academic standpoint which had most strongly influenced him in youth (Philippson [111] 1173 ff.) but which he had departed from in the 50s; it would then have been an embarrassment for him to issue *Leg.*, and it was presumably published posthumously.

haunt
The lucid interspace of world and world,
Where never creeps a cloud, or moves a wind,
Nor ever falls the least white star of snow,
Nor ever lowest roll of thunder moans,
Nor sound of human sorrow mounts to mar
Their everlasting calm.

These gods were paradigms of the undisturbedness (ἀταραξία) to which we should aspire; it would have been fatally impaired, if they had had to weary themselves with operating the mechanisms of nature or caring for mankind; in truth they could do nothing to help or harm us, while our own calm of mind was disturbed by the false notion that we had cause to fear them in life or after death. Prayers and sacrifices to them could not then fulfil the functions they performed in popular conceptions.

Critics could contend that by removing the notions of divine providence and benevolence the Epicureans totally subverted religion. For Posidonius, who thought the Epicurean theology too absurd to be embraced by a rational man, the Epicureans were atheists at heart, who dared not avow their true opinions for fear of the hostility that would be provoked; Cicero seems to make his Academic spokesman concur. The language of Lucretius, who makes *religio*, and not *superstitio*, a great source of evil, could have given colour to this imputation. Yet it was no more just than that which turned Epicureans into mere voluptuaries. Epicurus himself had faithfully fulfilled all traditional religious practices; he offered prayers and sacrifices in conformity with the laws, participated in religious festivals, was actually initiated into the Eleusinian Mysteries (fr. 169 Us.), insisted on fidelity to oaths, and was careful in invoking the names of gods when appropriate (fr. 142). But all this was not due simply to fear of social disapproval, or worse. He held that it was proper 'not only because of the laws but for reasons in conformity with Nature' (frs. 13; 387). In acts of piety and especially in festivals the wise man comes more vividly to apprehend and share the joy of the gods. True piety consists in perceiving what the divine nature really is, honouring it, and modelling one's own life on it (fr. 386). The mind must of course be free from unwarranted fear of the gods, for then 'nec delubra deum placido cum pectore adibis' (Lucr. VI. 75 ff.). The Epicurean had his own version of 'seeking to make himself like god' (ὁμοίωσις τῷ θεῷ κατὰ τὸ δύνατον (Pl. *Theaet.* 176 B). But no doubt it remained true that his attitude was commonly misunderstood and that a partial acquaintance with the dogmas of the School might make men negligent of the cults.[26]

By contrast the Stoics were strong on the divine governance of the world ordered for the benefit of man. But what did they mean by 'divine'? God was taken to be a material substance, of the purest kind, *aither* or fire, that penetrates the entire material world which it has made and holds together in its present form; it can be equated therefore with nature or the law of nature, which we can see from the design of the structure to be intelligence and reason, the same reason indeed in which men in some measure consciously participate and which for their own good they are bound to obey; the moral law is also for them the law of nature. Thus the Universe is itself divine; as in Pope's exposition of a later Stoicizing deism, divinity—

> Lives through all life, extends through all extent,
> Spreads undivided, operates unspent.

The Universe is also eternal, though consumed by periodic conflagrations into its primordial divine element. But the element is found, as it were, in a purer form both in the reason of men and still more in other individual beings in which it is still less adulterated, and which we can call gods, though they are not eternal but subject to dissolution in the periodic conflagrations; similarly the souls of men or at least of good men may survive death at least for a time, though they too must perish eventually in the same way. These gods include the constellations and the elements, and are present in all the processes of nature and even in apparently inanimate things providentially designed for our benefit, or in any manifestations of the universally benevolent divinity. This makes it appropriate to render cults, as the Romans did, to such abstractions as Mens and Fides. On a similar basis we may accept the 'constitution' as gods of men who conferred benefits on their fellow-men (above, n. 24) and the existence of 'daimons', fragments as it were of the

[26] See esp. criticisms of Academics and Posidonius *ap. Nat. D.* I. 115–24, III. 3.

cosmic God, which are present in each man's soul, if not identifiable with his reason, and whose function it is to keep him in tune with the Universe; a Roman could doubtless equate such a 'daimon' with the Genius of family cults, described by Horace as the 'naturae deus humanae' (*Ep.* II. 2. 183 ff.). The traditional worship of deities which were supposed to be responsible for natural phenomena, and many of the Greek myths allegorically interpreted, could be treated by the Stoics, with the help of fanciful etymologies of divine names, as indications that men had long had a dim understanding of the philosophic truths which Stoic teaching revealed. It was therefore open to them to participate in traditional modes of worship as symbolizing their reverence for true divinity (cf. below, n. 28). However, their gods were very different from those of popular belief; none was in human form, and they were rather 'naturae rerum', the essences of things, than 'figurae deorum', divine personalities (*Nat. D.* III. 63). They were unfailingly beneficent to mankind, but this beneficence consisted in the providential order of the world, of which they were, so to speak, component parts, rather than in their ability to confer special favours on their votaries.[27] Piety, a species of justice, governing the relation of men to gods, which could be defined as 'knowledge of the service of gods', was proper to the sage, who was indeed the only true priest and alone expert in sacrifices, consecrations, and purifications.[28] However, sages were few; it was actually doubtful if the type had ever been instantiated, and the Epicurean Philodemus could assert that on Stoic views the mass of men were so hateful to the gods and so devoid of intelligence that they had not the faintest notion of rendering them due honour.[29]

At one time Stoics had actually expressed opinions overtly hostile to conventional religion. Zeno's ideal *polis* contained no temples or images of the gods; there was, he said, nothing holy in the products of vulgar craftsmen. Here he was probably

[27] *SVF* ii. 1178–80; cf. Sen. *Ep.* 95. 50 (below).

[28] D.L. VII. 119, 124; *SVF* ii. 1017; iii. 604. Note iii. 660 (Stob.): 'Stoics say that the good man keeps a festival, since a festival is a particular time in which it is right to be concerned with the divine for the sake of honour and appropriate symbolism (ἐπισημασίας); hence the celebrant ought to accommodate himself with piety to such an appointed occasion.' Cf. below, n. 36. For similar non-Stoic definitions of piety and the like cf. *Nat. D.* I. 116; [Pl.], *Def.* 412 E 14; 414 A 12: 415 A 9.

[29] Phld. *Mus.* IV, XXI. 1–6, quoted in *SVF* iii. p. 233 under Diogenes fr. 86.

adopting a Cynic attitude; we read that Diogenes did not regard it as sacrilegious to steal from a temple; he also ridiculed divination, religious purifications, prayers for material benefits, and votive offerings; some ascribed to him, others to Diagoras of Melos, the notorious atheist, the saying that there would have been far more thank-offerings to Posidon on Samothrace if those who had been drowned as well as those who had been saved had set them up.[30] None of these tales has any demonstrable authenticity, but at least they tell us what Cynic attitudes made it plausible to ascribe to the founding father of the sect. However, I need not concern myself here with the Cynics, as it does not seem that they were active commonly, if at all, in Republican Rome.[31]

Stoics later on did not think it right to shock people in the Cynic manner; it is, for example, significant that Chrysippus proscribed urinating on a shrine (*SVF* iii. 754). But they could still criticize conventional religious practices. Seneca says that they offered precepts on the proper worship of the gods (*Ep.* 95. 47 f.); all such precepts for men's conduct were useful, according to Cleanthes, whom later Stoics followed, in pointing out particular practical duties for any one who understood the basic doctrines, the 'decreta ipsa philosophiae et capita' (*Ep.* 94. 1–4). But the precepts for worship that Seneca cites are prohibitions of the sort of superstition caricatured by Theophrastus (*Characters* XVI) and later pronounced by the Platonist Plutarch to be worse than atheism, since it implied fear of divine malevolence.[32] In the view of Seneca 'deum colit qui novit' (*Ep.* 95. 47); it was essential only to believe in the existence and kindly benevolence of the gods, who were protectors of the human race, though sometimes indifferent to individuals (*Ep.* 95. 50). The *caveat* in the last phrase would have disturbed those who expected special favours for their prayers and offerings (cf. above, n. 27). Posidonius and Hecato indeed said that the wise man would pray for 'good things' from the gods (D.L. VII. 124), but 'good things' ought to have been limited to virtues, since for Stoics nothing else was truly good. In fact Stoics like Marcus

[30] Zeno: *SVF* iii. 264–7; Diogenes, D.L. VI. 24, 42, 59, 63, 73.

[31] Dudley [78] ch. 6.

[32] Plut. *Mor.* 164 E and *passim*. (It is evident that there were atheists in his time among ordinary Greeks.)

Aurelius (above, n. 23) might thank the gods for other blessings, but then they were not sages but errant human beings. If the sage was the only true priest, it was perhaps because he alone understood what to ask or thank the gods for. Seneca could say that if you wished to propitiate the gods, you must be virtuous: 'satis illos colit quisquis imitatus est' (*Ep.* 95. 50), but that it was idle to lift up your hands in prayer to heaven or to images of the gods: 'prope est a te deus, tecum est, intus est (*Ep.* 41. 1); expiations, since the fates are immutable, serve only to console sick minds (*QNat.* II. 35. 1). In his lost essay on superstition he repudiated the consecration of images, the deification of disgraceful human emotions like Pavor, the frenzies of Oriental rites, and even some practices at the temple of Jupiter Capitolinus (August. *CD* VI. 10). Still, he could write of the traditional cults: 'omnia sapiens servabit tamquam legibus iussa, non tamquam diis grata' (*Ep.* 95. 50). Mere obedience to the laws (which in itself could have been regarded as a moral duty) was hardly the only justification that Stoics could have given for conformity. Epictetus, in a context in which he insists that piety consists above all in holding true opinions about the gods and cheerfully accepting the dispensations of divine providence, also requires conscientious and pure-hearted performance of the traditional libations and sacrifices (*Ench.* 31); I feel sure that he thought this a way of showing that thankfulness to God, which, as he says elsewhere, men should never cease expressing all their lives (*Diss.* I. 16. 15–21; III. 26. 28 f.; IV. 1. 108 f.).

In *De Natura Deorum* Cicero sets out the Epicurean theology, then the Stoic; each is traversed by Cotta, the spokesman for the Academy, who contends that their arguments are not cogent, and the Epicurean conclusions actually ludicrous (above, p. 177). Some of his points would have been familiar to the general public; for example, the claim that the prosperity of the wicked and sufferings of the virtuous are incompatible with a benevolent providence of the gods; he can quote Ennius: 'nam si curent, bene bonis sit, male malis, quod nunc abest' (III. 79). It is evident that Cotta relays the arguments of Carneades, and identical or similar arguments re-appear in Sextus Empiricus (above, n. 20). But the scepticism of Carneades, unlike that of Sextus, permitted him to admit certain propositions as *probabilia*, i.e. one could see persuasive, though not conclusive, reasons for accepting them. Cicero remarks that Carneades himself was not an atheist (*Nat. D.* III. 44). This hardly needed saying if it meant only that he did not absolutely deny the existence of gods: that would have been dogmatism. What more than this did Cicero intend? Perhaps that Carneades allowed that there were better reasons for accepting than for denying the existence of some divinity. This appears to have been Cicero's own judgement even in his sceptical phase, for he gives his personal opinion at the end of Cotta's speech that the Stoic thesis was 'ad veritatis similitudinem propensior' (III. 95). Or perhaps Carneades did not discountenance actual worship of the gods; in that case he was not an atheist in the sense that the Christians were to be accused of atheism, for their refusal to participate in the cults. This accords with the attitude imputed to Cotta. He looks to philosophy to supply a *ratio religionis*, and finds that the Stoics fail, hardly less than the Epicureans, but still, in default of such a *ratio*, he will adhere to both the beliefs and the cults of 'our ancestors'. Hence, as Cicero suggests, Cotta's arguments are not such as to destroy men's religion, for even if they cannot be refuted, they do not require men to abandon the traditional forms of worship (*Div.* I. 8). This is indeed what Cotta is made to say emphatically: as a Roman and a *pontifex* (and Cicero of course had it in mind that he himself was an augur), he saw it as his duty to 'defend the beliefs we have inherited from our ancestors, and the sacred rituals and ceremonies'. He insists on this repeatedly; he is 'persuaded that Romulus by instituting the auspices and Numa by establishing the public rites had laid the foundations of our state, which could certainly never have risen to such greatness but for our efforts to placate the immortal gods' (*Nat. D.* III. 5–7, 9 f., 14 f.).

One argument most Stoics deployed for the divine order of the universe was the possibility of divination; Panaetius indeed questioned it (*Div.* I. 6), and it was not essential to their theology any more than to any other theistic doctrine. Divination is defined by Cicero as 'praesensio et scientia rerum futurarum' (*Div.* I. 4). The definition did not accurately cover the Roman notion that auspices and other omens and signs given by the gods 'announce what will happen in the absence of precautions' (I. 29); this sort of warning, except for its supernatural origin, is analogous to that which an architect may give that a projected building will collapse unless you lay the foundations sufficiently deep. In different forms divination was universally practised; this was one argument for its validity (I. 2–4, 86–96; II. 81). Most philosophers accepted it, though contemporary Peripatetics like Cratippus restricted it to a kind of extra-sensory perception in dreams and ecstasies, it was denied by the Epicureans, and questioned like everything else (I. 5 f.) by Carneades. The case for it was largely empirical; history abounded in examples; failures in the art could be ascribed to want of human skill, the kind of deficiency you could find in other arts, medicine for example. Cratippus even said that a single instance of foreknowledge in dreams would suffice to establish that in principle divination by dreams was possible (I. 17 f.). The sceptical contention that all cited instances were unauthenticated legends or deliberate fictions, like those which Cicero himself had introduced in his poem on his consulate (II. 47), was necessarily beyond proof. If no rational explanation could be found, that was also true of other beliefs which every one accepted, for instance belief in magnetism (I. 86). Of course hypothetical explanations were advanced. On Posidonius' view in particular everything in nature was connected by 'sympathy' (II. 34, 124, 142), so that there would be a link between the flight of birds or the state of a sacrificial victim's liver and an impending clash of arms. That brings us to Stoic doctrines of fate, to the ineluctable chain of events, which indeed include human volitions, and which they tried to accommodate to freedom of the will or at least to the subjective illusion of freedom. Their reasoning could lead to the conclusion that if Caesar had attended to the omens on the Ides of March, he could have foreseen his death but not prevented it. Cicero remarked that such foreknowledge would simply add to the sum of human misery, aggravating the pains of suffering with those of anticipation (II. 22 f.); if the gods were truly benevolent, they would 'from all creatures hide the book of Fate | All but the page prescribed, their present state'.

In any event divination in this sense had none of the practical utility which supposedly belonged to the Roman art. No doubt many, if not all, Stoics would have agreed with Epictetus (*Diss.* II. 7) that if we apply to diviners, it should be only to know the future path which Providence has marked out for us, and not to affect decisions on our conduct which must be governed by duty. This view of divination did not justify the traditional Roman belief that it enabled men to take precautions against errors they would otherwise have fallen into.

At the end of his dialogue *De Divinatione* Cicero re-affirms that his own school, the Academy, laid down no authoritative doctrine but left inquirers free to judge for themselves which arguments were most persuasive. However, he had given the case for divination to his brother Quintus, and had then traversed it in his own person, ultimately making Quintus recant (II. 100). I cannot believe that any Roman reader would have supposed that he himself was merely a dramatic figure in a dialogue, expressing views that were not necessarily his own, or that he did not mean that he had been personally engaged in uprooting superstition (II. 148). In *De Natura Deorum* he conveys the strongest impression that he found Epicurean theology absurd, and inclined to Stoic; equally in *De Divinatione* he intimated his personal agreement with the Epicureans that belief in divination was irrational. Others shared such incredulity. Among his fellow-augurs only Appius Claudius professed that the augurs retained knowledge of the art of divination; Cicero himself had rejected this, even when he still averred that divination was in principle possible and had once been practised by the augurs; another member of the college, Gaius Marcellus, denied that too (*Leg.* II. 31–3). If Cicero opines that the *ius augurum* had been established in sincere conviction, though preserved merely for political reasons (*Div.* II. 75), this opinion is of course consistent with an unstated proposition that the original conviction was itself erroneous. Appius was derided by his colleagues, who held that augury was no more than an astute device to influence the minds of the vulgar (I. 105). Cicero himself suggests that it was designed for political expediency (II. 43), and he makes Quintus concede that the augurs are ignorant of the art (I. 25); speaking himself, he says that it is retained 'as corresponding to popular beliefs and for its great services to the state' (II. 75). Here we have an indication of a cleft in religious mentality that had opened up between the élite and the masses; similarly, he tells us that no magistrate or men of rank any longer had recourse to the *sortes Praenestinae*, as the common people evidently still did (II. 86 f.). All this suggests that it would not be at all surprising if Cicero personally had no belief in divination (and his letters suggest as much by their absolute silence), though Academic scepticism prevented him from stating this categorically. But in that case it is all the more significant that in *De Divinatione* he more or less repeats Cotta's declaration on the necessity of preserving all ancestral religious practices; in the context this must include all the traditional practices of divination (II. 148). At the same time he also reaffirms his acceptance of the doctrine that the beauty and order of the world compels him to admit the existence of some excellent and eternal being (*naturam*) which deserves our veneration. This vague faith is far removed from the beliefs that underlay the traditional cults, which none the less he wishes to be maintained.[33]

Thus for Cicero, speaking through Cotta or in his own person, theoretical agnosticism or outright disbelief has no practical consequences for religious institutions. Is he speaking as a Roman rather than as a sceptical philosopher? Perhaps not. Sextus too, though he follows sceptics who would not, like Carneades, concede that any propositions in any field of inquiry were more plausible than any others, says that sceptics would undogmatically conform to the way of living in their society, in order that they might not be precluded from doing anything at all. This holds good for religious as for other practices; indeed in ordinary discourse the sceptic will actually *say* that gods exist, as well as do everything that pertains to their veneration (*PH* I. 23 f., 226; *M.* IX. 49). He can even ingeniously argue that they escaped the imputations of impiety that those of every dogmatic school properly incurred; for the latter were bound to attribute either total or partial foreknowledge of all events to the gods; but if it was partial, they were imperfect beings, and if it was total, they must either be impotent to prevent the evils in which the world abounded, or be responsible for those evils, and thus be malignant; and all these contentious ranked as

[33] My remarks on Cic. *Div.* are substantially the same as drafted before I had read the articles by Beard [320] and Schofield [325]; the former I find unhelpful, the latter acute and judicious, but I differ from him at least in nuance on Cicero's personal attitude. As to this, Jonathan Barnes reminds me of Lord Melbourne's remark: 'I am a strong supporter of the Established Church: I support it, like a buttress, from the outside.' (Theology was his favourite reading.)

impious (*PH* III. 9–12). Thus sceptics, as well as dogmatists who could attach some symbolic significance to the received forms of worship, would not in outward behaviour seem to deny their efficacy.

No doubt this kind of attitude was highly sophisticated, and there might be others whose readiness to conform was undermined by their knowledge that wise men had questioned or rejected traditional beliefs. Long ago the Stoic Aristo had been accustomed to say that excellent philosophic teaching could do harm to hearers who misinterpreted or perverted it (Cic. *Nat. D.* III. 77); Epictetus was to attribute a pernicious influence on ordinary men at least to that of Epicureans and Academics, which he abhorred (*Diss.* II. 20. 32–5). For Varro 'the natural theology' of philosophers, even if it might present a truer conception of the divine than that commonly entertained, was superfluous for the masses. It was therefore to be confined to the schools, not ventilated in the forum (above, nn. 2 f.). Cicero concurred. He makes Cotta admit that he would not voice his agnosticism on the existence of the gods in a public meeting (*Nat. D.* I. 61), and he says in *De Divinatione* that he and Quintus can freely discuss whether there is any possibility of divination because they are conversing in private (II. 28). Of course these dialogues were to be published, but they would not be expected to have a wide readership. Whatever speculations we may adopt on the diffusion of literacy or on the cost of books, it is unlikely that many had the capacity to understand philosophic disquisitions. Cicero himself said that philosophy was satisfied with the judgement of the few, and deliberately shunned the multitude, which viewed it with suspicion and hostility (*Tusc.* II. 4). Commenting on this, Lactantius was to remark that though both Stoics and Epicureans professedly sought to convert all and sundry, they could not succeed. Philosophy, he thought, required prior training in grammar, rhetoric, geometry, music, and astronomy. Be that as it may, Epicurean and Stoic theology involved comprehension of their theories on the physical world, and particularly in the case of Stoicism, of logic. We may recall Lucian's Hermotimus, who had spent twenty years to no avail in pursuing the Stoic path to wisdom and at the end of it was convinced by a sceptic that he had better simply share in the everyday life and abandon 'strange puffed up pretensions'. Lactantius was surely right that the systems of the schools were accessible only to the leisured class, and could seldom reach women, slaves, and the poor in general, whose time was fully occupied in getting their daily bread in the fields and workshops.[34] As we have seen, there are indications in Cicero's *De Divinatione* that the masses were more credulous than educated men.

There was the less risk that very many people would be corrupted, since philosophers of every complexion were ready to set their inferiors a good example by outward conformity. Socrates, according to Xenophon (*Apol.* 10–13), could have effectively met the charge that he did not recognize the city's gods by saying that everyone had seen him sacrificing at the common festivals and public altars; this was a complete answer. This conformism disgusted Christians like Origen and Augustine who set it down to fear and hypocrisy.[35] In some cases their accusation may have been true, but they did not reckon with the possibility that philosophers put their own interpretation on the conventional acts of worship they performed. With no comprehension of the special position of Christians, bound like the Jews to make no graven images and worship no pagan gods (*Deut.* 5: 7–9), Celsus could see no reason why they should not do likewise.[36] It was of course in public, when men were fulfilling the duties of office or participating in state festivals, that they were actually required to conform. In private life there may have been many a 'parcus cultor deorum et infrequens', uncensored and unremarked, though Horace's phrase, if pressed, suggests only that he had not been scrupulous in carrying out *all* the traditional private cults, rather as professed and believing Christians of modern times may think it enough to communicate at Easter and to resort to the rites of the Church for baptism, marriage, and burial.

In Christian countries there have been men in every age negligent of prescribed worship or of the precepts of the Church, of whom relatively few could have adduced (or can now adduce) rational grounds for incredulity; in modern times many have no doubt been affected by the assumption that Christianity has

[34] Lact. *Div. Inst.* III. 25; Lucian, *Hermotimus*, esp. 2, 84.

[35] Origen, *c. Celsum* V. 35, 43; VI. 4; VII. 6, 44, 66; cf. August. *CD* VI. 1 and 10.

[36] *c. Cels.* VIII. 66, cf. 2: in praising Helios or Athena one could really be revering the one true God.

been discredited by those whose judgement deserves most respect. In the Graeco-Roman world too there must have been *indocti*, a term that can include all who had not carefully studied philosophy, who were influenced by vague awareness of critiques of traditional religion; such men were probably more often to be found among persons of *some* education than among the masses.[37] In so far as the hold of the old religion ever weakened in the people at large, we may have to look for explanations other than the impact of rational inquiry; at all times mere experience of unanswered prayers and unrequited sacrifices might induce a loss of faith in ancestral gods (cf. above, n. 18), sometimes succeeded by hope that other gods might render more effectual aid.

We may also ask the question, though we can hardly answer it, how many of those who assented to any particular set of philosophic dogmas were inexpugnably assured of their truth, especially as each was open to plausible objections. How many were 'light half-believers of their casual creeds'? What can we make of the alleged Epicureanism of an Atticus, occupied in all the anxieties of money-making, or of a L. Piso or C. Cassius, still determined despite the teaching of the Master:

> *contendere nobilitate,*
> *noctes atque dies niti praestante labore*
> *ad summas emergere opes rerumque potiri?*

Or how many could feel, confusedly, with Virgil:

> *felix qui potuit rerum cognoscere causas.*
> *fortunatus et ille deos qui novit agrestis?*

The sceptic, who did not claim to know anything, was not even in a theoretical position from which he could deny the possibility that the cults were efficacious: was it not a prudent insurance to act as if they were, especially as their efficacy was not deemed to depend on inward faith? Such doubts might arise even in the mind of a committed unbeliever. Plutarch tells us (*Brut.* 39) that the evil omens that heralded the first battle of Philippi were gradually carrying Cassius away from his Epicurean doctrines. The stroke of lightning in a clear sky that turned Horace back to religion may be a fiction of autobiography, and

[37] We may thus understand the variety of opinions among the *indocti* to which Cicero refers (*Nat. D.* I. 5).

yet convey some more general truth, showing how easy it was in those days to pierce the thin armour of rationalism.

However all this may be, it is clear that philosophically educated Romans like Varro and Cicero thought it necessary to maintain the traditional religion, whatever its errors. To say no more of Varro, Cicero passed in *De Legibus* from laying down a Stoic doctrine of the divine law that rules the Universe to prescribing a code of sacred laws for his model city, which with minor amendments is expressly based on Roman institutions; like Varro he made not the slightest attempt to show that these laws could be deduced from, or were even consistent with, the general theological system he had accepted. There is a curious difference here between his procedure and that of Plato whom he was consciously rivalling in the construction of an ideal state. Plato was bent on banning or persecuting heretical opinions; Cicero has nothing of this, and indeed religious *opinions* as such were never proscribed by the Roman state, not even those of the Christians, until Christianity itself took the state over. But whereas in the *Republic* Plato in a casual sentence left it to Delphi to determine all religious usages in his model city, and in the *Laws* only refers offhand to prayers and sacrifices.[38] obviously of the ordinary kind, for Cicero the institutions are all-important; he is concerned with what men do, not with what they think. As we have seen, he was just as insistent in his later sceptical vein that the established ceremonies should be kept up. He takes occasion to record that as consul he had been careful to observe them 'summa cum religione' (*Div.* I. 103). His overt actions, and the frequent appeals to piety in his speeches (which cannot be taken as evidence of personal convictions), would make more impression than ratiocinations which were known to comparatively few.

The historian is perhaps well advised in general to adopt the standpoint of Carneades and not to hope for certainty. At any rate it is only in 'Academic' terms that I dare answer the question with which I began. It seems *probable* that the theological doubts and contradictions of the philosophic schools had little effect on Roman religious practices, or so far as concerns the mentality of most Romans, on the beliefs associated with them.

[38] Pl. *Rep.* 427 B; *Laws* 738 B–E, 828 A, 909 B–E; Panhellenic religious festivals accepted, 947 A, 950 E.

# 8

# Plutarch: Roman Heroes and Greek Culture

CHRISTOPHER PELLING *

## I

A TYPICAL Roman response to anything Greek or cultured was to steal it, to destroy it, or just occasionally to liberate it. *Marcellus* centres on the destruction and the theft, as Marcellus ransacks the shrine of Syracuse and brings the treasures to Rome. This is central to Plutarch's moral evaluation of his hero, and he discusses it in *Marc.* 21:

Marcellus enjoyed all the better reputation with the common people, because he adorned the city with works of visual art which were delightful in their Hellenic grace and their truth to nature. On the other hand it was Fabius Maximus who earned the approval of the older people, because after he had captured Tarentum he did not disturb or remove anything of the kind: he carried off all the city's money and other valuables, but allowed all the statues to remain in place, adding the famous remark, 'Let us leave the Tarentines their angry gods'. Such people blamed Marcellus, firstly for rendering the city vulnerable to envy, if not only men but even gods were to be paraded like captives in his triumphal procession; and secondly because until then the people had spent their time either in warfare or in agriculture and had never tasted luxury or leisure, so that their character had been like that of Euripides' Heracles, 'Simple, unpolished, but good in the

* This paper was heavily indebted to work which was at the time unpublished. I discussed many points with Simon Swain, whose thesis dealt with precisely this topic: much of his work has since been published (347a-f). I have indicated those points which I am conscious of drawing from him, but there is doubtless much else besides. He too emphasises the linking of Hellenic education with an interest in control of the passions. John Moles generously allowed me to exploit the draft of his commentary on Plutarch's *Cicero* [338a]. I owe much to this (especially the point about 'the two lives' in *Cic.*), and also to his Oxford D.Phil thesis on *Brutus* (1979). Dr Moles also read and commented on an earlier draft of this paper, as did Father Frederick Brenk: I am most grateful. Some of my translations are adapted from the Penguin versions of Ian Scott-Kilvert and Rex Warner.

greatest things.' Now Marcellus was filling them with idleness and chatter, so that they spent most of the day in urbane discussion about art and artists. Yet Marcellus himself spoke with pride of this even to the Greeks, saying that he had taught the ignorant Romans to respect and admire the marvellous achievements of Greek art.

Several things are interesting about this. First, that this episode is so important to Plutarch: indeed, he has been preparing for this moment from the very beginning of the Life, when—doubtless with no evidence at all except for what Marcellus finally did to Syracuse—he had stressed that Marcellus was primarily a soldier, but 'had enough enthusiasm for Greek culture and literature to make him respect and admire those who excelled in them, though he himself never had the leisure to study or learn these subjects as much as he would have wished' (1. 3). Little touches then reinforce the impression: for instance, at 2. 5 his good-looking son is also 'admired by the citizens for his wise restraint *and his education*'—a point that adds nothing to the immediate story, but fills out the picture of a most civilized family. As very often with Plutarch, Hellenism matters greatly, and the hero's attitude to Greek culture is made a crucial theme.

In this Life, indeed, the contrast between Greek and Roman is strongly felt, and there is an unusual interest in stressing the qualities of Rome as a city at the time: so bellicose, so unsophisticated, so primitive—so very different, indeed, from the Thebes of the paired Life *Pelopidas*.[1] For instance, Roman *superstition* is made a recurrent theme of *Marcellus*,[2] and at one point the exceptional Roman human sacrifice of the day is contrasted with the more enlightened views of the Greeks (3. 6). That picks up a theme already familiar from *Pelopidas*, where in chapters 21–2 it is surely supposed to emerge that human

[1] Note particularly *Pel.* 19. 2, where the laudable erotic aspect of the Sacred Band captures something which Rome clearly lacks: 'it was right that they should claim the child of Ares and Aphrodite for the city: for, if the element of warfare and valour keeps particular company with persuasion and gracefulness, that is when everything combines through Harmony into the most appropriate and ordered of states'. The contrast with Rome, where everything had to serve the interests of continual warfare (*Marc.* 1. 4–5), is very clear.

[2] Besides 3. 6 note also 4. 7, explicitly stressing Roman religiosity; that is then developed in 5 (esp. 5. 4–7); 6. 11–12; 7. 4, 8; 10. 6 (οὐχ ὅσιον, a suggestive choice of words); 12. 2; 27. 2–3; 28. 2; 29. 8–11.

sacrifice is barely tenable for an enlightened Greek: at least, the sequel at Leuctra vindicates the more humane path taken by Pelopidas, who sacrifices a foal instead. Then in Syracuse Marcellus' generosity 'to the Greeks' is put in those terms (20. 1); a little earlier Plutarch has made great play with the clever little Greek Archimedes, with his intricate systems of pulleys, completely baffling the stolid Romans, as he hoisted up their massive galleys in the air, swung them around, and then toppled them over: and the bewildered Romans looked on, seeming very bellicose and very primitive indeed (14–18. 1). The whole thing is told with much more gusto by Plutarch than for instance by Livy, whose account (XXIV. 34) is distinctly more dignified and less boisterous; or by Polybius, probably Plutarch's major source for the passage, whose account is much more clinical (VIII. 6). So not merely is Marcellus' attitude to the Greeks, and to Greek culture and works of art, central to the Life: the elaborate contrast of the two worlds also gives it particular point.

Yet, secondly, very little is made of looking at this from the Syracusan point of view. The pathos of their plight is felt, sometimes quite strongly (as when Marcellus bursts into tears at 19. 1–2, thinking of what they are going to suffer)—but actually in many ways rather *less* strongly than it is even in Livy.[3] When Plutarch weighs up the arguments for or against Marcellus' action, it is clearly seen from the Roman viewpoint: he dwells on the adornment Marcellus brought the city which the people liked, and the possibility that he might bring dishonour and even divine displeasure on the city; but the main issue is what he has *done* to the people, filling them with all this idle chatter. Hellenism matters, but Plutarch does not write as an outsider looking in, estimating Marcellus by what he has done to the Greek city. It will all turn on what he has done to *Rome*. When writing about a Roman public figure, Plutarch enters into the spirit of the thing, and in some ways the standards he adopts could well be those that a civilized Roman could also adopt.

But only in some ways, for also the precise form the criticism of Marcellus takes is extremely *un*-Roman. This is one of those cases where we can see Plutarch thinking for himself, confronting

[3] Below, p. 204.

one of the great *topoi* of Roman historiography—the disastrous and debilitating effect of foreign, especially Greek, culture—and giving it a rather unexpected tweak. Livy's treatment, and for that matter Polybius', of the same theme is decidedly more sombre: that was the start of the disastrous habit of admiring Greek arts, heralding all sorts of perilous excess.[4] We should not expect Plutarch to be keen on that particular *topos*: he after all thinks Rome should have learnt a great deal more from Greek culture;[5] and in fact he turns it upside down. Plutarch may not come down explicitly for or against Marcellus in the passage quoted, but still the way he puts the criticism—'he was filling them with laziness and chatter, so that they spent most of the day in smart discussion about art and artists'—seems very mild, and there is a great deal in the surrounding narrative that helps to tilt the scales Marcellus' way. In the first part of the chapter Plutarch has been dwelling on the wretchedly primitive and bellicose state of Rome at the time; then, in the next chapter he goes on at some length to discuss the Roman distinction of triumph and *ovatio*, leaving a heavy hint that the Spartans judged matters better when they reserved their highest honours for victories won by the arts of peace. Marcellus protests that he is *civilizing* these people, and Plutarch is carefully making it clear that these Romans need civilizing. And he has prepared the ground in other ways, organizing his narrative in a way which tends very much to Marcellus' favour: as we shall see, he indeed seems to be justifying him in rather more unqualified terms even than Livy does in his parallel narrative.[6] When Marcellus is then accused in Rome, it is all stirred up by petty political enemies (23): the reader is reminded of an even more petty scene in the *Pelopidas*, where Menecleidas is clearly stigmatized for arraigning Pelopidas when he returns after the Leuctra campaign, *Pel.* 25. Memories of that *Pelopidas* incident also perhaps help to prejudice us in Marcellus' favour. In fact, all the texture of the

[4] Livy XXV. 40. 1–3; Polyb. IX. 10. I elaborate this point in [340] 185–7.

[5] Cf. esp. *Mar.* 2; *C.mai* 23. 3 (quoted below, pp. 206–7, 215).

[6] Besides the instances discussed later in the text, notice that at 19. 3–6 Plutarch defends Marcellus against the charge of responsibility for the ransacking; Livy XXV. 25. 5–9 has much the same material, but makes the point less insistently. Then at 20. 2 the outrages elsewhere in Sicily are dismissed very blandly; Livy XXIV. 37–9 leaves a different impression.

narrative seems to allow Marcellus to get away with his defence at 23. 6, 'that in return for all the outrages that the Syracusans committed against the Romans, they have suffered nothing more than it is impossible to prevent men defeated in war from suffering'. Certainly, Plutarch knows and says that Marcellus was criticized, and that the 'older generation'—whom he might normally expect to be right, especially with Fabius on their side (21. 5)—thought Marcellus was wrong; later, in the *Synkrisis* with Pelopidas, he will indeed compare Marcellus unfavourably in precisely this respect with the generosity of Epaminondas and Pelopidas. Yet in the narrative itself the moral issue is relatively simple. For Plutarch, Marcellus at least deserves credit for caring about Greek culture; and what he does for Rome is civilizing rather than debilitating.

The issues seem decidedly more complex in Livy's account, which Plutarch very probably knew.[7] With Livy's larger canvas, the question of Syracusan guilt is explored more carefully: at XXIV. 32. 2–6 he brings out how careworn and divided the city was about supporting the tyrants Hippocrates and Epicydes (an emphasis he may well draw from Polybius, if we may judge from Polyb. VII. 5. 3–5)—though Livy is certainly clear that it was not just the tyrants who favoured defection from Rome: the *plebs* too were blindly enthusiastic for that

[7] Or, if he did not know Livy himself, he at least knew something very like it. Cf. Scardigli [346] 38–41, 169–70, and works she cites. Much of Plutarch's detail is very close to Livy's, and this tradition was evidently his major source for much of the narrative; it is of course supplemented from elsewhere, especially from Polybius (himself Livy's source for much of the Syracusan material), Posidonius, and some extraneous material concerning Archimedes—possibly based on oral tradition rather than a separate Archimedes-biography, as e.g. Scardigli [346] 39 assumes. But there are a few places where Plutarch seems to derive detail from Livy's annalistic source(s) rather than Livy himself: cf. esp. Klotz [338], who assumes rather gratuitously that this source was Valerius Antias. The similarities between Plutarch and Livy still suggest either (1) that Plutarch is extensively using Livy as well as (?)Antias; or (2) that Livy is himself following (?)Antias very closely indeed; or indeed both, as Klotz assumed. If (1), then Plutarch knew Livy and read him closely; if (2), then he was using an account so similar that Livy conveys an almost exact impression of what it was like. If Plutarch in fact knew Livy's annalistic source(s) for the trial instead of Livy himself, then he would probably not have come across the quizzical treatment of Manlius Torquatus: however closely Livy was following his source, that is surely his own. But most of the rest of the argument would still hold, and Livy would still afford an interesting comparison of how the material *could* be treated. The position in *Fabius* is similar: in [340] 183–4 n. 103, I argue that it is there more likely that he knew Livy directly. If so, then that is probably the case in *Marcellus* too.

course (cf. also XXIV. 21. 1). In Plutarch the Syracusans are much more straightforwardly in the wrong (14. 1–5), and his perfunctory ἐκράτουν γὰρ οἱ περὶ τὸν Ἱπποκράτην, 'Hippocrates' party was in the ascendant', gives no hint of the agonizing. When it comes to the sack itself, Livy's colouring is again complex. He has no doubt about the *legitimacy* of Marcellus' despoiling—'hostium quidem illa spolia et parta belli iure' (XXV. 40. 2)—but he does dwell on the disastrous consequences for Rome itself. When Marcellus is arraigned, the Syracusan complaints are hardly felt as justified, and their speech wholly falsifies the facts as we know them from Livy's own earlier narrative.[8] Marcellus' view of the matter—'quicquid in hostibus feci ius belli defendit' (XXVI. 31. 2, cf. 31. 9)—is closely similar to Livy's own at XXV. 40. 2 (quoted above), and for that matter to the implications of Plutarch's narrative, as we have seen. And yet in Livy the pathos of the Syracusan misery is still felt, and their ambassadors' horror when Sicily once more falls to Marcellus seems wholly genuine (XXVI. 29. 1–3). In Plutarch, as we saw, the accusations are wholly inspired by Marcellus' Roman political enemies (23. 1); in Livy the Syracusans' mission seems to be their own affair, though the politicians certainly exploit it (XXVI. 26. 5–6; 29. 1–5). Then, after Marcellus has replied, it is interesting that it is T. Manlius Torquatus who takes the opposite view. Torquatus before has emerged as an *extreme* defender of tradition, whose judgement can be at odds with justice or humanity. The most conspicuous instance was his opposition to the proposal to ransom the Roman prisoners after Cannae, XXII. 60: 'priscae ac nimis durae, ut plerisque uidebatur, seueritatis', indeed, as he was then introduced (XXII. 60. 5). But Torquatus' defence of tradition could not then be dismissed: it touched on the core of Roman pride, dignity, and resilience, the qualities so vital to Rome's survival. Now too Torquatus cannot simply be wrong. Certainly, his view of

[8] Thus at XXVI. 30. 1–2 they argue that Hieronymus was killed 'prope publico consilio' largely because of his favour for Carthage: that does not really square with XXIV. 21. 1, where his death (however popular, XXIV. 7. 7; 21. 2–3) does not affect the Syracusan stance. Leontini had not in fact been 'crudeliter direpti' (XXVI. 30. 4, cf. XXIV. 30. 7); nor had XXV. 23. 6–7 really suggested that Marcellus' delay was responsible for the death of the seventy or eighty noble conspirators (XXVI. 30. 3). The 'principes Syracusanorum' had not in fact been so ready to desert (XXVI. 30. 5), as Marcellus fairly points out (31. 4–6).

Syracusan guilt or innocence is over-simple (XXVI. 32. 2–3), but then so was Marcellus' own (31. 3); certainly, his supporters include some who are motivated by simple vindictiveness (32. 5, echoing 29. 5). But his appeal to Hiero's memory still strikes a chord: just as after Cannae, he is giving an off-key version of something that is true and important. Marcellus is not clearly to be condemned for what he has done to Syracuse; but what he has done to Rome is badly amiss. His great days are over, and we know it.[9]

The comparison with Livy has had to be lengthy, because Livy's moralism is itself so elaborate: but it surely suggests something of how Plutarch *might* have treated the theme. Such moral complexity is not beyond him: if Plutarch were asked, for instance, whether it was good for Caesar to conquer Pompey, or for Octavian and Antony to defeat Brutus, or for Philopoemen to fight for freedom against Rome, he could hardly give an unequivocal answer. Here the theme is hardly less central to the Life; yet it is not Plutarch, it is the Roman Livy, who feels that this devastation of a Greek city is morally agonizing.

One further point is important. As we saw, Marcellus was initially characterized as interested in Greek culture, but without time to pursue it; instead he was 'warlike in his experience. powerful in his body, naturally bellicose (φιλοπόλεμος), and with a lordly pride and assurance on the battlefield . . .' (1. 2–3). Exactly what Rome needed at the time, in fact: and his extraordinary courage in single combat is then stressed in the early chapters, especially of course the *spolia opima* passage where he kills the Gallic king (7). But it all turns sour at the end, where his uncontrollable desire to fight Hannibal gets the better of him (strongly stigmatized in 28, cf. *Pel.* 2, *Snk.* 3. 6–8); and then we see the culpable rashness with which he allows himself to be isolated, ambushed, and killed, almost a failed

[9] So W. Hoffmann, *Livius und der zweite Punische Krieg* (Berlin, 1942) 65: '. . . wie sich die Kurve seines Lebens abwärts bewegt'. Cf. then XXVII. 20. 10. In view of Torquatus' role here and after Cannae, XXIII. 22 is thought-provoking, when along with Fabius Maximus he opposes any notion to extend the Roman citizenship to the Latins. The time will come when that too will be right, but the old men's feeling for tradition is right too. Later the elder Cato sometimes plays a similar role: cf. esp. Livy XXXIV. 1–4, where his speech on the *Lex Oppia* is surely meant to sound overstated, even silly—yet Book XXXIV goes on to explore the move of Rome into Greece, and the exposure to precisely that debilitating foreign culture which Cato was right to fear.

monomachy.[10] This is of course another, much clearer link with the *Pelopidas*, but Marcellus is criticized rather more fiercely and forthrightly for his rashness than Pelopidas; at *Snk.* 3. 3 Plutarch explicitly claims that Pelopidas' death was the more excusable, on not specially good grounds. This inability to control a particular *pathos*, here the bellicosity, is another thing which we shall very often find in Roman Lives concerned with Hellenism: that point is made strongly by Simon Swain in a series of important works.[11] When we find a Roman gentleman with Hellenic tastes and education, that predisposes us to inquire about his ability to control himself and his passions. Education should teach him that control, but here and often elsewhere it does not. The point is made most explicitly in the introductions to *Coriolanus* and *Marius*:

The same man (Coriolanus) bore witness to the truth of the view that a naturally generous and noble disposition, if it lacks education (παιδεία), will produce many evil fruits along with the good, in the same way as naturally good soil which is not tilled. Coriolanus' energy and strength of mind constantly led him to attempt ambitious exploits, the results of which were good for Rome; but these qualities were combined with violent rages and uncompromising strokes of self-assertion (θυμοῖς . . . ἀκράτοις καὶ φιλονεικίαις ἀτρέπτοις), which made it difficult for him to combine with others. . . . Of all the blessings which men enjoy through the favour of the Muses, there is none so great as the process of taming and humanizing the natural instincts through education and study (ὑπὸ λόγου καὶ παιδείας), so that by submitting to reason we acquire balance and avoid excess. (*Cor.* 1. 3–5)

Marius is said never to have studied Greek literature, or to have used the Greek language for anything serious, saying that it was absurd to learn a language whose teachers were other men's slaves. . . . Plato would often say to the philosopher Xenocrates, who had the reputation of being too surly and uncouth, 'My dear Xenocrates, do please sacrifice to the Graces'; and in the same way, if Marius had been persuaded to sacrifice to the Greek Muses and Graces, he would not have brought his career, with its glorious commands and political achievements, to so ugly a conclusion, cast aground by rage and by untimely ambition on the shores of a most savage and brutal old age

[10] For an interesting speculation concerning the historical truth about Marcellus' curious death, cf. M. Caltabiano, *CISA* 3 (1975) 73–4.

[11] See introductory note.

(ὑπὸ θυμοῦ καὶ φιλαρχίας ἀώρου καὶ πλεονεξιῶν ἀπαρηγορήτων εἰς ὠμότατον καὶ ἀγριώτατον γῆρας ἐξοκείλας). (*Mar.* 2. 2–4)

And both *Coriolanus* and *Marius* go on to illuminate the catastrophic effect of those rages and ambitions in political life.[12] Marcellus is of course not so stigmatized; anyway, unlike at least Marius, he can hardly be blamed for his lack of education, for his opportunities in this warlike period were so very limited (1. 3–5). But this curious link of an interest in Hellenism and an interest in impetuosity and lack of self-control is something that we shall certainly find again.

Marcellus' death is pathetic and shamefully rash: it also shows some curious similarities to the death of Archimedes at Syracuse, which Plutarch has lavishly recounted earlier in the Life (19). Archimedes too died in a tragic and rather random way; his body too was brought to his great adversary, in his case Marcellus himself, just as Marcellus' body is now brought to Hannibal; the adversary's respect and even regret is carefully traced. It is the sort of thing that Plutarch sometimes does elsewhere, developing points of contact between the moment of greatest achievement and the moment of catastrophe: indeed, he had done something the same in the *Pelopidas*, where there are elements in Pelopidas' death which remind us of many of his most glorious moments (especially the liberation of the Cadmeia), and the much more salutary personal courage he had shown in those earlier triumphs.[13] In the *Marcellus* it encourages us to take the fall of Syracuse and Marcellus' own death very closely together. And that is not simply casual: it is fundamental to Plutarch's conception to see how the same

[12] In *Cor.*, cf. esp. 15. 4–5; 21. 1–2; 22. 3; *Alc.* 41(2); Russell [344]; at 34. 3 it is again πάθος which overcomes him as he collapses before his womenfolk, again something of which Plutarch does not wholly approve (*Alc.* 43(4) ). In *Marius*, cf. esp. 10. 9; at first his θυμοῦ σφοδρότης is an advantage, 14. 1, and he strikingly knows how to control the θυμός of others, 16. 1–17. 1; then esp. 28. 1–2; 34. 5–7; 41. 6; 43–4; 45. 10–12.

[13] Thus *Pel.* 31. 4 recalls 8. 5–8 and 20. 4–22 (unpleasant omens before the Cadmeia and Leuctra; notice that at 8. 5–8 it is the more unequivocally disagreeable omen that Plutarch here selects from the more elaborate list in *De Gen. Socr.* 587–8); 31. 6 recalls 7. 1–2. As at the Cadmeia, the fight is for freedom and against 'tyrants'; Pelopidas' monomachy is glorious at 11. 9, catastrophic at 32. 9–11 (a very similar effect to that in *Marcellus*). The posthumous vengeance at 35. 4–12 is again very similar to the Cadmeia plot. There are also echoes of Tegyra (32. 2 recalls 17. 2); Tegyra in its turn recalls the Cadmeia (17. 11–13 recalls 13. 5–7). Pelopidas now falls victim to that θυμός (32. 9; cf. 28. 10) which it was the purpose of his glorious Sacred Band to inflame (19. 5).

basic traits produce both the capture of Syracuse, where both the military brilliance and the Hellenic tastes emerge at their strongest even as the Greeks suffer so terribly, and the catastrophe, where we rather see the limitation of that bellicosity and that Hellenic education.

## II

*Philopoemen and Flamininus* takes us from theft and destruction to liberation: and once again the two Lives need to be taken very closely together.[14] The continuity of themes through the pair is perfectly clear, and once again is centrally concerned both with Hellenism, or perhaps rather 'what each did to Greece', and with the control of the passions. Here the crucial passions are different: 'Philopoemen's faults arose through contentiousness (φιλονεικία), Flamininus' through ambition (φιλοτιμία)', says Plutarch in the first chapter of the epilogue (*Flam.* 22(1). 4), and he has done his best to characterize the two figures with these two neighbouring traits. He introduces Philopoemen's φιλονεικία strongly at *Phil.* 3. 1:

> The ambition in his character was not altogether pure of contentiousness or free of anger, but, although he wished to emulate Epaminondas above anyone else, he managed to imitate his energy, intelligence, and incorruptibility but could not keep his gentleness or gravity or humanity in politics. That was because of his anger and contentiousness: and he seemed more attuned to military than to political virtue.

And Plutarch again relates this to his education—his lack of enthusiasm for the philosophical education he received, his preference for reading military manuals. (Plutarch smartly raps him over the knuckles for this at 4. 10; the theme recurs at 13. 5.) Such philosophy as he imbibed is in fact rather hard to trace; perhaps it does help to explain his unpretentious personal appearance (2. 2–4), his incorruptibility (15. 7–12), and particularly his devotion to freedom. But we once again find the negative ethical points as well, especially concerning the passions: and these are presumably related to that early impatience with his philosophical learning. For instance, he finds

[14] This section expands some remarks in my [341] 85–8. Rather than obscure the argument with extensive cross-reference, I have preferred to repeat some material here.

it difficult to control his anger:[15] that helps to explain the culpable impetuosity that led to his death (18–20). But particular emphasis is laid on his ambition (φιλοτιμία), which can sometimes be laudable (e.g. 6. 10) but can also so easily shade off into φιλονεικία.[16] That is most conspicuous at 17. 7, where Philopoemen is so eager that he, rather than Flamininus and the Romans, should be the one to restore the Spartan exiles. The days of Greek contentiousness were really over (18. 2, cf. *Flam.* 11, quoted below). Philopoemen is 'the last of the Greeks' (1. 7); and in more ways than one.

Yet that episode of the Spartan exiles also brings out how closely similar the qualities of φιλονεικία and φιλοτιμία are: it has so much in common with various actions of Flamininus which Plutarch attributes to φιλοτιμία, in particular his anxiety to retain his Greek command rather than allow any successor to step in and gain all the credit (*Flam.* 7. 2; 13. 2). Still, for most of the Life Flamininus is devoting his φιλοτιμία to a more laudable end, freeing the Greeks and then leading them to peace and harmony. Plutarch does not romanticize this liberation as sentimentally as he might have done; he brings out clearly that such freedom was a matter of political necessity for the Romans, particularly given the way that Philip and Antiochus had maltreated the Greeks.[17] Once again as in the *Marcellus*, he views the whole question from the side of Rome and the Roman general, at least as much as from the side of Greece itself. But at the same time Flamininus' guiding motive is not really the desirable political result, nor anything more altruistic or sentimental: it is rather that distinctive desire for honour, φιλοτιμία. Plutarch then dwells on the honours, including divine honours, which the Greeks paid Flamininus (and, incidentally, on his chagrin when the Aetolians did not pay him enough, or when Philopoemen himself seemed to Flamininus to be winning more than his fair share of the acclaim).[18]

[15] Cf. 13. 8; 17. 5; and then esp. *Flam.* 22(1). 5–7—not quite the same emphasis as in the narrative of 16 and 18 (cf. [341] 88), but the narrative at least evinces the same ethical worry.

[16] Other equivocal acts of φιλοτιμία at 7. 1–2 and 13; apparently laudable, but still thought-provoking, at 17. 6–7.

[17] Cf. esp. *Flam.* 2. 3–5; 5. 1–2; 12. 6; E. Badian, *Titus Quinctius Flamininus, Philhellenism and Realpolitik*, Semple Memorial Lecture (Cincinnati, Ohio, 1970) 53–7.

[18] *Flam.* 12. 8–10; 13. 3–9 (cf. *Phil.* 15. 1–3); 16. 5–17. 2.

Flamininus had always been *φιλοτίμος*, and these are the answering *τίμαι*. Yet it is interesting that this personal character of Flamininus' motives does not seem to cast any shadow over the liberation. In their different ways both Polybius and Livy were concerned about the notion that Flamininus was at several points prepared to end the war prematurely rather than let a successor get the honour: Polybius comments with some fascination on the shrewd way in which Flamininus was able to combine his own interest with that of Rome (*πάνυ γὰρ ἀγχίνους, εἰ καί τις ἕτερος Ῥωμαίων* . . ., XVIII. 12. 3); and Livy, clearly embarrassed, tries to play down the theme.[19] Plutarch states that motivation without any concern at 7. 2 (cf. 13. 2). His point is rather different: he is *assuming* that *φιλοτιμία* and starting from it, and bringing out how it can in certain circumstances have extremely desirable and noble results. Elsewhere too Flamininus' *φιλοτιμία* in Greece may seem a little morally problematic,[20] but still Plutarch at the end of the Greek section hastens to his defence: his *φιλοτιμία* was not enough to hinder the splendid effects of his natural reasonableness and humanity (*ἐπιείκεια ἤθους*, 17. 1–3). But, as we shall see, there are other occasions where its consequences are much more uncomfortable.

The themes of freedom, and of Greece, are themselves further links between the two Lives. Philopoemen fights for liberty (his series of wars *against tyrants* is particularly stressed);[21] 'the last of the Greeks' indeed revives Greece's glory long after its time, and he is concerned to fight for its freedom even against Rome (*Phil.* 17. 3). But it is then the Roman Flamininus who *gives* the Greeks their liberty, at that splendid scene at the Isthmian Games (*Flam.* 10–11). Plutarch, like Polybius XVIII. 44–6 (who is presumably his main source) and Livy XXXIII. 33. 5–7, stops to recreate the thoughts of those present at that great occasion. Polybius and Livy concentrate on the *Romans*—their greatness of spirit, their clemency, their altruism. This time Plutarch focuses more on Greece than on Rome:

[19] Polyb. XVIII. 10. 11–12; 39. 3–4; Livy XXXII. 32. 5–8, XXXIII. 13. 5, with J. Briscoe, *Commentary on Livy xxxi–xxxiii* (Oxford, 1973) 22 n. 4, 26–7, 227–8, 274–5.

[20] *Flam.* 9; 13. 1–4.

[21] *Phil.* 8. 3; 10; 12. 2; 12. 4–6; 16. 5; 19. 2; *Flam.* 24(3). 2.

They thought about Greece and all the wars it had fought for freedom; and now it had come almost without blood and without grief through the championship of another people, this finest and most enviable of prizes. . . . Men like Agesilaus, Lysander, Nicias, and Alcibiades had been great warriors, but had not known how to use their victories to noble and glorious ends; if one discounted Marathon, Salamis, Plataea, and Thermopylae, and Cimon's victories at the Eurymedon and in Cyprus, all Greece's wars had been fought internally for slavery, every trophy had been also a disaster and reproach for Greece, which had generally been overthrown by its leaders' evil ways and *φιλονεικία*. (*Flam.* 11. 3–6)

Then he turns, rather briefly, to the Romans, these foreigners who had finally brought Greece their freedom, 'liberating them from their harsh despots and tyrants'. That stress on *φιλονεικία* is telling, for that is of course the word for Philopoemen; and indeed that final phrase 'liberating them from harsh despots and tyrants' in many ways suits the emphases of *Philopoemen* rather than *Flamininus* (for Flamininus conspicuously *failed* to carry through the war against the Spartan tyrant Nabis, 13. 1–4). Plutarch will return to some of the themes of this chapter in the epilogue, where he will stress that Philopoemen's battles were themselves 'against other Greeks'—'Philopoemen killed more Greeks as general of the Achaeans than Flamininus killed Macedonians when fighting for Greece', and so on (*Flam.* 22 (1). 3). Plutarch is surely developing a theme throughout the pair, stressing the uncomfortable consequences for Greece of such contentiousness, even when it is found in so admirable a man as Philopoemen; its more healthy equivalent was Flamininus' *φιλοτιμία*, at least when he devoted it to winning the Greeks their freedom and their peace.[22]

So far the moralism seems rather crude: *φιλοτιμία* and Flamininus seem much better and worthier of imitation than *φιλονεικία* and Philopoemen. But in the epilogue Plutarch does not state the contrast in anything like so unqualified a fashion, and in fact finds it rather difficult to decide between Greece's champion Philopoemen and its liberator Flamininus; and other aspects of his treatment of Flamininus make one pause. It is of course characteristic of Plutarch to bring out how the same

[22] This is carefully explored by J. J. Walsh in *Phil.* 136 (1992), 208–33.

qualities contribute both to a man's greatness and his flaws: the elder Cato's anti-Hellenism, his attitude to wealth, his austerity, his lack of compromise; Antony's warmth, his spontaneity, his soldierliness, and his fundamental simplicity. We have already seen something of this with Marcellus, too. So it is here with Flamininus, and Plutarch shows us the weakness as well as the strength of that φιλοτιμία. That certainly emerges in his brush with Cato over the fate of his disreputable brother:

> And so the two men fell into incurable hostility towards one another. Yet Cato was a fine citizen who was only administering his office according to the laws; and it was all for the sake of a man who may have belonged to Titus' family, but was still unworthy of him and deserving of his punishment. I cannot believe that this was a good and statesmanlike act of Titus. (*Flam.* 19. 7)

The φιλοτιμία is even more disquieting in Flamininus' final execution of Hannibal. Plutarch does give some space to the justifications which might be given, but still clearly disapproves:

> Flamininus' natural φιλοτιμία won credit, as long as it had sufficient scope in the wars I have described . . . But when he gave up his command he was criticized, as one who could not restrain his intense lust for glory even when the rest of his life did not allow for action. In this way he became hateful to most people because of his violent move against Hannibal. . . . (*Flam.* 20. 1–3)

And Plutarch goes on to give an elaborate and vivid description of Hannibal's death—surprisingly elaborate, as this seems to be in danger of unbalancing the Life (he has nothing at all to say of Flamininus' own death, for instance). Perhaps he is just making the most of whatever material he can to fill out an unsatisfactory gap in his sources, who clearly had little to say of Flamininus' old age; but there is surely more to it than that. For the description of Hannibal's death has some clear parallels with the end of *Philopoemen*, where Plutarch gives a similarly lavish account of Philopoemen's own last days (18–21). It is in fact rather the same trick as in the *Marcellus*, with the points of contact there between the deaths of Archimedes and Marcellus himself. Here Philopoemen, like Hannibal, seemed set for a peaceful old age; but his character would not let him rest, and when already in his seventies and in poor health he set off on a new campaign against the Messenians. He was captured, and kept prisoner in an underground cave (*Phil.* 19. 4): just as Hannibal met his end in underground caves, again carefully described (*Flam.* 20. 7–8). Philopoemen, like Hannibal, was beset by a relentless and unforgiving personal foe; in both cases Plutarch dwells on the last words, as the hero takes the fatal chalice; and in both cases the killers meet with strong criticism from their own countrymen for such lack of magnanimity to a great adversary (*Phil.* 21. 1–2, *Flam.* 21. 1–6). It does not look as if these parallels can be coincidental: once again Plutarch is encouraging us to compare Philopoemen and Flamininus in their leading characteristics, and trace the consequences. Here the moral implications are rather different. Flamininus' φιλοτιμία inflicts on another the sort of final undignified humiliation which Philopoemen's φιλονεικία brings on himself. In both cases, it is a sort of patriotism that drives them on, Philopoemen against the Messenians, and Flamininus against Hannibal; their φιλονεικία (or φιλοτιμία) will not let them rest even in old age, and in each case leads them to this final humiliation, suffered in the one case, inflicted in the other. Earlier Flamininus' φιλοτιμία brought great gifts to a great people, the Greeks, and consequent credit to himself; now it is killing a great person and disgracing himself. The pattern is a very neat one; and again brings out how close is the unity of the pair.

So what comes out of these two Lives? Many of the same points as with the *Marcellus*. Hellenism matters, vitally: but 'what each of them does to Greece' is not the only or decisive concern. It is equally important to see how both control their similar passions, that ambition that can easily topple over into contentiousness (Philopoemen) or can easily bring discredit and disaster rather than glory (Flamininus). Once again, the interest in Hellenism goes very closely with this evaluative analysis of passion and self-control. Of course, such analysis is in some ways typical of Plutarch, but it would be a mistake to think that he *always* examines self-control so critically: Pompey, for instance, can be harshly criticized for his outbursts (e.g. *Pomp.* 47. 8), or Fabius for his final demagogy (*Fab.* 25–6); and it is clearly questionable whether Gaius Gracchus was justified in harrying the nobles quite so fiercely in vengeance for his brother. But in none of these Lives is the analysis of passions quite so thoughtful as in the cases we have been examining. The moral failings may be important to the Lives,[23] but they are often simply *presented* to us, without this sort of careful analysis. When Hellenic education is in point, Plutarch tries a little harder to *understand* the flaws, and to relate them to corresponding moral strengths.

It is easy to extend this analysis to other second-century Lives: the *Cato maior*, for instance, where his anti-Hellenism becomes a major theme. His proud attachment to Roman tradition is initially seen as a source of strength:

> A man who followed the ancestral custom of working his own land, who was content with frugal meals and an uncooked breakfast and simple clothing and an ordinary cottage, who thought it more admirable to renounce luxuries than to acquire them—such a person was rare indeed. By now the Roman Republic had already grown too large to preserve its original purity; the very power which it exercised over so many realms and peoples constantly brought it into contact with a great diversity of modes of living, and provided examples of many different sorts of lives. (*C.mai.* 4. 2)

But notice how the threats are there described, Rome 'brought into contact with a great diversity of modes of living, and examples of many different sorts of lives'. This is not the typical Roman stress on *Oriental*, especially *Greek*, culture; at this stage of the Life Cato is coming out well, and to specify the foreign influences as Greek would suggest too many complicating and qualifying notions. His attitude to Greek culture itself is, at this stage of the Life, treated accordingly (2. 3–6). Though he is said to have been a latecomer to Greek education, no reason is given (2. 5), and Plutarch does not yet suggest any *hostility* to Greek. The emphasis here is different: how the young Cato was filled with enthusiasm for the Greek philosopher Nearchus; how he was always able to exploit Greek stories and ideas in his writings; how in old age he learnt something from Thucydides and Demosthenes. The hostility only emerges at 12. 5, and then especially when the theme of debilitating foreign culture comes back towards the end of the Life. By that time Hellenic influences are specifically in point, and that is because this time

[23] Cf. e.g. [340] 184–5, on *Fabius*.

the qualifications are meant to be felt. Plutarch indeed makes them explicit:

> He tried to turn his son against Greek culture, and allowed himself a remark which was much too intemperate for an old man: he pronounced with all the solemnity of a prophet that, if ever the Romans became infected with the literature of Greece, they would lose everything. Time has shown that this ominous prophecy was wrong; for the time when the city reached the height of its power was the time when it was receptive to Greek learning and Greek culture. (*C.mai.* 23. 1–3)

By then Plutarch is bringing out how strengths as well as weaknesses spring from this exclusiveness and this anti-Hellenism, and various excesses, even perhaps his overdone asceticism, can be related to it. It is most interesting that this passage on Cato's anti-Hellenism is immediately preceded by the discussion of his treatment of his slaves (21): Plutarch clearly feels that this was deficient in humanity, and he has earlier contrasted it with the humanity which enlightened Greeks showed even to animals (5. 3–5). Then it is immediately followed by the notice of Cato's intemperate marriage to a much younger woman, another episode which moves Plutarch to moral disquiet (24. 1–8, cf. 33 (6) ). In each case Cato comes out poorly, though in each case one can relate the failings to analogous virtues (the economic austerity, the warmth of his family life); in each case the control of the passions seems defective; and that is exactly what we might expect of an unenlightened anti-Hellenist.

Not that Romans always come out badly in this evaluation of their passions. *Aemilius*, for instance, portrays a very civilized man, who although he receives only a Roman education himself, at least shows what favour to Greece he can (27–8); then he takes pains to secure a Greek education for his *sons* (6. 8–10). At 28. 11 he takes from Perseus' treasure only the books: for his sons, once again. The boys continue to be important, for it is the coincidental death of two sons, at the moment of Aemilius' triumph, that presents him with the greatest challenge to his rationality and self-control. He responds marvellously, with exemplary speeches on human vulnerability and the ways of Fortune. He is a *natural* philosopher, indeed, who is systematically contrasted with the despicable Perseus; and the contrast is given particular point by the prominence afforded to Perseus' sons as well, especially in the account of the triumph (33. 7–34. 2). Where Hellenism and philosophy come into point, Plutarch is simply more ready to gauge Romans on this particular moral scale: he does not always mark them down.

## III

It is time to turn to cases where people *do* receive Hellenic education: something that Marcellus had no time for, that Aemilius himself missed out on, and that Cato rejected. It is really only with the middle and later second century that Plutarch can assume Greek education was readily available at Rome[24]—it was open to Aemilius' sons, for instance; but it is particularly with the first-century heroes that it becomes crucial, with *Cato minor*, *Brutus*, and especially *Cicero*.

In the early chapters of *Cicero* Plutarch puts more weight on philosophical than on rhetorical education, and this marks a considerable difference from Cicero's own account in his *Brutus*:[25] Plutarch is even interested enough to include a sentence on why Antiochus of Ascalon drifted away from Carneades and the New Academy, and to note that Cicero disapproved of this new-fangled doctrine (4. 1–3). One other difference is that Plutarch has even less than the *Brutus* account on what Cicero *learnt* from those philosophers: Cicero himself for instance explains how he acquired some useful dialectical skills from the Stoic Diodotus (*Brut.* 309). Cicero admittedly has little enough of this, but Plutarch has even less: he is interested, not in 'what Cicero got from philosophy', but in the idea of a 'clash of *βίοι*', the two lives which were open to Cicero.[26] When things were bad in the Sullan civil war he returned 'to that academic and contemplative life, and kept company with Greek scholars and attended to his studies' till Sulla won (3. 3); then he rushed home to take on Chrysogonus. A bold step, one might think, and one that showed a real moral courage; still, Plutarch does not seem to imply that this was inspired by his

[24] This is demonstrated in detail by Swain [347e]

[25] Cf. Griffin, above, p. 24 n. 37.

[26] This is brought out very well by Moles in his commentary on *Cic.* [338a]. There is something in Cicero's *Brutus* too on the clash of lives, especially in connexion with Philo at 306, but Plutarch develops the emphasis more exclusively.

moral philosophy. It is 'a fine and splendid opportunity to make his mark in politics', no more (3. 6): a spectacularly bland statement, but one which again brings out Plutarch's lack of interest in what Cicero *got* from his philosophy. A little later, mainly because of fear, Cicero came back to Greece and philosophy, here Antiochus of Ascalon:

> Cicero approved of the older doctrines, thinking that, if ever he dropped out of public life, he would move his life from the forum and political affairs, and live out his life in peace with philosophy. (*Cic.* 4. 3)

And this is surely the principal reason why there is so little on rhetoric in these early chapters. In this contrast between public life and philosophy, rhetoric belongs on the side of public life, and Cicero develops it as an instrument for politics (*ὥσπερ ὄργανον*, 4. 4). It is duly that rhetorical skill which Plutarch stresses as winning Cicero his early success (5). In these chapters Plutarch is dwelling on the studies, and on the contemplative life which Cicero is to put aside. Here, philosophy must come first.

The 'clash of lives' comes back interestingly just before the Civil War, as Cicero calls at Rhodes and Athens on the way back from Cilicia:

> Sailing back from his province he first put in at Rhodes and then stayed some time in Athens, which he was glad to do through yearning (*πόθῳ*) for his old pastimes. After associating with the foremost men of culture and greeting his friends and companions of the past, and after receiving from Greece the appropriate marks of admiration, he returned to the city, where the civil war was already breaking out as if under a violent inflammation. (*Cic.* 36. 7–9)

It is a poignant little interval at so tense and crucial a moment: Moles[27] comments that the two lives are temporarily harmonized—but also that that yearning, that *πόθος* for what is distinctively absent, brings out how difficult the two ways of life are normally to reconcile. *Cicero* really is a good Life, and Plutarch had a specially sensitive understanding of his subject: Cicero was Plutarch's kind of man, and from personal experience Plutarch understood this conflict of *βίοι* particularly well.

[27] [338a], note on 36.7.

When Cicero first entered public life, he consulted the Delphic oracle and asked how he could become ἐνδοξότατος, 'most renowned'; he was told, rather tartly, to follow his own nature rather than popular renown (5. 1). Thus Plutarch introduces another vital theme: Cicero will so often win that renown, but will also so often spoil everything for its sake. A chapter later, when full of self-satisfaction he returns from Sicily and realizes that no-one knows where he has been, he reflects that the renown for which he is contending has no bound or limit:

> but it is still true that his extraordinary delight in being praised, and his over-susceptibility to fame (πρὸς δόξαν ἐμπαθέστερον ἔχειν), stayed with him all his days, and often wrecked many of his fine designs. (*Cic.* 6. 6)

And so once again we find that distinctive connexion between an interest in Hellenism, here particularly Hellenic philosophy, and a man's ability to control a destructive emotion (πάθος). Here the interest in Hellenism is different: that 'clash of lives' was barely felt in the other biographies we looked at—perhaps there was a hint of it in *Marcellus*, but no more. The emotion is a little different too, though it has something in common with Flamininus' φιλοτιμία. But the connexion of biographical interests is still very much the same.

When one measures Cicero on the scale of control of the passions, he does not come out too well. During his exile:

> Many men visited him in their goodwill, and the Greek cities contended with one another in their embassies to him—but still he spent most of the time dispirited and deeply grieved, gazing towards Italy like those hopelessly in love. He was too mean-spirited, too humbled, too diminished by what had happened: one would not have expected this from one who had lived with so much culture. And yet he often asked his friends to call him not an orator, but a philosopher: he had picked philosophy as his task, rhetoric as a mere tool (ὄργανον) for political necessities. But glory is extraordinarily able to wash rationality like a dye out of one's soul, and infect one with the passions of the many, because it is with these that politicians must keep their regular company—unless one keeps firm guard and reacts to externals as one who will play a part in the affairs themselves, but not in the passions which customarily attend them. (*Cic.* 32. 5–7)

It is the *Greek* cities that are courting him, the cities where he might well go and spend his life in contemplative bliss; but by now his public life has taken over too exclusively, and the passion for glory is out of control. The contemplative alternative no longer appeals; and Cicero is the poorer man for it. He is given a similar poor press for his self-control when the war itself is under way. The last years of his life are presented as a series of dispiriting choices, and they are presented very starkly: should he support Pompey or Caesar? Should he fight in the war? Should he beg pardon from Caesar? And finally should he support Octavian, despite all the risks? One can see Plutarch adapting his material to present the choices *more sharply*. Should Cicero support Pompey or Caesar?—

In the letters he says that he is uncertain which way to turn: Pompey's cause is the better and finer, but Caesar is the more capable man of affairs, and the better able to save himself and his friends; so he has someone to flee, but no-one to flee to. (*Cic.* 37. 3)

Yet, if one looks at the letters Plutarch seems to be quoting,[28] the issues are much more blurred. There are so many complicating strands: the thought, for instance, that Pompey's strategy is so inadequate (though Cicero does not understand it very lucidly); or that he is personally no less ambitious than Caesar himself. Plutarch's formulation 'Caesar is better able to save himself *and his friends*' again makes his cause less ethically impossible than Cicero in fact thought; in the letters the point is rather that Caesar is proving a most unreliable friend (e.g. *Att.* VII. 3. 3). In fact, Plutarch seems to be going out of his way to present the choice in as pointed, striking, and morally demanding a way as possible.

The passage goes on to mention an exchange of letters with Trebatius:

[28] Cic. *Att.* VIII. 7. 2, 'ego uero quem fugiam habeo, quem sequar non habeo', is especially in Plutarch's mind, but that letter does not give the description of the two men's causes; that seems to be adapted from such letters as *Fam.* VII. 3. 1–3, *Att.* VII. 12. 3, VII. 13. 1–2, etc. The issue is complicated: cf. D. R. Shackleton Bailey, *Cicero's Letters to Atticus* i (Cambridge, 1965) 61–2. It may even be that Plutarch is quoting a quite different letter where Cicero used the *mot* again, but it is much more likely that he is conflating several letters from memory, as at *Brut.* 22: cf. [343] 93. At all events, we need not doubt that Plutarch knew the important letters at first hand (cf. [343] 88–9), and consequently knew that Cicero's formulation of the choice was less clear-cut than he here suggests.

Trebatius, one of Caesar's friends, wrote to him to say that in Caesar's view the right thing would be for Cicero to range himself on his side and share his hopes; but that, if he felt himself too old for this, then he ought to go to Greece and live there quietly, without participating on either side. Cicero was amazed that Caesar did not write himself, and angrily replied that he would do nothing unworthy of his past political career. (*Cic.* 37. 4)

Here Plutarch seems to be going on *Att.* VII. 17. 3–4;[29] if he is, then the alterations are telling. Caesar in fact asked Cicero just to stay near Rome: it is Plutarch who imports the notion that 'if Cicero rejects that through his old age, let him withdraw *to Greece* . . .'—a suggestive revival of the old 'clash of lives' point. The final point is also interesting, where Cicero is so piqued that Caesar has not written himself: and that pique seems crucial in deciding him against Caesar. In the letter itself it is *Atticus* whom Cicero tells he will not act unworthily of his past: it is not a peremptory response (πρὸς ὄργην) to Trebatius, but actually rather dignified.[30] And, though Cicero certainly *was* angry and offended (and says so), he also did not reject Caesar's feelers completely: 'I do not despise Trebatius' letter', he says: in history, this certainly did not decide the matter. So Plutarch phrases the choice between Pompey and Caesar in this ethically challenging way—and then distorts the evidence to make Cicero show himself unable to live up to the demands made by so bemusing a choice, and reach his final decision for curiously unworthy reasons in a curiously unworthy way.

The unworthiness goes on: Cicero's bad behaviour in the camp at Pharsalus, making too many poor jokes (38); his attempt to slink away rather than take on a command after the defeat, which brought him into a brush with Cato (39. 1–2: perhaps it *was* the right thing for him to bail out even at so late

[29] This is again difficult: cf. Shackleton Bailey on *Att.* VII. 17. 3–4. It is certainly possible that Plutarch has seen a different letter, the one to Trebatius to which the Atticus letter refers. Still, Plutarch's phraseology is in parts very close indeed to the Atticus letter; and, if that is his source, the alterations are consistent with Plutarch's interests in this Life, and no more startling or extensive than he is prepared to make elsewhere. Moles ad loc. assumes that the Atticus letter is the source: I find his remarks on the passage very acute, and here follow them closely.

[30] Shackleton Bailey on *Att.* VII. 17 comments that 'Plutarch's account (*Cic.* 37), according to which Cicero replied to his letter in anger, is notably careless if based upon this passage'; but the alterations do not come from carelessness.

a stage, but one understands the impatience of his fellows); his timidity when approaching Caesar in Italy, compared with Caesar's own magnanimity (39. 3–5); and then a further, more elaborate discussion of how unworthy Cicero was of his own philosophy, when he rather disgraced himself in his treatment of Terentia and (particularly) his response to Tullia's death. Plutarch is again forthright in his criticisms:

When he began to write Rome's history, he found himself entangled in many public and private affairs and passions (πάθη), for which he himself was mainly to blame . . .

Many philosophers[31] consoled him on Tullia's death, but he took it too hard (βαρέως ἄγαν). (*Cic.* 41. 1, 8)

The similarities with his poor showing in exile are indeed clear.

The next great choice comes after the Ides of March: should he lend himself to Octavian or not? The various arguments are laid out very carefully, but then Plutarch states clearly that 'the *real* reason'—a slight echo of Thuc. 1. 23. 6, indeed!—was, first, his hatred for Antony, and then his susceptibility to flattery and the honours he thought the alliance would bring his way (45. 1): and Brutus' criticisms of Cicero's vanity are then given a lot of space. Once again, the stress is on a difficult choice: but, once again, Cicero fails to live up to the demands of that choice, and comes out very badly. And his reprehensible πάθη again bring catastrophe, this time to him personally: his desolation as he realises how he has been tricked is sensitively traced.

Even the clash of βίοι comes back at the end, in poignantly different ways. First, a false start: under Caesar's monarchy he withdrew from politics and devoted himself to philosophically-minded young men (τοῖς βουλομένοις φιλοσοφεῖν τῶν νέων)—but these unexpectedly became a source of *political* strength, for they were so well-connected (40. 1). The two lives are beginning to intertwine in unpredictable ways. But the second point is much more menacing, the contrast between Cicero's way of life and *Antony*'s: Antony is particularly hostile because of 'the dissimilarity and divergence of their lives', τὴν τῶν βίων ἀνομοιότητα καὶ διαφοράν (43. 2). The destructive contrast turns

[31] In view of the Life's themes, Ziegler and Moles are clearly right to keep the manuscripts' φιλόσοφοι rather than emend, with Volkmann and Flacelière, to the limp φίλοι.

out to be, not that between philosophy and public life, but that between dignified public life (the sort a philosophical gentleman ought to lead) and the sort favoured by Antony. And, thirdly, it is a final irony that a crucial role in betraying Cicero is played by a slave-boy whom, from his own kindness of spirit, he was educating in liberal studies. The boy's name was Philologus. Cicero's own culture played a strange part in his downfall.

To sum up on *Cicero*: once again, culture matters, but not in the sense that it explains any political line Cicero took. It matters because it provides an alternative way of life, which suggestively interweaves with the life Cicero in fact adopted. It matters, too, because once again, as Plutarch moves into the register of culture and Hellenism, he also moves into a particular register of moral evaluation, one which centres on control of the πάθη; here, that takes the form of dwelling on a series of particularly agonizing and ethically demanding choices, to which Cicero finally showed himself unequal. And what a very good way this was of doing Cicero!

## IV

*Brutus* is in many ways similar, but in some ways different. Here too we have very much 'the *philosopher*' in action, rather than any particular type of philosopher, and there is little interest in tracing what Brutus derived from any specific school. Here too we certainly have a great interest in moral evaluation. What we do not get, though, is any emphasis on the morally *problematic* quality of the various choices that Brutus made, even though they might seem to lend themselves to that: whether he should support his father's murderer Pompey, whether he should kill Caesar who had done him so much good, whether he should commit suicide.

First, the philosopher in action. The great impression of Brutus left by Plutarch (and thence perhaps by Shakespeare too) is very Stoic indeed:

> Because of his virtue, they say that the many felt affection for Brutus, his friends loved him, the best people admired him, and not even his enemies hated him: for he was outstandingly gentle, great-hearted, unmoved by any anger, pleasure, or greed, and kept his mind upright

and unbending in defence of what was noble and what was right. (*Brut.* 29. 3)

'Unmoved by any anger, pleasure, or greed . . .', *πρὸς πᾶσαν ὀργὴν καὶ ἡδονὴν καὶ πλεονεξίαν ἀπαθής*: just as we have had a great stress on his *ἀπαθεία* on the morning of the Ides of March (14. 6), as he delivered his judgements with relentless concentration and fairness while waiting for Caesar to arrive, and bore with extraordinary fortitude the *πολλὰ θορυβώδη* (15. 1), the 'many disconcerting events'—even the false report of his own wife's death (15. 5–9). His *ἀταραξία* may not be complete; at home in the days before the conspiracy, his wife Porcia could see that he was 'full of an unaccustomed *ταραχή*' (13. 3) and at the news of her death once again *συνεταράχθη*(15. 9); but even then 'he did not desert his public duty, and was not driven by his emotion (*πάθος*) to dwell on his private concerns' (15. 9); and he duly kept his nerve better than the others as the critical moment approached (16). The moral vocabulary, at least, seems distinctively Stoic; these are the terms in which we are invited to evaluate his emotional control; and it is hard to avoid being impressed. Then of course there is his own final death-scene, which seems to take its place in the martyrological tradition of the suicidal Stoic sages.

Yet Plutarch himself stresses at the beginning that Brutus was an Academic, not a Stoic at all. That is the linking theme with the paired life, the *Dion*, where Plato himself plays quite an important part; and Plutarch lays great stress on this at the beginning of the pair (*Dion* 1–2). *Both* of them came 'from the Academy', and it is duly one of Plato's *dicta* that Plutarch there gives as a sort of motto for the pair: that fortune and power must combine with wisdom and justice so that deeds can have both glory and greatness. (Admittedly a rather undistinguished *dictum* to pick, but there is a reason for this: Plutarch likes to start with relatively crude and unsophisticated formulations, and to re-define and deepen them as he proceeds.) There is then a certain bending of the narrative in *Brutus* 2 to make Brutus more of an enthusiast for the Old Academy than he really was.[32] Plutarch's general stress on Brutus as an Academic

[32] So Moles ad loc. (see introductory note): 'Babut' [333] '198–200, demonstrates that the somewhat hostile account of Antiochus in *Cic.* 4. 1–2 more truly represents Plutarch's own views than *Brut.* 2. 3 and *Luc.* 42. 3. It follows that Plutarch is deliberately

seems to be substantially correct, though his Stoic leanings were also doubtless recognized, even in his own life-time: that does give special point to Horace's 'cum fracta uirtus' of Philippi (*Carm.* II. 7. 11).[33] But for us the point is how extraordinarily undeveloped Plutarch leaves this contrast of schools. We are surely not meant to feel any incoherence, nor even any particular point in this combination of the Academic and the apparently Stoic; we are not, for instance, supposed to develop an idea of a young Academic developing into a Stoic sage under the pressure of events, interesting though such a treatment might have been. It is natural for the Academic stress to be established so strongly in the opening chapters: the opening chapters are after all the ones closest to *Dion*, and as often the linking themes of the pair are here at their most elaborate. But then this Academic emphasis is left undeveloped, and the themes that come out rather suit *any* philosopher: the sort of man who will show the gentleness (πραότης) and control of θυμός so distinctly lacking in his famous ancestor (1. 2–3); who will put personal enmities behind him in preferring Pompey to Caesar in 49 (4. 1–3); who will know that Caesar must be killed because his country's freedom demands it, no matter how well Brutus himself has fared at Caesar's hands (especially 7. 6–8. 4; 9. 5–10); who will try to limit bloodshed, even where an Antony or a C. Antonius is concerned (18. 3–6; 20. 2; 26. 5–8; 28. 1–2); who will at least have the decency to feel distress at the sufferings of Xanthus (31); and who will above all be unbending in his opposition to tyranny and his devotion to freedom. It *might* have been stressed that the Academics particularly prided themselves on their attachment to freedom (cf. e.g. *Phil.* 1. 3–4 as well as the *Dion*): but it does not really emerge from *this* Life. Here Brutus is surely just the philosopher in action, with his absolute commitment to high moral standards; and the apparently Stoic colouring just goes along with that. It is pre-eminently the deep moral commitment which *any*

playing down the controversial aspects of Antiochus in order to portray Brutus as a relatively orthodox Academic. At this juncture in the Life he does not wish to give Brutus Stoic characteristics. He has to say that Brutus was a follower of Antiochus and the "Old Academy", because he was, but he says as little as possible about Antiochus, and puts the stress instead upon his more amiable brother Aristus, a much less important philosopher.'

[33] Moles [350] esp. 64.

philosopher ought to show, and is not to be interpreted in the sense of any real clash or contrast between Academic and Stoic principles or behaviour. Again in *Dion* 1 Plutarch quotes the remark of the trainer Hippomachus, who said he could recognize his athletes even if he only saw them carrying meat away from the *agora*: 'thus it is reasonable for the intellect of the cultured person to attend his actions, showing a sort of harmony and rhythm along with decorum in what he does . . .' There is simply something about a philosopher, *any* philosopher, something about the way he acts: that harmony, rhythm, and decorum.

The point becomes particularly interesting at *Brut.* 40, the discussion of Brutus and Cassius before Philippi:

> The two generals came out and met in the space between their armies. Cassius said to Brutus, 'May this day bring us victory, Brutus, and may we share our success for the rest of our lives. But since the greatest of human affairs are the most uncertain, and since we may never see one another again if the battle goes against us, what have you decided to do if you have to choose between flight and death?' Brutus answered, 'When I was young, Cassius, and knew very little of the world, I was led, I do not know how, into throwing out a vast judgement in philosophy. I blamed Cato for taking his own life, because I thought it was impious and unmanly to try to evade the divine course of things and not to accept fearlessly whatever may befall, but to run away from it. But now in the present state of my fortunes, I see things differently. If the gods do not give their verdict in our favour, I have no desire to try other hopes or plans. I shall die content with my destiny. On the Ides of March I gave up my life to my country, and since then for her sake I have lived another life which is free and glorious.' At this Cassius smiled. Then he embraced Brutus and said, 'Now that our minds are made up, let us march against the enemy, for either we shall conquer, or, if we lose, we have nothing to fear.' (*Brut.* 40. 5–9)

This would seem to be a prime case where a discussion could have been developed in terms of particular schools: the Academic Brutus and the Epicurean Cassius coming together, and under the force of circumstances coming to virtually a Stoic view.[34] And there was a particular reason to present it this way:

[34] On the attitudes of the various schools, see now esp. Griffin [192] and Grisé [193] 167–244; the classic treatment is that of Hirzel [194]. On *Brut.* 40 in particular, cf. Moles [196] and Griffin, above, p. 11 n. 18.

for in the very preceding chapter Plutarch had developed the idea that Cassius' Epicurean principles were shaken by a sequence of bad omens, and his tendency to believe in them (39. 6, cf. *Caes*. 66. 2–3). The Epicurean, at least, is ripe for conversion. But, once again, this clash of schools does not seem to emerge clearly from the discussion of suicide itself: there is no capital made, for instance, of the fact that the Epicurean Cassius should not really assent to this so easily. Of course the arguments deployed against suicide—those Brutus *once* believed in, but has now given up—have many points of contact with those developed by Plato in the context of Socrates' death:[35] it might even be argued that they would so readily be identified as 'Academic' that the 'from Academic into Stoic' interpretation would immediately be understood by Plutarch's audience, so that he did not need to trouble with labelling the different arguments and approaches. But it seems unlikely. Brutus' 'philosophy' makes it appropriate to ponder the issues in this register: it gives him the arguments and the facility in deploying them, it enables him to play with this 'big philosophical λόγος' (§7) and see the issues particularly clearly. That is all.

What is more, we are surely supposed to think (along with Cassius) that Brutus has now got it right. The rhythm of the whole Life demands that this will be a worthy death, with exemplary final words, courage, and dignity; it is interesting, for instance, that in the famous story of Lucilius it is *assumed* that Brutus would naturally take his own life. When the soldiers took Lucilius and thought he was Brutus, 'some felt pity for his fortune, others thought him unworthy of his reputation, now that his φιλοψυχία had left him a prey to barbarian enemies' (50. 4): φιλοψυχία, they thought he was clinging on to life.[36] Then Lucilius was brought before Antony:

> 'No enemy', said Lucilius, 'has taken Marcus Brutus, nor could they ever take him: may fortune never conquer his virtue to that extent. He will be found alive—or dead, and lying worthily of himself. (*Brut*. 50. 5–6)

[35] Cf. Pl. *Phd*. 61 B–62 D.

[36] For the dismissive character of the word cf. LSJ s.v. and e.g. *Brut*. 43. 7; *Ant*. 76. 5 (though also notice 83. 7); *Nic*. 26. 4; *Mar*. 46. 9.

The emphasis is clear: Brutus' suicide was noble, worthy, and *right*. The notion that the decision was problematic is not developed, though it clearly could have been:[37] the decision is consonant with the moral courage and moral virtue he has always shown.

Here we have come on to the difference from *Cicero*. There, we noticed, it was precisely the problematic quality of so many decisions that Plutarch stressed, making them morally sharper and more demanding than they were in life—even if then Cicero tended to show himself unworthy in the motives that eventually swayed him one way or another. In *Brutus* there is much less moral problematic. When Brutus decides that his benefactor Caesar needs to be murdered, that simply displays the same disdain for personal considerations which brought him to Pompey's side in the first place, the side of his father's murderer: the link between the two incidents is implicit in the narrative and explicit at *Synkrisis* 3. 8. Plutarch is of course aware that this was conventionally an immense moral problem in estimating Brutus' act;[38] he indeed develops it in that way in the *Synkrisis* (3. 4 ff.)—does this make him better or worse than Dion, who had no similar personal favours binding him to Dionysius? But there is no hint of any real problematic in the narrative itself. Once again, Brutus has simply got it right: just as we surely feel he was right in the famous quarrel with Cassius over the despoiling of the Asian cities (34–5), where it was left for Shakespeare to make the moral issue more complex.

This does not mean that there are no hints of criticism in the Life at all: of course there are. There is moral criticism, especially when Brutus allows Sparta and Thessalonica to be publicized as the fruits of victory for his troops: that is the one unforgivable (ἀναπολόγητον) blemish on Brutus' reputation, even though Plutarch explains how he found himself forced into doing it (46). There is practical criticism too, most notably in the strong hint that he was wrong to spare Mark Antony on the Ides of March: one cannot believe that the gentle Plutarch

[37] *Cleom.* 31 gives an interesting idea of what *might* have been said. On Plutarch's own views, cf. Babut [333] 100: on the whole, he appears to accept that suicide can in certain circumstances be acceptable. (*Mor.* 476 A–B is here important, but also difficult: cf. Brenk [335] 176.)

[38] Cf. Rawson [343].

would *morally* approve of such a murder, but he is well enough aware that the political consequences were decidedly unfortunate (20. 1–2, linking this with the similar mistake in allowing Antony to deliver his funeral speech). Once again, as in a way with *Marcellus*, we see Plutarch entering into the spirit of the thing, adopting the standards of public political life in judging a public political man, even one with so firm a background in moral philosophy. More substantially, there is even the doubt that killing Caesar was a good thing to do in any case: Rome after all needed a monarchy, and Caesar was the 'gentlest of doctors' for the ills of the Roman state, and Rome could not really hope for anything better (*Snk*. 2. 2). But it is again interesting that that train of thought is developed in the *Synkrisis* chapters, where it makes a particular point in contrasting the fortunes of Brutus and Dion, in the tyrants they had the lack to run up against; the idea is not at all insistent in the narrative itself. Such reservations would have left too much of a shadow over the whole ethical question of the tyrannicide: Plutarch prefers to allow the moral issue to be much clearer, and Brutus to be much less ambiguous in his virtue. It is clearly a different form of moralism from the *Cicero*: here we have a hero who is more exemplary—and perhaps the less human for it. This is a protreptic rather than descriptive form of moralism, a greater concern to set up a model for imitation than to point a truth about the fragility and vanity of human nature—that nature which could generate so great and cultured, but also so vain and fragile, a figure as Cicero.

*Cato minor* is a little different again. In its moralism, it lies somewhere between *Brutus* and *Cicero*. As in *Brutus*, it is hard to avoid being impressed by the man's moral courage. That is particularly true at the end, when he is resolved on death but his first thought is still for the safety of Utica; but throughout his life Cato *has* managed to keep to his principles, and that was not easy as the Republic crumbled around him. Still, Plutarch is here more ready to criticize than in *Brutus*. It may be domestic matters, his drunkenness or—particularly—his management of his womenfolk (6; 24. 4–25. 13; 52. 8; cf. 73. 2–4 on the sexual antics of his son). More substantially, there are doubts about his whole political style. In the introduction to the pair Plutarch recalls Cicero's notion that Cato sometimes appeared to be speaking in Plato's Republic rather than the sewer of the Roman state (*Phoc.* 3. 2): the Life develops the idea. It really is hard for others to take such an ostentatious and tactless parade of principle (9. 10; 14. 7–8; 36. 5–37; 39. 2; 44. 11); there are times when it endangers the whole state. In 60, Cato rejected a marriage-alliance with Pompey, and Plutarch's view of the matter is clear:

If one may judge from the sequel, Cato missed the mark completely: by rejecting the alliance he allowed Pompey to turn to Caesar, and contract a marriage which united the power of the two men and shortly overturned the Roman state and destroyed the constitution. None of this would perhaps have happened, if Cato had not felt fear at the minor wrongs of Pompey and overlooked the greatest of them all, in allowing him to add his power to that of others. (*C.min.* 30. 9–10)

And the clash between principle and practicality is interestingly developed, for instance in several exchanges with Cicero—32. 8–11, where in 59 BC Cicero prevails on Cato to yield to circumstances and take the oath; 35. 1, where Cato responds with rather similar advice to Cicero himself; then 50. 2–3, where Cicero presses him to show more affability in his canvassing, for the state needs men like him in power. Where Cato does bring himself to compromise, he seems to win Plutarch's approval: in the shrewd corn-dole of 26. 1, for instance, or in supporting Pompey for his sole consulship in 47. 2–4. Here, certainly, the issues do not seem simple: this indeed is the sort of development that Plutarch might have given to the quarrel of *Brutus* 34–5, but did not. Even in *Cato* Plutarch could have done a little more of this: it is for instance in the other Lives, not in *Cato* itself, that he makes his reservations clear about the optimate behaviour at the beginning of the Civil War, forcing the issue and playing into Caesar's hands.[39] The overall enthusiasm for Cato, too, is so clear that one could not feel the same sort of ethical reservations that Plutarch suggests about Cicero. But the moral questions do seem a little less clear-cut than in *Brutus*.

One further point concerning *Cato*: here, for once, the influence of a particular school is felt. Cato is identifiably a Stoic

[39] Contrast the rapid *C.min.* 51. 6–52. 1 with e.g. *Ant.* 5. 3; 5. 8; *Caes.* 31. 1; 33. 4.

to the end. That helps to explain his scruffiness, something which Plutarch himself clearly feels reservations about (cf. especially 44. 1); but at least Cato was 'accustoming himself to feel shame only at what was shameful, and to scorn anything else that was conventionally of ill repute' (6. 6). But in fact it is at the end (naturally enough) that the Stoic colouring is especially strong. Before he dies Cato paradoxically claims that he is the true victor and Caesar the vanquished, in what was fair and honourable (64. 8–9). After that it is no surprise to find Cato, on his last evening alive, discoursing on 'the so-called paradoxes of the Stoics', holding with fierce intensity that only the good man is free, and the worthless are all slaves—'so that it was clear to everyone that he was about to end his life, and free himself from the present troubles' (67. 2–3). His behaviour may still not be beyond Stoic reproach: he does after all lose his composure, and angrily strikes a slave (68. 5). But the initial decision to kill himself remains unquestionably right. It is appropriate, indeed, for the people of Utica to respond to the news of his death by hailing him as 'their benefactor, their saviour, the one man who is truly free and unvanquished' (71. 1). This is once again an unproblematic and, on the whole, a noble suicide. This time, it is identifiably a Stoic suicide too.

## V

*Cato* reminds us how difficult it is to generalize about Plutarch's biographical technique; but *Cato* does remain the exception. Normally the treatment of Hellenic culture is strikingly lacking in this sort of explanatory force: one rarely feels one has come to *understand* why a hero acted in any way simply because of his particular philosophy or education. We may admire a man more warmly, we may judge him more critically; we seem rather rarely to understand him with any more insight. Ancient writers *could* analyse personality more informatively. Marcus Aurelius, for instance, and indeed Horace in the *Satires* can explain what they derived from their philosophy, just as they can set out what they learned from more personal influences, particularly their fathers.[40] But this does not seem to be Plutarch's way.

[40] Cf. esp. Marc. Aurel. *Med.* 1. 17; Hor. *Serm.* 1. 6.

Perhaps here Christopher Gill's distinction between 'personality-viewpoints' and 'character-viewpoints' may be useful.[41] If we speak of 'character', we are usually more concerned to evaluate; we of course wish to describe a person, but may often do this with comparatively little concern to understand him; and, in our descriptions, we quite often tend to subsume an individual to a class (one can usually put some sort of adjective in front of 'character'—'irascible', 'generous', 'surly', 'vain', etc). 'Personality', in contrast, tends to be more individuating, more concerned with isolating what makes a man different from anyone else, and often with understanding what makes him the way he is. Gill suggests that the fundamental contrast between Plutarch and modern biography can helpfully be put in these terms: Plutarch is typically more concerned with character, modern biography with personality. Now it may be that some reservations should be made about the distinction itself: it is not at all clear how far the various things we associate with 'personality' and 'character' are simply English semantic accidents, rather than belonging together in some sort of intrinsic logical bundle. Plutarch too is not just concerned with 'character' in our terms: for instance, his Coriolanus is very much a 'personality', and Plutarch's analysis of his debt to his dominant, bellicose mother has a good deal in common with modern approaches. Sometimes Plutarch individuates (Alcibiades or Timoleon), sometimes makes his heroes closer to a class (Crassus or Numa); sometimes he is both individuating and evaluating (Pompey or Nicias), sometimes really doing neither (Alexander or Caesar). But still the distinction, however rough, can sometimes be illuminating, and a lot of the argument of this paper could be summarized by saying that Hellenic culture, *when it is present*, is made much more a question of character than of personality. It encourages us to ask more evaluating questions; it counts as a plus, but not always a decisive one, on the moral scale; it possibly tends to make some (but only some) of the figures more akin to types (Brutus, perhaps, possibly even Flamininus, though not really Cicero, nor Marcellus, nor the elder nor even the younger Cato). What it does not particularly do is help us to understand

[41] [336], [348], [349].

them, though it may help us (in Cicero's case) to understand some of the tensions and temptations he felt. An absence of education by contrast does rather help us to understand people as personalities, at least in the sense that it offers an explanation why a Marius or a Coriolanus or even a Marcellus found a certain passion more difficult to control: it also encourages us to dwell on the ways in which certain critical flaws cohere closely with moral strengths, so that we develop a stronger, more integrated picture of a man's nature. It may not go all that deep, but at least it is something.

Still, this is only to re-phrase the question, not to answer it. Plutarch is interested in culture and education; he has the resources to analyse people's personality, and to suggest the influences which explain a way a man is different from his fellows—Coriolanus is enough to demonstrate that. So *why* does he so rarely exploit cultural background to illuminate these questions? I suspect the answer should be sought, not in the ancients' views of culture or philosophy, but in their perceptions of personality and (especially) childhood. But that, as Plutarch would say, is matter for another treatise.[42]

[42] I discuss this in [342].

# 9

# Roman Rulers and the Philosophic Adviser

†ELIZABETH RAWSON*

THERE has been a great deal of discussion of the clash between philosophers, or those under the influence of philosophers, and Roman emperors whom they regarded as tyrants. Much less attention has been paid to the other side of the coin, and to the philosophers who were, or were claimed to have been, honoured political advisers to the emperors and other great Romans.

Dio Chrysostom's 49th *Discourse* is one of the fullest expressions of the belief of so many philosophically inclined Greeks that, if a ruler could not himself be a Platonic philosopher king (*εὕροι δ' ἄν τις σπανίως μὲν φιλοσόφους ἄρξαντας ἐν τοῖς ἀνθρώποις*), he should become the pupil of a philosopher, or take a philosopher as his *σύμβουλος*, and while giving orders to others accept orders from him as to *ἃ δεῖ πράττειν καὶ τίνων ἀπέχεσθαι*.[1] It is not possible, of course, to keep the ideas rigidly distinct; the ruler who accepts a philosopher's advice slides easily into the ruler who is a student of philosophy, and he into a philosopher king.

The Epicureans, says Plutarch, wrote treatises on kingship to teach us to avoid living with kings[2] (Philodemus' *On the Good King according to Homer* is written by the author rather as poet and critic than as Epicurean philosopher[3]); and if the Cynics sometimes had views on the good king, they were often not themselves *hoffähig*. But behind Dio is a tradition running back to the fourth century BC, and above all to Plato's conviction

* I am grateful to members of the Seminar, and to Mrs Griffin and Dr M. Dzielska, for criticism and suggestions; also to members of the Corpus Classical Seminar, to whom the revised version was read.

[1] Dio Chrys. 49. 3, 5–8.

[2] Plut. *Mor.* 1127 A.

[3] Murray [141].

that philosophers alone knew the true Good, and so how to rule well, running back also to his own and his pupils' attempts to teach and advise a variety of rulers. Isocrates' definition of philosophy was very unlike Plato's, but he told Nicocles of Cyprus that in order to gain a thorough understanding of what kings should know, he should choose advisers who have been educated according to some kind of philosophy, and so can deliberate well; he needs φιλοσοφία as well as ἐμπειρία.[4] The treatise on kingship addressed by Aristotle, or supposedly addressed by Aristotle, to the active and uncontemplative Alexander claimed that philosophy was not necessary for the king himself, but even a hindrance; he should however listen to and obey philosophers.[5] Chrysippus held that if the wise man (himself already a true king) cannot rule himself, he may live with a king, and the Stoics Sphaerus and Persaeus are the best known of those who attached themselves to royal courts in the Hellenistic period.[6] As well as the philosophers who became, or lived with rulers, there were those who simply addressed letters or dedicated treatises on kingship or other symbouleutic works to them.[7]

It is true that Plutarch shows in his essay *That philosophers should consort with rulers* (in order to benefit the largest number of people) that some hesitated to do so since it made them liable to charges of flattery and personal ambition;[8] and he was writing after a period of severe tension between Roman emperors and (primarily Stoic and Cynic) philosophers, which may have made the latter fearful of approaching the former. And there were always some Greeks who distrusted philosophy and its practitioners; so the historian Cassius Dio makes Maecenas advise Augustus not to trust philosophers just because he has found his friend Areus a good man. Dio is staging a debate in which, significantly, Augustus' advisers on the best form of government—a commonplace of philosophic discussion—are not philosophers, but his Roman friends and assistants in prac-

[4] Isoc. *Nic.* 35, 50.

[5] Arist. fr. 647 Rose.

[6] Chrysippus *SVF* iii. 691, 702.

[7] J. Klek, *Symboulutici qui dicitur sermonis historia critica* (Diss. Freiburg-i.-Br., 1919). But there seems to be nothing on σύμβουλοι themselves.

[8] Plutarch, *Mor.* 776 B.

tical affairs, Agrippa and Maecenas.[9] But in the Greek world, unlike the Roman, such sceptical voices are isolated.

What I want to do is to ask how far Greeks tried to persuade, or succeeded in persuading, Roman statesmen, particularly Roman emperors (frequently called 'kings' in Greek), to take philosophic advisers in the art of ruling. Or how far did they claim subsequently but unjustifiably to have done so? And what did they think the rulers learnt? The investigation may tell us most, perhaps, about the ideas of some of Rome's Greek subjects, and their attempts to secure patronage and status (or the status of their subject and even their race) but it will throw some light on the actual standing and influence of philosophy and philosophers in the Roman world. Oswyn Murray has rightly noted that from the time of the Second Sophistic there was a tendency to equip all important (rather, all 'good') emperors of the past with a philosophic adviser.[10] He notes some earlier examples of the habit; in fact we must start the story at a much earlier date.

In the discourse we began with, Dio Chrysostom starts with Agamemnon and Nestor and goes on to mention numerous Greeks who had sage advisers or who were pupils of philosophers. It is because Philip studied in Thebes with Lysis the Pythagorean that he excelled previous Macedonian Kings; Pericles was a pupil of Anaxagoras; the kings of the Persians, Egyptians, Indians, and Celts had their magi, priests, brahmins, and druids.[11] If he does not here mention Plato's involvement with Syracuse, or Alexander's relations with Aristotle and other philosophers, other sources often do (though many philosophers later condemned Alexander as bloodthirsty and tyrannical); but naturally classicizing Greek writers of the imperial period are inclined to omit the Hellenistic figures.

Dio's only Roman example is that of King Numa, whom 'some say partook of the wisdom of Pythagoras'. When and where this idea arose is uncertain.[12] It was based, as Plutarch's *Life of Numa* shows, on the belief that many of Rome's tradi-

[9] Cassius Dio LII. 1–41.

[10] Murray [355].

[11] See above, n. 1.

[12] Pythagoras appears to have been known in Rome at least since the fourth century BC, Pliny, *NH* XXXIV. 26.

tional customs were Pythagorean in origin.[13] Cicero in the *De Re Publica* suggests that the story was an 'inveteratus error' in 129 BC, the dramatic date of the dialogue. He was not sorry 'non esse nos transmarinis nec importatis artibus eruditos sed genuinis domesticisque virtutibus';[14] and Livy, a little later, is delighted that he must reject the tale, and that Numa's virtue was not drawn from 'peregrinis artibus', but 'disciplina tetrica ac tristi veterum Sabinorum'.[15] The learned Varro of course had the chronology right; Ovid, as a poet, can ignore it, but it is noteworthy that he takes Numa to Croton in search not of political wisdom, but of wisdom 'de rerum natura', and has him listen to lectures on vegetarianism, metempsychosis, physics, meteorology, and paradoxology—only.[16] Later Roman sources omit the tale; but among the Greeks, though Dionysius of Halicarnassus tries to suggest that he has worked out the chronological incompatibility himself for the first time,[17] others abandon it with regret or not at all—Plutarch appeals to a work attributed to Epicharmus (a παλαιὸς ἀνήρ and a Pythagorean himself) which said Pythagoras was given Roman citizenship and which therefore presumably took him to Rome.[18]

The contrasting attitudes of Greeks and Romans to this story serve to set the scene; we move on to the late Republic. We will consider only those figures whom Greek authors describe as philosophic advisers on how to rule; other philosophers in touch with great Romans may of course have taken up the part, or been seen as doing so, for example Blossius with Tiberius Gracchus, or M. Crassus' stingily treated Peripatetic Alexander, but there is no evidence that this is so.[19]

Plutarch was always anxious to find philosophic inspiration for his heroes and to show Romans as admirers of Greek culture; at different places in the *Moralia* Scipio and Panaetius, Cato and Athenodorus, and Cicero and Nigidius Figulus all

[13] Plut. *Num.* 8. 7, cf. Cic. *Tusc.* IV. 2.

[14] Cic. *Rep.* II. 28–9. Plut. *Aem.* 2. 1 shows the Aemilii (perhaps in the early second century BC) claimed descent from Pythagoras.

[15] Livy I. 18. 4.

[16] Ovid *Met.* XV. 1–481.

[17] Dion. Hal. II. 59.

[18] Plut. *Num.* 8. 9.

[19] Plut. *Ti. Gracch.* 8. 4–5. cf. Cic. *Amic.* 37; Plut. *Crassus* 3. 3.

exemplify the ideal relationship between statesman and philosopher.[20] In another list Aelian, writing in the late second or early third century AD, notes *σύμβουλοι* from Antenor, the adviser of Odysseus, onwards: the Romans mentioned include Lucullus, who gained advantage from Antiochus of Ascalon, as Maecenas did from Areus, Cicero from Apollonius (not however a philosopher), and Augustus from Athenodorus; elsewhere Aelian says that Caesar did not disdain to frequent the doors of Aristo, or Pompey those of Cratippus, for from them they could get the most benefit: *οὐ γὰρ ἄρχειν, ὥς ἔοικεν, ἀλλὰ καλῶς ἄρχειν ἐβούλοντο.*[21]

The great devotee of the view that all good Roman statesmen and rulers had philosophical advisers was Themistius, who in the fourth century AD was one such himself, honoured by every emperor from Constantius II to Theodosius I, who made him City Prefect and tutor to his son, the future Emperor Arcadius. In one or another of his speeches the emperor he is addressing is reminded not only that Philip and Alexander favoured philosophers, but that Scipio was associated with Panaetius, that Augustus honoured and employed Areus of Alexandria, Tiberius Thrasyllus, Titus Musonius, Trajan Dio Chrysostom, and the two Antonini Epictetus; Marcus also relied on Rusticus.[22] Julian, in his *Letter to Themistius*, picks up a number of these examples for discussion.[23]

Let us look at these instances, recalling that while Greek philosophers would advise any ruler, whatever his title, in political theory the ideal single ruler was always called a king; while great Roman nobles of the later Republic regarded themselves, and were regarded by others, as the equals of Hellenistic kings, or even, especially as consuls or proconsuls, as in a sense kings themselves.[24]

The younger Scipio's friendship with the distinguished Stoic Panaetius is attested above all by Cicero. But though Cicero

[20] Plut. *Mor.* 777 A, 797 D.

[21] Ael. *VH* XII. 25; VII. 21.

[22] Themist. 13. 173b–c, 5. 63d, 11. 145b, 34. 31–2. Themistius' own grandfather held the same position in Byzantium, 5. 63d.

[23] *ad Them.* 265c; cf. *Caesares, passim.*

[24] Rawson [357]. Of course philosophers—notably Dio Chrysostom—may also advise cities; and non-philosophers may advise kings, often to much the same effect as philosophers.

did of course believe that a philosophic education—in not only ethics and politics but dialectic too—was essential to the complete orator, who is the true statesman, he was too convinced of the essential superiority of the Roman moral and political tradition to visualize Scipio tamely accepting advice in that field from Panaetius. In the *De Re Publica* Scipio carefully distances his friend from politics: I wish he were here to tell us about astronomy, but I don't entirely approve of his devotion to these matters and think Socrates, who rejected them, was wiser. Later it is said that Scipio has discussed the *res publica* with Panaetius and Polybius, and found arguments to show the superiority of the Roman form to all others; but grammatically, it is he, not Panaetius, who has done this.[25] Cicero elsewhere tells us that Panaetius was Scipio's only companion on the latter's embassy to the East, and highly honoured by him.[26] But it is modern scholars who see Panaetius' function, especially on the journey, as that of a practical adviser on Greek affairs, and who think that he provided a justification of Rome's rule over her subjects, as that of a superior over inferiors.[27] In a speech, however, Cicero said (perhaps not very seriously) that Panaetius' effect on Scipio was to make him 'lenissimus'. This evokes the commonest of all *τόποι* involving the philosophic adviser.[28]

The case of Lucullus is not unlike that of Scipio. Cicero has a good deal to tell us in the *Lucullus* about Lucullus' friendship with Antiochus of Ascalon, the founder of the so-called Old Academy, in reaction against the sceptical New Academy.[29] But this is part of a desperate attempt to argue that Lucullus and other great Romans are suitable participants in a technical dialogue on epistemology; and the other connections between Roman nobles and Greek philosophers that Cicero adduces in this work serve the same end. Again, it is modern scholars who argue that Lucullus, who twice took Antiochus to the East with him, used him as an adviser on Greek affairs,[30] rather than, as Cicero might imply, in order to discuss the extent to which

[25] Cic. *Rep.* I. 15, 34.
[26] Cic. *Luc.* 5.
[27] e.g. Walbank [358].
[28] Cic. *Mur.* 66.
[29] Cic. *Luc.* 4.
[30] Esp. Glucker [71]; cf. Barnes above, pp. 56–7; 58–9; 62.

Philo of Larissa had misrepresented Academic tradition. It is true that leading philosophers in this period were often men of wealth and position (for example it was fitting for Cicero when passing through Athens to stay in the house of Antiochus' brother, and in some sense successor, Aristus).[31] Such men are therefore plausible advisers on Eastern affairs for great Romans, and may have felt it their duty to give practical counsel if possible. But in advising a foreign power *qua* Greeks rather than *qua* philosophers, as modern scholars seem to assume they do, they would have been stepping outside the traditional role of the philosophic σύμβουλος.

Aelian, as we saw, assigns Apollonius as adviser to Cicero—Apollonius Molon, the rhetor who only knew Cicero in the East when he was young and of little political importance, and who in fact wrote against philosophy.[32] However, Plutarch (who curiously omits from his *Life* the philosophers Cicero studied with in youth) says that he himself stated that as consul in 63 he made use in saving his country of the advice of the philosopher Nigidius Figulus.[33] Nigidius was a senator who was soon to rise to the praetorship, and as such an entirely suitable member of a Roman consul's *consilium*. Plutarch ignores this; but though Nigidius is by most of the Roman sources remembered as an astrologer and magician, he had a right to the title of philosopher—he claimed to be a Pythagorean, and Cicero calls him a *physicus*, a scientist or natural philosopher; the fragments of his zoological work show use of Aristotle as well as magical sources.[34] Cicero's lost account in Greek of his consulship was probably Plutarch's source for Nigidius' role in 63; the label of philosopher in this context is surely Plutarch's own. Cicero himself never suggests he needed philosophical aid in his political career;[35] and he did not even like Nigidius' esoteric brand of philosophy, claiming to have argued with him from a sceptical point of view.[36] He aimed higher—intimating to his brother

[31] Cic. *Att.* v. 10. 5.

[32] Cic. *Brut.* 312, 316; Schol. Aristoph. *Nub.* 144.

[33] Plut. *Mor.* 797 D.

[34] Rawson [94] 181 ff.

[35] Cic. *Timaeus* 1.

[36] Cassius Dio XXXVIII. 18 ff. thought he needed one when in exile and brings on a perhaps fictional Athenian friend Philiscus (not actually called a philosopher) to staunch his laments and imbue him with σοφία.

that he had as consul perhaps actually incarnated the Platonic ideal of a philosophic ruler. This letter, an essay on good rule addressed to Quintus as governor of Asia, has been shown by Klek to draw much from the tradition of the philosopher's letter of advice to a ruler; to have an ex-philosopher-ruler acting as philosophic *σύμβουλος* to another philosopher-ruler (as Quintus is politely described) is a nice twist.[37] Cicero also liked to compare himself with Demetrius of Phaleron, whom he saw as uniting theory and practice as ruler of Athens in the late fourth century BC.[38] In the preface to the *De Re Publica* however he suggests that practical statesmen—lawgivers—are both anterior and superior to philosophers: they have discovered and put into practice what the philosophers preach.[39]

Near the end of his life, himself powerless in politics, he returned to the role of philosophic adviser, basing a letter to Caesar on Aristotle's and Theopompus' addresses to Alexander: '*συμβουλευτικὸν* saepe conor'.[40] He seems also to have read Antisthenes' *Cyrus*, on Kingship, for this purpose.[41] But he had no luck with this work; Caesar's agents Oppius and Balbus vetoed its dispatch.[42]

Plutarch's *Life of Cato* gives a full account of his subject's involvement with various philosophers, which we need not reproduce here; they are not represented as advising him how to rule, and indeed Cato, who never reached the consulship or governed a province, is the least plausible of the great Republican nobles in the role of king. But in the essay on the philosopher's duty to engage with rulers Plutarch notes his sailing *ἀπὸ στρατίας* to find the philosopher Athenodorus ('Cordylion', the first of the two Tarsian Stoics of the name).[43] The motif of the great man going to seek out the philosopher at home is an old one; the secular thus recognizes the superiority of the spiritual power.

Similarly, Aelian said, as we saw, that Pompey frequented the house of Cratippus—the distinguished Peripatetic who

[37] Cic. *Qfr.* I. I. 29; Klek (above, n. 7) 82 ff.
[38] Cic. *Leg.* III. 14; *Off.* I. 3.
[39] Cic. *Rep.* I. 3.
[40] Cic. *Att.* XII. 40. 2; cf. XIII. 28. 2 'aliquid consili dari'.
[41] Cic. *Att.* XII. 38a. 2.
[42] Cic. *Att.* XIII. 27, 28.
[43] Plut. *Mor.* 777 A.

taught Cicero's son in Athens and was given Roman citizenship by Caesar.[44] The only occasion on which we hear that Pompey and he met is that on which Pompey put in at Lesbos on his flight after Pharsalus; Cratippus came to pay his respects and to discuss πρόνοια, according to Plutarch.[45] It is unlikely that there is anything of substance behind Aelian's words, though the two men may have met in Mitylene fifteen years earlier when Pompey was on his way home from the Mithridatic Wars.

Pompey, however, though his education had been cut short by an early entry on public life, had a vast respect for learning. It is surprising that his relationship with the great Stoic savant Posidonius is not picked up by imperial sources. I have argued elsewhere that Pompey may have felt that, just as he was a second Alexander, so Posidonius was his Aristotle—indeed, Strabo compares the two philosophers, and with his wide interests Posidonius was not too unworthy of the role.[46] But Pompey's visits to Posidonius in Rhodes were brief ones: the sage is recorded as lecturing Pompey and his suite on the rhetorical doctrines of Hermagoras and on vice as the only real evil, and as advising the great general, in Homer's words, αἰὲν ἀριστεύειν καὶ ὑπείροχον ἔμμεναι ἄλλων.[47]

It is modern scholars who have connected Pompey's humane resettlement of the defeated pirates with Posidonius' Stoicism. Mildness is what philosophers are expected to advise; but *parcere subiectis* was traditional Roman policy.

And certainly neither Posidonius nor Cratippus can have been long-term political advisers to Pompey. That role, for Greek affairs, was played by Theophanes of Mitylene, an ἀνὴρ πολιτικός according to Strabo, and author of a highly-coloured history of Pompey's deeds in the East.[48] In Roman affairs too Pompey had his advisers, and even tended to disappear behind them; but they were such men as L. Lucceius, Scribonius Libo, and others, Romans of the senatorial class, if also cultivated men (more prone to historiography than philosophy).

As for Caesar, it is hard to conceive of him listening patiently

[44] Plut. *Cic.* 24. 5.
[45] Plut. *Pomp.* 75. 4.
[46] [94] 106; Strabo XIII. 617.
[47] Plut. *Pomp.* 42. 5; Cic. *Tusc.* II. 61; Strabo XI. 492.
[48] Strabo XIII. 617.

to ethical commonplaces or to lectures on tyranny or the mixed constitution, and contemporary sources associate him with no philosophers. Modern scholars have tried to make him an Epicurean, largely on the tenuous evidence of the speech given him in Sallust's *Catilinarian War* with its doubts of a future life; he did have Epicurean friends, such as Matius.[49] But Plutarch would probably have told us if Caesar had studied with any philosopher as a young man. References and jokes in Cicero's letters to him are literary, not philosophical (contrast the letters to the Epicurean Cassius) and what they discussed at dinner was 'φιλόλογα multa'.[50] Caesar's lost literary works derive from Alexandrian scholarship. But Aelian, undaunted, provides us, as we saw, with the name of a philosophical adviser—Aristo.

*Πολλοὶ μὲν οἱ Ἀρίστωνες*, as Lucian observes.[51] This is Aristo of Alexandria, a member of the philosophic gathering there in Lucullus' time evoked in Cicero's *Lucullus*. The key is provided by the historian Appian, who (probably using a Roman source) tells us in Book II of his *Civil Wars* that, when in Alexandria, Caesar listened to the philosophers, modestly standing with the other auditors.[52]

Caesar would hardly have cared for the commentaries on Aristotle's logical works for which Aristo, who left Antiochus to become a Peripatetic, is best remembered; but he might have been interested in a possible work on the Nile.[53] Advice on how to rule seems improbable. Caesar returned to Rome without, so far as we know, Aristo in his train, though given the development of Aristotelian studies in Italy at this time Mariotti thinks the philosopher may have visited it.[54] It is true that Caesar now offered citizenship to Greek teachers in Rome and wished to harness intellectuals, both Roman and Greek, to the service of the state; but these are largely technical specialists—the Romans mostly lawyers, with Varro who was to form the first public library in Rome; the Greeks headed by the astronomer Sosigenes, who worked on the reform of the calendar; and if we

[49] Sall. *Cat.* 51. 20.

[50] Cic. *Att.* XIII. 52. 2.

[51] Lucian, *Lexiphanes* 1.

[52] App. *B. Civ.* II. 89.

[53] I. Mariotti, *Aristone d'Alessandria* (Bologna, 1966) 37 (Caesar will not be found in his index, nor Aristo in that of Gelzer's *Caesar*).

[54] Ibid. 25.

may trust a late source, a team of 'philosophers' recruited to map the Empire.[55] It is conceivable that it was Caesar who brought Areus of Alexandria to Rome and made him tutor to his young grand-nephew Octavius; but it was only, it seems, Apollodorus of Pergamum, the rhetorician, who was in attendance on Octavius at Apollonia when the news of Caesar's death arrived.[56]

The establishment of the principate is a turning point for our subject. The Roman political system had collapsed and Roman virtue was thought to be in decay. If the Romans had less to learn in some fields from the Greeks—and by now had plenty of experience of ruling them—what these had to teach about kingship might seem more relevant than before, since both Greeks and, after a while, Romans were in no doubt that a king was what they now had.

The relationship of Augustus to Areus and Athenodorus (the other Athenodorus of Tarsus, the son of Sandon, who had been in Rome since possibly the fifties[57]) is central to the later justification of good emperors by means of philosophy. It is what Julian is alluding to in the *Caesares* when he shows Apollo turning the chameleon-like and haughty Octavian into *ἄνδρα ἔμφρονα καὶ σώφρονα* by handing him over to Zeno, who recites over him some of his doctrines *ὥσπερ οἱ τὰς Ζαμόλξιδος ἐπῳδὰς θρυλοῦντες*.[58] In Augustus' own speech later in the work one of his chief claims to pre-eminence among all the Emperors is that he showed himself so gentle to the guidance of philosophy that he put up with, nay enjoyed, Athenodorus' *παρρησία*, and revered the man as his *παιδαγωγός* and own father, while Areus was his *φίλος* and *συμβιωτής*. In brief, he never sinned against philosophy.[59]

This is an unexpected view of Augustus for anyone who begins from the Roman sources. Suetonius simply says that Augustus drew knowledge of various forms of erudition from the philosopher Areus and his sons Dionysius and Nicanor; and notes, under the general heading of his subject's writings,

[55] Julius Honorius, *Geographi Latini Minores* 21.
[56] Nic. Dam. *Vita Aug.* 17. 44.
[57] Cic. *Att.* XVI. 11. 4 (44 BC); perhaps *Fam.* III. 7. 5 (51 BC).
[58] Julian, *Caesares* 309 b–c.
[59] Ibid. 326 a–b.

*Exhortationes ad Philosophiam* (possibly juvenile).[60] Seneca observes that Livia found her chief consolation for the death of Drusus in a work of Areus. But neither Tacitus in the favourable version of the summing up of Augustus' rule, nor the fuller and more whole-heartedly positive Velleius (a soldier by profession) have anything to say about philosophic advisers.[61]

The Greek writers here show us the sort of thing that these were expected to contribute. According to Cassius Dio (and numerous other authors) Octavian told the Alexandrians on the city's capture that he spared it partly for Areus' sake. It is often stated by the ancient sources that he had placed Areus beside him on the dais.[62] According to Plutarch he forgave many persons in the city at his friend's request, including Philostratus—Cleopatra's court philosopher and a brilliant improviser but (Octavian thought) a fraud as an Academic. It was Areus, goes on Plutarch, who advised Octavian to kill Caesarion, saying οὐκ ἀγαθὸν πολυκαισαρίη. Julian observes that Areus was far from ambitious and refused a high position in Egypt; according to Plutarch he was, however, made ἐπίτροπος (procurator?) of Sicily.[63] Why Aelian called him Maecenas' friend and adviser is unknown; Maecenas was emphatically no Stoic. Areus' professional work, suitably for an imperial adviser, seems to have been largely on ethics, and not original. Stobaeus preserves extracts from a general study of previous philosophical views, and a work on the doctrines of Plato.[64] It would be highly significant if Areus (Areus Didymus) wrote a polemical work on Cicero's *De Re Publica*, as Oswyn Murray suggested; establishing the best form of constitution is exactly what the philosophic adviser does. But could he openly advise monarchy, rather than Cicero's mixed constitution, so early in the Principate—even in Greek?[65]

[60] Suet. *Aug.* 89. 1; cf. 85. 1.

[61] Sen. *Consol. ad Marc.* 4; Tac. *Ann.* I. 9; Vell. Pat. II. 59, etc.

[62] Cassius Dio LI. 16, etc.

[63] Plut. *Ant.* 81. 2; Julian, *ad Them.* 265 C–D, 266 A. Bowersock [97] 41, argues that Areus was offered the post of Idios Logos in Egypt. [Plut.] *Mor.* 207 B; in Sicily Areus replaces a Theodorus whom Augustus thought corrupt, so not likely to be Athenodorus *pace* C. Cichorius, *Römische Studien* (Leipzig, 1922) 281.

[64] Diels, *Doxog. Gr.* 447 ff.

[65] Murray [356] 175 n. 1. Didymus Chalcenterus (Amm. Marc. XXII. 16. 16, Suidas s.v. *Τράγκυλλος*) is certainly a surprising author for such a work; Claudius Didymus, another grammarian, has also been suggested, L. Cohn, *RE* V (1905) 471.

According to [Lucian] *Macrobioi* Athenodorus was Octavian's *διδάσκαλος* (along with Apollodorus the rhetorician).[66] He does not appear at all in Suetonius or the Roman historians. But Dio Cassius and others tell how he convicted Augustus of lax security by having himself carried, bearing a dagger, into the presence in a covered litter supposed to contain a lady. And [Plut.] *Apophth.* has the tale that, on receiving permission to return home because of advanced years, he left as his parting advice the suggestion that, whenever he felt angry, Augustus should repeat the letters of the alphabet before doing or saying anything—by which Augustus was so struck that he seized the philosopher's hand, crying 'I still need you', and kept him a further year.[67]

The story may be apocryphal, for Athenodorus' return to Tarsus, admittedly when elderly, was made so that he could reorganize the city; he obtained tax relief for it and finally a hero-cult for himself. In the light of this and his role at court his view, discussed by Seneca, that the wise man should not take part in politics is a puzzle.[68] We also know that he dedicated a work to Octavia, perhaps a consolation on Marcellus' death; and he wrote, like Posidonius, on tides; also on his home town, Tarsus. Cicero may refer to a work *Περὶ εὐγενείας*. Athenodorus further commented to Strabo on the law-abiding nature of the inhabitants of Petra in Arabia.[69] Themistius, in another passage, produces yet another philosophic adviser to Augustus, in Thrasyllus, who is more commonly associated with Tiberius; Themistius links him with Areus—Augustus was great because he took Areus and Thrasyllus around with him. But Suetonius only shows the Emperor joking with Thrasyllus (whom he describes as 'Tiberi comitem') on Capri about a line of Greek verse.[70]

Augustus is said to have been a friend of several other philosophers, though they are not formally represented as advisers. One is yet another Stoic, C. Julius Theon of Alexandria, called the 'successor' of Areus (it is not clear in what role). He

[66] [Lucian] *Macr.* 21.
[67] [Plut.] *Mor.* 207 C.
[68] Sen. *Tranq.* 3.
[69] Strabo XVI. 779.
[70] Themist. 5. 63 d; Suet. *Aug.* 98. 4.

received large estates in Egypt, where he was ἀρχιερεύς and possibly Idios Logos. Strabo says that Xenarchus, a Peripatetic from Seleucia on the Calycadnus who taught at Rome, was a friend of Augustus, and it was surely Augustus who had to approve the appointment of the Academic Nestor of Tarsus and Athenaeus the Peripatetic to teach Marcellus. Nestor later ruled Tarsus in succession to Athenodorus.[71]

Tiberius was an even more ambiguous figure than Augustus. In the pages of Velleius, he appears as the ideal ruler. But he is not associated with philosophers. For Velleius the question of *adiutores imperii* is vital, both for Augustus and Tiberius: 'raro eminentes viri non magnis adiutoribus . . . usi sunt'. But the examples are the two Scipios employing the two Laelii, and Augustus his family, with Agrippa and Statilius Taurus; Tiberius has lost Germanicus and Drusus, but now has Sejanus.[72]

Tiberius' policy in the East was not unsuccessful, and this might be why he is viewed with enough favour by Themistius to be given a philosophic adviser: Thrasyllus. Julian was outraged, taking the traditional Roman line that Tiberius was tyrannical and φύσει χαλεπός; Thrasyllus would have been discredited by his association with him if his works had not shown his true character.[73] Thrasyllus is remembered by the Roman sources, and by Dio Cassius, simply as an astrologer, and as such influential on Tiberius. But he is pretty certainly to be identified as the Platonist responsible for a new edition of Plato's dialogues—a Pythagorean who wrote on the first principles of Pythagoreanism and Platonism, and on the musical τόνοι; also a work on the heavenly bodies: a typical *oeuvre* for a Platonist of his time.[74] His abstruse interests suggest that his position might not be that held by Augustus' Stoics; would he have been offered administrative posts? Would he even have felt able to give political advice?

Contrary to what scholars who believe that he was a wise administrator of the provinces might lead one to expect, Claudius is not regarded by any Greek source as a good ruler (indeed his enslavement to base desires and unworthy dependents might

[71] For all these see Bowersock, [97].

[72] Vell. Pat. II. 127. I.

[73] Julian, *Letter to Themist.* 265 b–266 a.

[74] Dillon [73] 184–5.

seem deeply unphilosophic). He thus has no philosophic adviser, though one might have been found for him in Claudius Balbillus, if the *amicus principis* found in an Egyptian context in his reign is the astronomer and savant attested under Nero and given great honours, including games, at Ephesus with Vespasian's permission.[75]

With Nero we arrive at the tyrant who persecutes the philosopher, which is not our subject. Themistius insists that Nero *Σενέκᾳ οὐ συνῆν*: it was the dancers Pylades and Metrobius with whom he associated—with fatal results.[76] But on the whole the Greek sources do not count the highborn Roman amateur Stoics as philosophers;[77] Musonius Rufus was closer to being a professional, and better known in the Greek world (he wrote in Greek). Themistius duly has him trying to stop Nero playing.[78]

There were however people at Rome who did think of Seneca as a philosophic adviser, for in the *De Clementia* he finds it necessary to insist that Stoics are not harsh and thus unable to give good counsel to *principes* and kings.[79] And the playwright of the *Octavia*, writing soon after his death, shows him as a philosopher and trying as such to get Nero to control his passions, and not to destroy distinguished men.[80] He had, however, been retained to teach Nero oratory, and Agrippina, taking the Roman distrust of philosophy to extremes, actually barred him from teaching it to the young prince at all.[81] His position of power was based on the fact that he was an ex-consul and an *amicus principis*, a leading light in the Emperor's *consilium*. Tacitus introduces him with general reference to his *studia* and to *praecepta eloquentiae*; philosophy is only mentioned when Suillius attacks his wealth as inconsistent with its profession, and when Seneca's retirement and death are being

[75] H. Musurillo, *The Acts of the Pagan Martyrs* (Oxford, 1954) 130 ff.

[76] Themist. 6. 72 d; 13. 173 b.

[77] Plut. *Frag. Incert.* 211 Sandbach probably identified Julius Canus, put to death by Gaius, as *ἕνα τῶν Στωϊκῶν*, but he is not an adviser. In Philo *Leg.* 41 ff. Macro gives advice on kingship of a familiar philosophic kind to Gaius, but of course the praetorian prefect cannot be described as a philosopher: Goodenough [354] 13, 103 ff.

[78] Themist. 34. 48—'zum mindesten zweifelhaft', K. v. Fritz, *RE* xvi (1935) 894.

[79] Sen. *Clem.* II. 5. 2; there was a genuine problem here, as the Stoic sage was not supposed to be moved by the emotions, including pity.

[80] Anon. *Octavia* 440 ff.

[81] Suet. *Ner.* 52. She thought it *imperaturo contrariam*.

described—in connection, therefore, with his private affairs.[82] Suetonius never mentions Seneca's philosophy at all, but notes that he was already a senator when he began to teach Nero (what he taught him is not made clear).[83]

Themistius (like other fairly sober sources) has nothing to say about Vespasian, who ended by finding the Stoics impossible to deal with; he put Helvidius Priscus to death and banished Musonius. But he was usually regarded as a 'good' emperor. So Philostratus in the early third century gave him a splendid philosophic adviser at Alexandria at the start of his reign, in the shape of the Pythagorean and mage Apollonius of Tyana; indeed he claims that the story grew up that one of the main reasons that Vespasian went to Egypt at all was to seek out Apollonius; and a debate of philosophers—Apollonius, Dio Chrysostom, and the Stoic Euphrates—advising on policy is staged for his benefit. Here we have entered the world of historical fiction; though Euphrates, to judge from Pliny's picture of him, might have liked to be an imperial adviser, and did encourage the Younger Pliny in his administrative duties by assuring him that they formed the best part of philosophy.[84]

Fiction or no, let us see what Apollonius is supposed to have said. He argues against the other two that monarchy is the only practical constitution for Rome now, and Vespasian has the justice and temperance proper to a ruler. Pleased, the emperor asks to be instructed in the virtues of the good king. These are not to be taught, says the sage, but despise your wealth, use it to succour the poor, and keep the property of the rich secure. Be moderate in the use of power, do not destroy distinguished men, show rebels they will be punished, obey the law yourself, revere the gods, see your sons obey you, try discreetly to reform Roman luxury, end the pride of the imperial freedmen, choose governors by merit, and see that those ruling Greece can speak Greek.[85]

[82] Tac. *Ann.* xii. 8. 2; xiii. 2. 1, 42. 4; xiv. 56. 3; xv. 62. 2.

[83] Suet. *Ner.* 7. 1; 35. 5.

[84] Philostr. *VA* v. 27 ff. Pliny, *Ep.* i. 10. 10. Euphrates possibly a pupil of Musonius, Fronto p. 115 Naber (not to be pressed). For the semi-factional character of Philostratus' Apollonius see esp. Bowie [352] and Dzielska [353], and of his Demetrius, Billerbeck [79] 52.

[85] Philostr. *VA* v. 35–6.

Apollonius also praises Vespasian's son Titus for σωφροσύνη, and is soon invited to Tarsus to meet him. Titus says his father has told him about the advice he has been given, and asks ἐμοὶ δὲ . . . περὶ ἄρχης καὶ βασιλείας τί ὑποθήσῃ; Obey your father and grow like him, says Apollonius, and proposes to give Titus as his companion in Rome Demetrius the Cynic, now teaching there, who will tell him τί δεῖ πράττειν τὸν ἀγαθὸν ἄρχοντα. Titus is unenthusiastic at the prospect of a Cynic councillor, but Apollonius writes off to Demetrius. He also gets Titus, described as πρᾶος καὶ χρηστός, to give the Tarsians great favours (and prophesies the circumstances of Titus' death).[86]

Titus too counted as a 'good' emperor; and Themistius had another candidate for his adviser, Musonius, perhaps not much more solid than Apollonius or Demetrius. Titus did recall Musonius from exile, and we know from Tacitus that Vespasian had under Nero been friendly with the Stoic aristocrats Thrasea and Barea Soranus, which makes it just possible that Titus had had some association with Musonius in youth.[87] But he was a tempting figure for the role of philosophic adviser, for we possess his address to a client king in Syria on the duty of a ruler to study philosophy.[88]

Domitian, to some extent in fact as well as in fiction (Philostratus again) is the tyrant who oppresses philosophers. Thus later sources do not note that he favoured some, at least for a time, such as the Flavius Archippus only known from Pliny's letters to Trajan. Apollonius pops up again as a friend of Nerva, who writes to ask him to come to Rome as his adviser, but only gets a letter ξύμβουλον περί τῶν ἀρχικῶν and containing deep secrets, shortly before the death of both parties.[89]

With Trajan we return to earth, though not to certainty. There was clearly no prospect of turning the unlearned and soldierly Trajan into a philosopher-king, but the new emperor was not only anxious to avoid tyranny, but (it seems) to end the quarrel between philosophy, especially that of the so-called 'Stoic opposition', and the principate; Julian says that he revered philosophy, though himself too fond of ease, wine, and

[86] Ibid. VI. 29–34.
[87] Tac. *Hist.* IV. 7.
[88] Musonius ed. Hense 8, tr. in Lutz [155]; cf. van Geytenbeek [154] 124 ff.
[89] Philostr. *VA* VIII. 27–8.

boys.[90] The position of philosophic adviser might seem open. There may have been competition for the job; Dio Chrysostom has to deal with rivals, who attack him as a flatterer. Scholars disagree as to whether Dio really delivered any or all of his four orations on kingship before Trajan (and then reworked and repeated them before audiences in Greek cities as he seems to imply in *Or.* 57—a splendid way to impress them with one's importance).[91] But Dio was at least half a sophist, and to sophists actual delivery was crucial; he claimed to be an old friend of Nerva's, and for personal contact with Trajan we have the story (probably not precisely true) that the emperor once took him in his chariot and said that though he did not understand what he said he loved him as himself.[92]

Not that Trajan would have failed to understand the orations on kingship, unless his Greek was weaker than is likely, though they are somewhat allusive and provide problems for us. We cannot discuss them seriously here. Semi-Cynic in tone, especially 1 and 4, they stress the value of *πόνος*, and argue that excessive learning is not necessary for the ruler (music is not morally efficacious); 4 plays down military glory, probably with the projected Eastern wars of Trajan in mind. There can be little doubt at least that the ruler they evoke is meant to be Trajan, and the advice given is thought of as relevant to his case. The kings called up as precedents are primarily Philip and Alexander, and Dio seems to see himself as Aristotle and Diogenes; but elsewhere he can masquerade as Nestor the adviser of Agamemnon, sage and experienced, but not strictly a philosopher.[93]

It is also uncertain to what extent there were direct relations between Trajan and Plutarch. There were certainly later thought to have been; and they had common friends, notably Sosius Senecio. We have seen that Plutarch was interested in the figure of the philosophic adviser; but the pamphlet known as *Ad principem ineruditum*, though its title might suggest it was addressed to Trajan, is concerned with rulers in general,

[90] Julian, *Caesares* 311c, 327c, 328b. Cf. Pliny *Pan.* 47. 1; he honours teachers of rhetoric and philosophy.

[91] Desideri [166]; Jones [167] esp. 115 ff; Moles [168] and [169].

[92] Philostr. *VS* 1. 488.

[93] Dio Chrys. 56. 8 ff.

including city magistrates, while that already mentioned, urging philosophers to consort with rulers, is addressed to a philosopher who has embraced an unknown ruler whom the MSS call Sorcanus.[94] But it is not surprising that the author of the spurious *Apophthegms of Kings and Generals* should claim to be Plutarch, sending the little work to Trajan as the κοιναὶ ἀπαρχαί of philosophy, quicker to read than the *Parallel Lives* and useful for understanding ἡγεμονικοί.[95] This forgery may date from not too long after Plutarch's death, but the notorious *Institutio Traiani* quoted by John of Salisbury in the twelfth century, and regarded by him as Plutarch's, seems to be a Latin work of the fourth century AD.[96]

Hadrian knew various philosophers, perhaps including Epictetus,[97] but was probably more interested in other aspects of intellectual life; he liked to appear cleverer than anyone else, quarrelled with various learned men, including two who are called philosophers,[98] and was subject to passions of an unphilosophic kind; no-one seems to have tried to fix him up with a philosopher as a real σύμβουλος, and Julian calls him a sophist, i.e. a cultured practitioner of show oratory.[99] It is also significant that Themistius, in spite of some chronological improbability, assigns Epictetus not to Hadrian but to Antoninus Pius and Marcus Aurelius.[100] Though Marcus by his own account read and valued Epictetus' works he clearly never knew him personally,[101] and while Epictetus had important Roman pupils and visitors, he is more concerned with rooting out the ambition to be a φίλος Καίσαρος than to qualify anyone for the post or claim it himself, though he did, as a good Stoic, hold that it could be a duty to hold office.[102]

[94] Plut. *Mor.* 776 B.

[95] [Plut.] *Mor.* 172 C–E.

[96] S. Desideri, *La 'Institutio Traiani'* (Genoa, 1958).

[97] SHA *Hadr.* 16. 10.

[98] Ibid. 15. 5; Philostr. *VS* I. 489. Cf. Daly and Suchier [159] for a second- or third-century question-and-answer dialogue in Latin between Hadrian and Epictetus, and a similar one between Hadrian and the 'silent philosopher' Secundus, who writes his answers; neither has any political material (and Hadrian in the second is rather tyrannical).

[99] Julian, *Caesares* 311 d.

[100] Themist. 5. 63 d.

[101] *Med.* I. 7; VII. 19.

[102] Starr [163]; Millar [161].

Themistius' other suggestion, where Marcus is concerned, is better; Rusticus was indeed one of his teachers of philosophy, highly valued by him, as the *Meditations* reveal, and the *Historia Augusta* may not be far out in saying that Marcus shared public as well as private business with him.[103] But Q. Junius Rusticus, of an old senatorial family, twice consul and finally urban prefect, was a Roman aristocrat as well as a philosopher.

As for Marcus himself, it was easy to see, in his own time as after it, his devotion to philosophy. Many praised him for it; the rebel Avidius Cassius, we are told, did not.[104] But the *Historia Augusta* is hardly right to say that Plato's remark about the philosopher king was always in his mouth. A single passage of the *Meditations* suggests that flatterers had indeed called him that, but shows that he suspected that some claimants to the role were play-acting, ἐτραγῴδησαν, rather than living in accordance with nature; he need not emulate them. At any event, one did not live in Plato's Republic; one must be content with small advances; the work of philosophy is humble and modest.[105]

After his death there was for a long time no emperor with an ear, or, as the problems of the third century mounted, any leisure for the traditional lessons of philosophy. We will not pursue our subject into late antiquity: it is time to try to sum it up.

G. Bowersock, in his *Augustus and the Greek World*, is inclined to see philosophers as simply one group among the highly educated Greeks of whom late Republican dynasts, and then the first emperor, made use; and he treats Augustus' philosophers with other 'pedagogues' of his.[106] In a slightly different way E. L. Bowie, dealing with a later period and mainly concerned to refute Bowersock's views on the political importance of sophists as such, tends to reduce all Greek intellectuals, from the public point of view, to Greek magnates, in contact with emperors and other great Romans primarily in virtue of their social standing, and the education common to their class.[107] It

[103] SHA *M. Ant.* 3. 4.

[104] *ILS* 5163. 26; Cassius Dio, LXXI. 1; SHA *M. Ant.* 1. 1, 2. 6, 8. 1, 16. 5; *Avidius Cassius* 1. 8, calling Marcus 'philosopham aniculam', cf. 3. 5, 14. 5.

[105] SHA *M. Ant.* 27. 6–7; Marc. Aur. *Med.* IX. 29.

[106] [97].

[107] Bowie [178].

is true that we must be aware of the context in which the philosophers work, and of the overlap between different roles; it is true also that many of them were of good social standing. But philosophers have a tradition behind them which sets them somewhat apart from others. They can take a higher line. Augustus is praised for submitting to Athenodorus' *παρρησία*, and that is a crucial concept.[108] (Is it the explanation of Marcus' remark that he was often angry with Rusticus?) To look ahead for a moment, Synesius' *Περὶ βασιλείας*, which has a programme of reform so radical that we hardly can believe it was actually delivered before Arcadius, justifies its boldness at the opening by stating that it is the product of one who is a philosopher, not a rhetorician.[109] What rhetors and sophists did was, primarily, to praise—though that might provide a model for the ruler to follow; what envoys did was to request (and praise too). Philosophers might warn.

They had therefore a particular manner; what of their matter? Plato and his immediate disciples, anxious to teach rulers to know the true Good, had embarked on the full programme, starting with mathematics—something that did not exactly take, for example at the court of Macedon, which preferred horseplay and heavy drinking.[110] The fare was soon made easier. The fundamental principle was that kingship could only be justified as the rule of a supremely good man. He must be guided by reason, not the desires, and must be loving, merciful, and beneficent to his subjects. Sometimes he is represented as obedient to law, sometimes as himself embodying the law. The philosophers we have considered concerned themselves, in their role as advisers, occasionally with discussions as to the best form of constitution—though this was never really an open question at Rome; but chiefly with basic moral commonplaces: the ruler must possess the four cardinal virtues (courage, justice, temperance, and prudence), live in accordance with nature, control his passions, and above all show mercy. Areus' advice to put Caesarion to death seems to be the only case in which a philosopher is recorded as recommending severity to a Roman ruler, though we saw that Seneca had to

[108] Above, n. 59.

[109] T. D. Barnes, 'Synesius in Constantinople', *GRBS* 27 (1986) 93–112.

[110] Athen. XI. 508 d–e, quoting Theopompus on Euphraeus at the court of Perdiccas.

defend the Stoics from a charge that they were not likely to show pity, and Apollonius is imagined as telling Vespasian to make it clear he will punish rebels. But Numa was always seen as mild compared with Romulus; Athenodorus had advice for Augustus on keeping his temper; Lucian's amiable (and possibly fictional) Demonax tells an unnamed Roman governor who asks πῶς ἄριστα ἄρξει not to become angry (and to talk little and listen much), and persuades another governor to pardon an impertinent Cynic.[111] Even Cicero, and here it appears the advice was greatly needed, has a lot to say to his brother about mildness.

If the king needs courage, it is, according to Musonius, so that he should not fear death or toil. Philosophers prefer peace to war. Beside Dio, who says the king should be πολεμικός but not φιλοπόλεμος, we may place the fictional Apollonius, who tells the Parthian king (another recipient of his advice) not to go to war with Rome over a small piece of territory.[112] There is little about relieving the poor, though Apollonius instructs Vespasian to use his wealth to do so, as well as not to oppress the rich or take their property—traditional behaviour of tyrants, but also typical of recent emperors.

Oswyn Murray has argued that Philodemus, in *The Good King according to Homer*, adapted Hellenistic kingship-doctrine to the Roman Republic, by conceiving of his kings, as Homer did, in the plural, and paying unusual attention to the conception of the council of state.[113] However, most of the advice we have seen being given to Romans, either in fact or in fiction, can be paralleled in our fragments of the vast ruler-literature addressed to Greek kings or other potentates—which does not mean that it was necessarily valueless. Cicero of course writes to his brother as a man experienced in Roman administration (how to control the *negotiatores*); Apollonius, it turns out, is rather more specific than some, and a firm Hellenophile; not only does he tell Vespasian to choose suitably educated governors for Greek-speaking provinces, but breaks with him when he revokes Nero's gift of freedom to Greece.[114] But other philosophers get benefits for their own city (notably Areus).

[111] Lucian, *Demon.* 51, 50.

[112] Philostr. *VA* I. 37.

[113] Murray [141]; Grimal [138] interprets the work differently.

[114] Philostr. *VA* V. 41.

Court philosophers had occasionally been used in the Hellenistic world for political posts; thus Persaeus governed Corinth for Antigonus Gonatas. Was it as such that Areus and the others got from Augustus important administrative positions in the East? It should be remembered in the case of Egypt, where Areus was offered and Theon given a post, that at that time there were still few Romans with experience of a country that was very much a law unto itself; both men, it seems, were natives (though it is true that it was in Sicily that Areus was actually employed). As for Tarsus, it had to be reformed, but it was a free city, and Augustus could hardly send in a Roman official; Athenodorus and Nestor were Tarsians. It is possible that this is not the whole story, that Augustus made public use of philosophers to impress Greek opinion—perhaps in conscious contrast to Antony, who had employed dubious intellectuals and artists: Boethus, a bad poet who embezzled olive oil, to rule Tarsus, a citharode Anaxenor to collect revenues, and possibly the grammarian Nicias to govern Cos, while he enriched such figures as the scurrilous rhetorician Sex. Clodius from Sicily—though of course the poor press these men have received may be unjust.[115]

The Romans were familiar with the notion of the philosophic ruler and the philosophic adviser; but, as we have seen, many of them were not very interested in these ideas. They expect great men, including emperors, to be generally cultured, and to support learning and the arts; there is nothing wrong with 'Greek studies' (in moderation)—Suetonius states approvingly that Augustus pursued Greek and Latin studies alike, and even the military man Velleius notes Octavian's remarkable talent for liberal studies and that Tiberius was 'optimis studiis maximoque ingenio instructissimus'.[116] But philosophy is not singled out (even in the case of Marcus some of the Latin sources put it on a level with oratory or Greek letters in general).[117] And Andrew Wallace-Hadrill has shown that Roman propaganda, numismatic and other, about the virtues of the emperor, does not stress the four cardinal virtues so familiar from Greek philo-

[115] Strabo XIV. 674; R. Syme, *Roman Papers* ii (Oxford, 1979) 521–8.

[116] Suet. *Aug.* 89. 1; Vell. Pat. II. 59. 4, 94. 2. Cf. Pliny, *Pan.* 47: Trajan favours rhetoric, philosophy and all *studia*.

[117] Aurelius Victor, *Caes.* 16. 1; *Epitome de Caes.* 16. 7.

sophy;[118] while, as Miriam Griffin points out (above, pp. 21–2), the emperors were slow to give philosophers the same exemption from tax as the more obviously useful *grammatici* and rhetoricians.

Nor is philosophy seen as the qualification for an *amicus* or an *adiutor*. We have seen Velleius' views on the matter, and how Cassius Dio, who was, though a Greek, a senator, makes Maecenas and Agrippa Augustus' advisers on the best form of government. The friends whom Trajan is praised by the Latin sources for honouring and trusting are Sura, Palma, Senecio, not Plutarch or Dio Chrysostom.[119] The philosophers who do rise to high office, Seneca and Rusticus, are Romans of good position, and technically amateurs; Tacitus only mentions Seneca's philosophy à propos of his personal life; the *Historia Augusta* notes Rusticus' Stoicism but does not formally cast him as a philosophic adviser. There is, it seems, a tendency for those Romans who do not share the traditional distrust of philosophy to regard it primarily as the medicine of the soul, helping one to withstand oppression and the shocks of fortune, and to die well. The step from the philosophic gentleman to the philosophic political adviser or indeed the philosophic ruler was not a large one, but our surviving Latin sources at least do not often take it. Nor, of course, do all the Greek philosophers themselves; though Epictetus in this is perhaps reflecting the approach of the 'Stoic opposition'.

Finally, many of the advisers provided for great Romans by Greek writers are pretty dubious candidates for the post—though by no means all as fanciful as Pythagoras and Apollonius of Tyana. Either a personal link is not to be proved, or if it is, its nature is uncertain; perhaps Tiberius *was* really only interested in Thrasyllus' astrological skill or other recondite learning. But too negative a conclusion may be unjustified. The tradition that a philosopher should advise the ruler he was associated with πῶς ἄριστα ἄρχειν was so strong in the Greek world that when one was so associated he probably felt he should at least try to live up to expectations.

And, as we saw at the start, there is the written, as well as the

[118] Wallace-Hadrill [359].

[119] Pliny, *Pan.* 85–6; Aur. Vict., *Caes.* 13. 8; *Epit.* 13. 5.

spoken word. Demetrius of Phaleron advised Ptolemy I to read works on kingship because he would find in them what his friends did not dare tell him.[120] We know too little of Roman reading habits, but Xenophon's *Cyropaideia* was a favourite with great Romans of the Republic; it could at a pinch be called a philosophic work on kingship.[121] We know also that though Plutarch wrote his *Political Precepts* specifically for a young man of Sardis, and much of its deals realistically with the problems of a Greek city under Rome (Plutarch deplored philosophers who insist on advising but give no solid advice), yet at least one important Roman, Cornelius Pulcher, often had it in his hands.[122]

We need not altogether agree with the suggestion that, because they controlled educated opinion and the judgement of posterity, and taught that only virtue and beneficence could legitimize a king, and because by claiming the right to be advisers themselves they helped to keep rulers out of the hands of priests and fanatics, the philosophers were major benefactors of humanity.[123] (In fact they tended to accept learned foreign priests as equivalents of themselves, while their harsh judgement of Alexander did not prevent him from mesmerising posterity.) But it is likely that even in the Roman world, where philosophy had a limited hold on public opinion, they had some influence for good.

[120] Plut. *Mor.* 189 D.

[121] K. Münscher, *Xenophon in der griechisch-römischen Literatur*, Philol. Suppl. 13 (1920) 74–5.

[122] Or so its author claimed, Plut. *Mor.* 86 C–D.

[123] Murray [356] 308 ff.

# Bibliography

## *compiled by Philippa Smith, revised by Maddalena Bonelli and Ben Morison*

THE bibliography does not aim at completeness. It serves two purposes. First, in Sections I–III, there is an introduction to the literature on the general subject-matter of *Philosophia Togata*. This is complemented by Section IV, which lists four specialist bibliographies. (Many of the items cited contain extensive bibliographies of their own.) Secondly, in Sections V–XIII, there are lists of items relevant to the particular topics of the individual papers. These Sections include a few items to which the papers do not refer and they omit a few items which, though referred to in the papers, are of marginal relevance to the main topic of *Philosophia Togata*. The assignment of an item to one Section rather than another is sometimes arbitrary: the various cross-references will do something to mitigate this fact.

Numbers which are followed by a letter (e.g. [18a]) indicate the revisers' additions to the original bibliography.

### I. TEXTS

The texts of the major authors are mainly to be found in OCT, Teubner and Loeb editions. There is a valuable anthology, equipped with an excellent bibliography in:


[1] Long, A. A., and Sedley, D. N., *The Hellenistic Philosophers*, 2 vols (Cambridge, 1987).


For papyrus texts of ancient philosophers, see:


[1a] *Corpus dei papiri filosofici greci e latini* (Florence, 1989–)


For Stoic texts see:


[2] Arnim, H. von, *Stoicorum Veterum Fragmenta*, 4 vols (Leipzig, 1903–24).

[3] Hülser, K., *Die Fragmente zur Dialektik der Stoiker* (Stuttgart/Bad Cannstatt, 1987).

[4] Straaten, M. van, *Panaetii Rhodii fragmenta*³ (Leiden, 1962).

[5] Edelstein, L., and Kidd, I. G., *Posidonius*, vol. 1 *The Fragments*, vol. 2 *Commentary* (Cambridge, 1972 and 1988).

[6] Theiler, W., *Poseidonios: die Fragmente* (Berlin, 1982).

For Epicurus see:

[7] Arrighetti, G., *Epicuro: Opere*$^2$ (Turin, 1973).
[8] Usener, H., *Epicurea* (Leipzig, 1887).

and also:

[9] Sedley, D. N., 'Epicurus *On Nature* Book XXVIII', *Cronache ercolanesi* 3 (1973) 5–83.

Further Epicurean texts:

[10] Vogliano, A., *Epicuri et Epicureorum Scripta in Herculensibus papyris servata* (Berlin, 1928).
[11] Angeli, A., and Colaizzo, M., 'I frammenti di Zenone Sidonio', *Cronache ercolanesi* 9 (1979) 47–133.
[12] Angeli, A., 'I frammenti di Idomeneo di Lampsaco', *Cronache ercolanesi* 11 (1981) 41–101.
[13] Longo Auricchio, F., *Philodemi de Rhetorica libri primus et secundus*, in Sbordone, F., *Ricerche sui papiri ercolanesi* vol. 3 (Naples, 1977).
[14] Spina, L., 'Il trattato di Filodemo su Epicuro ed altri (PHerc 1418)', *Cronache ercolanesi* 7 (1977) 43–83.
[15] Dorandi, T., 'Filodemo, *Gli Stoici* (PHerc 155 e 339)', *Cronache ercolanesi* 12 (1982) 91–133.
[16] —— *Filodemo: il buon re secondo Omero* (Naples, 1982).

New texts of the Herculaneum papyri are frequently published in *Cronache ercolanesi*. The papyri are catalogued (and given an extensive bibliography) in:

[17] Gigante, M., *Catalogo dei papiri ercolanesi* (Naples, 1979).

See also:

[17a] Blank, D., Janko, R., and Obbink, D., *Philodemus' Aesthetic Works* (Oxford, forthcoming).
[18] Casanova, A., *I frammenti di Diogene d'Enoanda* (Florence, 1984).
[18a] Gigante, M. (ed.), *La Scuola di Epicuro* (Naples, 1978–).

For *testimonia* to the Academy see:

[18b] Dorandi, T., 'Four Testimonia on the Academy', *Classical Quarterly* 28 (1988), 576–8.

[18c] Gaiser, K., *Philodems Academica* (Supplementum platonicum I, Stuttgart and Bad Cannstadt, 1988).
[19] Gigante, M., 'Polemonis Academici fragmenta', *Rendiconti della Accademia di archeologia, lettere, e belle arti di Napoli* 51 (1976) 91–144.
[20] Mette, H. J., 'Zwei Akademiker heute: Krantor von Soloi und Arkesilaos von Pitane', *Lustrum* 26 (1984) 7–94.
[21] —— 'Weitere Akademiker heute: von Lakydes bis zu Kleitomachos', *Lustrum* 27 (1985) 39–148.
[22] —— 'Philon von Larisa und Antiochos von Askalon', *Lustrum* 28–9 (1986/7) 9–63.

## II. GENERAL STUDIES

The standard history of philosophy, old but still indispensable for the prosopography of the period, is:

[23] Zeller, E., *Die Philosophie der Griechen in ihrer geschichtlichen Entwicklung*,[5] iii. 1 (Leipzig, 1923).

Two shorter histories have recently appeared:

[24] Hossenfelder, M., *Die Philosophie der Antike 3: Stoa, Epikureismus und Skepsis*, vol. 3 of Röd, W. (ed.), *Geschichte der Philosophie* (Munich, 1985).
[25] Long, A. A., *Hellenistic Philosophy: Stoics, Epicureans, Sceptics*[2] (London, 1986).

See also:

[26] Baldry, H. C., *The Unity of Mankind in Greek Thought* (Cambridge, 1965).
[26a] Dillon, J. M., and Long, A. A., *The Question of Eclecticism: Studies in Later Greek Philosophy* (Berkeley, 1988).
[26b] Donini, P.-L., 'The History of the Concept of Eclecticism', in [26a], 15–33.
[27] Sedley, D. N., 'Diodorus Cronus and Hellenistic Philosophy', *Proceedings of the Cambridge Philological Society* 23 (1977) 74–120.

The proceedings of the Symposia Hellenistica contain some of the best recent work done by philosophers in the area:

[28] Schofield, M., Burnyeat, M. F., and Barnes, J. (edd.), *Doubt and Dogmatism: Studies in Hellenistic Epistemology* (Oxford, 1980).
[29] Barnes, J., Brunschwig, J., Burnyeat, M. F., and Schofield, M.

(edd.), *Science and Speculation: Studies in Hellenistic Theory and Practice* (Cambridge/Paris, 1982).

[30] Schofield, M., and Striker, G. (edd.), *The Norms of Nature: Studies in Hellenistic Ethics* (Cambridge, 1986).

[30a] Barnes, J., and Mignucci, M. (eds), *Matter and Metaphysics* (Naples, 1988).

[30b] Brunschwig, J., and Nussbaum, M. C. (eds), *Passions and Perceptions: Studies in Hellenistic Philosophy of Mind* (Cambridge, 1993).

[30c] Laks, A., and Schofield, M. (eds), *Justice and Generosity* (Cambridge, 1995).

See also:

[31] Flashar, H., and Gigon, O. (edd.), *Aspects de la Philosophie Hellénistique*, Entretiens Hardt 32 (Geneva, 1985).

### (i) *Epicureanism*

There are several book-length studies of Epicureanism, among them:

[32] Asmis, E., *Epicurus' Scientific Method* (Ithaca, 1984).

[33] Bailey, C., *The Greek Atomists and Epicurus* (Oxford, 1928).

[34] Bignone, E., *L'Aristotele perduto e la formazione filosofica di Epicuro*² 2 vols (Florence, 1973).

[34a] Castner, C., *Prosography of Roman Epicureans between the second century BC and the second century AD* (Frankfurt, 1988).

[35] Diano, C., *Scritti epicurei* (Florence, 1974).

[36] Festugière, A. J., *Epicurus and his Gods* (New York, 1955).

[37] Frischer, B., *The Sculpted Word* (Berkeley, 1982).

[38] Gigante, M., *Scetticismo e epicureismo* (Naples, 1981).

[39] Goldschmidt, V., *La doctrine d'Épicure et le droit* (Paris, 1977).

[39a] Hossenfelder, M., *Epikur* (Munich, 1991).

[40] Konstan, D., *Some Aspects of Epicurean Psychology* (Leiden, 1973).

[40a] Mitsis, P., *Epicurus' Ethical Theory* (Ithaca, NY, 1988).

[41] Müller, R., *Die Epikureische Gesellschaftstheorie* (Berlin, 1972).

[42] Schmid, W., *Epicuro e l'epicureismo cristiano* (Brescia, 1984).

[43] de Witt, N. W., *Epicurus and his Philosophy* (Minneapolis, 1954).

The best of these is Schmid [42] (Schmid had a thorough knowledge of the papyrus texts). Goldschmidt [39] and Müller [41] connect most nearly with the main concerns of *Philosophia Togata.*

There is an interesting collection of essays in:


[44] aa. vv., *ΣΥΖΗΤΗΣΙΣ: studi sull' epicureismo greco e latino offerti a Marcello Gigante*, 2 vols (Naples, 1983).


Among articles of a general nature note:


[45] Ardizzoni, A., 'Il saggio felice tra i tormenti', *Rivista di filosofia e di istruzione classica* 70 (1942) 81–102.

[46] Long, A. A., 'Pleasure and Social Utility—the Virtues of Being Epicurean', in [31].

[47] Momigliano, A., 'Epicureans in Revolt', *Journal of Roman Studies* 31 (191) 149–57; repr. in his *Secondo contributo alla storia degli studi classici* (Rome, 1960).

[48] —— 'Su alcuni dati della vita di Epicuro', *Rivista di filosofia e di istruzione classici* 63 (1935) 3–16; repr, in his *Quinto contributo alla storia degli studi classici* (Rome, 1975).

[49] Philippson, R., 'Die Rechtsphilosophie der Epikureer', *Archiv für Geschichte der Philosophie* 23 (1910) 289–337, 433–46; repr. in his *Studien zu Epikur und den Epikureern* (Hildesheim, 1983).


See further Sections III (ii), VIII, and IX; and items [189], [197], and [329]–[332].

### (ii) *Stoicism*

Among books on Stoicism, see:


[50] Edelstein, L., *The Meaning of Stoicism* (Cambridge, Mass., 1966).

[51] Forschner, M., *Die stoische Ethik: Über die Zusammenhang von Natur-Sprach- und Moralphilosophie im altstoischen System* (Stuttgart, 1981).

[52] Kargl, J., *Die Lehre der Stoiker vom Staat* (Erlangen, 1912).

[53] Pohlenz, M., *Die Stoa*$^{2}$ (Göttingen, 1959).

[54] Reesor, M., *The Political Theory of the Old and Middle Stoa* (New York, 1951).

[55] Rist, J. M., *Stoic Philosophy* (Cambridge, 1969).

[56] Sambursky, S., *Physics of the Stoics* (New York, 1959).

[57] Sandbach, F. H., *The Stoics* (London, 1975).

[58] —— *Aristotle and the Stoics*, Proceedings of the Cambridge Philological Society suppl. 10 (Cambridge, 1985).

[58a] Schofield, M., *The Stoic Idea of the City* (Cambridge, 1990).


Of these items, [53] remains a standard work; [52] and [54] are most pertinent to *Philosophia Togata.*

There are useful collections of articles in:

[59] Long, A. A. (ed.), *Problems in Stoicism* (London, 1971).
[60] Rist, J. M. (ed.), *The Stoics* (Berkeley/Los Angeles/London, 1978).
[61] Brunschwig, J. (ed.), *Les stoïciens et leur logique* (Paris, 1977).

Articles relevant to *Philosophia Togata* include:

[62] Baldry, H. G., 'Zeno's Ideal state', *Journal of Hellenic Studies* 79 (1959) 3–15.
[63] Chestnut, G. F., 'The Ruler and the *Logos* in Neo-Pythagorean, Middle Platonic and Late Stoic Political Philosophy', *Aufstieg und Niedergang der römischen Welt*, II 16. 2 (1978) 1310–32.
[64] Devine, F. E., 'Stoicism on the Best Regime', *Journal for the History of Ideas* 31 (1970) 323–36.
[65] Hunt, H. A. K., 'The importance of Zeno's physics for an understanding of Stoicism during the late Roman Republic', *Apeiron* 1 (1967) 5–14.
[65a] Isnardi-Parente, M., 'Ierocle stoico', in W. Haase (ed.), *Aufstieg und Niedergang der römischen Welt*, II 36.3 (Berlin, 1989), 2201–26.
[65b] Obbink, D., and Vander Waerdt, P. A., 'Diogenes of Babylon: the Stoic Sage in the City of Fools', *Greek, Roman and Byzantine Studies* 32 (1990), 355–96.
[65c] Schofield, M., 'Two Stoic Approaches to Justice', in [30c], 191–212.

See further Sections III (iii)–(vii), VI, and X; and items [184]–[187], [201], [333], [351], and [355].

## (iii) *The Academy*

General accounts of Greek scepticism include:

[66] Brochard, V., *Les Sceptiques grecs*² (Paris, 1923; repr. 1969).
[67] Dal Pra, M., *Lo scetticismo greco*² (Bari, 1975).
[68] Stough, C. L., *Greek Skepticism* (Berkeley/Los Angeles, 1969).

For Academic scepticism in particular see:

[69] Striker, G., 'Sceptical Strategies', in [15].
[70] Ioppolo, A. M., *Opinione e Scienza* (Naples, 1986).

On the end of the Sceptical Academy (and much else) consult:

[71] Glucker, J., *Antiochus and the Late Academy*, Hypomnemata 56 (Göttingen, 1978).

See also Section VII. For the rise of Middle Platonism see:

[72] Theiler, W., *Die Vorbereitung des Neuplatonismus*² (Berlin, 1964).
[73] Dillon, J., *The Middle Platonists* (London, 1977).
[74] Dörrie, H., *Der Platonismus in der Antike*, vol. 1 (Stuttgart/Bad Cannstatt, 1987).

## (iv) *The Peripatetics*

The fundamental work is:

[75] Moraux, P., *Der Aristotelismus bei den Griechen*, 2 vols (Berlin, 1973 and 1984).

There is a useful survey article by:

[76] Wehrli, F., 'Der Peripatos bis zum Beginn der römischen Kaiserzeit', in Flashar, H. (ed.), *Die Philosophie der Antike* 3 (Basel/Stuttgart, 1983).

See also:

[76a] Gottschalk, H. B., 'Aristotelian Philosophy in the Roman World from the Time of Cicero to the End of the Second Century AD', in W. Haase (ed.), *Aufstieg und Niedergang der römischen Welt*, II 36.2 (Berlin, 1990), 1079–174.
[77] Lynch, J. P., *Aristotle's School* (Berkeley, 1972).

## (v) *Cynicism*

It is still worth referring to an old study:

[78] Dudley, D. R., *A History of Cynicism* (London, 1937).

Among more recent works see:

[79] Billerbeck, M., *Der Kyniker Demetrius: ein Beitrag zur Geschichte der frühkaiserzeitlichen Popularphilosophie*, Philosophia Antiqua 36 (Leiden, 1979).
[79a] —— 'Greek Cynicism in Imperial Rome', in M. Billerbeck (ed.), *Die Kyniker in der modernen Forschung* (Bochumer Studien zur Philosophie 15, Amsterdam, 1991), 147–66.
[79b] Goulet-Cazé, M.-O., 'Le Cynisme à l'époque impériale', in W. Haase (ed.), *Aufstieg und Niedergang der römischen Welt*, II 36.4 (Berlin, 1990), 2720–833.

[79c] —— and Goulet, R. (eds), *Le Cynisme ancien et ses prolongements* (Paris, 1993).

[79d] Griffin, M. T., 'Le Mouvement cynique et les romains: attraction et répulsion', in [79c], 241–58.

and items [207]–[208].

### (vi) *Philosophy at Rome*

A brief list of books which discuss, in fairly general terms, various aspects of this topic might include the following items:

[80] Balsdon, J. P. V. D., *Romans and Aliens* (London, 1979).

[81] Clarke, M. L., *The Roman Mind: studies in the history of thought from Cicero to Marcus Aurelius* (New York, 1968).

[82] Daube, D., *Roman Law: linguistic, social and philosophical aspects* (Edinburgh, 1969).

[83] Grilli, A., *Il problema della vita contemplativa nel mondo greco-romano* (Milan/Rome, 1953).

[83a] Grimal, P. (ed.), *La Langue latine: la langue de la philosophie* (Collection de l'École française de Rome 161, Rome, 1992).

[83b] Hahn, J., *Der Philosoph und die Gesellschaft* (Heidelberger Althistorische Beiträge 7, Stuttgart, 1989).

[84] Schulz, F. H., *The History of Roman Legal Science* (Oxford, 1953).

[85] Wirszubski, C., *Libertas as a Political Idea at Rome during the Late Republic and Early Principate* (Cambridge, 1950).

There are some useful collections of articles:

[86] Klein, R. (ed.), *Das Staatsdenken der Römer*, Wege der Forschung 46 (Darmstadt, 1966).

[87] Maurach, G. (ed.), *Römische Philosophie*, Wege der Forschung 193 (Darmstadt, 1976).

[88] Oppermann, H. (ed.), *Römische Wertbegriffe*, Wege der Forschung 34 (Darmstadt, 1967).

From innumerable studies of article length note:

[89] Boyancé, P., 'Le Stoicisme à Rome', in *Association Guillaume Budé: Actes du VII$^{e}$ Congrès* (Paris, 1964).

[90] Daly, L. W., 'Roman Study Abroad', *American Journal of Philology* 71 (1950) 40–58.

[91] Lind, L. R., 'The Tradition of Roman Moral Conservatism' in

Deroux, C. (ed.), *Studies in Latin Literature and Roman History* I (Brussels, 1979).

[92] Litchfield, H. W., 'National *exempla virtutis* in Roman Literature', *Harvard Studies in Classical Philology* 25 (1914) 1–72.

[93] Momigliano, A., review of [85], *Journal of Roman Studies* 41 (1951) 146–53; repr. in his *Quinto contributo alla storia degli studi classici* (Rome, 1975).

On the Republican period see especially:

[94] Rawson, E., *Intellectual Life in the Late Roman Republic* (London, 1985).

[94a] Wallace-Hadrill, A., review of [94], *Classical Philology* 85 (1988), 224–35.

and also:

[94b] Ferrary, J.-L., *Philhellénisme et impérialisme* (Bibliothèque des écoles françaises d'Athènes et de Rome 271, Rome, 1988).

[94c] Griffin, M. T., 'The Intellectual Developments of the Ciceronian Age', in J. A. Crook, A. Lintott and E. Rawson (eds), *The Cambridge Ancient History*, vol. ix (Cambridge, 1994), 689–728.

[95] Grimal, P., 'Les éléments philosophiques dans l'idée de monarchie à Rome à la fin de la République', in [31].

[96] Lind, L. R., 'The Idea of the Republic and the Foundations of Roman Political Liberty', in Deroux, C. (ed.), *Studies in Latin Literature and Roman History* IV (Brussels, 1986).

See further Sections III (i), V, and XI.

On the Imperial period:

[97] Bowersock, G. W., *Augustus and the Greek World* (Oxford, 1965).

[98] —— *Greek Sophists in the Roman Empire* (Oxford, 1969).

[99] Donini, P., *Le scuole l'anima l'impero: la filosofia antica da Antioco a Plotino* (Turin, 1982).

[99a] Fein, S., *Die Beziehungen der Kaiser Trajan und Hadrian zu den Litterati* (Stuttgart and Leipzig, 1994).

[100] MacMullen, R., *Enemies of the Roman Order* (Cambridge, Mass., 1967).

[101] Maier, B., *Philosophie und römisches Kaisertum* (Vienna, 1985).

[102] Toynbee, J. M. C., 'Dictators and Philosophers in the first century AD', *Greece and Rome* 13 (1944) 43–58.

See further Sections III (iii)–(viii), XII, and XIII.

## III. AUTHORS OF THE ROMAN PERIOD

This section lists some items dealing with particular authors: Lucretius is catered for by Section IX, Plutarch by Section XII, and Posidonius by Section VI.

### (i) *Cicero*

For a general account of Cicero see e.g.:

[103] Rawson, E., *Cicero: a Portrait* (London, 1975), and the papers collected in:

[104] Büchner, K. (ed.), *Das Neue Cicerobild*, Wege der Forschung 27 (Darmstadt, 1971).

See also:

[105] Martyn, J. R. C. (ed.), *Cicero and Virgil: Studies in Honour of Harold Hunt* (Amsterdam, 1972).

There is a useful bibliographical survey in:

[106] Douglas, A. E., *Cicero*, Greece and Rome: New Surveys in the Classics 2 (Oxford, 1968; with Addenda, 1978).

[106a] Gawlick, G. and Görler, W., 'Cicero' in [181a], 991–1168.

On Cicero as a philosopher and writer of philosophy, see, in general:

[107] Barnes, J., 'Cicero's *de fato* and a Greek Source', in Brunschwig, J., Imbert, C., and Roger, A. (edd.), *Histoire et Structure–à la mémoire de Victor Goldschmidt* (Paris, 1985).

[107a] Boes, J., *La philosophie et l'action dans la correspondance de Cicéron* (Nancy, 1990).

[107b] Fortenbaugh, W. W. and Steinmetz, R. (eds), *Cicero's Knowledge of the Peripatos* (Rutgers University Studies in Classical Humanities 4, New Brunswick NJ, 1989).

[108] Gigon, O., 'Cicero und die griechische Philosophie', *Aufstieg und Niedergang der römischen Welt*, I. 4 (1972) 226–61.

[108a] Giusta, M., 'Antioco di Ascalona e Carneade nel libro V del "De finibus bonorum et malorum" di Cicerone', *Elenchos* 11 (1990), 29–49.

[108b] Glucker, J., 'Cicero's Philosophical Affiliations', in [26a], 34–69.

[108c] —— 'Cicero's Philosophical Affiliations Again', *Liverpool Classical Monthly* 17 (1992), 134–8.

[108d] ——'*Probabile, Veri Simile*, and Related Terms', in [111a], 115–43.

[109] Görler, W., *Untersuchungen zu Ciceros Philosophie* (Heidelberg, 1974).

[109a] ——'Ein sprachlicher Zufall und seine Folgen. "Wahrscheinliches" bei Karneades und Cicero', in C. W. Müller *et al.* (eds), *Zum Umgang mit Fremdsprachlichkeit in der griechischen-römischen Antike* (Palingenesia 36, Stuttgart, 1991).

[109b] ——'Silencing the Troublemaker: *De Legibus* 1.39 and the Continuity of Cicero's Scepticism', in [111a], 85–113.

[109c] Griffin, M. T., 'Philosophical Badinage in Cicero's Letters', in [111a], 325–46.

[110] Hirzel, R., *Untersuchungen zu Ciceros philosophischen Schriften*, 3 vols (Leipzig, 1883).

[110a] Lévy, C., *Cicero Academicus: Recherches sur les "Académiques" et sur la philosophie cicéronienne* (Collection de l'École française de Rome 162, Rome, 1992).

[110b] Long, A. A., 'Cicero's Plato and Aristotle', in [111a], 37–61.

[110c] MacKendrick, P., *The Philosophical Books of Cicero* (London, 1989).

[111] Philippson, R., 'Marcus Tullius Cicero: die philosophischen Schriften', *Paulys Realencyclopädie* vii, A1 (1939) 1104–92.

[111a] Powell, J. G. F. (ed.), *Cicero the Philosopher* (Oxford, 1995).

[111b] ——'Cicero's Translations from Greek', in [111a], 273–300.

[112] Reid, J. S., Introduction to *M. Tulli Ciceronis Academica* (London, 1885; repr. 1984).

[112a] Ruch, M., *Le Préambule dans les œuvres philosophiques de Cicéron* (Paris, 1958).

[112b] ——'Nationalisme culturel et culture internationale dans la pensée de Cicéron', *Revue des études latines* 39 (1961), 158–71.

[113] Schmidt, P. L., 'Cicero's Place in Roman Philosophy: a Study of his Prefaces', *Classical Journal* 74 (1979) 115–127.

[113a] Sharples, R. W., 'Causes and Necessary Conditions in the *Topica* and *De Fato*', in [111a], 247–72.

[113b] Smith, P. R., ' "A self-indulgent misuse of leisure and writing"? How not to write Philosophy: did Cicero get it right?', in [111a], 301–23.

[113c] Stokes, M. C., 'Cicero on Epicurean Pleasures', in [111a], 145–70.

[113d] Strasburger, H., *Ciceros philosophisches Spätwerk als Aufruf gegen die Herrschaft Caesars* (Spudasmata 45, Hildesheim, 1990).

[114] Süß, W., *Cicero: eine Einführung in seine philosophischen Schriften (mit Ausschluß der staatsphilosophischen Werke)* (Mainz, 1966).

[114a] Tarán, L., 'Cicero's Attitude towards Stoicism and Skepticism in the *De natura deorum*', in K.-L. Selig and R. Somerville (eds.), *Florilegium Colombianum. Essays in Honor of P. O. Kristeller* (New York, 1987), 1–22.

On moral and political philosophy in particular, see:

[115] Barnes, J., 'Cicéron et la guerre juste', *Bulletin de la Société française de Philosophie* 80 (1986) 37–80.

[116] Brunt, P. A., '*Laus Imperii*: Conceptions of Empire Prevalent in Cicero's Day', in Garnsey, P., and Whittaker, C. R. (edd.), *Imperialism in the Ancient World* (Cambridge, 1978).

[117] ——'*Amicitia* in the Late Roman Republic', Proceedings of the Cambridge Philological Society 11 (1965) 1–20.

[118] De Lacy, P., 'Cicero's Invective against Piso', *Transactions of the American Philological Association* 72 (1941) 49–58.

[118a] Ferrary, J.-L., 'The Statesman and the Law in the Political Philosophy of Cicero; in [30c], 48–73.

[119] Gargiulo, T., 'Aspetti politici della polemica antiepicurea di Cicerone. Il *Laelius de amicitia*', *Elenchos* 1 (1980) 292–332.

[120] How, W. W., 'Cicero's Ideal in his *De Republica*', *Journal of Roman Studies* 20 (1930) 24–42.

[121] Howes, J. R., 'Cicero's Moral Philosophy in the *De Finibus*', in [79].

[122] Hunt, H. A. K., *The Humanism of Cicero* (Melbourne, 1954).

[123] Kerford, G. B., 'Cicero and Stoic Ethics', in [105].

[124] Keyes, C. W., 'Original Elements in Cicero's Ideal Constitution', *American Journal of Philology* 42 (1921) 309–323.

[124a] Long, A. A., 'Cicero's Politics in the *De Officiis*', in [30c], 213–40.

[125] Mitchell, T. N., 'Cicero on the Moral Crisis of the Late Republic', *Hermathena* 136 (1984) 21–41.

[126] Plezia, M., 'The First of Cicero's Philosophical Essays', in Michel, A., and Verdiére, R. (edd.), *Ciceroniana: hommages à Kazimierz Kumaniecki* (Leiden, 1975).

[127] Pöschl, V., *Römischer Staat und griechisches Staatsdenken bei Cicero: Untersuchungen zu Ciceros Schrift De Re Publica* (Berlin, 1936).

[127a] Powell, J. G. F., 'The *rector rei publicae* of Cicero's *De Re Publica*', *Scripta Classica Israelica* 13 (1994), 19–29.

[128] Rawson, E., 'The Interpretation of Cicero's *De Legibus*', *Aufstieg und Niedergang der römischen Welt*, I 4 (1973) 334–56.

[129] Sprute, J., 'Rechts- und Staatsphilosophie bei Cicero', *Phronesis* 28 (1983) 150–76.

[130] Steinmetz, F. A., *Die Freundschaftslehre des Panaitios nach einer Analyse von Ciceros 'Laelius de Amicitia'*, Palingenesia 3 (Wiesbaden, 1967).

[131] Valente, P. M., *L'éthique stoïcienne chez Cicéron* (Paris, 1956).

[131a] Wood, N., *Cicero's Social and Political Thought* (London, 1988).

[131b] Wright, M. R., 'Cicero on Self-Love and Love of Humanity in *De Finibus* 3', in [111a], 171–95.

See further Section X, and items [201], [228], [233], [236], [286], and [319]–[326].

(ii) *Philodemus*

There is a serviceable introduction in:

[132] De Lacy, P. H., and E. A., *Philodemus: on Methods of Inference* (Naples, 1978),

and it is still worth reading:

[133] Philippson, R., 'Philodemos', *Paulys Realencyclopädie* xix (1938) 2444–82; repr. in his *Studien zu Epikur und den Epikureern* (Hildesheim, 1983).

See also:

[133a] Asmis, E., 'Philodemus' Epicureanism', in W. Haase (ed.), *Aufstieg und Niedergang der römischen Welt*, II 36.4 (Berlin, 1990), 2369–406.

[134] Dorandi, T., 'Der "gute König" bei Philodem und die Rede des Maecenas vor Octavian (Cassius Dio LII 14–40)', *Klio* 66 (1985) 158–67.

[135] Gigante, M., *Ricerche filodemee*[2] (Naples, 1983).

[136] —— 'La biblioteca di Filodemo', *Cronache ercolanesi* 15 (1985) 5–30.

[137] —— *La Bibliothèque de Philodème* (Paris, 1987).

[138] Grimal, P., 'Le "bon roi" de Philodème et la royauté de César', *Revue des Études Latines* 44 (1966) 254–85.

[139] Kleve, K., 'Zu einer Neuausgabe von Philodem "Über die Götter", Buch 1 (PHerc 26)', *Cronache ercolanesi* 3 (1973) 89–91.

[140] Liebich, W., *Aufbau, Absicht, und Form der Pragmateiai Philodems* (Berlin, 1960).

[141] Murray, O., 'Philodemus and the Good King according to Homer', *Journal of Roman Studies* 55 (1965) 161–82.

[142] —— 'Rileggendo Il buon re secondo Omero', *Cronache ercolanesi* 14 (1984) 157–60.

[142a] Obbink. D. (ed.), *Philodemus and Poetry* (Oxford, 1995).

See also Section VIII, and items [238], [255]–[261], [300], and [331]–[332].

(iii) *Seneca*

[143] Avotins, I., 'Training in Frugality in Epicurus and Seneca', *Phoenix* 31 (1977) 214–17.

[144] Bodson, A., *La morale sociale des derniers stoïciens Sénèque, Epictète, et Marc Aurèle* (Paris, 1967).

[145] Currie, H. M., 'Seneca as Philosopher', in Dudley, D. R., *Neronians and Flavians: Silver Latin* I (London, 1972).

[146] Griffin, M. T., *Seneca: a philosopher in politics* (Oxford, 1976).

[147] Grimal, P., *Sénèque, sa vie, son œuvre, sa philosophie* (Paris, 1948).

[148] —— *Sénèque ou la conscience de l'empire* (Paris, 1979).

[148a] Inwood, B., 'Politics and Paradox in Seneca's *De Beneficiis*', in [30c], 241–65.

[149] Manning, C. E., 'Seneca and the Stoics on the Equality of the Sexes', *Mnemosyne* 26 (1973) 170–7.

[150] Motto, A. L., *Guide to the Thought of Lucius Annaeus Seneca* (Amsterdam, 1970).

[151] —— and Clark, J. R., 'Paradoxum Senecae: the Epicurean Stoic', *Classical World* 62 (1968) 37–42.

[152] Rozelaar, M., *Seneca, eine Gesamtdarstellung* (Amsterdam, 1976).

And [231].

(iv) *Musonius Rufus*

[153] Charlesworth, M. P., 'The philosopher (Musonius)', in his *Five Men: character studies from the Roman Empire* (Cambridge, 1936).

[154] Geytenbeck, A. C. van, *Musonius Rufus and the Greek Diatribe* (Assen, 1963).

[155] Lutz, C., *Musonius Rufus, the Roman Socrates* (New Haven, 1947).

(v) *Epictetus*

[156] Bonhöffer, A., *Epiket und die Stoa* (Stuttgart, 1890).
[157] —— *Die Ethik des Stoikers Epiktet* (Stuttgart, 1894).
[158] Brunt, P. A., 'From Epictetus to Arrian', *Athenaeum* 55 (1977) 19–48.
[159] Daly, L. W., and Suchier, W., *The Altercatio Hadriani Augusti et Epicteti Philosophi* (Urbana, 1939).
[160] Long, A. A., 'Epictetus, Marcus Aurelius', in Luce, T. J. (ed.), *Ancient Writers* II (New York, 1982).
[161] Millar, F., 'Epictetus and the Imperial Court', *Journal of Roman Studies* 55 (1965) 141–8.
[162] Moreau, J., *Epictète ou le secret de la liberté* (Paris, 1964).
[163] Starr, C. G., 'Epictetus and the Tyrant', *Classical Philology* 44 (1949) 20–9.

And [144].

(vi) *Dio Chrysostom*

[164] Arnim, H. von, *Leben und Werke des Dio von Prusa* (Berlin, 1898).
[165] Brunt, P. A., 'Aspects of the Social Thought of Dio Chrysostom and of the Stoics', *Proceedings of the Cambridge Philological Society* 19 (1973) 9–34.
[166] Desideri, P., *Dione di Prusa* (Messina, 1978).
[167] Jones, C. P., *The Roman World of Dio Chrysostom* (Cambridge, Mass., 1978).
[168] Moles, J., 'The career and conversion of Dio Chrysostom', *Journal of Hellenic Studies* 98 (1978) 79–100.
[169] —— 'The Date and Purpose of the Fourth Kingship Oration of Dio Chrysostom', *Classical Antiquity* 2 (1983) 251–78.
[170] —— 'The Addressee of the Third Kingship Oration of Dio Chrysostom', *Prometheus* 10 (1984) 65–9.
[170a] —— 'Dio Chrysostom, Greece, and Rome', in D. C. Innes, H. M. Hine, and C. B. R. Pelling (eds.), *Ethics and Rhetoric: Classical Essays for Donald Russell on his Seventy-Fifth Birthday* (Oxford, 1995), 177–92.
[170b] Trapp, M., 'Sense of Place in the Orations of Dio Chrysostom', in D. C. Innes, H. M. Hine, and C. B. R. Pelling (eds.), *Ethics and Rhetoric: Classical Essays for Donald Russell on his Seventy-Fifth Birthday* (Oxford, 1995), 163–76.

See also [85] and [93].

(vii) *Marcus Aurelius*

In addition to [144], [156], [157], and [160], see:

[171] Brunt, P. A., 'Marcus Aurelius in his *Meditations*', *Journal of Roman Studies* 64 (1974) 1–20.
[172] Farquharson, A. S. L., *Marcus Aurelius*² (Oxford, 1952).
[173] Noyen, P., 'Marcus Aurelius, the Greatest Practician of Stoicism', *Acta Classica* 24 (1955) 372–83.
[174] Rist, J. M., 'Are you a Stoic? The Case of Marcus Aurelius', in [252].
[175] Stanton, G. R., 'Marcus Aurelius: Emperor and Philosopher', *Historia* 18 (1969) 570–87.

(viii) *The Second Sophistic*

[176] Anderson, G., *Lucian: theme and variation in the second sophistic*, Mnemosyne suppl. 41 (Leiden, 1976).
[177] —— 'Lucian: a Sophist's Sophist', *Yale Classical Studies* 27 (1982) 61–92.
[177a] —— 'The Second Sophistic: Some Problems of Perspective', in D. A. Russell (ed.), *Antonine Literature* (Oxford, 1990), 91–110.
[178] Bowie, E. L., 'The Importance of Sophists', *Yale Classical Studies* 27 (1982) 29–59.
[178a] Brunt, P. A., 'The Bubble of the Second Sophistic', *Bulletin of the Institute for Classical Studies* 39 (1994), 25–52.
[179] Jones, C. P., *Culture and Society in Lucian* (Cambridge, Mass., 1986).
[179a] Swain, S., *Hellenism and Empire. Language, Classicism and Power in the Greek World of the Second Sophistic*, AD 50–250 (Oxford, 1996).

And [98].

## IV. BIBLIOGRAPHIES

There are excellent published bibliographies for Epicureanism in vol. 2 of [44] and for Scepticism in:

[180] Ferraria, L., and Santese, G., 'Bibliografia sullo scetticismo antico (1880–1978)', in Giannantoni, G. (ed.), *Lo scetticismo antico*, vol. 2 (Rome, 1980).

For the Stoics see:

[181] Epp, R. H., 'Stoicism Bibliography', in *Spindel Conference 1984: Recovering the Stoics*, Southern Journal of Philosophy suppl. 23 (Memphis, 1985).

But for the bibliographies covering most topics in Hellenistic Philosophy, see the revised Ueberweg:

[181a] Flashar, H. (ed.), *Hellenistische Philosophie* (Die Philosophie der Antike 4, 2 vols., Basel and Stuttgart, 1994).

Further material can be found in the bibliographical journals—*L'année philologique, Revue philosophique de Louvain, The Philosopher's Index*, and the rest.

## V. PHILOSOPHY, POLITICS AND POLITICIANS AT ROME

For the second century BC see the texts in:

[182] Garbarino, G., *Roma e la filosofia greca dalle origini alla fine del II secolo A. C.*, 2 vols (Turin, 1973),

and consult:

[183] Astin, A. E., *Scipio Aemilianus* (Oxford, 1967).

For possible philosophical influence on the Gracchi:

[184] Becker, J., 'The Influence of Roman Stoicism upon the Gracchi Economic Land Reforms', *La Parola del Passato* 19 (1964) 125–34.

[185] Dudley, D. R., 'Blossius of Cumae', *Journal of Roman Studies* 31 (1941) 92–9.

[185a] Erskine, A., *The Hellenistic Stoa: Political Thought and Action* (Oxford, 1990).

[185b] Hadot, I., 'Tradition stoïcienne et idées politiques au temps des Gracques', *Revue des études latines* 48 (1970), 133–79.

[186] Nicolet, C., 'L'inspiration de Tibérius Gracchus', *Revue des Études Anciennes* (1965) 142–58.

[187] Smuts, F., 'Stoisyne invloed op Tiberius Gracchus', *Acta Classica* 1 (1958), 106–16.

On Athenion:

[188] Badian, E., 'Rome, Athens and Mithridates', *American Journal for Ancient History* 1 (1976) 105–28.

On the late Republic in general, consult:

[189] Bourne, F. C., 'Caesar the Epicurean', *Classical World* 70 (1977) 417–32.

[190] Brunt, P. A., 'Cicero's *Officium* in the Civil War', *Journal of Roman Studies* 76 (1986) 14–17.

[191] Crawford, M., 'Greek Intellectuals and the Roman Aristocracy in the First Century BC', in Garnsey, P., and Whittaker, C. R. (edd.), *Imperialism in the Ancient World* (Cambridge, 1978).

[191a] Dettenhofer, M., 'Cicero and C. Cassius Longinus: Politische Korrespondenz ein Jahr vor Caesars Ermordung (Cic. fam. 15, 16–19)', *Historia* 39 (1990), 249–256a.

[192] Griffin, M. T., 'Philosophy, Cato, and Roman Suicide', *Greece and Rome* 33 (1986) 64–77, 192–202.

[193] Grisé, Y., *Le suicide dans la Rome antique* (Paris, 1982).

[194] Hirzel, R., 'Der Selbstmord', *Archiv für Religionswissenschaft* 11 (1908) 75–104, 243–84, 417–76.

[195] Jocelyn, H. D., 'The Ruling Class of the Roman Republic and Greek Philosophers', *Bulletin of the John Rylands Library* 59 (1976/7) 323–66.

[196] Moles, J., 'Some "Last Words" of M. Iunius Brutus', *Latomus* 42 (1983) 763–79.

[197] Mulgan, R. G., 'Was Caesar an Epicurean? (Sallust *BC* 51. 20)', *Classical World* 72 (1978/9) 337–9.

On Atticus:

[198] Leslie, R. J., *The Epicureanism of Titus Pomponius Atticus* (Philadelphia, 1950).

[199] Bailey, C., review of [198], *Journal of Roman Studies* 41 (1951) 163–4.

[200] Raubitschek, A. E., 'Phaidros and his Roman Pupils', *Hesperia* 18 (1949) 96–103.

For the Empire see:

[201] Brunt, P. A., 'Stoicism and the Principate', *Proceedings of the British School at Rome* 43 (1975) 7–35.

[202] Macleod, C. W., 'The Poetry of Ethics: Horace Epistles 1', *Journal of Roman Studies* 69 (1979), 16–27; repr. in his *Collected Essays* (Oxford, 1983).

[203] Malitz, J., 'Helvidius Priscus and Vespasian. Zur Geschichte der "stoischen" Senatsopposition', *Hermes* 113 (1985) 231–46.

[204] Mayer, R., 'Horace's Epistle I and Philosophy', *American Journal of Philology* 107 (1986) 56–73.

[205] —— 'Horace on Good Manners', *Proceedings of the Cambridge Philological Society* 31 (1985) 33–46.

[206] Winterbottom, M., 'Quintilian and the *Vir Bonus*', *Journal of Roman Studies* 54 (1964) 90–7.

And also [341].

On the Cynics see:

[207] Kindstrand, J. F., 'Demetrius the Cynic', *Philologus* 124 (1980) 83–98.
[208] Moles, J. L., '"*Honestius Quam Ambitiosius*?"–an Exploration of the Cynic's Attitude to Moral Corruption in his Fellow Men', *Journal of Hellenic Studies* 103 (1983) 103–23.
[208a] —— 'The Cynics and Politics', in [30c], 129–58.

## VI. POSIDONIUS AS PHILOSOPHER–HISTORIAN

The most influential study was:

[208b] Reinhardt, K., *Poseidonios* (Munich, 1921).

This became:

[208c] Reinhardt, K., 'Poseidonios von Apameia', *Paulys Realencyclopädie* XXII.1 (1953), cols. 558–825, which was printed separately as:
[209] —— *Poseidonios von Apameia* (Stuttgart, 1954).

Note that [5] above challenges [208b]–[209].
See also:

[209a] Kidd, I. G., 'Poseidonios', in F. Ricken (ed.), *Philosophen der Antike* (Munich, 1996).
[210] Laffranque, M., *Poseidonios d' Apamée (Paris,* 1964).

And, among articles:

[211] Dihle, A., 'Posidonius' System of Moral Philosophy', *Journal of Hellenic Studies* 93 (1973) 50–7.
[212] Dobson, J. F., 'The Posidonius Myth', *Classical Quarterly* 12 (1918) 179–95.
[213] Edelstein, L., 'The Philosophical System of Posidonius', *American Journal of Philology* 57 (1936) 286–325.
[214] Hijmans, B. L., 'Posidonius' Ethics', *Acta Classica* 2 (1959) 27–42.
[214a] Kidd, I. G., 'Posidonius on Emotions', in [59], 200–15.

[215] ——'Philosophy and Science in Posidonius', *Antike und Abendland* 24 (1978) 7–15.

[215a] ——'Moral Actions and Rules in Stoic Ethics', in [60], 247–58.

[216] ——'Poseidonius and Logic', in [61].

[217] ——'Posidonian Methodology and the Self-sufficiency of Virtue', in [31].

[218] Nebel, G., 'Zur Ethik des Poseidonios', *Hermes* 74 (1939) 34–57.

[219] Nock, A. D., 'Posidonios', *Journal of Roman Studies* 49 (1959) 1–16.

[220] Strasburger, H., 'Posidonios on Problems of the Roman Empire', *Journal of Roman Studies* 55 (1965) 40–53.

On Posidonius as a historian:.

[220a] Bringmann, K., 'Geschichte und Psychologie bei Poseidonios', in [31], 29–66.

[221] Fritz, K. von, 'Poseidonios als Historiker', in *Historiographia antiqua: Commentationes Lovanienses in honorem W. Peremans septuagenarii editae* (Louvain, 1977).

[221a] Halm, D. E., 'Posidonius' Theory of Historical Causation', in W. Haase (ed.), *Aufstieg und Niedergang der römischen Welt*, II 36.3 (Berlin, 1989), 1325–63.

[222] Malitz, J., *Die Historien des Poseidonios* (Munich, 1983).

[223] Reinhardt, K., 'Philosophy and History among the Greeks', *Greece and Rome* 1 (1954) 82–90.

[224] Schmidt, K., *Kosmologische Aspekte im Geschichtswerk des Poseidonios*, Hypomnemata 63 (Göttingen, 1980).

On other ancient approaches to history:

[225] Andreoni, E., 'Sul contrasto ideologico fra il *de re publica* di Cicerone e il poema di Lucrezio (la genesi della società civile)', in *Studi di poesia latina in honore di A. Traglia* (Rome, 1979).

[226] Kenney, E. J., 'The Historical Imagination of Lucretius', *Greece and Rome* 19 (1972) 12–24.

[227] Furley, D. J., 'Lucretius the Epicurean. On the History of Man', in [276].

[228] Hathaway, R. F., 'Cicero, *De Republica II*, and his Socratic view of history', *Journal for the History of Ideas* 29 (1968) 3–12.

[229] McKim, R., 'Myth against Philosophy in Ovid's Account of Creation', *Classical Journal* 80 (1984/5) 97–108.

[230] Manuwald, B., *Der Aufbau der Lukrezischen Kulturentstehungslehre* (Mainz/Wiesbaden, 1980).

[231] Motto, A. N., 'The Ideal of Progress in Senecan Thought', *Classical Journal* 79 (1983/4) 225–40.

[232] Pigeaud. J., 'Épicure et Lucrèce et l'origine du langage', *Revue des Études Latines* 61 (1983) 122–44.

[233] Rawson, E., 'Cicero the historan and Cicero the antiquarian', *Journal of Roman Studies* 62 (1972) 33–45.

[234] Schrijvers, P. M., 'La pensée de Lucrèce sur l'origine du langage', *Mnemosyne* 27 (1974) 337–64.

[235] Verbeke, G., 'Les stoïciens et le progrès de l'histoire', *Revue philosophique de Louvain* 62 (1964) 5–38.

[236] Wolf, R., 'Cicero as historian of philosophy', *Classical Bulletin* 36 (1960) 37–9.

## VII. ANTIOCHUS OF ASCALON

In addition to items [71]–[74], see:

[237] Cumont, F., 'Antiochus d'Athènes et Porphyre', *Annuaire de l'Institut de philologie et d'histoire orientales de l'Université libre de Bruxelles* 2 (1934) 135–56.

[238] Dorandi, T., 'Filodemo e la fine dell'Accademia (PHerc 1021 xxxiii–xxxvi)', *Cronache ercolanesi* 16 (1986) 113–18.

[238a] Görler, W., 'Antiochos von Askalon über die "Alten" und über die Stoa. Beobachtungen zu Cicero, *Academici Posteriores* I, 24–43', in P. Steinmetz (ed.), *Beiträge zur hellenistischen Literatur und ihrer Rezeption in Rom* (Palingenesia 28, Stuttgart, 1990).

[238b] —— 'Antiochus D'Ascalon', in R. Goulet (ed.), *Dictionnaire des philosophes antiques*, vol. i (Paris, 1994), 216–8.

[239] Hunt, H. A. K., 'The Ethical System of Antiochus', in [122].

[240] —— 'The Stoic and Antiochean Definitions of the Good', in [122].

[241] Luck, G., *Der Akademiker Antiochus*, Noctes Romanae 7 (Bern/Stuttgart, 1953).

[242] Lüder, A. M., *Die Philosophische Persönlichkeit des Antiochos von Askalon* (Göttingen, 1940).

[243] Müller, R., '*Βίος θεωρητικός* bei Antiochos von Askalon und Cicero', *Helikon* 8 (1968) 222–37.

[244] Sedley, D. N., 'The End of the Academy', *Phronesis* 26 (1981) 67–75.

[245] Strache, H. M., *Der Eklektizismus des Antiochos von Askalon*, Philologische Untersuchungen 26 (Berlin, 1921).

[246] Tarrant, H., 'Agreement and the Self-evident in Philo of Larissa', *Dionysius* 5 (1981) 66–97.

[247] —— *Scepticism or Platonism? The Philosophy of the Fourth Academy* (Cambridge, 1985).

[248] ——'The Stoicizing Epistemology of Antiochus of Ascalon', *Dialectic* 25 (1985) 34–49.

[249] ——'Peripatetic and Stoic Epistemology in Boethius and Antiochus', *Apeiron* 20 (1987) 17–37.

## VIII. PHILOSOPHICAL ALLEGIANCE IN THE GRECO-ROMAN WORLD

On the general issue of school allegiance, see:

[249a] Barnes, J., 'Metacommentary', *Oxford Studies in Ancient Philosophy* X (1992), 267–81.

[249b] Donini, P.-L., 'Testi e commenti, manuali e insegnamento: la forma sistematica e i metodi della filosofia in età postellenistica', in W. Haase (ed.), *Aufstieg und Niedergang der römischen Welt*, II 36.7 (Berlin, 1994), 5027–100.

[250] Longo Auricchio, F., and Tepedino Guerra, A., 'Aspetti e problemi della dissidenza epicurea', *Cronache ercolanesi* 11 (1981) 25–40.

[251] Longo Auricchio, F., 'La scuola di Epicuro', *Cronache ercolanesi* 8 (1978) 21–37.

[252] Meyer, B. F., and Sanders, E. P. (edd.), *Jewish and Christian Self-Definition* vol. 3 (London, 1982).

[253] Nock, A. D., *Conversion* (Oxford, 1933).

[254] Tarán, L., 'Amicus Plato sed magis amica veritas', *Antike und Abendland* 30 (1984) 93–124.

For the Epicurean attitude to rhetoric consult:

[255] Angeli, A., 'L'esattezza scientifica in Epicuro e Filodemo', *Cronache ercolanesi* 15 (1985) 52–84.

[256] Barnes, J., 'Is Rhetoric an Art?', *darg Newsletter* 2 (1986) 2–22.

[257] Ferrario, M., 'La conezione della retorica da Epicuro a Filodemo', in *Proceedings of the XVI International Congress of Papyrology* (Chico, 1981).

[258] Hubbell, H. M., 'The *Rhetorica* of Philodemus', *Transactions of the Connecticut Academy of Arts and Sciences* 23 (1920) 243–382.

[259] Isnardi Parente, M., *Techne* (Florence, 1966).

[260] Longo Auricchio, F., 'Epicureismo e scetticismo sulla retorica', in *Atti del XVII congresso internazionale di papirologia* (Naples, 1984).

[261] ——'Testimonianze dalla "Retorica" di Filodemo sulla concezione dell' oratoria nei primi maestri epicurei', *Cronache ercolanesi* 15 (1985) 31–61.

Note in addition:

[262] Cavallo, G., *Libri, scritture, scribi a Ercolano* (Naples, 1983).
[263] Kindstrand, J. F., 'A Supposed Testimony of Bion of Borysthenes', *Classical Quarterly* 35 (1985) 527–9.
[264] Puglia, E., 'La filologia degli Epicurei', *Cronache ercolanesi* 12 (1982) 19–34.

IX. LUCRETIUS AND POLITICS

The classic commentary is:

[265] Bailey, C., *Titi Lucreti Cari De Rerum Natura Libri Sex*, 3 vols (Oxford, 1947).

There is a good bibliographical survey:

[266] Kenney, E. J., *Lucretius*, Greece and Rome: New Surveys in the Classics 11 (Oxford, 1977).

Among books on Lucretius and his art, see:

[267] Boyanceé, P., *Lucrèce et L'Épicurisme* (Paris, 1963).
[268] Clay, D., *Lucretius and Epicurus* (Ithaca, 1983).
[269] Fowler, D. P., and P. G., *A Companion to Lucretius* (Oxford, 1988).
[270] Masson, J., *Lucretius, Epicurean and Poet* 2 vols (London, 1907 and 1909).
[271] Minyard, J. D., *Lucretius and the Late Republic*, Mnemosyne suppl. 90 (Leiden, 1985).
[272] Nichols, J. H., *Epicurean Political Philosophy: the De Rerum Natura of Lucretius* (Ithaca, 1976).
[273] Sallmann, K. G., *Die Natur bei Lucrez* (Bonn, 1962).
[274] Snyder, J. M., *Puns and Poetry in Lucretius*' de rerum natura (Amsterdam, 1980).
[275] West, D., *The Imagery and Poetry of Lucretius* (Edinburgh, 1969).

There are collections of essays:

[276] Gigon, O. (ed.), *Lucrèce,* Entretiens Hardt 24 (Geneva, 1978).
[277] Classen, C. J. (ed.), *Probleme der Lukrezforschung* (Hildesheim, 1986).

Articles on the political aspects of Lucretius' work include:

[277a] Alberti, A., 'The Epicurean Theory of Law and Justice', in [30c], 161–90.

[278] Berns, G., 'Time and Nature in Lucretius' *de rerum natura*', *Hermes* 104 (1976) 477–92.

[279] Boyancé, P., 'Lucrèce et son disciple', *Revue des Études Anciennes* 52 (1950) 212–33.

[280] Cabisius, G., 'Social Metaphor and the Atomic Cycle in Lucretius', *Classical Journal* 80 (1984/5) 109–20.

[281] Davies, H. Sykes, 'Notes on Lucretius', *Criterion* 11 (1931/2) 25–42; repr. in [277].

[282] Desmouliez, A., 'Cupidité, ambition, et crainte de la mort chez Lucrèce (d.r.n. III 59–63)', *Latomus* 17 (1958) 317–23.

[283] d'Eufemia, M., 'Note sul pensiero politico dell' epicureismo romano', *Rivista di cultura classica e medioevale* 16 (1974) 87–96.

[284] Fellini, A., 'Risonanze del *de consolatu meo* ciceroniano nel poema di Lucrezio', *Rivista di filosofia e di istruzione classica* 29 (1951) 307–16.

[285] Grimal, P., 'Le poème de Lucrèce en son temps', in [276].

[286] Howe, H. M., 'Amafinius, Lucretius and Cicero', *American Journal of Philology* 72 (1951) 57–62.

[287] Kleve, K., 'Philosophical Polemics in Lucretius', in [276].

[288] Merrill, W. A., 'The Signification and Use of the Word *natura* by Lucretius', *Transactions of the American Philological Association* 22 (1891) xxxii–xxxv.

[289] Monti, R. C., 'Lucretius on Greed, Political Ambition and Society: *de rerum natura* 3. 59–86', *Latomus* 40 (1981) 48–66.

[290] Packman, Z. M., 'Ethics and Allegory in the Proem of the Fifth Book of Lucretius' *De Rerum Natura*', *Classical Journal* 71 (1975/6) 206–12.

[291] Perret, J., 'L'amour de l'argent, l'ambition et la crainte de la mort (Lucrèce, III 59–86)', in *Mélanges Ernout* (Paris, 1940).

[292] Pianazzola, E., 'Lucrezio: sopravvivenza e potere', *Rivista di cultura classica e medioevale* 19 (1977) 609–24.

[293] Roller, D. W., 'Gaius Memmius: Patron of Lucretius', *Classical Philology* 65 (1970) 246–8.

[294] Schmid, W., 'Lucretius Ethicus', in [276].

[295] Wiseman, T. P., 'The Two Worlds of Titus Lucretius', in his *Cinna the Poet and Other Roman Essays* (Leicester, 1974).

[296] —— '*Pete nobiles amicos*: Poets and Patrons in Late Republican Rome', in Gold, B. (ed.), *Literary and Artistic Patronage in Ancient Rome* (Austin, 1982).

Further on Epicurean political theorizing:

[297] Barigazzi, A., 'Sul concetto epicureo della sicurezza esterna', in [44].
[298] —— 'Un pensiero avveniristico nel Giardino di Epicuro', *Prometheus* 4 (1978) 1–17.
[299] Gigante, M., and Dorandi, T., 'Anassarco e Epicuro "Sul regno"', in Romano, F. (ed.), *Democrito e l'atomismo antico*, Siculorum Gymnasium 33 (Catania, 1980).
[300] Gigante, M., 'Filodemo e Pisone: de Ercolano a Roma', *Annali della Scuola Normale Superiore di Pisa, Classe di Lettere e Filosofia*[3a] 15 (1985) 855–66.
[301] Reich, K., 'Der historische Ursprung des Naturgesetzbegriffs', in *Festschrift E. Kapp* (Hamburg, 1958).

On Latin political vocabulary:

[302] Hellegouarc'h, J., *Le vocabulaire latin des relations et des parties politiques sous la république (Paris,* 1972).

See also:

[303] Long, A. A., 'Chance and Natural Law in Epicureanism', *Phronesis* 22 (1977) 63–88.
[304] Westman, R., *Plutarch gegen Kolotes, seine Schrift 'Adversus Colotem' als philosophiegeschichtliche Quelle*, Acta Philosophica Fennica 7 (Helsinki, 1955).

And note [226]–[227], [230], [232], and [329].

## X. CICERO ON STOIC MORAL PHILOSOPHY AND PRIVATE PROPERTY

On the Stoic material see, in addition to the items in Sections II (ii) and III (iii)–(vii):

[305] Bonhöffer, A., 'Die Telosformel des Stoikers Diogenes', *Philologus* 67 (1908) 582–605.
[306] Long, A. A., 'Carneades and the Stoic *telos*', *Phronesis* 12 (1967) 59–90.
[307] Striker, G., 'Antipater, or the Art of Living', in [30].

On Cicero, see Section III (i); and on the *De Officiis*, in addition to [190], consult:

[308] Dyck, A., 'Notes on Composition, Text and Sources of Cicero's *De Officiis*', *Hermes* 112 (1984) 215–27.

[309] Gärtner, H. A., *Cicero und Panaitios* (Heidelberg, 1974).

[310] Higginbotham, J., *Cicero on Moral Obligation* (California, 1967).

[311] Holden, H., *M. Tulli Ciceronis De Officiis Libri Tres* (Cambridge, 1899).

[312] Pohlenz, M., *Antikes Führertum: Cicero De Officiis und das Lebensideal des Panaetios* (Leipzig, 1934).

[313] —— 'Cicero, *de Officiis* III', *Nachrichten der Gesellschaft zu Göttingen, phil.-hist.Kl.* 1 (1934) 1–40; repr. in his *Kleine Schriften* I (Hildesheim, 1965).

[314] Tanner, R. G., 'Cicero on Conscience and Morality', in [105].

## XI. PHILOSOPHY AND RELIGION IN THE LATE REPUBLIC

Among general studies there are:

[314a] Beard, M., 'Religion', in J. A. Crook, A. Lintott, and E. Rawson (eds), *The Cambridge Ancient History*, vol. ix (Cambridge, 1994), 729–68.

[315] Latte, K., *Römische Religionsgeschichte* (Munich, 1960).

[316] Liebeschutz, J. H. W. G., *Continuity and Change in Roman Religion* (Oxford, 1979).

[316a] Potter, D., *Prophets and Emperors: Human and Divine Authority from Augustus to Theodosius* (Cambridge, Mass., 1995).

[317] Weinstock, S., *Divus Julius* (Oxford, 1971).

[318] Wissowa, G., *Religion und Kultus der Römer*[2] (Munich, 1912).

For Cicero's thoughts on religion see:

[319] Ardley, G. W. R., 'Cotta and the Theologians', *Prudentia* 5 (1973) 33–50.

[320] Beard, M., 'Cicero and Divination: the formation of a Latin Discourse', *Journal of Roman Studies* 76 (1986) 33–46.

[321] Denyer, N., 'The Case Against Divination: an Examination of Cicero's *De Divinatione*', *Proceedings of the Cambridge Philological Society* 31 (1985) 1–10.

[322] Luck, G., '*Studia Divina in Vita Humana*. On Cicero's "Dream of Scipio" and its Place in Graeco-Roman Philosophy', *Harvard Theological Review* 49 (1956) 207–18.

[323] Pease, A. S. (ed.), *M. Tulli Ciceronis De Natura Deorum* 2 vols (Cambridge, Mass., 1955 and 1958).

[324] ——*M. Tulli Ciceronis De Divinatione liber primus*, 2 vols (Urbana, 1920; repr. Darmstadt, 1973).

[325] Schofield, M., 'Cicero For and Against Divination', *Journal of Roman Studies* 76 (1986) 47–65.

[326] Turpin, J., 'Cicéron, *De Legibus I–II* et la religion romaine: une interprétation philosophique à la vieille du principat', *Aufstieg und Niedergang der römischen Welt*, II 16. 3 (1986) 1877–1908.

On Varro:

[327] Boyancé, P., 'Sur la théologie de Varron', *Revue des Études Anciennes* 57 (1955) 57–84.

[328] Cardauns, B., 'Varro und die römische Religion: zur Theologie, Wirkungsgeschichte und Leistung der *Antiquitates Rerum Divinarum*', *Aufstieg und Niedergang der römischen Welt*, II 16. 1 (1978), 80–103.

On Epicurean attitudes:

[329] Jope, J., 'Lucretius, Cybele and Religion', *Phoenix* 39 (1985) 250–62.

[330] Kleve, K., 'On the Beauty of God. A Discussion between Epicureans, Stoics and Sceptics', *Symbolae Osloenses* 53 (1978) 69–83.

[331] Luppe, W., 'Epikureische Mythenkritik bei Philodem—Götterliebschaften in PHerc. 243 II und III', *Cronache ercolanesi* 14 (1984) 109–24.

[332] ——'Zu zwei Papyri aus Philodem περὶ εὐσεβείας', *Philologus* 129 (1985) 186–91.

## XII. PLUTARCH—ROMAN HEROES AND GREEK CULTURE.

Of the secondary literature on Plutarch, the most pertinent items are:

[333] Babut, D., *Plutarque et le stoïcisme* (Paris, 1969).

[334] Barrow, R. H., *Plutarch and his Times* (London, 1967).

[335] Brenk, F. E., *In Mist Apparelled* (Leiden, 1977).

[335a] de Blois, L., and Bons, J. A. E., 'Platonic Philosophy and Isocratean Virtues in Plutarch's *Numa*', *Ancient Society* 23 (1992), 159–88.

[335c] Gallo, I., *Aspetti dello stoicismo e dell'epicureismo in Plutarco* (Quaderni del giornale filologico ferrarese 9, Ferrara, 1988).

[335d] Georgiadou, A., 'Bias and Character-Portrayal in Plutarch's Lives of Pelopidas and Marcellus', in W. Haase (ed.), *Aufstieg und Niedergang der römischen Welt*, II 33.6 (Berlin, 1992), 4222–56.

[336] Gill, C. J., 'The Question of Character-development: Plutarch and Tacitus', *Classical Quarterly* 33 (1983) 469–87.

[336a] Hershbell, J., 'Plutarch and Stoicism', in W. Haase (ed.), *Aufstieg und Niedergang der römischen Welt*, II 36.5 (Berlin, 1992), 3336–52.

[336b] —— 'Plutarch and Epicureanism', in W. Haase (ed.), *Aufstieg und Niedergang der römischen Welt*, II 36.5 (Berlin, 1992), 3363–83.

[337] Jones, C. P., *Plutarch and Rome* (Oxford, 1971).

[338] Klotz, A., 'Die Quellen der plutarchischen Lebensbeschreibung des Marcellus', *Rheinisches Museum* 83 (1934) 289–318.

[338a] Moles, J. L., *Plutarch's Life of Cicero* (Warminster, 1988).

[339] Pelling, C. B. R., 'Plutarch's Method of Work in the Roman Lives', *Journal of Hellenic Studies* 99 (1979) 74–96. Reprinted in [346a], 265–318.

[340] —— 'Plutarch and Roman Politics', in Moxon, I., Smart, J. D., and Woodman, A. J. (edd.), *Past Perspectives–studies in Greek and Roman historical writing* (Cambridge, 1986). Reprinted in [346a], 319–56.

[341] —— 'Synkrisis in Plutarch's Lives', *Quaderni del Giornale filologico ferrarese* 8 [*Miscellanea Plutarchea*] (1986) 83–96.

[341a] —— 'Aspects of Plutarch's Characterisation', *Illinois Classical Studies* 13 (1988), 257–74.

[342] —— 'Childhood and Personality in Greek Biography', in [342a], 213–44.

[342a] —— (ed.), *Characterization and Individuality in Greek Literature* (Oxford, 1990).

[342b] —— 'Truth and Fiction in Plutarch's Lives', in D. A. Russell (ed.), *Antonine Literature* (Oxford, 1990), 19–52.

[342c] —— 'The Moralism of Plutarch's Lives', in D. C. Innes, H. M. Hine, and C. B. R. Pelling (eds.), *Ethics and Rhetoric: Classical Essays for Donald Russell on his Seventy-Fifth Birthday* (Oxford, 1995), 205–20.

[343] Rawson, E. D., 'Cassius and Brutus: the memory of the Liberators', in Moxon, I., Smart, J. D., and Woodman, A. J. (edd.), *Past Perspectives—studies in Greek and Roman historical writing* (Cambridge, 1986).

[344] Russell, D. A., 'Plutarch's Life of Coriolanus', *Journal of Roman Studies* 53 (1963) 21–8. Reprinted in [346a], 357–72.

[345] —— *Plutarch* (London, 1973).

[346] Scardigli, B., *Die Römerbiographien Plutarchs* (Munich, 1979).

[346a] —— (ed.), *Essays on Plutarch's Lives* (Oxford, 1995).

[347] Swain, S., 'Plutarch and Rome: three studies', D.Phil. Thesis (Oxford, 1987).
[347a] —— 'Character Change in Plutarch', *Phoenix* 43 (1989), 62–8.
[347b] —— 'Plutarch: Chance, Providence and History', *American Journal of Philology* 110 (1989), 272–302.
[347c] —— 'Plutarch's Aemilius and Timoleon', *Historia* 39 (1989), 314–44.
[347d] —— 'Hellenic Culture and the Roman Heroes of Plutarch', *Journal of Hellenic Studies* 110 (1990), 126–45. Reprinted in [346a], 229–64.
[347e] —— 'Plutarch's Lives of Cicero, Cato, and Brutus', *Hermes* 118 (1990), 192–203.
[347f] —— 'Plutarch's Characterisation of Lucullus', *Rheinisches Museum* 135 (1992), 207–16.
[347g] Titchener, F. B., 'Critical Trends in Plutarch's Roman Lives, 1975–90', in W. Haase (ed.), *Aufstieg und Niedergang der römischen Welt*, II 33.6 (Berlin, 1992), 4128–53.
[347h] Walsh, J. J., 'Syzygy, Theme, and History: a Study in Plutarch's *Philopoemen* and *Flamininus*', *Philologus* 136 (1992), 208–33.

And also [196].

See in addition:

[348] Gill, C. J., 'The Question of Character and Personality in Greek Tragedy', *Poetics Today* 7 (1986) 251–73.
[349] —— 'The Character-Personality Distinction', in [342a], 1–31.
[350] Moles, J. L., 'Politics, Philosophy and Friendship in Horace *Odes* 2, 7', *Quaderni Urbinati* 25 (1987) 59–72.
[351] Walsh, P. G., 'Livy and Stoicism', *American Journal of Philology* 79 (1958) 355–75.

## XIII. ROMAN RULERS AND THE PHILOSOPHIC ADVISER

Much of the relevant bibliography has already been listed, especially in Section V. See also:

[352] Bowie, E. L., 'Appollonius of Tyana', *Aufstieg und Niedergang der Römischen Welt*, II 16. 2 (1978) 1652–99.
[353] Dzielska, M., *Apollonius of Tyana in Legend and History* (Rome, 1968).
[354] Goodenough, E. R., *The Politics of Philo Judaeus* (New Haven, Conn., 1938)

[355] Murray, O., 'The *Quinquennium Neronis* and the Stoics', *Historia* 14 (1965) 41–61.
[356] —— *Περὶ βασιλείας*, D.Phil. Thesis (Oxford, 1971).
[357] Rawson, E. D., 'Hellenistic Kings and their Roman Equals', *Journal of Roman Studies* 65 (1975) 148–59.
[358] Walbank, F. W., 'Political Morality and the Friends of Scipio', *Journal of Roman Studies* 55 (1965) 1–16.
[359] Wallace-Hadrill, A., 'The Emperor and his Virtues', *Historia* 30 (1981) 298–323.

# Index Locorum

The index is selective. Passages are listed if they are quoted or paraphrased, or if they are discussed or commented upon, or if they are referred to in more than one context.



* *Acad.* = *Academici Libri* (*Acad. Post.*, *Varro*). *Luc.* = *Lucullus* (*Acad. Prior.*).

* *Luc.* = *Lucullus* (*Acad. Prior.*). *Acad.* = *Academici Libri* (*Acad. Post., Varro*).

# Index of Names

# General Index

This index is intended as a supplement to the *Index of Names* which includes many general items. Philosophical terms in Greek have been inserted into the alphabetical sequence according to the conventional transliteration, e.g. φ as ph and ψ as ps.